Ethics, Meaningfulness, and Mutuality

There is an urgent need to understand how private and public organisations can play a role in promoting human values such as fairness, dignity, respect, and care. Globalisation, technological advance, and climate change are changing work, organisations, and systems in ways that foster inequality, alienation, and collective risk. Against this backdrop, organisations are being urged to make their contribution to the common good, take account of the interests of multiple stakeholders, and respond ethically as well as efficiently to complex challenges that transcend traditional organisational and state boundaries.

Ethics, Meaningfulness, and Mutuality poses critical questions related to organisational design by challenging limits to current thinking, such as the neglect by political philosophers of markets, firms, and stakeholders or by organisational theorists of business ethics. In so doing, the book advances our understanding of the theory and practice of ethical organising. Specifically, meaningfulness and mutuality will be used to yield values and principles for a philosophy of ethical organising that includes an account of human values in morally desirable collective action and examines the relationship of collective action to the contested concept of shared value creation. Within a philosophy of ethical organising, mutuality permits an examination of the unavoidable relational nature of collective action, whereas meaningfulness addresses fundamental human concerns for significance and leading a life we have reason to value.

By addressing our status as relational beings with human needs for meaning, a philosophy of ethical organising brings critical thinking to the creation of morally informed organisational practices that are not only instrumentally beneficial for addressing wicked problems but are normatively desirable for human flourishing.

Ruth Yeoman is a Fellow at Kellogg College, University of Oxford, and an Associate Researcher at King's College, University of London. Ruth researches the concepts and application of meaningfulness and mutuality to work, organisations, and systems.

Routledge Studies in Business Ethics

Business ethics is a site of contestation, both in theory and practice. For some it serves as a salve for the worst effects of capitalism, giving businesses the means self-regulate away from entrenched tendencies of malfeasance and exploitation. For others business ethics is a more personal matter, concerning the way that individuals can effectively wade through the moral quagmires that characterise so many dimensions of business life. Business ethics has also been conceived of as a fig leaf designed to allow business-as-usual to continue while covering over the less savoury practices so as to create an appearance of righteousness.

Across these and other approaches, what remains critical is to ensure that the ethics of business is the subject of incisive questioning, critical research, and diverse theoretical development. It is through such scholarly inquiry that the increasingly powerful purview of corporations and business activity can be interrogated, understood and, ultimately, reformulated. This series contributes to that goal by publishing the latest research and thinking across the broad terrain that characterised business ethics.

The series welcomes contributions in areas including: corporate social responsibility; critical approaches to business ethics; ethics and corporate governance; ethics and diversity; feminist ethics; globalization and business ethics; philosophical traditions of business ethics; postcolonialism and the ethics of business; production and supply chain ethics; resistance, political activism and ethics; sustainability, environmentalism and climate change; the ethics of corporate misconduct; the politics of business ethics; and worker's rights.

The Rise of Business Ethics
Bernard Mees

Ethics, Meaningfulness, and Mutuality
Ruth Yeoman

For more information about this series, please visit: www.routledge.com/Routledge-Studies-in-Business-Ethics/book-series/SE0900

Ethics, Meaningfulness, and Mutuality

Ruth Yeoman

Routledge
Taylor & Francis Group

NEW YORK AND LONDON

First published 2020
by Routledge
52 Vanderbilt Avenue, New York, NY 10017

and by Routledge
2 Park Square, Milton Park, Abingdon, Oxon, OX14 4RN

Routledge is an imprint of the Taylor & Francis Group, an informa business

Library of Congress Cataloging-in-Publication Data
A catalog record for this book has been requested

ISBN: 978-0-8153-8040-5 (hbk)
ISBN: 978-1-351-12512-3 (ebk)

Typeset in Sabon
by Apex CoVantage, LLC

MIX
Paper from
responsible sources
FSC® C013056
www.fsc.org

Printed and bound in Great Britain by
TJ International Ltd, Padstow, Cornwall

I dedicate this book to:
My daughters, Hannah and Abigail.

And Peter, Rachel, Tim, David, Rachel, and Max; my nephews, Alex and Georgie; my god-daughter, Bethany; and their many local and international friends.
With love, respect, and hope.

Contents

Preface   xi

Overview: Ethics, Meaningfulness, and Mutuality   1

The Sustainability Imperative 1
Motivating Humanity 6
A Human Capability for Ethical World-Building 8
  Meaningfulness and Mutuality 9
Towards a Philosophy of Ethical World-Building 10
  Organisations and Organising 12
  Becoming World-Builders 13
Overview of Chapters 14

1   The Realm of Values   22

Relational Conception of Values 25
  Eudaimonic Reflection and Cosmopolitan Morality 27
  Organisational Values 30
  Values-Work 32
Values in Ethical Organising 34
  Moral Free Space 35
  Liberal Value Pluralism 36
Moral Progress 39
  Moral Imagination 40
  Meanings, Understanding, and Knowledge 41
  Common Knowledge 43
  Changing Values 44

2   **The Meaning of Value**   51

Value and the Sustainability Imperative 51
The Meaning of Value 52
  Forms of Value 53
Value Worth Creating 58
  Worth 59
  Integrative Worth and Publicness 61
  Ethical Worlds 63
Creating Life Value 64
  Live Worth Living in the Anthropocene 65
  Valuing in Life Value Organisations 66
The Life Value Model 68
  Materialist Ethics 69
  Framing Life Value Organisations 69
  Elements of the Life Value Model: Source, Target,
    Process, and Significance 71

3   **Meaningfulness and Mutuality**   81

The Value of Meaningfulness 81
  Meaningfulness: Objective, Subjective, Hybrid 83
  Sources of Meaning and Public Meaningfulness 86
  Practical Reasoning 88
  Ethic of Care 89
  Domination and Alienation 90
Mutuality as an Organising Principle 92
  Roots of Mutuality 93
  Mutuality and Reciprocity 94
  Constrained and Expansive Mutuality 96
Dimensions of Mutuality 98
  Ethical Orientations: Fairness, Care, and
    Flourishing 100
Voice: Democratic World-Building 103
  Structures and Institutions 103
  Mêtis: Overcoming Muteness and Harnessing
    Mutancy 107

4   **Collective Action: Integrity, Purpose, Work**   117

Normatively Desirable Collective Action 118
Collective Moral Agents 120

Integrity 121
Emotions and Reasons 123
Morally Worthy Organisations 124
  Philosophy of Purpose 125
  Organisational Purpose 128
  Aspects of Purpose and Purposing 129
Work: Complex Contribution 132
Agonistic Republicanism 135
  Consensus and Conflict 136
  Agonism: Constructive Conflict 137
  Republicanism: Responsible Difference-Making 138

5   Judging, Responsibility, and an Ethic of Care   146

Judging as Thinking and Feeling 146
Objects 149
  Concern for Objects 149
  Bringing Objects into View 150
Responsibility to Create Collective Moral Agents 152
  Duties to Organise 154
  Responsibility to See Others 156
Ethic of Care 158
  Materialist Ethics of Care 160
  Becoming a Self-Determining Being 161
Ethic of Care and Systems of Social Cooperation 162
  Separations of Distance, Power, and Culture 163
  Supply Chains as Systems of Social Cooperation 164

6   A Philosophy of Ethical Organising: Justice, Capabilities,
    Meaningfulness   173

Capability Justice 173
Social Constructivism and Justice 175
  Seeing Ourselves as World-Builders 179
  Constructing Basic Structures 180
  Contesting Ethical Worlds 182
A Capability for Ethical World-Building 185
  Individual Capabilities 186
  Collective Capabilities 188
  Organisational Capabilities 190
  Life Capabilities 195
Ethical Organising at the Base of the Pyramid 197

7   The Society of Meaning-Makers: Dignity, Empathy, Power   206

The Society of Meaning-Makers 207
  All Affected 209
  Mutuality in the Society of Meaning-Makers 211
Creating the Moral Community 214
  The Capacity to Dignify 215
  Moral Expansiveness and Empathy 217
  Empathy and Organisational Emotions 220
Distributed Power System 222
  Organisational Power 223
  Relational Power 225
  Discursive Authority 227

Conclusion: Towards an Empirical Research Agenda   233

Creating Mutual Organisation 238
Mutual Public Service Economy 241
The Meaningful City 245

Index   253

Preface

I have written this book through turbulent times that will be transformative and generational in their impact. The 2018 United Nations IPCC Global Warming Report set down the gauntlet for my thinking about the implications of the sustainability imperative for ethical organising and our prospects for living meaningful lives in the Anthropocene. I have also been mindful of how post-EU referendum populism has corrupted the body politic of the United Kingdom. At times, it has felt as if reason and common feeling has departed our political institutions and is more likely to be found in the many private and public organisations that are striving to fulfil their public promises to care for and sustain animals, people, societies, and our natural world. These organisations are made by grandmothers, grandfathers, parents, sons, and daughters, neighbours, colleagues, and friends. It is their skill, craft, and knowledge that maintains the entire complex economic and social order upon which we all depend to survive and flourish. It is therefore my fundamental concern that we establish the morally viable conditions for people to make life value organisations, in ways that develop their capabilities for ethical world-building, and also contribute to the meaning and purpose of their lives. In this endeavour, I recognise that many organisations are failing to make the necessary changes to their business and organisational models. For people connected to such organisations, they can only do the best they can—whether to work against, hold to account, attempt to reform, or speak up, possible. They will find support if exemplar organisations are prepared to lead the way. Finally, my concept of ethical organising relies upon an extension of democratic participation to all kinds of organisations. In this regard, I am part of the Tocquevillian democratic tradition that looks to the potential of voluntary associations to become schools of democracy. John Dewey thought of democracy as a way of life, and, as such, democracy remains a rich resource for human progress that we have yet to fully exploit.

I would like to thank Dr Milena Mueller Santos (Oxford) and Dr Lauren McCarthy (Royal Holloway, University of London), with whom I have worked on several research projects related to supply chains and the meaningful city. I have also benefited immensely from a number of academic collaborations. With Professor Katie Bailey, Dr Adrian Madden, Dr Marc Thompson, Professor Marjo Lips-Wiersma, and Dr Neil Chalofsky, I have worked on several publication projects related to meaningful work. With Professor Jari Stenvall (University of Tampere), Dr Marc Thompson (University of Oxford), and Ilpo Laitenen (University of Tampere), I developed a research project exploring the concept of The Meaningful City. For Professor Colin Mayer at the Saïd Business School, I set up the Mutuality in Business Programme, sponsored by Mars Inc. The Centre for Mutual and Co-owned Business at Kellogg College, University of Oxford, directed by Professor Jonathan Michie, has provided an intellectual base for my work. However, none of this would have been possible without the generous participation of many organisations: notably, Rochdale Boroughwide Housing, Cheshire West and Chester Local Authority, Hermes Investment Management, Argent LLP, Mars Inc., Primark, CottonConnect, SEWA (self-employed women's association), Agilysis, and Formation Architects. I have learnt much from them about the realities, strains, and pleasures of ethical organising in practice. I am grateful to Oxford's John Fell Fund for supporting my research on meaningful work, mutual organisations, and the cotton supply chain in India. I have also been the fortunate award holder of a British Academy/Leverhulme small grant to examine employee-owned organisations.

I am thankful to my parents, family, and friends for tolerating the months of neglect that comes with being associated with an academic writer. Most especially, I am deeply grateful to my partner, Dr Roger Harrison, who supported me through tricky times, listened to my attempts to formulate my thoughts, and supplied insights that have helped me to complete the task.

I have dedicated this book to the young adults in my life.

Ruth Yeoman
Chartridge, United Kingdom

Overview
Ethics, Meaningfulness, and Mutuality

The Sustainability Imperative

We urgently need to understand what kinds of organisations are capable of transitioning humanity to sustainable social and economic ways of living, using change processes that are fair, inclusive, and just. Today, we organise under the pressure of climate change, biodiversity collapse, widening social and economic inequalities, technological shifts, and political fragility. Such problems lead Hirst (2007) to ask: 'How does one govern a society divided into large organisations that are struggling to cope with complex activities and volatile conditions?' (p. 30). I argue that we do so by drawing upon all the talents: harnessing the values, meanings, norms, and relationships of diverse voices and perspectives into building the shared knowledge and understanding needed for learning, innovation, and cooperation. As Paul Polman, ex-CEO of Unilever, says:

> The issues we face are so big and the targets are so challenging that we cannot do it alone, so there is a certain humility and a recognition that we need to invite other people in. When you look at any issue, such as food or water scarcity, it is very clear that no individual institution, government or company can provide the solution.
>
> Paul Polman (Confino, 2012)[1]

We must invite people to contribute what is theirs to contribute in ways that respect and care for their humanity, and show concern for what matters to them. Caring concern extends to the manifold of valuable beings and things that make our lives worth living and for which we have responsibilities to steward, repair, maintain, and nurture, depending upon what actions will promote their welfare. To fulfil such responsibilities requires an uplift of human capability development, especially, I argue, a human capability for ethical world-building that enables us to create and maintain the many organisations through which we encounter valuable beings and things, incorporating them into the meaningfulness of our lives. Human beings possess a 'will to form', which Burrell (2013) describes as 'a deliberate plan and purpose that deal practically and functionally with the coordination of elements into an orderly structure that is in working order' (p. xxi). He describes the will to form as a continual process of 'constant organizing of organizations' (p. xxi) that seeks to 'order the world into meaning' (p. xix). This drive constitutes a general capacity for organising that can be translated into a human capability for ethical world-building, via mediating institutions and conversion factors derived from a synthesis of meaningfulness and mutuality. Such multi-level, multi-perspectival organising must draw upon the whole range of human motivations, and this includes, particularly, our fundamental human need for meaning (Yeoman, 2014a, 2014b). However, this need has been neglected in social and economic theory. In developing a human capability for ethical world-building, I reassess the role that meaningfulness, as a moral value, plays in practical reasoning, especially in the social processes of organising needed for expansive social cooperation.

The recent United Nations IPCC report (2018) summarises the likely impacts of 1.5% temperature rise above pre-industrial levels. Subsequent studies have started to examine not only the material effects upon ecosystems and biodiversity but also the psychological effects upon mental health and the relational fabric of human societies. For example, the 2019 Greenlandic Perspectives Survey documents a community suffering from ecological grief, as Greenlanders' mental health is put under pressure by the loss of animals, habitats, and a way of life they value.[2] Such felt material, social, and psychological harms means that the tide is turning on organisational neglect of 'ethics, morals and laws' (Burnes and Cooke, 2012). The ethical demands that the sustainability imperative makes on our capacity to organise means that ethical abstinence (Jaeggi, 2018) in the organisational realm is no longer a viable long-term strategy. Ethical organising is not a 'nice to have'—something we get round to once the important business of the day has been dealt with. Rather, the sustainability imperative entails fundamental shifts in organisational models, aimed at creating life value and undertaken *in medias res*, or 'in the middle of things', out of which we act together. Following Donaldson (2008), ethical organising requires a 'Normative Revolution' to establish 'the normative basis of markets in general, and for the normative basis of the corporation' (p. 174).

Ethical organising attends to perplexing situations that overspill traditional boundaries and stretch organisational capabilities for multi-scalar, multi-partner collaboration. Such situations have already produced a valuable resource of organisational innovations, including, for example, sustainable business models in the circular economy; urban labs in smart cities; social enterprises, cooperative platforms, and mutual ownership; multi-stakeholder partnerships in the collaborative governance of natural resources; base-of-the-pyramid initiatives; and ESG (environment, social, and governance) impact investing. These innovations are often characterised by hybrid organising that cuts across standard assumptions of what constitutes private and public value creation, in the process reshaping conventional organisational forms. For example, the UN Global Compact has adopted ten principles to support business contributions to the SDGs (sustainable development goals).[3] Unilever has applied these principles to their Sustainable Living Plan, described by the company as aiming to 'set out to decouple our growth from our environmental footprint whilst increasing our positive social impact' and included human rights and workplace reforms, as well as supply chain sustainability.[4] Moves such as these are contributing to a shift in the investor ecosystem, propelling initiatives such as Climate Action 100+, a coalition of investors that is targeting 100 'systemically important emitters'. Although not a member of Climate Action 100+, BlackRock has an emergent strategy focussed on long-term investment in organisations demonstrating a social purpose.[5] In his 2019 CEO letter, BlackRock CEO Larry Fink says: 'Purpose is not a mere tagline or marketing campaign; it is a company's fundamental reason for being—what it does every day to create value for its stakeholders'. Blackrock uses ESG investing to direct capital towards organisations working to create long-term social and environmental value.[6] With respect to the SDGs, the Business & Sustainable Development Commission, established by leading corporations in partnership with the United Nations, comments:

> This is new territory. Moving business to a sustainable growth model will be disruptive, with big risks as well as opportunities at stake. It will involve experimenting with new 'circular' and more agile business models that can grow exponentially to shape new social and environmental value chains.
>
> (Business and Sustainable
> Development Commission, 2017: 6)

We must examine new approaches to concerns of *synoikismos*, or how we are to live together, that incorporate a wider range of human motivations than rational self-interest. In his writings on the city, Soja (2003) uses *synoikismos* to describe the city as a gathering or a habitation for dwelling together, calling us to a moral concern for 'the conditions that derive from dwelling together in a particular home place or space' (p. 273). In ethical organising, I conceive of ethical worlds as habitations for ensembles of morally valuable beings and things, and apply our need for meaning to describe the motivational basis for constructing ethical worlds through which we take care of valuable beings and things that make our lives worth living. From the perspective of materialist ethics, Noonan (2012) argues that all value is derived from the life-ground, or the 'general conditions of maintaining and developing terrestrial life' (loc. 213), where 'what is good is what enables life to develop and survive' (loc. 213). Noonan (2012) distinguishes between instrumental life value, or the 'resources, institutions, relationships, and practices that maintain life', and intrinsic value, or the 'expression and enjoyment of the capacities that the satisfaction of life-requirements enables' (loc. 285). Drawing upon the motivations implied by our need for meaning, life value defines economic activity as the provisioning of those life goods we need to fulfil our responsibilities to care for valuable beings and things.

Sustainability in the provisioning of life goods must become the core objective of value creation models (Breuer et al., 2018), where the value created is life value, or those life-requirements produced within planetary boundaries needed for survival and flourishing. Systematic reordering of our socio-ecological system requires new shared meanings, values, and narratives to bind us into a common concern for valuable beings and things and motivating us to make our contribution to constructing social cooperation that expands our circles of moral concern. Drawing upon a wider range of human motivations means creating a 'metaphysical reconstruction of economics' (McCarraher, 2011: 110), where economic models of human behaviour account for relationality (Mir, 2019). However, Brenkert (2019) comments that 'normative business ethics has little to say about how to correct motivational ethical problems' (p. 919). The business case appeal to self-interest neglects many other sources of motivation, including our need for meaning and purpose. From the viewpoint of organisational theory, Greenwood and Freeman (2017) call for a 'broadening of the intellectual base of business ethics' (p. 1) that will help us to develop our ethical knowledge of businesses as societal institutions. In particular, the fact of value pluralism means differences over purpose, values, and ways of living can no longer be regarded as intrusions into effective organising that must be dissolved away through negotiation, socialisation, or suppression. In his 2019 address to the Investment Association of Canada, John Ruggie (2019) argues that ESG investing has neglected the S, or social dimension, making it the 'weakest pillar of the three'. Ruggie describes the S dimension as being 'about people', who are 'workers, including in supply chains; customers; and people in affected communities', as well as shareholders.

More broadly, the S dimension is the relational infrastructure of ethics, values, and meanings that motivate social cooperation. Himes and Muraca (2018) identify the relevant human values for evaluating ecosystem services with relational values. These are described by the IPBES (Intergovernmental Platform on Biodiversity and Ecosystem Services) as: 'imbedded in desirable (sought after) relationships, including those between people and nature' (p. 1). Narotzky and Besnier (2014) argue that lives worth living depend upon 'structures of provisioning' (p. 4), underpinned by social relations of trust and care. Gibson-Graham (2014) provide a minimal list of relational values that inhere in heterogeneous economies, including 'trust, care, sharing, reciprocity, cooperation, coercion, bondage, thrift, guilt, love, equity, self-exploitation, solidarity, distributive justice, stewardship, spiritual connection, and environmental and social justice' (p. 151).[7] Given the multiplicity of values at work, Burford et al. (2013) argue that a fourth pillar, described by values-based intersubjectivity, needs to be added to the three pillars (environmental, economic, and social) of sustainable development. The intersubjective conditions of this in-between space of relational values can be evaluated and tracked as another dimension of sustainable development. Viable relational values are sustained by a dialogic intersubjective realm, or a 'human 'interworld [. . .] of shared meaning that transcends individual consciousness" (p. 3045). This interworld of shared meanings underpins the transmission of narratives that inform identities, ways of living, and ultimately judgements that life is meaningful and worth living.

The value of meaningfulness contributes to the values-based reasoning for collective action aimed at life value creation when certain organisational conditions pertain. I show that these conditions are provided by the relational resources of mutuality, taken to be an organising principle for orchestrating long-term collaboration between disparate collectives. Ethical organising goes beyond organisational self-interest by bringing to ethics and economics the concept of life value organisations as entities, structured by integrity, values, and purpose, and formed from the joint contributions of all those who are affected by the organisation's activities (Driver, 2006). Life value organisations are pluralist, relational, and power-sharing entities that are socially constructed by their members, who are entitled to exercise their human capability for ethical world-building, in order to create and maintain the organisation as a collective moral agent. In creating life value organisations, world-builders gather valuable beings and things into assemblages with the aim of solving vexing problems related to matters of common concern. John Dewey (1927) defines the public as the domain of 'all those who are affected by the indirect consequences of transactions to such an extent that it is deemed necessary to have those consequences systematically cared for' (pp. 15–16). Caring for consequences is not the sole responsibility of states but lies with all of us who are simultaneously the deciders, producers, and users of goods and services necessary for life value. Becoming practised in caring for consequences is civilising. It trains us in the arts of being human— of complex living that develops our capacities and ultimately justifies the worth of human civilisation.

Given the complexity of the many problems that world-builders are called upon to address, organisations are becoming increasingly connected into associational ecosystems. I argue that the sustainability imperative demands that all these should be collective moral agents, characterised by integrity and organisational emotions, where the social basis for these features is the society of meaning-makers. In this way, creating life value provides organisations with a morally viable purpose or an enduring reason to exist that is worthy of their member contributions. With this in mind, I develop a capability justice account of ethical organising, arguing that people have responsibilities to contribute to creating life organisations as collective moral agents, to the extent that their contributions are structured by the goods of meaningfulness. The goods of meaningfulness include freedom as non-domination, autonomy as non-alienation, and dignity as being seen as a particular person with a life of one's own to lead (Yeoman, 2014).

Motivating Humanity

In outlining my case for a philosophy of ethical organising, I draw upon Dewey's (1917) concept of pragmatic idealism, of which he says: 'We pride ourselves upon a practical idealism, a lively and easily moved faith in possibilities as yet unrealized, in willingness to make sacrifice for their realization' (p. 9). Ethical organising is *pragmatic*, because our best option for sustaining human civilisation, whilst preserving equity, justice, and dignity, is to make full use of our already existing interdependence, collective knowledge, and innovative capacity to solve global problems, and it is *idealistic* because the necessary form of planetary-scale organising relies upon a cosmopolitan moral expansiveness and uplift of human capabilities for values-based cooperating. Such pragmatic idealism requires richer models of human motivation than those that rely solely on rational self-interest. For example, Hirschman (1970) calls for a more complex approach to economics that reaches into the 'murky realms' of culture, affect, and meaning. He urges economists to 'complicate some categories of economic discourse' (p. 89), so as to illuminate 'the incredible complexity of human nature' (p. 95). Ostrom (2010) says that economics needs a theory of human behaviour which accounts for the relational dimensions of action, and recognises people as 'learning and norm-adopting individuals' (p. 432). More recently, economists have become interested in how we are motivated by concepts, ideas, meanings, values, and narratives that evoke emotional and cognitive responses in the social interactions of everyday action (Shiller, 2017).

Meaningfulness and meaning-making are neglected features of human motivation and a source of ethical behaviour. Brandom (2009) observes that, as 'concept-mongering' and 'normative creatures', we 'live and move [. . .] in a normative space' (p. 33). As unavoidably normative creatures, justifying the objective value of meanings that underpin our subjective experience of meaningfulness is of 'utmost importance to us' (Nozick, 1981: 571). Success in advancing claims of objective value and subjective attachment depend upon meaning-making as an 'activity which brings value to human life' (Karlsson et al., 2004: 63). A sense of meaning shapes how we see ourselves in the world and is an important factor in economic behaviour and social cooperation: 'People want to believe that they have some control over their behaviour and hence their destiny—they want to feel as if they are more than the sum of nerve firings happening in obscure parts of their brain' (p. 70). Karlsson et al. (2004) propose that the connection between the desire for meaning and human behaviour can be modelled along a number of dimensions, including the opportunity to make free choices; reducing uncertainty about preferences; the search for higher meaning; and the ability to make (moral and prudential) sense of the world.

However, the motivational importance of meaningfulness as a prudential and moral value and the role of meaning-making in human rationality have yet to be incorporated into economic and organisation theory: 'If economics do not take into account meaning, it runs the risk of missing something important in the understanding of human behaviour' (Karlsson et al., 2004: 73). Cassar and Meier (2018) suggest how economic models can incorporate meaningful work by accounting for non-monetary incentives, such as corporate purpose. Lepisto and Pratt (2017) argue that the ideal of meaningful work operates as a source of justification when seeking to ease our 'uncertainty and ambiguity regarding the value or worth of one's work' (p. 8). People involved in corporate social responsibility initiatives generate meaningfulness through sense-making (Aguinis and Glavas, 2019). However, meaningfulness can be thwarted if employees are required to take part in CSR initiatives, making these look like organisational vanity projects when employees' own work is of poor quality or unfairly rewarded. Meaningfulness is less likely to be experienced in organisations that make no attempt to secure mutuality in production and distribution, consistent with fairness, trust, and concern.

In my philosophy of ethical organising, I specify a social architecture of meaningfulness and mutuality that converts the general capacity to organise into the human capability for ethical world-building. The value of meaningfulness manifests at multiple scales of work, organisations, and systems, when mutual organisation is used to create meaning-making processes that connect to our 'desire to make sense of our immediate experience, our life, and our world' (Chater and Loewenstein, 2015: 137). The drive for sense-making underpins our ability to create and justify 'responsibilising narratives' (Bénabou et al., 2018: 1) and, via these narratives, transmits the social norms needed for expansive social cooperation. Di Paolo et al. (2010) argue that sense-making is interactive, joint, and participatory, such that people 'intertwine their sense-making activities, with consequences for each other in the process, in the form of the interactional generation of new meanings and the transformation of existing meanings' (p. 72). However, sense-making, itself, does not provide a moral basis for evaluating, selecting, and incorporating meanings. For this, the value of meaningfulness must be incorporated into our practical reasoning regarding 'what we ought to do'.

Meaningfulness enters into deliberation as a prudential value that illuminates what is valued by a person living a particular life and also as a moral value in evaluating the worth of the objects constituting her life and reflecting upon how morality requires her to respond to the intrinsic worth of those objects. Economic and organisation theory can contribute to our understanding of the value of meaningfulness in practical reasoning by proposing the normative design of dialogic practices that sensitise people to the prudential and moral significance of the meanings constituting their activities and interests. From democratic theory, Mansbridge et al. (2010) show how deliberation can be expanded by using constrained self-interest, or interests limited by moral commitments, to bring information into problem-solving, thereby aiding the formation of 'an aggregative common good or conflict' (p. 73). Interest is an 'enlightened preference' (p. 68), constructed from commitments that are self-, other-, and ideal-regarding. Such interests are mutable, susceptible to transformation through exploration of different perspectives upon conflictual and problematic situations and, when filtered through the moral value of meaningfulness, provide confidence that interests incorporate things of objective worth and subjective appeal. This joint investigation of interests often takes place among people who must act together in troubling situations, where the relevant dialogic spaces are created when ethical worlds are ordered by the mutuality principle.

A Human Capability for Ethical World-Building

In ethical organising, mutuality and meaningfulness assume the role of meta-values. These are values invested with a fertile historical and cultural diversity of meanings that have the capacity to orchestrate other values into value-systems. In her capability theory of justice, Nussbaum (2000) gives two architechtonic capabilities—practical reason and affiliation—a special role because they 'organise and suffuse all the others, making their pursuit truly human' (p. 82). In order to establish a human capability for ethical world-building, I outline a social architecture of meaningfulness and mutuality, consisting of an integrated network of normative elements, including: agonistic republicanism, the society of meaning-makers, public meaningfulness, the goods of meaningfulness, liberal value pluralism, and the status and capabilities for becoming a meaning-maker. The social architecture of meaningfulness and mutuality operates as normative technology for incorporating interactive processes of meaning-making into ethical world-building, using core practices of mutual organisation, such as voice and purposing (see Chapter three).

The synthesis of meaningfulness and mutuality considers a variety of motivational drives other than rational self-interest to be relevant to human behaviour. The purpose of ethical organising is to create collective moral agents that will enable us to experience ourselves as whole people when assembling morally valuable beings and things into ethical worlds and generating duties of care towards them. In capability justice, exercising the capability for ethical world-building satisfies our entitlement to make our contribution to solving shared problems related to caring for beings and things that matter to us. This is a responsibility, provided certain normative conditions consistent with the value of meaningfulness are met. These conditions are: firstly, that organising aims at objectively valuable objects which are subjectively attractive and, secondly, that collective action is structured by the goods of meaningfulness (freedom, autonomy, and dignity). The value of meaningfulness in practical reasoning provides the basis for a critical evaluation of ends, or whether our activity addresses morally valuable objects and, if so, what means we should deploy to take care of those objects. Mutual organisation generates practices, such as a durable voice-system, that activate meaning-making in practical reasoning.

Meaningfulness and Mutuality

In a synthesis of meaningfulness and mutuality, I use Wolf's (2010) hybrid account of meaningfulness, which integrates objective and subjective elements, such that 'meaning arises when subjective attraction meets objective attractiveness' (p. 9). The experience of meaningfulness is more likely to occur when a person becomes actively connected to a worthy object, or something or someone of value, such that they are 'gripped, excited, involved by it' (Wolf, 1997: 208). I take meaningfulness to be collectively constructed from the materials of everyday living, and make an ethic of care the standpoint for evaluating the moral viability of meanings. Morally legitimate collective action, aimed at promoting the welfare of worthy objects, must be structured by the goods of meaningfulness (freedom, autonomy, and dignity). Such collective action permits the exercise of complex capabilities that are productive of a life we have reason to value, or as Wolf (2010) puts it, 'to live a life worth living' (p. 10). By acting together on problems or objects of common concern, people create meaningfulness for themselves and others. But because we encounter problems and objects in specific contexts, the meanings generated are plural and often conflicting, leading to diverse experiences of meaningfulness. Meanings are translated into the experience of meaningfulness via integrative processes of social construction where social interactions have ethical features of mutual recognition, respect, and care.

Meaningfulness is related to having life-grounded projects that provide us with the material for the narrative formation of our lives, directing us to the responsibilities we have to act appropriately towards the objects for the sake of which such projects exist. Thus, meaningfulness does not come from the aggregation of individual goods, but from long lasting *appropriate orientations* towards particular objects, such as persons, animals, or activities, where orientations may be judged to be appropriate when they point us towards the responsibilities we have to further the good for those objects (see Yeoman, 2014a). Mutuality is an organising principle that affords normative resources for designing organisations that contain ground projects and social processes, enabling us to incorporate the value meaningfulness into collective practical reasoning. The objective of mutual organisation is to distribute among all affected stakeholders a fair share of the benefits and burdens arising from their shared activities. In a mutual organisation, distribution is determined through fair procedures in which all affected stakeholders have a voice in influencing the rules governing such distributions and furthermore are invested with joint control rights in determining the purposes and actions of the organisation. Mutuality unlocks meaningfulness by supplying the intergrative meaning-making processes that connect to repositories of purposes, values, and meanings. Voice is a core practice for mutual organisation, where voice involves sharing with the others the responsibility and authority for forming the purpose, making the rules and implementing the tasks necessary for promoting the good for worthy objects, or those objects for the sake of which the organisation exists. The practices of mutuality help life value organisations engage their members in diverse sources of meanings, thereby giving such organisations an advantage in producing the common goods or the facilities we need to fulfil our responsibilities to care for morally valuable beings and things.

Towards a Philosophy of Ethical World-Building

Ethical world-building involves a critical examination of how our ideas concerning the relationship between ethics, organisations, and economics shape human lives, including the values, meanings, needs, interests, capabilities, and relationships by which people orientate themselves to morally valuable beings and things, gathering them into relational ensembles for solving shared problems and creating life value. Nelson (2016) says that ethics and economics cannot be kept separate and that if we are to 'survive and flourish, as a species as well as individuals, we have to act as whole people, body and soul together' (p. 8). The divide between ethics and economics mirrors that between morality and ethics in moral theory. Jaeggi (2018) says ethics must be concerned with critical evaluation of forms of life, which she defines as 'complex bundles (or ensembles) of social practices geared to solving problems that for their part are historically contextualized and normatively constituted' (p. 29). Such an ethical inquiry must be concerned with how any given form of life can make progress towards becoming a 'just cohabitation' (p. ix). Moral learning arises out of perplexing situations, characterised by messy entanglements of people, things, urgencies, ideas, experiments, and interpretations, where sustainable social change is a particular kind of normatively desirable process, through which people enrich their experience of others, expand their moral circles of concern, and develop their own and others' ethical capabilities.

Thus, a rapprochement between ethics, organising, and economics equips world-builders with a critical normativity suitable for creating life value organisations. Drawing upon the case of the Tea Party, White (2017) develops a critical theory perspective on associational life that has been corrupted by an interior malignancy, understood as 'systematically invasive, not directly willed by anyone, and may be lethal to its host' (p. 132). Systematic malignancy is a type of logic maintained by wilful blindness, cognitive dissonance, and other failures of ethical competence. By distorting and appropriating our meaning-making capacities, this logic undermines the normative core of social organisation. However, malignancy can be overcome by a 'richer narrative of human capaciousness' (p. 134) that acknowledges the need for openness to difference when working for the reform of existing social and political orders. Capaciousness resists the experience of *dearth* as the 'sense of becoming vivid of our condition of finitude' (p. 66) that interacts with a 'brute insufficiency of meaning' (p. 94) and manifests as a threat to one's identity. We can ease eco-anxiety arising from *dearth* by seeing ourselves as responsible for cultivating capacious connections in ensembles of beings and things directed towards life value creation as a generative source of meaning and purpose.

Organisations are potent sources of meaning abundance. As 'thought worlds' (Douglas, 1986), they shape the cognitive processes that are the building blocks for any social order. However, to overcome tendencies to malignancy, meaning abundance must be harnessed into ethical world-building. Stark (2009) characterises organisations as 'cognitive ecologies that facilitate the work of cognitive reflection' (p. 5), through which people articulate 'what is valuable, what is worthy, what counts' (p. 4). Reflection shaped by constructive conflict and responsible difference-making taps into the immanent potential of organisations, or the interior normative richness of organisational life that forms part of our 'relational sociomaterial totality' (Tsoukas, 2019: 11). As a source of change, immanence is activated through morally desirable collective action, structured by mutual organisation practices, such as democratic voice, justice, and dignity. An organisational meaning-system that avoids malignancy is maintained in organisations where people are relational and cooperative, dissent and difference are respected, and directors are integrators and communicators. Douglas (1986) emphasises that 'a truly complex ordering is the result of sustained effort' (p. 56); it takes hard human work to hold together the dynamic tensions and contradictions that maintain any organisation. The result is a 'collective achievement'—something to be valued, nurtured, and taken pride in.

Organisations and Organising

Activating the emancipatory possibilities of ethical organising requires a view of organisations as entities that are susceptible to human agency, realised through member participation in the processes of organising. Organisations are objects in the human world of things we value. Dewey (1981) argues that organisations are both entities and interactions of people: 'A corporation is neither a mental state nor a particular physical event in space and time. [. . .] It is an objective reality which has multitudinous physical and mental consequences. [. . .] It would not exist [. . .] apart from the interaction of human beings with one another' (p. 154). Perrow (1972) describes organisations as tools by which people exercise power and get things done: 'Organizations are multipurpose tools for shaping the world as one wishes it to be shaped. They provide the means for imposing one's definition of the proper affairs of men [sic] upon other men' (p. 14). Elsewhere, Perrow (1991) says of organisations that they are 'the key phenomenon of our time' (p. 725), and he specifies three questions relevant to understanding the organisation society: how do organisations begin, grow and die; how are they organised internally and how might this be improved to benefit all stakeholders; and what impact do they have on society (Perrow, 2000: 469–470).

Applying these questions to the formation of life value organisations means retrieving the organisation as an object of design that is manifested through co-creative, polyphonic world-building. Lopdrup-Hjorth (2015) describes the loss of the organisation as an object of inquiry as 'organisation-phobia' (p. 439). He attributes this to problematising organisations as dangerous and all powerful entities. Du Gay and Lopdrup-Hjorth (2016) argue that a 'fear of the formal' (p. 6) has led to the hollowing out of organisations, and they call for formal design to be reclaimed, in order to establish organisations capable of instituting authority and responsibility. The stakeholder theory of the firm provides a jumping off point for developing the concept of the life value organisation (Freeman et al., 2010). Stakeholder theorists argue that corporations ought to be managed to the benefit of all stakeholders (Freeman, 1984), such that 'firm performance might be defined as the total value created by the firm through its activities, which is the sum of the utility created for each of a firm's legitimate stakeholders' (Harrison and Wicks, 2013: 102). Boatright (2002) develops a stakeholder perspective by characterising the 'nexus of contracts' as corporate constituencies where each constituency of employees, customers, suppliers, and investors 'provides some asset in return for some gain' (p. 1838). Given this, Boatright argues that stakeholder theory is consistent with contract theory, such that 'all stakeholders are regarded as contractors with the firm, with their rights determined through bargaining' (ibid.). Harrison and Wicks (2013) define the legitimate stakeholders of the firm as 'those groups to whom the firm owes an obligation based on their participation in the cooperative scheme that constitutes the organization and makes it a going concern. They include customers, communities in which the firm operates, suppliers of capital, equipment, materials, and labor' (p. 102, cf. Phillips, 2003).

Human interaction is of central importance to the creation of organisational value, particularly life value. O'Donnell et al. (2003) find that 'almost two thirds of organizational value is perceived to be intellectual and that half of this IC value is perceived to stem directly from the people dimension' (p. 82). However, to be consistent with ethical organising, not any kind of interaction will do, but rather these interactions should be morally viable relationships. Donaldson and Preston (1995) argue that 'managers should acknowledge the validity of diverse stakeholder interests and should attempt to respond to them within a mutually supportive framework, because that is a moral requirement for the managerial function' (p. 87).

Organisations possess general features that can be subjected to ethical evaluation. Hodgson (2006) considers organisations as a special type of institution, where institutions are human-made creations consisting of 'systems of established and prevalent social rules that structure social interactions' (p. 2, cf. North, 1991). From the perspective of public value theory, Bozeman (2013) argues that both public and private organisations are public to the extent that they are all shaped by public power and that publicness/privateness are dimensions of organisations rather than categories. The blurred distinction between public and private organisations means that all organisations are taking on aspects of hybridity. Following Wittgenstein's family resemblances view on businesses, Herzog (2018) argues that all organisations share similar clusters of productive practices. In my development and application of the social architecture of meaningfulness and mutuality, I share Herzog's view that there are general features of all organisations that can be critically evaluated using ethical criterion.

Becoming World-Builders

Organising is what human beings do in order to pursue purposes and interact with objects that they value. Yet moral and political theory has little to say to ethical concerns regarding who makes organisations, how they do so, and with what consequences. In organisational theory, normative reflection upon the moral agency of employees, suppliers, customers, and other stakeholders is overshadowed by the focus on managerial, entrepreneurial, or investor agency. Human agents have become invisible in theories of organising, which tend to privilege organisations as 'hyper-muscular supermen, single handed in their efforts to resist institutional pressure, transform organizational fields and alter institutional logics'

(Suddaby, 2010: 15). Greenwood and Miller (2010) argue that organisational theory needs to retrieve its core concern which is 'understanding
the management of collective effort through organization design' (p. 78),
including complex organisations such as 'transnational organizations,
vertically disintegrated firms, and network, modular, or even virtual organizations' (p. 80). In other words, human agency in ethical organising must
be designed into organisations.

Organisations belong to all of us. None of us should be allowed to do anything we like to entities constructed from collective human effort, the assets
of other living creatures, and the materials of the earth, in which dwell our
most precious objects and concerns. We are entitled to contribute to making organisations that are worthy of our involvement with them and that
give meaning to our lives. Furthermore, in the social processes of organising,
no one should be permitted to usurp someone's capacity for organising or
thwart its conversion into the human capability for ethical world-building.
To do so is extractive world-building that assumes a person's general capacity for organising can be co-opted to serve means and ends defined by others.
Such capability appropriation transgresses that person's entitlements to the
goods of meaningfulness. Organisations that are worthy of our contributions are life value organisations, and these are constructed from a human
capability for the ethical world-building as an element of capability justice.

Overview of Chapters

This book outlines a philosophy of ethical organising that identifies the
general organisational features of the expansive social cooperation needed
to address the sustainability imperative. Chapter 1 examines the realm of
values and the role that human values play in ethical organising. Values
are conceptualised as relational, dynamic, and constituted by meanings
and as socially constructed in moral free spaces that are repositories for
ethical resources, such as liberal value pluralism. When structured by the
social architecture of meaningfulness and mutuality, moral free spaces are
proliferated in life value organisations. Moral free spaces provide arenas
for meaning-making that connects values, knowledge, and understanding
via positive narrative formations. People are equipped to judge narratives as morally viable or unviable when the value of meaningfulness is
incorporated practical reasoning and where mutuality is employed as an
organising principle for collective action.

In Chapter 2, I draw upon McMurtry (1998, 2002) and Noonan's
(2012) materialist ethics to conceptualise value as life value, where such
value is worth creating when it contributes to the fundamental conditions
for life to happen and to flourish. Although value creation is central to
organisational theory, value is poorly understood, frequently conceived
in simplistic terms, and emptied of normative content. This chapter will
take a philosophical approach to examining the meaning of value in

organisations and systems, using this to outline the general features of an organisational model for life value creation.

Meaningfulness and mutuality provide the social basis for equipping people with the capability for the ethical world-building they need to develop life value organisations. In a philosophy of ethical organising, meaningfulness and mutuality are conceptualised as meta-values for structuring life value organisations. Using meaningfulness and mutuality as meta-values, Chapter 3 specifies elements of a social architecture of meaningfulness and mutuality that translates the general capacity for organising into a human capability for ethical world-building. The value of meaningfulness is taken up into practical reasoning by participants in collective action who must jointly determine what they ought to do. Mutuality as an organising principle institutes meaning-making processes, and in turn these processes activate the value of meaningfulness in practical reasoning, both at the organisational level and in the inter-organising of associational ecosystems.

In the proposed philosophy of ethical organising, collective action conforms to normatively desirable characteristics, derived from the social architecture of meaningfulness and mutuality, when the ends and means of joint activities promote human emancipation and ecological repair. Chapter 4 argues that such normatively desirable collective action depends upon life value organisations being created by their members as collective moral agents. Collective moral agency is developed when organisations become sensitised to values through processes of empathetic thinking and feeling that augment the moral emotions of their members and establish integrity as the organisation's independent moral presence in society. Such an organisation is worthy of the interactions and contributions of its members. Purposing as a social process incorporating multiple participants is discussed, using the concept of agonistic republicanism to admit constructive conflict and responsible difference-making into collective deliberations.

Values connect collective action to value creation through multi-perspective evaluations of what is worth creating. Chapter 5 explores questions related to moral judgement and responsibility by applying a materialist ethic of care to the question of 'how well we doing' in looking after those beings and things that we know to be morally valuable. This will be combined with Young's (2010) social connection theory of responsibility, which identifies how structural injustice arises from the cumulative decisions and actions of individuals. Practices of judging and responsibility are incorporated into a conceptualisation of complex systems, such as supply chains, as unfolding systems of social cooperation. Meaningfulness and mutuality are used to illuminate the relationality between persons, even across separations of distance, culture, and power.

In Chapter 6, I develop further the social constructivist elements of ethical organising. The capability for ethical world-building is subject to capability justice, thereby entitling each person, as a self-determining, interdependent, and vulnerable being, to a contributive share in determining the means and ends of ethical world-building, and affording them the status as co-authorities for judging between constructed worlds. Worlds are ethical when they are instituted by a just basic structure. Justice in the social construction of ethical worlds demands fairness, care, and flourishing in the social processes of unfolding human action through which the basic structure comes into being.

In Chapter7, I draw upon Gewirth's (1996) use of mutuality in a community of rights to examine what is needed to create a society of meaning-makers. The society of meaning-makers is central to capacity-building in organisations and systems that seek to put into practice the philosophy of ethical organising. Slote's (2007) ethic of care will be used to examine how practices of empathetic understanding contribute to the social learning needed to develop a sense of emotional connectedness and responsibility, including the capacity to make judgements on 'how well are we doing'. A distributive power system is proposed that involves relational power as being open to be influenced by the differences of others.

Finally, I use the social architecture of meaningfulness and mutuality as a normative lens to examine three troubling situations that illuminate the dimensions of ethical organising. The sustainability imperative requires system-level change that closes the space of opportunity for organisations to act against the interests of enduring human civilisation. In 'the arc of the moral universe', Cohen (1997) argues that the moral vacuity of the slave system produced its inherent structural weakness, leading ultimately to its collapse. The moral interests of slaves in 'material well-being, autonomy and dignity' conflicted with the interests of the slave system. However, the powerlessness of slaves meant that they were not able to give informed and free consent to any agreements constituting slavery as a system of social cooperation (p. 94). This injustice rendered slavery as an institutional system unstable and illegitimate—structurally, the system lacked the ethical viability needed for social cooperation to survive over generations: 'Its Nature of wickedness is its manifest Destiny of Ruin' (p. 95). In order to avoid a destiny of ruin for our children and grandchildren, a pragmatic idealist approach to ethical organising must open-heartedly include our fellow world-builders in the practical and moral evaluation of the forms of organising that will best sustain human civilisation upon the earth.

Notes

1. Confino, J. (2012, April 24). 'Unilever's Paul Polman: Challenging the Corporate Status Quo'. *The Guardian*. www.theguardian.com/sustainable-business/paul-polman-unilever-sustainable-living-plan
2. See Greenland Perspective, Natural History Museum of Denmark. https://kraksfondbyforskning.dk/wp-content/uploads/2019/08/2019_08_11_Greenlandic_Perspectives_Climate_Change_Final_Report_Reduced.pdf [accessed 27 August 2019].

3. See United Nations Global Impact, '87 Major Companies Lead the Way Towards a 1.5°C Future'. www.unglobalcompact.org/
4. See Unilever, 'Sustainable Living'. www.unilever.co.uk/sustainable-living/
5. In his 2018 CEO letter, Larry Fink cites Deloitte research, which finds that 63% of millennial workers believe the primary purpose of business is to improve society.
6. See Coalition for Inclusive Capitalism, 'Embankment Project for Inclusive Capitalism'. www.ey.com/Publication/vwLUAssets/ey-at-embankment-project-inclusive-capitalism/$FILE/EY-the-embankment-project-for-inclusive-capitalism-report.pdf
7. Patterson et al. (2018) highlight a tension between social justice and sustainability objectives. Whilst social justice is essential to humanising social and economic transitions, interpretations of social justice that prioritise, for example, jobs growth may have unintended political consequences that divert attention from climate change urgencies.

Bibliography

Agle, R. A., Donaldson, T., Freeman, R. E., Jensen, M. C., Mitchell, R. K., & Wood, D. J. (2008). Towards a Superior Stakeholder Theory. *Business Ethics Quarterly*, 18 (2): 153–190.

Aguinis, H., & Glavas, A. (2019). On Corporate Social Responsibility, Sensemaking, and the Search for Meaningfulness Through Work. *Journal of Management*, 45 (3): 1057–1086.

Bénabou, R., Falk, A., & Tirole, J. (2018). *Narratives, Imperatives and Moral Reasoning*. IZA Discussion Papers 11665, Institute of Labor Economics (IZA).

Boatright, J. R. (2002). Contractors as Stakeholders: Reconciling Stakeholder Theory with the Nexus-of-Contracts Firm. *Journal of Banking and Finance*, 26 (9): 1837–1852.

Bozeman, B. (2013). What Organization Theorists and Public Policy Researchers Can Learn from One Another : Publicness Theory as a Case-in-Point. *Organization Studies*, 34 (2), 169–188.

Brandom, R. (2009). *Reason in Philosophy*. Cambridge, MA: Harvard University Press.

Brenkert, G. G. (2019). Mind the Gap! The Challenges and Limits of (Global) Business Ethics. *Journal of Business Ethics*, 155 (4): 917–930.

Breuer, H., Ludeke-Freund, F., & Brick, C. (2018). *Business Model Innovation in the Era of Sustainable Development Goals*. Conference Paper: The ISPIM Innovation Conference, The Name of the Game, Stockholm, Sweden, 17–20 June.

Burford, G., Hoover, E., Velasco, I., Janoušková, S., Jimenez, A., Piggot, G., Podger, D., & Harder, M. K. (2013). Bringing the "Missing Pillar" into Sustainable Development Goals: Towards Intersubjective Values-Based Indicators. *Sustainability*, 5: 3035–3059.

Burnes, B., & Cooke, B. (2012). Review Article: The Past, Present and Future of Organization Development: Taking the Long View. *Human Relations*, 65 (11): 1395–1429.

Burrell, G. (2013). *Styles of Organizing: The Will to Form*. Oxford: Oxford University Press.

Business and Sustainable Development Commission (January 2017). *Better Business Better World Executive Summary*. http://report.businesscommission.org/uploads/Executive-Summary.pdf [accessed 1 August 2019].

Cassar, L., & Meier, S. (2018). Nonmonetary Incentives and Implications of Work as a Source of Meaning. *Journal of Economic Perspectives*, 32 (3): 215–238.

Chater, N., & Loewenstein, G. (2015). The Under-Appreciated Drive for Sense-Making. *Journal of Economic Behavior & Organization*, 126: 137–154.

Cohen, J. (1997). The Arc of the Moral Universe. *Philosophy & Public Affairs*, 26 (2): 91–134.

Confino, J. (2012, April 24). 'Unilever's Paul Polman: Challenging the Corporate Status Quo'. *The Guardian*. www.theguardian.com/sustainable-business/paul-polman-unilever-sustainable-living-plan

Cortes, M., & Londono, S. (2009). What Sense Can the Sense-Making Perspective Make for Economics? *Integrative Psychological and Behavioral Science*, 43 (2): 178–184.

Crosby, B. C., & Bryson, J. M. (2010). Special Issue on Public Integrative Leadership: Multiple Turns of the Kaleidoscope. *Leadership Quarterly*, 21: 205–208.

Dewey, J. (1993 [1917]). The Need for a Recovery of Philosophy. In: Morris & Shapiro (eds.), *John Dewey: The Political Writings*. Indianapolis & Cambridge: Hackett Publishing Company, 1–9.

Dewey, J. (1927). *The Public and Its Problems*. Athens: Swallow Press & Ohio University Press.

Dewey, J. (1981). Experience and Nature. In: Boydston, Jo Ann (ed.), *John Dewey: The Later Works 1925–1953*. Carbondale: Southern Illinois University Press.

Dewey, J. (2008). Experience and Nature. In: Boydston, Jo Ann (ed.), *The Later Works of John Dewey, Volume 1: 1925–1953: 1925*. Carbondale: Southern Illinois University Press.

Di Paolo, E. A., Rohde, M., & De Jaegher, H. (2010). Horizons for the Enactive Mind: Values, Social Interaction, and Play. In: Stewart et al. (eds.), *Enaction: Towards a New Paradigm for Cognitive Sciences*. Cambridge, MA: MIT Press, 33–87.

Donaldson, T., & Preston, L. E. (1995). The Stakeholder Theory of the Corporation: Concepts, Evidence, and Implications. *The Academy of Management Review*, 20 (1): 65–91.

Douglas, M. (1986). *How Institutions Think*. Syracuse, NY: Syracuse University Press.

Driver, M. (2006). Beyond the Stalemate of Economics Versus Ethics: Corporate Social Responsibility and the Discourse of the Organizational Self. *Journal of Business Ethics*, 66 (4): 337–356.

du Gay, P., & Lopdrup-Hjorth, T. (2016). Fear of the Formal. *European Journal of Cultural and Political Sociology*, 3 (1): 6–40.

Freeman, R. E. (1984). *Strategic Management: A Stakeholder Approach*. Boston: Pitman/Ballinger.

Freeman, R. E., Harrison, J. S., Wicks, A. C., Parmar, B., & de Colle, S. (2010). *Stakeholder Theory: The State of the Art*. Cambridge: Cambridge University Press.

Gewirth, A. (1996). *The Community of Rights*. Chicago: University of Chicago Press.

Gibson-Graham, J. K. (2008). Diverse Economies: Performative Practices for Other Worlds. *Progress in Human Geography*, 32: 613–632.

Gibson-Graham, J. K. (2014). Rethinking the Economy with Thick Description and Weak Theory. *Current Anthropology*, 55 (9): 147–153.

Greenwood, M., & Freeman, R. E. (2017). Focusing on Ethics and Broadening our Intellectual Base. *Journal of Business Ethics*, 140 (1): 1–3.

Greenwood, R., & Miller, D. (2010). Tackling Design Anew: Getting Back to the Heart of Organizational Theory. *Academy of Management Perspectives* (November): 78–88.

Harrison, J. S., & Wicks, A. C. (2013). Stakeholder Theory, Value, and Firm Performance. *Business Ethics Quarterly*, 23 (1): 97–124.

Herzog, L. (2018). *Reclaiming the System: Moral Responsibility, Divided Labour, and the Role of Organizations in Society*. Oxford: Oxford University Press.

Himes, A., & Muraca, B. (2018). Relational Values: The Key to Pluralistic Valuation of Ecosystem Services. *Current Opinion in Environmental Sustainability*, 35: 1–7.

Hirschman, A. O. (1970). *Exit, Voice, and Loyalty: Responses to Decline in Firms, Organizations and States*. London: Harvard University Press.

Hirst, P. (2007). Can Associationalism Come Back ? *Critical Review of International Social and Political Philosophy*, 4 (1): 15–3.

Hodgson, G. (2006). What are institutions? *Journal of Economic Issues*, 40 (1): 1–25.

Hodgson, G. M. (2015). On Defining Institutions: Rules versus Equilibria. *Journal of Institutional Economics*, 11 (3): 497–505.

IPCC (2018). Summary for Policymakers. In: V. Masson-Delmotte, P. Zhai, H.-O. Pörtner, D. Roberts, J. Skea, P. R. Shukla, A. Pirani, W. Moufouma-Okia, C. Péan, R. Pidcock, S. Connors, J. B. R. Matthews, Y. Chen, X. Zhou, M. I. Gomis, E. Lonnoy, T. Maycock, M. Tignor & T. Waterfield (eds.), *Global Warming of 1.5°C: An IPCC Special Report on the Impacts of Global Warming of 1.5°C above Pre-Industrial Levels and Related Global Greenhouse Gas Emission Pathways, in the Context of Strengthening the Global Response to the Threat of Climate Change, Sustainable Development, and Efforts to Eradicate Poverty*. www.ipcc.ch/site/assets/uploads/sites/2/2019/05/SR15_SPM_version_report_LR.pdf

Jaeggi, R. (2018). *Critique of Forms of Life*. Cronin (trans.). Cambridge, MA, & London: Harvard University Press.

Karlsson, N., Loewenstein, G., & McCafferty, J. (2004). The Economics of Meaning. *Nordic Journal of Political Economy*, 30: 61–75.

Lepisto, D. A., & Pratt, M. G. (2017). Meaningful Work as Realization and Justification Toward a Dual Conceptualization. *Organizational Psychology Review*, 7 (2): 99–121.

Lopdrup-Hjorth, T. (2015). Object and Objective Lost? Organization-Phobia in Organization Theory. *Journal of Cultural Economy*, 8 (4): 439–461.

Mansbridge, J., Bohman, J., Chambers, S., Estlund, D., Føllesdal, A., Fung, A., Lafont, C., Manin, B., & Martí, J. L. (2010). The Place of Self-Interest and the Role of Power in Deliberative Democracy. *Journal of Political Philosophy*, 18: 64–100.

McCarraher, E. (2011). We Communists of the Old School. In: Pabst (ed.), *The Crisis of Global Capitalism: Pope Benedict XVI's Social Encyclical and the Future of Political Economy*. Eugene, OR: Wipf & Stock.

McMurtry, J. (1998). *Unequal Freedoms: The Global Market as an Ethical System*. Toronto: Garamond.

McMurtry, J. (2002). *Value Wars: The Global Market versus the Life Economy*. London: Pluto.

Mir, K. (2019). *Ethics and Economic Theory*. Oxford & New York: Routledge.

Narotzky, S., & Besnier, N. (2014). Crisis, Value, and Hope: An Introduction to Supplement 9. *Current Anthropology*, 55 (August): 4–16.

Nelson, J. A. (2003). Separative and Soluble Firms: Androcentric Bias and Business Ethics. In: Ferber & Nelson (eds.), *Feminist Economics Today: Beyond Economic Man*. Chicago & London: University of Chicago Press.

Nelson, J. A. (2016). *Economics for Humans*. Chicago & London: University of Chicago Press.

Noonan, J. (2012). *Materialist Ethics and Life-Value*. Montreal & London: McGill-Queen's University Press.

North, D. C. (1991). Institutions. *Journal of Economic Perspectives*, 5 (1): 97–112.

Nozick, R. (1981). *Philosophical Explanations*. Cambridge, MA: Belknap Press, 1981.

Nussbaum, M. C. (2000). *Women and Human Development: The Capabilities Approach*. Cambridge & New York: Cambridge University Press.

O'Donnell, D., O'Regan, P., Coates, B., Kennedy, T., Keary, B., & Berkery, G. (2003). Human Interaction: The Critical Source of Intangible Value. *Journal of Intellectual Capital*, 4 (1): 82–99.

Ostrom, E. (2010). Beyond Markets and States: Polycentric Governance of Complex Economic Systems. *The American Economic Review*, 100 (3): 641–672.

Patterson, J. J., Thaler, T., Hoffmann, M., Hughes, S., Oels, A., Chu, E., Mert. A., Huitema, D., Burch, S., & Jordan, A. (2018). Political feasibility of 1.5°C societal transformations: the role of social justice. *Current Opinion in Environmental Sustainability*, 31: 1–9.

Perrow, C. (1972). *Complex Organizations: A Critical Essay*. Glenview, IL: Scott.

Perrow, C. (1991). A Society of organizations. *Theory & Society*, 20 (6): 725–762.

Perrow, C. (2000). An Organizational Analysis of Organizational Theory. *Contemporary Sociology*, 29 (3): 469–476.

Ruggie, J. (2019). ESG Investing: Coming into its Own—and Not a Moment Too Soon. Responsible Investment Association of Canada Annual Conference Keynote Address Montreal, April 24, 2019. https://www.business-humanrights.org/sites/default/files/documents/Montreal%20RIA_John%20Ruggie%20speech.pdf [accessed 5 August 2019].

Shiller, R. (2017). Narrative Economics. *American Economic Review*, 107: 967–1004.

Schiller, R. J. (2019). *Narrative Economics: How Stories Go Viral and Drive Major Economic Events*. Princeton & Oxford: Princeton University Press.

Slote, M. (2007). *Ethics of Care and Empathy*. Abingdon, UK: Routledge.

Soja, E. W. (2003). Writing the City Spatially. *City*, 7: 269–280.

Stark, D. (2009). *The Sense of Dissonance: Accounts of Worth in Economic Life*. Princeton & Oxford: Princeton University Press.

Suddaby, R. (2010). Challenges for Institutional Theory. *Journal of Management Inquiry*, 19 (1): 14–20.

Tsoukas, H. (2019). *Philosophical Organization Theory*. Oxford: Oxford University Press.

Walsh, J. P., & Ungson, G. R. (1991). Organizational Memory. *Academy of Management Review*, 16: 57–91.

Weick, K. E., & Roberts, K. H. (1993). Collective Mind in Organizations: Heedful Interrelating on Flight Decks. *Administrative Science Quarterly*, 38: 357–381.

White, S. (2017). *A Democratic Bearing: Admirable Citizens, Uneven Justice, and Critical Theory*. Cambridge: Cambridge University Press.

Wolf, S. (1997). Happiness and Meaning: Two Aspects of the Good Life. *Social Philosophy & Policy*, 14: 207–225.

Wolf, S. (2010). *Meaning in Life and Why It Matters*. Princeton, NJ: Princeton University Press.

Yeoman, R. (2014a). *Meaningful Work and Workplace Democracy: A Philosophy of Work and a Politics of Meaningfulness*. London: Palgrave Macmillan. Yeoman, R. (2014b). Conceptualising Meaningful Work as a Fundamental Human Need. *Journal of Business Ethics*, 125 (2): 235–251.

Young, I. M. (2011). *Responsibility for Justice*. Oxford: Oxford University Press.

1   The Realm of Values

The sustainability imperative imposes moral obligations upon us to direct social cooperation towards a global regime of environmental, social, and technological organisation and governance. With this in mind, Frederick's (2006) observation regarding our need for a shared realm of human values to address civilisational threats remains timely and urgent. He says: 'As human societies are drawn ever closer together by electronic and other technologies, and as they face the multiple threats posed by the unwise and heedless use of these devices, it will become ever more necessary to reach agreement on the core values and ethical principles that permit a human life to be lived by all' (p. 122). In my account of ethical organising, I show that individuals have a moral obligation to play their part in establishing collectives and organisations that can address sustainability challenges provided they are equipped with the human capability for ethical world-building. Hedberg (2018) argues that sustainability is a political commitment that everyone should share. However, I extend this obligation beyond the political realm to everyday organising including the diverse roles that people assume in work, communities, families, and societies. Commitments to sustainability represent values that motivate people to undertake collaborative work in order to bring together multiple levels and spheres of organising. Ehrlich and Ehrlich (2013) argue that climate change threatens the food systems upon which our complex, interconnected civilisation depends. To avoid breakdowns, such as mass famines, we must radically alter our use of energy, water, and land infrastructures, including how we value and relate to such life systems. For Ehrlich and Ehrlich (2013), behavioural change at the planetary scale demands a revolution in societal norms, values and narratives, in order to counter 'growthmanic cultures' (p. 4) and to establish sustainability as the core principle for economic and social organising.

Committing to values, as well as to the changes to motivational structures this entails, immerses moral agents in dilemmas, tensions, and sometimes irresolvable conflicts regarding what must change and what must stay the same. Tainter (2006) distinguishes sustainability from resiliency, where sustainability is 'the capacity to continue a desired condition or process, social or ecological', and resiliency is 'the ability of a system to adjust its configuration and function under disturbance' (p. 92). He draws upon an *Oxford English Dictionary* definition of sustainability, understood as, 'To support life in; to provide for the life or bodily needs of; to furnish with the necessities of life; to keep' (Orion, 1955: 2095). Tainter (2006) comments that 'people sustain what they value, which can only derive from what they know' (p. 92). In other words, we assign values to beings and things that promote particular ways of life we value. However, the values underlying resiliency, or the capacity for change in response to disturbances, may conflict with sustainability, or the capacity to keep or maintain the necessary conditions of lives and things we value. Sustainability is a form of everyday work where we must grapple with this tension between stability and change. Tainter (2006) argues that we solve the problems this throws up by applying new information and knowledge into increasingly complex techno-social institutions. However, doing so presents us with a conundrum because sustaining ways of life by adding complexity is costly, resulting in 'diminishing returns to complexity' (p. 94). Tainter (2006) shows that societies manage such costs either by achieving resiliency through simplification or by achieving sustainability using new resources to increase complexity. Thus, to sustain ways of life we value, we must use complexity to solve problems, even though the increasing costs of doing so may eventually outrun the capacity for sustainability itself. In ethical organising, we negotiate these tensions by using the meanings that inhere in values to create narratives which transmit knowledge and understanding to diverse, interdependent, but indirectly connected problem-solvers, who must find ways to cooperate across separations of distance, power, and culture. I use a synthesis of meaningfulness and mutuality to describe the general features of life value organisations needed to equip these problem-solvers with the capability for ethical world-building, so that they can fulfil their moral obligations to contribute to sustainability outcomes, through resiliency processes that demonstrate fairness and care to all those affected by change.

Although values are frequently evoked in the organisational and business ethics literature, we require further elaboration of what we mean by them and what they imply for ethical organising. Indeed, Jensen (2008, in Agle et al., 2008) says, with respect to values in groups, organisations, and societies, we know 'almost nothing about how values arise and most importantly, how they create conflict and destruction' (p. 171). I consider values to be socially constructed through collective action, with some values assuming the role of meta-values in complex systems. People bring about changes to value-systems by learning to act as moral agents in collective organising. This raises moral concerns regarding how people are affected by their participation in organising, especially how the structures and processes of organising determine their relationship to beings and things that they have incorporated into the meaningfulness of their lives. To address these moral concerns, I invest moral agents with a human capability for ethical world-building, where the aim of ethical world-building is life value creation, or those common goods needed to sustain human life and civilisation, whilst at the same time instituting the changes needed to repair and extend natural life systems.

I develop a relational conception of values as temporarily stable networks of meanings, where meanings connect understanding and knowledge when we act together to solve problems. If we value what we know, then acquiring values for sustainable ways of living must involve expanding our knowledge and understanding of how our lives are maintained by relational connections to other beings and things, possessing interests, claims, and concerns that are just as important as our own. By recognising the independent value of these objects, we bring more of them into our circles of moral concern, forming the relational basis for ethical world-building, or gatherings of beings and things into life value organisations. Life value organisations can be small or large, ranging from informal groups through to organisational bureaucracies, international networks, and associational ecosystems. Despite their diversity, they share common features as pluralistic, relational, and power-laden entities and are marked throughout their life cycle by moral concerns regarding the conditions under which world-building entangles human and non-human beings and things in webs of mutual dependence. For example, Tsing (2015) describes how global capital shapes the world of mushrooms and mushroom pickers, who are thrown into 'shifting assemblages of human and non-human: the very stuff of collaborative survival' (p. 19). By participating in such human and non-human worlds of production and reproduction, we are made vulnerable to these others through 'unpredictable encounters' that 'remake us as well as our others' (p. 19). We come to understand such entanglement through exploration of our responsibilities to look after morally worthy objects and entitlements to contribute to world-building in ways that enable us to experience our lives and work to be meaningful. That implies we need to be engaged in activities where morally desirable ends are sought through morally viable means.

Ethical world-building requires us to reason together regarding the means and ends of organising. Millgram (2001) describes practical reasoning as 'reasoning directed towards action: figuring out what to do, as contrasted to figuring out how the facts stand (p. 1). I argue that bringing the value of meaningfulness to bear upon practical reasoning provides moral resources for ethical world-building. These resources are supplied by reflecting the objective and subjective dimensions of meaningfulness in considerations of 'what beings and things matter to us, and how well are we doing to take care of them'. Practices of mutual organisation, such as voice, activate practical reasoning as collective evaluations of 'taking care', through which people draw upon diverse meaning-sources to craft and justify acts of care. These meanings-in-use feed into the common-pool resource of public meaningfulness and fertilise the social and organisational narratives motivating collective action. Mutual organisation facilitates this process by proliferating polyphonic moral spaces, which are structured for meaning-making. In such moral free spaces, participants are confirmed as equal meaning-makers, and invested with the co-authority and capabilities for meaning-making. By participating in moral free spaces, people become sensitised to values, endorsing those values that influence their thinking and feeling when acting into troubling situations. Values are worth valuing when they facilitate the creating together of culture, history, narratives, and experiences that make social cooperation viable for mutual learning and moral progress. Ethical organising taps into the ways in which social cooperation is motivated by our need for meaning in life and work, where such needs are satisfied by taking care of morally valuable objects or matters of common concern. This requires collective problem-solving capabilities to be created through organisational practices that recognise, preserve, and proliferate abundant meaning-sources and establish the interactive processes by which people adopt these meanings into their joint deliberations. Such social cooperation is scaled to larger social and economic entities when people come to see one another as equally capable meaning-makers, who bring vital differences, insights, and knowledge into the practical reasoning needed to solve complex problems.

I propose an account of values to support this philosophy of ethical organising as follows: firstly, describing a relational conception of values, including organisational values; secondly, exploring the value of meaningfulness in practical reasoning that draws upon Wallace's (2006) concept of eudaimonic reflection; thirdly, arguing that a key task for mutual organisation is to proliferate moral free spaces, constituted by liberal value pluralism; and fourthly, examining the connection between values, meanings, and knowledge in the moral progress needed to scale up social cooperation and address the sustainability imperative.

Relational Conception of Values

Values are internally complex and dynamic entities, constituted by evolving networks of meanings and temporarily stabilised through intersubjective meaning-making. As such, values are 'sedimented valuations that have become attitudes or dispositions, which we come to regard as justified' (Sayer, 2011). People as valuers generate and regenerate values through their participation in social processes, such as judging, appreciating, purposing, appraising, and caring, where values evoke in valuers cognitive and emotional orientations towards the beings and things that give their lives meaning. Harvie and Milburn (2010) maintain that values derive from 'that which people hold dear, esteem or cherish' (p. 632) and that we organise values into value-systems, according to our 'modes of relating to one-another' (p. 633). Hence, values are not simply preferences, or objects of desire, or even enduring beliefs (Rokeach, 1973) but are 'guiding principles in the life of a person or other social entity' (Schwartz, 1994: 21) that constitute relational orientations to valuable beings and things. Despite their emergent, processual character, values are not endlessly interpretable. Rather, they possess a certain independent authority over our thinking, feeling, acting, and being by structuring our moral and affective connections to those things that matter to us. However, Raz (2001) argues that even though the value that something has for us depends upon its independent significance, this connection is not automatic. Rather, we must actively engage with things of independent value and make them part of the meaningfulness of our lives:

> The personal meaning of objects, causes and pursuits depends upon their impersonal value, and is conditional upon it. But things of value have to be appropriated by us to endow our lives with meaning, meaning which is a precondition for life being either a success or a failure.
>
> (p. 20)

Moral agents become open to the authority of values when they are equipped with the capacity for moral attention, or the ability to look upon reality with 'a just and loving gaze' (Murdoch, 2001: 427). Moral attention, awareness, and imagination are practices needed for harnessing 'normative-descriptive talk in the presence of a common object' (p. 426) or the continual work of moral learning through which we build up 'structures of value around us' (p. 429). When such normative-descriptive talk is activated by the social architecture of meaningfulness and mutuality, moral learning is directed towards excavating the meanings that help world-builders develop understanding and knowledge of what constitutes the good for morally valuable objects.

In collective action, values are adopted as public promises made to ourselves and to others that signal our intention to act in certain understandable and justifiable ways. As such, they bind us into commitment networks of self, others, and objects, through which we distribute responsibilities of care (van Staveren, 2013). Nozick (1981) describes the relational dynamic of values as a 'push-pull' in which 'my value fixes what behaviour should flow from me; your value fixes which behaviour should flow towards you' (p. 401). Arendt (1958) puts this in terms of being simultaneously a doer and a sufferer in relational encounters: 'To do and to suffer are like opposite sides of the same coin, and the story that an act starts is composed of its consequent deeds and sufferings' (p. 190). Nozick (1981) says that 'values themselves lack causal powers' (p. 436). Rather, causal power resides in the 'objects that realize values' (ibid.), and 'it is people who can perceive values and be moved by them' (ibid.). Von

Scheve (2015) argues that values are connected to action via 'socially structured evaluative feelings' that are formed from a dual process of reasoning involving, firstly, 'unconscious, rapid, automatic, and high capacity' processing and, secondly, 'conscious, slow, and deliberative' processes (Evans, in von Scheve, p. 184). Thus, learning how to respond to the values that inhere in beings and things is a developmental process, involving both cognitions and emotions, and where meaning-making is a transmission route for values to become widely shared in organisations and society.

The presence of values influences our thinking and feeling, stimulating and expanding our awareness of the significance of value-laden, meaning-rich, morally worthy objects, and organising our engagements with such objects. Thus, values play a sensitising role in guiding the collective action of valuers who identify, investigate, and solve joint problems through 'intricately structured complex activities' (Nozick, 1981: 437). Benabou et al. (2018) identify two ways in which we increase our moral sensitivity to values, firstly, narratives, or the stories we tell ourselves and one another that give meaning to our experiences and, secondly, imperatives, or the general rules specifying how we ought to behave. Both narratives and imperatives provide us with justificatory reasons for why we should behave in one way rather than another. But as they are disseminated through social worlds, narratives can have positive or negative moral effects, either generating a 'cascade of prosocial behaviors' (p. 4) or reinforcing dysfunctional organisational habits of wilful blindness or exploitation. Realising positive effects from narrative dispersal depends upon recipients of narratives developing their moral agency as meaning-makers. By using the value of meaningfulness in practical reasoning that involves the development of evaluative emotions, meaning-makers become morally attuned to the positive values that inhere in narratives and therefore are more able to act out of those values for morally desirable ends. In this way, life value organisations can avoid or transform negative narratives by incorporating the value of meaningfulness into their collective practical reasoning.

Eudaimonic Reflection and Cosmopolitan Morality

Moral philosophy focusses on individual moral agency in direct interpersonal relations, but this is challenged by the modern condition of complexity, risk, and specialisation, in which our lives are affected by myriad relationships with people and things across separations of culture, power, and distance. To bring forward relevant dimensions of indirect interpersonal morality, Wallace (2019) argues that we need a conception of other people as 'equally real', possessing an equal standing and inhabiting lives that are just as important as our own. This understanding is developed when we expand our moral sensitivity to include the particularities of other lives, where these lives are connected to our own via the numerous personal, professional, and social roles that constitute belonging to social practices, or what Jaeggi (2018) calls forms of life. Wallace (2019) says that this awareness makes morality fundamentally relational, where relationality is described by the concept of the normative nexus, or 'complex of directed obligations and claims' (p. 97), through which we are connected to 'each of the persons who might potentially be affected by what we do' (p. 1). The normative nexus is a form of interpersonal morality that arises because 'we inhabit a common world together with other agents' (p. 1). Wallace confines this common world to sentient beings, but in a materialist ethics, our common world is populated by a multiplicity of material and immaterial, living and inanimate objects. Evaluating how matters stand for these objects involves investigating the tension between stability and change, sustainability and resiliency, whilst recognising that we have ongoing responsibilities to care for the ensemble as a whole, as well as individual beings and things.

In order to fulfil the responsibilities we have towards those beings and things connected to us in any given normative nexus, we must extend normative evaluation to indirect, as well as direct encounters with morally valuable beings and things. Such critical evaluation of the relational nexus is facilitated by incorporating the value of meaningfulness into practical reasoning. This is similar to what Wallace (2006) calls 'eudaimonistic reflection', which asks 'whether engaging in these pursuits is *worthwhile*, something that makes our own lives choice-worthy as human lives' (p. 395). Eudaimonistic reflection incorporates into practical reasoning the objective and subjective dimensions of meaningfulness, thereby allowing us to include in moral deliberation not only those values associated with impartial morality but also those values we derive from our particular projects, people, and other things, such that we 'find ways of integrating the various objectives that matter, bringing them together in a single life that makes appropriate room for each' (p. 404).

Activities we judge to be meaningful possess a degree of public, as well as personal importance. When we draw upon sources of public meaningfulness to make claims for the objective worth of objects we have incorporated into the meaningfulness of our lives, our personal connection to these objects is filtered through processes of public valuing. However, public valuing is an interactive process that is vulnerable to appropriation by more powerful agents. For instance, meaningfulness can be undermined if organisations make it obligatory for employees to adopt valuations of worth from the standpoint of organisationally specified values and meanings that they have not endorsed. This can have serious consequences. For example, in a UK parliamentary examination of abuse scandals involving Oxfam staff, Caroline Thompson, chair of Oxfam GB, observed that the organisation had prioritised protecting its reputation with donors ahead of ensuring accountability. Moreover, employees will judge management demands to conform to corporate-defined ethical valuations as illegitimate or self-indulgent if their own work is of poor quality or unfairly rewarded. In other words, meaningfulness is less likely to be incorporated into practical reasoning when organisations make no attempt to secure mutuality in structures and processes of the normative nexus, consistent with relational values such as fairness, trust, and concern.

Expansive social cooperation can draw upon this relational conception of moral agency by which we 'define obligations that govern our conduct toward people with whom we have never before interacted' (Wallace, 2019: loc. 487). Wallace (2019) extends the concept of the normative nexus to the cosmopolitan condition of morality: 'regulating our relations to a maximally inclusive notional community of individuals whose interests are considered equally important' (loc. 493). However, people are more likely to be able to adopt a cosmopolitan perspective when they see themselves as immersed in common worlds connecting particularist values, interests, and identifications to their responsibilities to care for morally valuable objects. For example, in caring about a particular friend, we are caring about treating the particular friend according to the standards and values that determine the practice of friendship. The connections between personal and cosmopolitan morality help us to *see* others, in the sense that they 'individuate the claimholder, making foreseeable to agents the persons to whom they are linked in a specific relational nexus' (Wallace, 2019: loc. 4097).

Hence, practical reasoning in ethical organising involves a conception of others as individuals, with lives that are just as important as our own. A conception of the self in relation to others is fostered when we become members of shared commitment networks, oriented to others through our equal standing as claims-makers and collectively directed towards matters of common concern. When collectivising our concern for valuable beings and things, we join our capability for ethical world-building to that of others. However this renders us vulnerable to several moral harms; for example, some are afforded opportunities to frame the background conditions of collective action to their advantage, to assign poor-quality work to marginalised others in the division of labour, or to appropriate the gains of social cooperation. To mitigate these moral risks, I use the social architecture of meaningfulness and mutuality as a type of normative technology to specify how collective action contexts connect individual and shared values to organisational values. This social architecture yields structural and processual elements that ensure capability justice when people form and exercise their human capability for ethical organising, including public meaningfulness, the society of meaning-makers, the goods of meaningfulness, liberal value pluralism in interactive processes of meaning-making, and agonistic republicanism in mutual organisation (see Chapter 3).

Organisational Values

Despite increasing organisational hybridity, the division of labour between state and market, public and private, continues to shape our thinking regarding the values we should promote in social and economic production (Smith, 2018). However, as we seek to address the sustainability imperative by adding more complexity to social organisation, efforts to maintain separate spheres are breaking down. As a result, we must learn to navigate the simultaneous publicness and privateness of the associational ecosystems now emerging in cross-domain organising by incorporating into ethical organising those values, as forms of commitments, that 'express one's care for one's valuable ends' (van Staveren, 2001: loc. 555). Van Staveren (2001) identifies three economic value domains and associated values—exchange/freedom, distribution/justice, and giving/care (loc. 1282)—which imply a set of ethical capabilities for commitment, emotion, deliberation, and interaction. She finds that people interact with these domains through their multiple roles as parents, workers, citizens. In so doing, people do not seek to maximise value in a single domain but rather struggle to achieve an internal equilibrium or balance between their roles and the conflicting values within roles, leading them to invest in '*all* ethical capabilities in *each* of the domains' (loc. 3533). Individual struggles to cohere personal values across multi-domain activities are reflected in the meaning-making they bring to creating organisational values, which is frequently characterised by tension, contradiction, and incommensurability. In ethical world-building, these struggles manifest in life value organisations that depend upon the co-creative contributions of multiple stakeholders. Life value organisations resist making efficiency, profit, or competition the master value, instead drawing upon diverse meanings to organise and constrain such values in value-systems that focus on what is needed to sustain life requirements. This requires organisations to create interactive processes of valuing that guard against degrading common-pool sources of meanings by silencing, distorting, and eliminating meanings connected to life value creation.

The dependence of life value organisations upon the contributions of their multiple members demands a distinctive approach to developing organisational values, which I argue is provided by incorporating the social architecture of meaningfulness and mutuality into ethical world-building. Different forms and types of organisational values exist in dynamic relation to one another. Bourne and Jenkin (2013) define organisational values as 'aggregations of personal values that reveal shared cognitive structures' (p. 504) which guide behaviour. They identify four value forms: espoused (given by top management), attributed (taken by members to be representative of the organisation), shared (aggregated from members' values), and aspirational (values that members believe the organisation ought to have). These value forms connect at different levels of the organisation, depending upon how organisational members are oriented to values through their shared need to address matters of common concern. In life value organisations, internally and externally located stakeholders use meaning-making to translate espoused, attributed, shared, and aspirational value forms into collective action. To undertake such values-work, stakeholders require access to diverse meaning-sources that are enriched when life value organisations proliferate polyphonic moral free spaces. In valuations of ecosystem services, Ranger et al. (2016) show how shared values are forged when people make connections between meanings and the significance of natural environments, where types of shared values include transcendental, cultural/social, communal, group, deliberative and other regarding values, and value to society. Shared values thus constitute a common resource for ethical world-building. Herzog (2017) argues that organisations have sector-level responsibilities to maintain inter-organisational commons including reputation, trust, and shared values. Such collective goods are produced through common work operating across inter-organisational boundaries.

Organisational values reflect relational power imbalances when advancing interpretive differences, resulting in aggregations of individual valuations that marginalise weaker voices and obscure the importance of collectives and groups for the social cooperation needed to take care of natural systems. At an organisational level, Hinings et al. (1996) show how managerially defined 'values underpin organizational structure and give it meaning' (p. 885), where these values describe the organisation's preferences for particular action pathways to deliver desired outocmes. Individual preferences for values are filtered through the interpretive meanings of a group, often invested with hierarchical privilege. Value-systems function as 'interpretive schemas' in organisational design and change, and these schemas are frequently supplied to organisational members by more powerful others, with the aim of conforming behaviour to unified, tensionless goals. Greenwood and Hinings (1988) describe the pluralistic, hybrid nature of organisations in somewhat pejorative terms as a stage of 'schizoid incoherence' in organisational change, where 'structures and processes reflect the tension between two contradictory set of ideals and values' (p. 304) and are relieved when the organisation achieves values coherence. But tensions arising from incommensurable values are rarely resolved, except temporarily, and Smith and Lewis (2011) have described the dynamic interaction between paradoxes, tensions, and sustaining organisations over time.

Although Malbašić et al. (2015) propose that plural organisational values can be balanced, the presence of paradoxes or 'the simultaneous presence of interrelated opposition' (p. 198) in multiple objective, power-dispersed, and pluralistic organisations generate paradoxes makes balancing an unviable strategy for every case of value conflict. In Indymedia—a new organisation set up to express idealistic values of equality, dignity, and voice—Perkmann and Spicer (2014) track how organisational values operate as focussing and filtering devices for negotiating tensions and differences. Struggles to maintain organisational values were translated into processes of 'organizational bricolage' by which organisational members stitched together diverse organisational forms to create a distributed power form fitted to their aspirations. In this endeavour, organisational values 'encapsulate the overall worldview that organizational members hold and the associated goals that they which to pursue' (p. 1799). They provided a 'yardstick' for evaluating different organisational forms and have 'structuring effects' on the emerging organisation (p. 1799). I explore next the values-work needed to create moral free spaces, constituted by liberal value pluralism, where valuers grapple with difference, producing interpretive variety in meanings and values, which are taken up into practical reasoning via the value of meaningfulness.

Values-Work

In life value organisations, valuers undertake values-work in moral free spaces, using the practices of mutual organisation to assemble valuable beings and things into commitment networks. This work depends on people recognising one another as equal meaning-makers, who carry into practical reasoning interpretations of meanings that shape understanding and knowledge and who are themselves a source of value. Mutual organisation structures polyphonic moral spaces, constituted by liberal value pluralism, and distribute meaning-making power to all those with an interest in contributing to the problem at hand. In practical reasoning, the value of meaningfulness provides the standpoint for examining meaning claims regarding how to further the good for the target of our actions. Mutual organisation expands the scope of meaning-makers to the maximal extent required to solve the problem at hand.[1] This involves meaning-makers in surfacing, interpreting, and naming the meanings that inform the understanding and knowledge they need to *see* one another across separations of distance, power, and culture. In other words, organisations that succeed in bridging such separations between self, others, and objects pluralise meanings and values by restoring the power of naming (Tirrell, 1993) to all those affected by its activities. However, Talisse (2015) points out that the sheer fact of value pluralism 'entails nothing about what we ought to do' (p. 1070) and that 'to derive a prescription, one must conjoin value pluralism with an additional premise' (p. 1071), such as welfare or human flourishing. Talisse describes the tyrannical value pluralist who recognises 'a plurality of objective, incommensurable values' (p. 1070) but regards domination, control, hierarchy, and other authoritarian values as constituting the desirable diversity of values. In life value organisations, orchestrated by the social architecture of meaningfulness and mutuality, the relevant values are pluralised by what is needed for all persons to lead meaningful lives in the Anthropocene, constrained by the need of each person for freedom, autonomy, and dignity.

Mutual organisation generates moral free spaces, constituted by liberal value pluralism, in the intra-organisational and inter-organisational locations where people must grapple with common problems. People who are affected by the organisation's activities have both an obligation and an entitlement to be involved in the problem-solving related to morally valuable objects constituting the meaningfulness of their lives and work. Blanc (2014) argues that workers need an expanded moral space to exercise their moral agency, or 'the socially shaped opportunities for action that can be enacted or endorsed from a comprehensive perspective' (p. 474), thereby affording them the ability to make their work 'part of their lived conception of the good' (p. 476). An absence of moral free spaces deprives workers of opportunities to contribute to collective action in ways that foster their moral agency.

In life value organisations, the space for moral agency extends to all those affected by the activities of the organisation. For the most part, people are permitted access to organisations according to corporate defined criteria. For example, stakeholder groups are often selected for inclusion in corporate-sponsored multi-stakeholder initiatives against one-dimensional criteria of cultural pluralism, associated with affected communities. This narrow pluralisation tames and constrains meaning-making, making it easier to cohere values with corporate defined objectives. However, in ethical organising, the basis of stakeholder pluralisation is broadened to include: firstly, members' collective self-determination in shaping the framing rules governing their interactions with corporations, governments, and civil associations and, secondly, their contributions to the joint creation of practices, processes, and structures needed to realise models of sustainable organisation. Pluralisation of the spaces for moral agency enhances opportunities for valuers to engage in values-work, where they assess 'what is of value, why it is valued, and how it is made recognizable' (Gehman et al., 2013: 86). With this in mind, Gehman et al. (2013) adopt a performative understanding of values situated in networks of practices that are 'the sayings and doings in organizations that articulate and accomplish what is normatively right or wrong, good or bad, for its own sake' (p. 84). They identify four processes for values work as follows: 'dealing with pockets of concern, knotting local concerns into action networks, performing values practices, and circulating values discourse' (p. 85). Such processes generate new roles for stakeholders, centred around the work of maintaining relationships based upon trust and social capital. For example, in transnational corporations with globally extended supply chains, specialised roles and structures include boundary spanners, often situated in ethical trading teams and who connect disparate stakeholders across organisational boundaries. Such roles and structures create the interdependencies, interactions, and knowledge needed to negotiate pluralism in the space between internal and external organisational members.[2]

In order to bring espoused, attributed, shared, and aspirational values to bear upon their collective problem-solving, valuers as organisational members require polyphonic moral spaces, constituted by liberal value pluralism, that permit expressive variety in reason-giving. In many circumstances, values cannot be reconciled into a unitary system without remainder. Berlin (1969) argues that the clash between values is unavoidable, requiring us to choose between ultimate ends, and that this always results in some degree of loss: 'The world that we encounter in ordinary experience is one in which we are faced with choices between ends equally ultimate, and claims equally absolute, the realization of some of which must inevitably involve the sacrifice of others' (Berlin, 1969: 168).[3] Moore worries that value pluralism leads to an inevitable slide into relativism, undermining conditions for social and political cooperation since collective action depends upon there being at least some minimal basis for principled agreement. He proposes a 'layered pluralism' (p. 254), which uses 'thin bases of cooperation' (p. 254) to foster diverse pathways for collective action. These bases are grounded in some minimal set of shared values and moral principles against a societal backdrop that assumes people behave according to individual self-interest. As people come to know one another through repeated cycles of interactions, the social bases of cooperation are thickened by mutual respect, providing the solidaristic basis for more ambitious social development and moral learning. This is similar to my developmental escalation of mutuality from becoming to cooperating to flourishing (see Chapter 3).

Values in Ethical Organising

Values are potent with activated and latent meanings.[4] When activated by the normative elements of mutual organisation, the hybrid value of meaningfulness provides valuers with a capacious moral space to investigate meanings constituting values and to incorporate them into commitment networks. Commitment networks are temporarily stable value-systems, which help to establish the coordination needed for diverse participants to cooperate. For example, multi-stakeholder partnerships (MSPs) in sectors such as palm oil, forestry, and fisheries management rely upon the formation of shared value-systems among business, government, and civil society to address wicked problems characterised by knowledge uncertainty, value conflicts, multiple stakeholders, and dynamic complexity (Dentoni et al., 2018). Valuers must engage with value pluralism, and this requires freedom to participate in moral free spaces where interpretive differences in values and meanings are generated and rendered productive for problem-solving directed towards sustaining and taking care of morally valuable beings and things.

Moral Free Space

In multi-stakeholder contexts, public and private organisations cannot evade attending to value pluralism. This leads Ehrnström-Fuentes (2016) to argue for a pluriversal perspective on corporate social responsibility, which permits different forms of life to exist alongside commercial profit-focussed activity. In their social contract theory of business, Donaldson and Dunfee (1999) seek to manage values-conflicts by using the device of moral free space to conform micro-social contracts of local agreements to macro-social contracts of hypothetical agreements between 'rational members of a community' (p. 19). Moral free space is the 'area bounded by hypernorms in which communities develop ethical norms representing a collective viewpoint concerning right behavior' (p. 83), where hyper-norms are defined as fundamental principles, or 'settled understandings of deep moral values' (p. 27). Moral free space allows moral agents to reflect in their collective action their particular and local values arising from different conceptions of living: 'The freedom of individuals to form or join communities and to act jointly to establish moral rules applicable to members of the community' (p. 38).

Hartman (2009) argues that hypernorms are important, not just because they may be action guiding but also because 'they raise questions and challenges that help us arrive at legitimate local norms and make good ethical decisions' (Hartman, 2009: 707), where a norm is a 'piece of practical knowledge' (p. 708) containing information about 'how to do things right' (ibid.). In moral free space, businesses and communities may adopt either a norm-taking approach by drawing upon local norms and values or a norm-making approach to craft moral innovations (De los Reyes et al., 2017). Donaldson and Dunfee (1999) constrain norm-generating activities on the part of business managers and community leaders by the requirement to gain the consent of all those who will be subject to the norm, guaranteed by voice or exit. However, the norm-creating role afforded to privileged groups begs the question of how norm change comes about and what power relations this entails. Brenkert (2019) argues that ethically motivated business behaviour requires a change in background institutions shaping the distribution of 'power, influence and authority' (p. 925). He draws upon Gaventa's (2006) visual, hidden, and invisible forms of power to show how organisations harness rules, constrain decision-making, and shape meanings and ideologies in order to coerce, persuade, and influence people to adopt the values and principles they have defined. In moral free space, only certain kinds of people, such as managers and community leaders, are afforded moral agency, and are therefore able to define values, norms, and rules on behalf of others, such as employees, suppliers, or community members. Even though Dempsey (2011) maintains that 'ISCT is genuinely pluralistic and not just a modified version of universalism' (p. 258), the choice freedom that is implicit in Donaldson and Dunfee's moral free space licenses to only a few the right to occupy the realm of value selection, interpretation, and invention. The assumption that a value-free space is available to be populated by values selected by corporations and communities is morally unconvincing. Rather, moral free space is a relational, polyphonic, power-infused arena of already existing values and meanings, inhabited by a complex ensemble of living beings and other important things and tied to historical and cultural conflicts over morally legitimate forms of life.

Liberal Value Pluralism

I expand moral freedom beyond the freedom of some to fill morally vacant space with values for their own advantage, to the freedom of all those affected by the organisation's activities to co-produce the reservoirs of values and meanings constituting the variety of lives that can be regarded as choice-worthy (Wallace, 2006). I conceptualise the freedom of moral space as the freedom to co-determine the values and meanings of the social worlds that shape the kinds of persons we are and the possible lives we can lead. This type of freedom requires collective self-determination of the framing rules in order to specify who should be included in determining values and what procedures they will use. From the perspective of psychology, Stern (2004) asks: 'when does freedom happen?' (p. 231). He says that freedom is an interactive achievement that is manifested through intersubjective encounter where people craft 'consciously accessible conflict as personal and social meaning' (p. 228), involving 'a conflict of purpose, interests and desires' (ibid.). Stern (2002) shows that the self is a relational, multiple, 'intersubjectively constituted' entity (p. 963), marked by internal conflicts that are a source of energy, freedom, and initiative because they stimulate problem-solving and moral learning. Benjamin (2004) incorporates Stern into a general 'trajectory of intersubjective development' involving a process of co-creating 'thirdness', which she describes as a vantage point for building 'relational systems' and 'intersubjective capacities' (p. 7). Co-creating thirdness in the relational nexus of self, other, and object involves overcoming the doer/done-to relation by becoming mutually open and available to those beings and things with which we are interconnected. This implies a readiness to be influenced by the intersubjectively generated differences invested in the co-construction of the shared position, for the sake of moral values and principles that hold together ensembles of self, other, and objects.

Ethical organising requires organisational spaces that provide intersubjective conditions for mutual influencing through which people experience themselves as free moral agents. I use Kekes's (1993) account of moral free space and liberal value pluralism, in order to capture our interest in freedom as a type of expressive faculty in discerning, exploring, and enjoying difference. Kekes (1993) describes how an enlarged moral space fertilises our interior lives with a plurality of meanings. He defines a good life in terms that are consistent with the hybrid value of meaningfulness: a life is good 'only if it is both personally satisfying and morally meritorious' (p. 9), within which values are "humanly caused benefits that human beings provide to others' (p. 44). This makes engaging with value pluralism a good to be encouraged because of the role that pluralism plays in creating good lives:

> For the plurality of values enriches the possibilities for our living good lives, increases our freedom, motivates us to assert greater control over the direction of our lives, and enlarges the repertoire of conceptions of life that we may recognize as good.
>
> (p. 12)

The morally relevant form of value pluralism for ethical organising is liberal value pluralism, which ensures that the value of meaningfulness maintains the widest possible space for multiplying the range of possible lives that are valued and available to be lived: 'That our pursuits are plural is worthy of celebration because it makes life interesting, rich, full of possibilities, and provides one of the strongest motives why we should be interested in each other' (p. 30).[5] Value conflicts cannot be avoided, but conflicts can be rendered productive and fertile for moral and social development when a value-system is 'sufficiently agile, flexible, and hospitable to a plurality of values' (p. 27). This makes liberal value pluralism conducive to freedom and moral learning because 'the pluralistic ideal is that we should *make* a good life for ourselves' (p. 14), rather than the monistic ideal where 'we should *find* the one life that is good for all of us' (p. 14). Kekes (1993) argues that pluralism is limited by the extent to which priority is given to some values because of their context independence. Such context-independent values are primary and secondary, where *primary* values protect us from harms such as starvation, humiliation, and exploitation, and *secondary* values address a broader set of vulnerabilities arising from the minimum requirements of living a good life in particular traditions:

> We might say that primary values are the content, while secondary values give form to them; or that primary values are satisfactions of brute, blind, uninterpreted needs, while secondary values provide

their interpretations which take into account the surrounding facts; or that primary values are derived from primitive urges, while secondary values are derived from the necessary attempt to civilize them.

(p. 33)

When incorporated into a pluralistic commitment network, primary and secondary values are conducive to moral progress because they help people learn how to make evaluative judgements in contested, conflicted situations, often involving divergent value-systems. Graeber (2013) says that value claims arise when different worlds clash or 'universes collide' and notes that 'in the end, political struggle is and must always be about the meaning of life' (p. 228). In such moments, we discover the value of values, which lies 'precisely in their lack of equivalence; they are used as unique, crystallized forms' (p. 224). For example, in instances of economic exchange, the non-comparability of values and their resistance to conversion into money make them standpoints for critical evaluation, and justification attempts that advance claims to society for pursuing particular forms of value rather than others. Graeber (2013) proposes that interior values, or 'infravalues', of a 'thousand totalities' (p. 233) are the route by which metavalues are created. For example, food security is a bundle of infravalues that facilitates metavalues, such as truth and beauty. As worlds interact and overlap, leading to mutual constitution, frictional differences can result in infravalues metamorphosing into metavalues. Infravalues, or instrumental values such as efficiency, are the means to the creation of metavalue, or final value. Graeber gives the example of Ortiz's (2013) study of securities analysts, who interpreted their activities as 'just technical' and therefore neutral with respect to value judgements, but who nonetheless privileged efficiency as a political, moral, and economic concept of value, thereby 'effectively making claims to ultimate value on a planetary scale' (Graeber, 2013: 234). In ethical organising, the meaning-making that enables infravalues to be transformed into metavalues is subject to critical evaluation using the value of meaningfulness in multi-perspectival practical reasoning.

People acquire ethical competence when they are participants in action contexts that reduce internal and external impediments to the expression of their moral agency, such as 'impoverished imagination' and 'repressive conventions' (Graeber, 2013: 140). The interaction between internal and external conditions for making pluralism part of our conceptions of living is explained in Kitwood's (1990) psychological work on the relational conditions of moral free space that is manifested between two or more people when they use what Kitwood calls free attention. Kitwood (1990) describes free attention as a relational orientation enabling us to 'be close to another with a kind of caring objectivity' (p. 5). The result is a moral free space where freedom is an expansive intersubjectivity between intersecting but separate lives, involving a kind of morality as 'complete particularism' (p. 6) or accepting another person in his or her unique-ness to the extent that each has the capacity to apprehend the other. An enlarged space of moral encounter is generated that goes beyond mutual respect or even equality, where people learn to see the other not as a 'simple unitary subject' but as 'a sentient being with all the complexities and disjunctures in subjectivity which that implies' (p. 9). Such encoun-ters are fostered in social settings low in 'structured domination' but high in expressiveness, or 'the free expression of desires, feelings, emotions' (pp. 7–8).

Kitwood (1990) argues that an ethics of attention expands moral space, stimulates social justice, and therefore brings about social change, through the 'healing of psychic wounds' at a social level (p. 10). This echoes Arendt's (1958) space of appearances, or the in-between space of deeds and words in which we help each other to disclose ourselves in our 'specific uniqueness' (p. 181). In revealing ourselves to one another, we explore, challenge, and develop our *inter-ests* (p. 82), or those vital ends for living a human life that we cannot provide for ourselves alone and that therefore motivate us to act together with others. This shared inves-tigation of *inter-est*, or what joins us to others because of our interdepen-dence, generates co-active power, or the power we need to act in concert. However, by opening ourselves to be influenced by one another in the midst of action, we make ourselves vulnerable to the unpredictability of collective action, in which we never quite manage to achieve purposes in the way we envisage, or even at all. Arendt (1958) argues that these risks can be alleviated by the twin practices of promising and forgiving. Promising is possible when we put forward values as commitments, or as binding public statements regarding the kind of person we see ourselves to be. When these accumulate into commitment networks constituted by liberal value pluralism, they provide the relational basis for the moral freedom that makes ethical organising possible.

Moral Progress

People deepen their knowledge of valuable objects by examining and reflecting upon the meanings imbued in their relationship to the object and the place this object has in their lives as a whole. Our relational worlds are constituted by multiple intersubjectivities between self, others, and objects, generating relational values that constrain how people and things can be treated. Meanings underpin these relational values. Mean-ings can be lively, dormant, forgotten, suppressed, and disturbed. They represent a generative surplus of our common heritage—a reservoir of human history and experience that we investigate, claim, struggle over, and exploit in order to connect values, understanding, and knowledge into collective action. In complex adaptive systems, the pattern of values constitutes a type of strange attractor that guides but does not determine how a chaotic system behaves. Attractors are not single points but rather basins of attraction, or 'sets of uncountable points that represent a force of attraction' (van Staveren, 2001: loc. 4490). Meanings that pattern values are the myriad points in basins of attraction providing open systems, such as organisations and associational ecosystems, with evolutionary pathways poised between randomness and equilibrium.

Moral Imagination

Valuers use moral imagination to access these reservoirs of meanings that pattern values. Kekes (1993) describes moral imagination as 'a psychological process involved in the mental exploration of our possibilities' (p. 99), where moral imagination illuminates the diversity of human lives: '[T]he moral imagination [. . .] reveals to us the complexity, the difficulty, and the interest of life in society, and best instructs us in our human variety' (Trilling, in Kekes, 1993: 100). Valuers use moral imagination to augment moral understanding and create new knowledge by collecting information about the acting and being of others, as well as what different possibilities for living this illuminates. At an organisational level, Werhane (1999) describes moral imagination as 'the ability to discover, evaluate, and act upon possibilities not merely determined by a particular circumstance, or limited by a set of operating mental models, or merely framed by a set of rules or rule-governed concerns' (p. 93). In multi-stakeholder partnerships, collaborative working is fostered by cultivating moral imagination with the aim of creating 'conceptual frameworks grounded in an effort to address the challenge of making sense of myriad, contested values and claims within complex, multi-layered stakeholder networks' (Calton et al., 2013: 722). In supply chains and bottom-of-the-pyramid (BoP) initiatives, practices of moral imagination use social and normative technologies such as mental models and 'faces to places' (Bevan and Werhane, 2011) to decentre the focal organisation and bring the lives of others out from the shadows. Mental models help stakeholders organise the knowledge and understanding that they derive from their inquiries into particular situations. They 'serve as selective organizing, filtering and focusing technologies through which we construct meaning' (Calton et al., 2013: 724). As such, mental models are a source of power and control, as well as formative of moral sensitivity to values. For example, Calton et al. (2013) argue that the Grameen Bank model of microlending was interpreted by some Indian banks through a lens of traditional banking profitability in which the male borrower is endowed with collateral, rather than as a social approach to augmenting the local economic ecosystem by improving the lives of women. The result was an increase of debt among the poorest and a damaged bottom line for the banks. Calton et al. (2013) describe this as an example of an incomplete mental model that might have achieved more values-sensitive outcomes for both banks and customers if moral imagination had been applied to the whole network of stakeholders.

Meanings, Understanding, and Knowledge

Values supply meanings with their moral content, and meanings supply values with their capacity to sensitise people to what matters. Sayer (2011) describes meanings as essential to collective action: 'meanings serve not only as external descriptions of the world but are constitutive of social practices, enabling people to act together in ways that would be impossible in the absence of those meanings' (p. 115). When people make use of meanings to justify or signify the importance of things, they crystallise meanings into values and translate values into commitment networks. In other words, values are formed from complex webs of meanings, layered with history and culture, which alert valuers to the contextual embeddedness of morally valuable objects, helping them work out how to fulfil their responsibilities of care for those objects. Values without meanings are motiveless; meanings without values lack moral viability.

In ethical organising, meaning-making in moral free space must conform to certain normative conditions, given by the social architecture of meaningfulness and mutuality: firstly, organising aims at objectively valuable objects that are subjectively attractive; secondly, collective action is structured by the goods of meaningfulness; and thirdly, polyphonic voice practices enact interactive processes of meaning-making, through which valuers engage with sources of meanings and activate values for ethical world-building. When faced with perplexing situations, valuers use meaning-making to bridge knowledge and understanding. In the absence of meaning-making, there are 'only events and no meanings' (Hansen, 2004: 7), and life becomes 'dumb, preposterous, destructive' (Dewey, 1922: 280). By investigating the meanings implicated in problematic situations, valuers construct understanding and knowledge, in the process easing their anxieties regarding the troubling nature of events. By adding new knowledge to complexity, they seek to sustain what they value by making the world into a home in which they can dwell, together with the beings and things that matter to them: 'For you will have developed a frame of mind which gives meaning to things that happen; and to find a meaning, to understand along with others, is always a contentment, an enjoyment' (p. 279). Dewey (1922) observes that even if we take 'the most extreme view about the inability of imputed meanings to make a difference to things, [. . .] it still remains true that they make all the difference in the world to us' (p. 277). However, under conditions of deep interdependency, complexity designed to sustain our world also increases risks of breakdowns, locking us into vicious circles of anxiety, from which emerge dysfunctional forms of organising, such as political populism and authoritarianism.

Arendt (1954) shows that when we populate moral spaces with matters of common concern, we generate meaning, knowledge, and understanding through cycles of encounter, mediated between self, others, and objects. In problematic situations, these mediated interactions are a source of interpretive differences in meaning-making that represent a preliminary understanding of the matter at hand: 'understanding is based on knowledge and knowledge cannot proceed without a preliminary, inarticulate understanding' (p, 310). Valuers use this preliminary understanding to make knowledge meaningful (p. 311), to evaluate judgements and assumptions, and to 'prepare a new resourcefulness of the human mind and heart' (p. 310). This constitutes a generative source of new or reinterpreted meanings that fuels further cycles of meaning-making. Arendt says that we can observe how meaning-making power proceeds when an event produces a new word that is accepted into popular language: 'the choice of new word indicates that everybody knows something new and decisive has happened' (p. 312). Arendt describes a two-step process of power over meaning-making that involves: firstly, naming the event and secondly, subduing or deselecting alternative meanings. This is a fragile process, easily appropriated to serve ideological formations that distort our ability to initiate new meanings, and even undermining our capacity to engage in the 'quest for meaning' itself (p. 317).

The 'power of naming', or the ability to excavate, describe, and communicate meanings, is crucial to world-building (Daly, 1973: 9). Tirrell (1999) shows how derogatory terms, such as 'nigger', are 'rich with their own history and reflect (in some sense) the history of the community in which they have meaning, and they are profoundly normative' (p, 42). For Tirrell (1999), what lies behind the use of such terms is a commitment to a system of expression and discourse that operates as a social practice. These terms are 'bully words with ontological force: they serve to establish and maintain a corrupt social system fuelled by distinctions designed to justify relations of domination and subordination' (p. 67). She argues that since such terms express established ways of living, their rehabilitation is 'a community wide achievement that takes time to occur' (p. 61). Meaning-making for ethical worlds must ensure that all those affected by world-building and its consequences have a say in determining the terms, concepts, norms, and values framing their world. To do so, people must be afforded the power of naming grounded in their status as co-authorities in meaning-making and invested with capabilities for meaning-making. This enables valuers to use the value of meaningfulness in practical reasoning in order to reconfigure the commitment network constituting the moral spaces that lie between the inhabitants of their worlds.

The power of naming surfaces and proliferates meanings, and where hospitable social and organisational conditions pertain, valuers appropriate these to the meaningfulness of their lives, using meanings to assess how well they are doing in taking care of worthy objects and to judge the moral worthiness of organisations they belong to. Repp (2018) maintains that 'a meaningful life is one that is rich in perceived sign meaning' (p. 404), where sign meanings are indispensable indicators of what things matter to us and thereby structuring how we value our lives. Sensitivity to sign meaning stimulates eudaimonistic reflection upon the context and nature of situations involving complex ensembles of beings and things. Aliveness and attentiveness to meanings underpins our ability to use signs to make meanings and is a form of knowledge about the problem at hand. This assumes that we have something to care about since 'meaningfulness only arises in a life in which things matter' (pp. 412–413). However, the connection between sign meaning and life meaning is vulnerable to domination, indifference, and disrespect. Organisational action contexts can result in meanings being appropriated, corrupted, or eliminated to serve the interests of some at the expense of others. Broken or distorted links between values, meanings, understanding, and knowledge alienate valuers from one another, their activities, and even their own selves: 'Without the interest, knowledge, or attention necessary to derive meanings from one's experiences, one is likely to feel estranged from the world' (p. 413). When sign meanings, for example, are harnessed to derogatory terms, the status of marginalised groups and individuals is undermined. Such words diminish the possibilities of living for everyone by disrupting the ways in which people translate common-pool sources of meanings into public meaningfulness. Poisoning moral space with negative meanings is the 'ruin of our categories of thought and standards of judgment' (Arendt, 1954: 318), corrupting the 'faculty of imagination' arising from the 'understanding heart' (p. 322). With implications for organisational breakdowns in mind, I discuss in Chapter 6 how we can train our moral sensibilities for seeing other persons and objects across separations of culture, power, and distance.

Common Knowledge

In dynamic systems, the ways in which valuers reinterpret meanings can have unpredictable consequences. Arendt (1958) says 'the smallest act in the most limited circumstances bears the seed of the same boundlessness, because every deed, and sometimes one word, suffices to change every constellation' (p. 190). Commitment networks are reconfigured when they fix around derogatory terms or dominating ideologies, which become a form of common knowledge. Charles Taylor argues that all facts exist as common knowledge between two or more people, or 'entre nous', 'between us', 'in public space' (Taylor, in Gilbert, 2008: 484). In professional practice, Edwards (2012) describes the role of relational agency and relational expertise in constructing common knowledge. Observing that 'working across practice boundaries on complex societal problems is now commonplace' (p. 22), Edwards focusses on joint activity in 'figured worlds' (p. 23), which entangle reason and emotion as people with diverse expertise build shared knowledge around their different interpretations of a situation. Inter-organisational collaborations such as integrated service provision, collaborative governance, or market shaping require complex cooperating, involving horizontal working to create the connections and structures for long-term joint production. Using activity theory, Edwards describes how complex cooperating is developed by focussing upon the common object of concern. During cumulative rounds of interaction, knowledge, data gathering, and emotional engagement with moral purpose is used to stimulate meaning-interpretation and difference-making.

Edwards (2012) identifies the general 'gardening tools' needed if inter-organisational and inter-individual collaboration is to 'create fluid and horizontal linkages between practices' (p. 23). These tools are relational expertise, common knowledge, and relational agency. Relational expertise as a form of empathetic orientation to others aligns motives for the co-production of common knowledge across practice boundaries, where relational agency mobilises common knowledge in order to 'represent the differences and dependences now of consequence and the ability of actors involved to use it' (p. 26). Boundary-crossing objects, or material and immaterial artefacts such as symbols, rituals, mission statements, and strategic plans, help people to transfer common knowledge across internal and external organisational boundaries. Lo and Eliasoph (2012) show that people's everyday acts of coordination are saturated with meanings that have the potential to travel up and into public meaning-making. When people act together, they activate meanings that influence the formation of shared coordinative structures and generate further meanings through repeated cycles of interaction. Through this process, people 'tinker their organisation together' (p. 15), allowing small changes to accumulate into new meanings that help them to 'actually know what to do together in the new few minutes, hours, or years ' (p. 782).

Changing Values

Lent (2017) says that 'culture shapes values and these values shape history' (p. 28). He ascribes social change and moral progress to the human capacity for patterning, or a search for meaning by creating narratives, constructing identities, and putting value on some things rather than others. In a review of the sustainability literature, Chang (2016) argues that we are seeing the emergence of a strong sustainability norm for 'reciprocity-based corporate sustainability', which directs business, government, and social organisations to securing multiple environmental, social, and economic objectives. However, values do not exist apart from people. Therefore, adopting new moral principles into system-level organising depends upon valuers becoming sensitised to values and equipped to incorporate values into collective action. This sensitising process is productive for problem-solving when moral free spaces adopt the value of meaningfulness as the motivational basis and evaluative standpoint for moral judgements. For example, Lips-Wiersma (2019) shows how Volkswagen's practices of weak sustainability 'substituted natural capital (clean air) for human capital (quality jobs, transport)' (p. 424) resulted from a failure to evaluate the moral worthiness of their activities and to create the relational conditions for using meaningfulness in practical reasoning: 'VW was poisoning the planet and showing blatant disregard for human health and well-being' (p. 423). The social architecture of meaningfulness and mutuality guards against such manifestations of wilful blindness by equipping people with moral free spaces that enable them to reflect the value of meaningfulness into their collective deliberations. Valuers are sensitised to values through values-work in the interactive processes of social construction that bring together the ethical-moral/objective and the cognitive-emotional/subjective dimensions of meaningfulness. Integrating the objective and subjective dimensions of meaningfulness is facilitated by the voice practices of life value organisations that adopt the mutuality principle into ethical organising.

In exploring norm change, Lessig (1996) makes a distinction between norm-talk and meaning-talk, arguing that norm-talk focusses on behaviour, whereas meaning-talk is attentive to both behaviour and context: 'we should allow norm talk to be thin and foreground-focussed, and we should use meaning talk to speak of the salience that particular norms have within a given social context' (p. 2184). Unlike norm-talk, meaning-talk provides participants with contextual information regarding the costs of social behaviour. Lessig (1996) notes that 'meaning talk is not cheap, at least epistemologically' (p. 2188). This is because shifts in meanings alters 'the interpretive context' and associated knowledge structures, making the costs of actions unclear (ibid.). Meaning-talk creates ambiguity, rendering a previously stable context malleable, thereby allowing the costs of behaviours to be understood in new ways (e.g. fines and prices). Ambiguity can be deliberately inserted into dialogic encounters through the presentation of new knowledge and deliberative mechanisms to stimulate meaning-making. For example, Verchick (2016) applies cultural cognition theory (CCT) to climate change scepticism, concluding that 'a person's attitude about climate change is not a risk assessment at all, but rather an expression of cultural values' (p. 971), where emotional pathways connect the meanings that constitute values to understanding and knowledge. Those advocating for norm change in climate change policies should therefore aim for expressive variety by bringing into public debate the different meanings that represent cultural interests and use diverse experts and values to communicate accurate information. However, knowledge of the mechanisms of moral emotions and the creation of normative technologies to harness emotional pathways into processes such as CCT raises new moral concerns. Without their endorsement and consent, such techniques could be experienced by recipients as manipulations of their meaning-making capacities that serve the interests of others.

Meaning-making is a form of social power that distributes meanings across a range, leading Lessig (1995) to ask, 'How does that range get made and, more importantly, changed?' (p. 955). In contentious contexts, we need a critical inquiry into who gets to make meanings, what influence they have over the interpretive processes of meaning-making, and how meanings are taken up into deliberation and narrative formation.

Kitwood (1990) says that 'no group, organization or society can be psychologically healthy in the long term unless it has the potential for the generation of moral space' (p. 12). In ethical organising, we must therefore ensure that moral free space allows for the equal opportunity of all affected participants to frame meaning-making, as well as their freedom to maintain connections between meanings and values regarding objects that contribute to the meaningfulness of their lives. The human capability for ethical world-building includes developing a view of ourselves as valuers engaged with others in practices of valuing in the production and maintenance of life organisations, where such organisations are vehicles for helping us to fulfil our responsibilities towards worthy objects, through means structured by the goods of meaningfulness. Such commitments to values help us hold together the tension between stability and change from which we create life value, or the life requirements for sustaining and repairing ethical worlds.

Notes

1. Delina and Sovacool (2018) argue that rapid scaling up of energy transitions requires a plurality of perspectives upon how to manage tensions and produce new knowledge.
2. Kivimaa et al. (2019) show how sustainability transitions depend upon intermediaries to pass work, knowledge, and resources to another across multiple organisations in order to build capacity for change into an associational ecosystem.
3. Moral value pluralism is distinct from political pluralism. The latter is concerned with what governments can require us to do and with what limits they can put on our freedom.
4. In *Nicomachean Ethics*, Aristotle notes the internal plurality of the good: '[T]he notions of honour and wisdom and pleasure, as being good, are different and distinct. Therefore, good is not a general term corresponding to a single idea' (*Nicomachean Ethics* I.6).
5. In the *Philebus* dialogue on what constitutes a good life, Socrates and Protarchus agree that a pluralistic perspective is to be preferred in which the best life will combine elements of living for pleasure and living for the pursuit of knowledge.

Bibliography

Agle, R. A., Donaldson, T., Freeman, R. E., Jensen, M. C., Mitchell, R. K., & Wood, D. J. (2008). Towards a Superior Stakeholder Theory. *Business Ethics Quarterly*, 18 (2): 153–190.

Arendt, H. (1954). Understanding and Politics (the Difficulties of Understanding). In: *Essays in Understanding 1930–1954*. New York: Harcourt Brace and Company, 1994, 307–327.

Arendt, H. (1958). *The Human Condition*. Chicago & London: University of Chicago Press.

Axtell, G. (2016). *Objectivity*. Cambridge and New York: Polity Press.

Benabou, R., Falk, A., & Tirole, J. (2018). *Narratives, Imperatives and Moral Reasoning*. IZA Discussion Papers 11665, Institute of Labor Economics (IZA).

Benjamin, J. (2004). Beyond Doer and Done to: An Intersubjective View of Thirdness. *Psychoanalytic Quarterly*, 73 (1): 5–46.

Berlin, I. (1969). Two Concepts of Liberty. In: Berlin (ed.), *Four Essays on Liberty*. Oxford: Oxford University Press, 118–172.

Bevan, D., & Werhane, P. H. (2011). Stakeholder theory. In: M. Painter-Morland & R. ten Bos (eds.), *Business Ethics and Continental Philosophy*. Cambridge: Cambridge University Press, 37–60.

Blanc, S. (2014). Expanding Workers' "Moral Space": A Liberal Critique of Corporate Capitalism. *Journal of Business Ethics*, 120 (4): 473–488.

Bourne, H., & Jenkins, M. (2013). Organizational Values: A Dynamic Perspective. *Organization Studies*, 34 (4): 495–514.

Brenkert, G. G. (2019). Mind the Gap! The Challenges and Limits of (Global) Business Ethics. *Journal of Business Ethics*, 155 (4): 917–930.

Calton, J. M., Werhane, P. H., Hartman, L. P., & Bevan, D. (2013). Building Partnerships to Create Social and Economic Value at the Base of the Global Development Pyramid. *Journal of Business Ethics*, 117 (4): 721–733.

Chang, S. J. (2016). Sustainable Evolution for Global Business: A Synthetic Review of the Literature. *Journal of Management and Sustainability*, 6 (1): 1–23.

Daly, M. (1973). *Beyond God the Father*. Boston: Beacon Press.

Delina, L.L. & Sovacool, B.K. (2018). Of Temporality and Plurality: An Epistemic and Governance Agenda for Accelerating Just Transitions for Energy Access and Sustainable Development. *Current Opinion in Environmental Sustainability*, 34: 1–6.

De los Reyes, G., Scholtz, M., & Smith, N. C. (2017). Beyond the "Win–Win": Creating Shared Value Requires Ethical Frameworks. *California Management Review*, 59 (2): 142–167.

Dempsey, J. (2011). Pluralistic Business Ethics: The Significance and Justification of Moral Free Space in Integrative Social Contracts Theory. *Business Ethics: A European Review*, 20 (3): 253–266.

Dentoni, D., Bitzer, V., & Schouten, G. (2018). Harnessing Wicked Problems in Multi-Stakeholder Partnerships. *Journal of Business Ethics*, 150 (2): 1–24.

Dewey, J. (1922). Events and Meanings. In: Jo Ann Boydson (ed.), *Essays on Philosophy, Education, and the Orient 1921–1922, the Middle Works of John Dewey 1899–1924*, Vol. 13. Carbondale: Southern Illinois University Press, 1988, 276–280.

Donaldson, T., & Dunfee, T. W. (1999). *Ties That Bind: A Social Contracts Approach to Business Ethics*. Boston, MA: Harvard Business School Press.

Edwards, A. (2012). The Role of Common Knowledge in Achieving Collaboration Across Practices. *Learning, Culture and Social Interaction*, 1 (1): 22–32.

Ehrlich, R. P., & Ehrlich, A. H. (2013). Can a Collapse of Global Civilization Be Avoided? *Proceedings of the Royal Society*, 280: 20122845.

Ehrnström-Fuentes, M. (2016). Delinking Legitimacies: A Pluriversal Perspective on Political CSR. *Journal of Management Studies*, 53 (3): 433–462.

Frederick, W. C. (2006). *Corporation Be Good! The Story of Corporate Social Responsibility*. Indianapolis, IN: Dog Ear Publishing.

Gaventa, J. (2006). Finding the Spaces for Change: A Power Analysis. *IDS Bulletin*, 37 (6): 23–33.

Gehman, J., Treviño, L. K., & Garud, R. (2013). Values Work: A Process Study of the Emergence and Performance of Organizational Values Practices. *Academy of Management Journal*, 56 (1): 84–112.

Graeber, D. (2013). It Is Value That Brings Universes into Being. *HAU: Journal of Ethnographic Theory*, 3 (2): 219–243.

Greenwood, M., & Freeman, R. E. (2017). Focusing on Ethics and Broadening our Intellectual Base. *Journal of Business Ethics*, 140 (1): 1–3.

Greenwood, R., & Hinings, C. R. (1988). Organizational Design Types, Tracks and the Dynamics of Strategic Change. *Organization Studies*, 9 (3): 293–316.

Hansen, D. T. (2004). John Dewey's Call for Meaning. *Education and Culture*, 20 (2): 7–24.

Hartman, E. (2009). Principles and Hypernorms. *Journal of Business Ethics*, 88: 707–716.

Harvie, D., & Milburn, K. (2010). Speaking Out: How Organizations Value and How Value Organizes. *Organization*, 17 (5): 631–636.

Hedberg, T. (2018). Climate Change, Moral Integrity, and Obligations to Reduce Individual Greenhouse Gas Emissions. *Ethics, Policy & Environment*, 21 (1): 64–80.

Herzog, L. (2017). No Company Is an Island: Sector-Related Responsibilities as Elements of Corporate Social Responsibility. *Journal of Business Ethics*, 146 (1): 135–148.

Hinings, C., Thibault, L., Slack, T., & Kikulis, L. (1996). Values and Organizational Structure. *Human Relations*, 49 (7): 885–916.

Horton Smith, D. (2017). The Global Historical and Contemporary Impacts of Voluntary Membership Associations on Human Societies. *Voluntaristics Review*, 2 (5–6): 1–125.

Jaeggi, R. (2018). *Critique of Forms of Life*. Cronin (trans.). Cambridge, MA, & London: Harvard University Press.

Kekes, J. (1993). *The Morality of Pluralism*. Princeton, NJ: Princeton University Press.

Kitwood, T. (1990). Psychotherapy, Postmodernism and Morality. *Journal of Moral Education*, 19 (1): 3–13.

Kivimaa, P., Sampsa Hyysaloc, S., Boond, W., Klerkxe, L., Martiskainena, M., & Schotf, J. (2019). Passing the Baton: How Intermediaries Advance Sustainability Transitions in Different Phases. *Environmental Innovation and Societal Transitions*, 31 (January): 110–125.

Lent, J. (2017). *The Patterning Instinct: A Cultural History of Humanity's Search for Meaning*. New York: Prometheus Books.

Lessig, L. (1995). The Regulation of Social Meaning. *University of Chicago Law Review*, 62: 943.

Lessig, L. (1996). Social Meaning and Social Norms. *University of Pennsylvania Law Review*, 144 (5): 2181–2190.

Lips-Wiersma, M. (2019). Does Corporate Social Responsibility Enhance Meaningful Work? A Multi-Perspective Theoretical Framework. In: Yeoman, Bailey, Madden & Thompson (eds.), *Oxford Handbook of Meaningful Work*. Oxford: Oxford University Press.

Lo, J., & Eliasoph, N. (2012). Broadening Cultural Sociology's Scope: Meaning-Making in Mundane Organizational Life. In: Alexander, Jacobs & Smith (eds.), *The Oxford Handbook of Cultural Sociology*. Oxford: Oxford University Press, 764–787.

Malbašić, I., Marimon, F., & Mas-Machuca, M. (2016). Is It Worth Having Focused Values? *Management Decision*, 54 (10): 2370–2392.

Millgram, E. (2001). Practical Reasoning: The Current State of Play. In: Millgram (ed.), *Varieties of Practical Reasoning*. Cambridge, MA & London: MIT Press, 1–26.

Moore, M. J. (2009). Pluralism, Relativism, and Liberalism. *Political Research Quarterly*, 62 (2): 244–256.

Murdoch, I. (2001). The Idea of Perfection. In: Millgram (ed.), *Varieties of Practical Reasoning*. Cambridge, MA, & London: MIT Press, 403–436.

Nozick, R. (1981). *Philosophical Explanations*. Cambridge, MA: Belknap Press.

Orions, C. T. (ed.). (1955). *The Oxford Universal Dictionary on Historical Principles* (3rd ed.). Cambridge: Oxford University Press.

Ortiz, H. (2013). Financial Value: Economic, Moral, Political, Global. *HAU: Journal of Ethnographic Theory*, 3 (1): 64–79.

Perkmann, M., & Spicer, A. (2014). How Emerging Organizations Take Form: The Role of Imprinting and Values in Organizational Bricolage. *Organization Science*, 25 (6): 1785–1806.

Ranger, S., Kenter, J. O., Bryce, R., Cumming, G., Dapling, T., Lawes, E., & Richardson, P. B. (2016). Forming Shared Values in Conservation Management: An Interpretive-Deliberative-Democratic Approach to Including Community Voices. *Ecosystem Services*, 21 (October): 344–357.

Raz, J. (2001). *Value, Respect and Attachment*. Cambridge: Cambridge University Press.

Repp, C. (2018). Life Meaning and Sign Meaning Life Meaning and Sign Meaning. *Philosophical Papers*, 47 (3): 403–427.

Rokeach, M. (1973). *The Nature of Human Values*. New York Free Press.

Sayer, A. (2011). *Why Things Matter to People: Social Sciences, Values and Ethical Life*. Cambridge: Cambridge University Press.

Schwartz, S. H. (1994). Are There Universal Aspects in the Structure and Contents of Human Values? *Journal of Social Issues*, 50: 19–45.

Shiller, R. (2017). Narrative Economics. *American Economic Review*, 107: 967–1004.

Smith, J. (2018). Navigating Our Way Between Market and State: 2018 Society for Business Ethics Presidential Address. *Business Ethics Quarterly*, 29 (1): 127–141.

Smith, W. K., & Lewis, M. W. (2011). Towards a Theory of Paradox: A Dynamic Equilibrium Model of Organizing. *Academy of Management Review*, 36 (2): 381–403.

Stern, S. (2002). The Self as a Relational Structure: A Dialogue with Multiple Self Theory. *Psychoanalytic Dialogues*, 12 (5): 693–714.

Stern, S. (2004). The Eye Sees Itself: Dissociation, Enactment and the Achievement of Conflict. *Contemporary Psychoanalysis*, 40 (2): 197–238.

Tainter, J. A. (2006). Social Complexity and Sustainability. *Ecological Complexity*, 3: 91–103.

Talisse, R. B. (2015). Value Pluralism: A Philosophical Clarification. *Administration & Society*, 47 (9): 1064–1076.

Tirrell, L. (1993) Definition and Power: Toward Authority without Privilege. *Hypatia*, 8 (4): 1–34.

Tirrell, L. (1999). Derogatory Terms: Racism, Sexism and the Inferential Role Theory of Meaning. In: Kelly Oliver & Christina Hendricks (eds.), *Language and Liberation: Feminism, Philosophy and Language*. Albany, NY: SUNY Press.

Trilling, L. (1976). *The Liberal Imagination*. New York: Scribner's.

Tsing, A. L. (2015). *The Mushroom at the End of the World*. Princeton, NJ, and Oxford: Princeton University Press.

Van Staveren, I. (2001). *The Values of Economics: An Aristotelian Perspective*. London and New York: Routledge.

Verchick, R. M. (2016). Culture, Cognition, Climate. *University of Illinois Law Review*, 969; Loyola University New Orleans College of Law Research Paper No. 2016–05.

Von Scheve, C. (2015). Societal Origins of Values and Evaluative Feelings. In: Brosch & Sander (eds.), *Handbook of Value: Perspectives from Economics, Neuroscience, Philosophy*. Oxford: Oxford University Press, 176–196.

Wallace, J. (2006). The Rightness of Acts and the Goodness of Lives. In: Wallace, Pettit, Scheffler & Smith (eds.), *Reason and Value: Themes from the Moral Philosophy of Joseph Raz*. Oxford: Oxford University Press, 385–411.

Wallace, R. J. (2019). *The Moral Nexus*. Princeton, NJ, & Oxford: Princeton University Press.

Werhane, P. H. (1999). *Moral Imagination and Management Decision-Making*. New York: Oxford University Press.

Yeoman, R. (2014). *Meaningful Work and Workplace Democracy: A Philosophy of Work and a Politics of Meaningfulness*. London: Palgrave Macmillan.

2   The Meaning of Value

Value and the Sustainability Imperative

In 1968, Robert Kennedy (1968) spoke of the moral poverty of gross national product as a societal goal. He said that, after the eradication of material poverty, we faced the further task of addressing 'the poverty of satisfaction—purpose and dignity—that afflicts us all', including how GDP 'measures everything [. . .] except that which makes life worthwhile'. To respond to the sustainability imperative, we require a concept of value which deepens our knowledge of beings and things constituting the lives we value, so that we can sustain those things whilst developing resiliency as the capacity for whole system change, or 'change that pervades all parts of a system, taking into account the interrelationships and interdependencies among those parts' (van Tulder and Keen, 2018). I draw upon McMurtry's (2011) and Noonan's (2012) concept of life value to provide a normative focus for judging the extent to which system change is morally worthy and for negotiating tensions arising from sustaining beings and things we value in rapidly changing contexts of interdependency. Noonan (2012) argues that 'all value is *rooted* in that which is required to maintain and develop life and its sentient, cognitive, imaginative and creative-practical capacities' (loc. 213). This means evaluating how the processes and outcomes of system change is experienced from the perspective of the beings and things through which change takes place, and for the sake of which change happens at all. In other words, change and transition must include a notion of social worth where 'Social worth is how a society values people: the value of people, but also the value obtained through people and the value invested and accumulated in people' (Narotzky, 2014).

The question of what value is worth creating can be applied to the varieties of 'grand challenges' associated with maintaining human civilisation within planetary boundaries. George et al. (2016) adapt the Grand Challenge Canada (2011) definition to describe grand challenges as 'specific critical barrier(s) that, if removed, would help solve an important societal problem with a high likelihood of global impact through widespread implementation'. Mobilising responses to such problems is developmental

because of the demands they make on human ingenuity and collaboration: 'the fundamental principles underlying a grand challenge are the
pursuit of bold ideas and the adoption of less conventional approaches
to tackling large, unresolved problems' (Colquitt and George, 2011:
432). Grand challenges straddle diverse but interconnected arenas, such
as urbanisation and human–natural systems (Alberti, 2017) or robotics
and impacts on heath and society (Yang et al., 2018). Adequate responses
demand global coordination and multi-level behavioural change; for
example, enabling technologies that are developed in large-scale projects involve many organisational partners in technical-social structures
orchestrated by new boundary spanning roles such as 'organisational
knowledge integrators' (Knudsen et al., 2019: 1). However, multi-participant change, such as cross-sector partnerships (CSPs), often draw upon top-
down, management-controlled change theories that are not appropriate
for complex partnering projects (van Tulder and Keen, 2018). Ferraro et
al. (2015) propose three structural features for designing system change:
participatory architecture, multivocal inscriptions, and distributed
experimentation. Kuhlmann and Rip (2018) highlight the importance of
governance practices, such as 'creative corporatism' (p. 451), in which
alliances of governmental institutions with private and public organisations orchestrate 'varieties of cooperation' (p. 449). They propose using
meta-governance to assemble people, organisations, and inter-organisational entities into co-active frameworks based upon 'tentative governance', or 'provisional, flexible, revisable, dynamic and open approaches
that include experimentation, learning, reflexivity, and reversibility'
(p. 450). Hollensbe et al. (2014) connect climate change adaptation to
organisational purpose and reorienting the purpose of business towards
stewardship, reciprocity, subsidiarity, plurality, solidarity, and dignity. In
this chapter, I associate system change that is judged to be morally worthy with life value creation. Valuers create such value when they exercise
their human capability for ethical world-building in life value organisations ordered by the social architecture of meaningfulness and mutuality.

The Meaning of Value

Value is not a settled concept. Indeed, economist Joan Robinson observes,
'The concept of value seems [. . .] to be a remarkable example of how
a metaphysical notion can inspire original thought, though in itself it is
quite devoid of operational meaning' (Robinson, 1942: xi). Robinson
(1962) also says that 'value is a relationship between people' (p. 32). With
this in mind, I take as my starting point the normative observation that
if there is to be value, it must be created, recognised, and understood by
valuers who, as relational beings, are the source and target of value. Value
is what is needed to produce people who, in the depth and range of their
relational connections to other valuable beings and things, are equipped

to navigate the challenges of their times and to create meaningful lives for one another, or lives they judge to be worth living. Korsgaard (1986) says, '[T]he only value there is that which human beings give their own lives. We must be the source of value' (p. 505). Indeed, creating our lives as a source of value and becoming a valuer who is capable of conferring value on beings and things is a moral responsibility because, without valuers, there is no value: 'even activities that seem most perfect to us, because we gain nothing apart from them and are able to take them as a giving point and meaning to our lives, must actually get their value from us valuing them' (pp. 504–505). Life value therefore involves making people who enact and express value in their beings and doings and who are equipped with the status and capabilities to evaluate what is of worth in the midst of action contexts thrown up by the sustainability imperative.

Forms of Value

I consider recent proposals for conceptualising value, including shared value, mutual value, public value, and collective value. All these forms of value share a common view that economic activity is undermining the life supports of human civilisation and the natural world, presenting critical problems to organisations seeking sustainable models of organising. These different perspectives on value translate into diverse proposals for what should be the purpose and activities of organisations, ranging from supplementing or replacing shareholder value with multiple or hybrid objective functions to radical system transformation, such as the 'regenerative economy' (Fullerton, 2013).

Shared value—The shared value creation (SVC) concept advanced by Porter and Kramer (2011) rests on its pragmatic appeal to corporate self-interest, and acceptance of the profit motive played out through competitive market relations. Porter and Kramer (2011) observe that corporate social responsibility (CSR) has failed to change corporate behaviour to any significant extent. In order to prompt corporate action on social, environmental, and economic concerns, they urge organisations to consider how the interests of different stakeholders can be reconciled through win–win exchanges. However, the SVC proposal has been subject to critical challenge, specifically in relation to change efforts that fail to address value pluralism and power imbalances, put corporate agency and interests centre stage, obscure how minimal gains keeps participants in exploitative relations, and concentrate upon managers as the key decision-makers (see Crane et al., 2014). In the context of ecosystem service value, Farber et al. (2002) note, 'While win-win opportunities for human activities within the environment may exist, they also appear to be increasingly scarce in a "full" global ecological—economic system' (p. 375). Given our unescapable need for fundamental life support systems, the planet cannot be considered as just another stakeholder, with interests to be weighed in the balance and traded off against other interests. Aakhus and Bzdak (2012) comment that SVC targeting of 'social value sweet spots leads to blind spots about what societies value' (p. 237), and Dembek et al. (2018) conclude that shared value has limited capacity for solving social problems. From a postcolonial perspective, Voltan et al. (2017) argue that CSV is rooted in Western norms and the interests of developed nations and expresses the business sector's 'view of how the world should be organized for the greater good of business' (Hastings, 2012: 3). Furthermore, due to the multidimensional nature of poverty, inequality, and powerlessness, little consideration is given to the many circumstances in which shared value is not produced or where minimal gains exploit weaker participants. By accepting standard practices of private enterprise—which assume the correctness of pursuing competitive advantage—SVC is unable to expand the strategic and moral imagination of managers who control the allocation of resources to the development of risky, innovative technologies, and novel practices. Given its focus on business interests, SVC has little transformative potential, offering valuers limited resources for evaluating how change sustains and repairs natural and human life-supports, including the justice of change in terms of its procedures, outcomes, and interactions (de los Reyes et al., 2017).

Mutual value—Mutual value creation is a variant of shared value, which shifts the focus of value creation from the interests of the most powerful corporate participants to a more inclusive perspective upon the concerns of all participants. In proposing a protocol for base-of-the-pyramid (BoP) initiatives, Simanis et al. (2005) describe mutual value as arising from a process of mutual learning between multinational corporations, NGO and other partners, and BoP participants, such that 'all parties must benefit in terms important to them' (p. 4). In examining BoP ventures, London et al. (2010) argue that the venture as a whole increases value when each participant is afforded opportunities to create and capture value, and where relational conditions allow participants to overcome producer productivity constraints and weak bargaining power. Hence, mutual value is concerned not just with the distribution of outcomes but also with the developmental possibilities of collaborative production process whereby '*co-creation* is the process by which *mutual value* is expanded together' (Ramaswamy, 2011: 195, original emphasis).

Gronroos and Helle (2010) connect mutual value creation to the adoption of a service logic in manufacturing, in which participants in associational ecosystems co-create inter-organisational common goods, such as governance, shared knowledge building, and shared expertise. Hussein (2018) describes common goods as 'those facilities—whether material, cultural or institutional—that the members of a community provide to all members in order to fulfil a relational obligation they all have to care for certain interests that they have in common'. These gains are not distributable through price mechanisms because they are produced through inter-organisational capabilities (Herzog, 2017) and often assume characteristics of publicness when providing common services to the whole system. For example, Fagioli et al. (2017) argue that the agri-food system must be understood as a multifunctional system, delivering 'extended value' across the whole food chain in several dimensions of social, environmental and financial sustainability, where multifunctionality 'goes beyond [the food chain's] primary function of supplying food and fibre, and provides various benefits to the environment and the socio-economic fields of society' (p. 91). Bonney et al. (2007) identify the following characteristics of sustainable value chains that produce mutual benefits: shared vision, aligned processes, structures and practices, sociocultural context of trust and open communication, and attention to the customer. Thus, mutual value creation involves multiple participants—corporations (collaborators and competitors), suppliers/producers, intermediaries, non-governmental organisations, institutions, and customers—in production processes that meet conditions of equality, mutual respect, and mutual concern. Ultimately, mutual value creation requires belief in the possibility of joint productivity gains, as well as trust that gains and losses will be fairly shared across repeated cycles of interaction.

However, despite the benefits of shifting the focus of value creation to the whole system, mutuality is not an unambiguous concept that can be adopted into the concept of mutual value creation without modification. In anthropology, mutuality has been used to conceptualise the social basis of kinship relations, such that kinship lies in 'diffuse, enduring solidarity' (Schneider, 1968) and is rooted in 'mutuality of being' (Sahlins, 2011). More recently, this concept of mutuality has been challenged by Goldfarb and Schuster (2016) who argue that mutuality involves 'durable exclusions' (p. 2), defined by participants through processes of power aimed at 'the 'wider stakes of relatedness' (p. 3) in a 'politics of value and semiotics' (p. 3). Whereas Sahlin's formulation associates mutuality with sameness, Goldfarb and Schuster (2016) argue that the mutuality embodied in mutual value is constitutively plural: 'Difference thus lives at the heart of kinship, enabling productive, dangerous, and pleasurable forms of identification and non-identification, mutuality and disassociation' (p. 8). The exclusionary potential of mutuality exposes a dark side to mutuality, involving anxieties of mutability, as unpredictable—and even monstrous—change. The fear of change tempts us to confine the social relations of mutuality to limited circles of concern, where outside of an immediate sphere of intimacy, we manage our relations to others through mutual gain as a calculation of individual advantage. Von Mises (1949) says that whether one engages in cooperation depends on one's assessment of the gains that will accrue to oneself. For Von Mises (1949), the social basis of cooperation is the motivation to secure individual benefits and to alleviative the sense of uneasiness that arises from the insecurities of interdependence. Cooperation is therefore a series of exchanges and bargains, through which individuals seek to settle their anxieties, fears, and restlessness.

Thomas Hobbes (1996) says that mutual fear is the defining characteristic of human societies, motivating the organisation of collective security. Mutual vulnerabilities multiply in complex systems where causal mechanisms are difficult to isolate from densely interconnected social, environmental, and economic contexts, leading to a rejection of interconnectedness (Runciman, 2018). However, rather than being seen as hazards to be avoided or opportunities to be translated into personal advantage, vulnerabilities can also be understood as generative of shared needs that are a source of collective value, where satisfying such needs motivates us to create collaborative systems, rooted in a culture of sociability and mutual aid. The starting point of cooperation may be mutual fear, leading to bargaining, and a scramble for individual gains, but this is not the whole of what cooperation becomes, as we learn to value other beings and things for their own sake and create a more expansive mutuality based on care and flourishing. Drawing on Kropotkin and others, Glassman (2000) describes how these thinkers on mutual aid came to the conclusion that: 'The only way a species can survive in a hostile environment over time is through extraordinary cooperation (p. 392)'. Kropotkin argues that rational self-interest alone does not motivate mutual aid, rather mutual aid is stimulated from within social activity itself, activated by the desire to 'find greater "joy of life" in community rather than out' (Glassman, 2000: 408).

Mutual vulnerability directs us to the value created when sustainability, in the form of lives we find to be meaningful, is achieved through just, inclusive resiliency, or change that is worth having because it increases the life value of all affected beings and things. Fineman (2008) describes vulnerability as a universal human condition that 'arises from our embodiment, which carries with it the imminent or ever-present possibility of harm, injury, and misfortune' (p. 9). We should therefore resist reducing individuals and groups to bundles of risk factors and instead consider vulnerabilities as arising from 'vulnerable life situations' including 'social processes, society and its institutions, including social work and the entire welfare service system' (Virokannas et al., 2018: 10). Confronted with the mutual dependence of humans and their environment, Fraser et al. (2003) urge us to consider the variables of 'environmental sensitivity' (p. 139), or sensitivity to changes in environmental conditions, and 'social resilience' (p. 140), or the ability of societies to respond to such changes. Food security is an example of a mutual vulnerability that needs to be viewed from different perspectives and scales of organising, where 'vulnerability is a multi-layered and multi-dimensional social space defined by political, social and institutional capacities' (Watts and Bohle, 1993: 46). We are vulnerable to disruptive changes in the condition of those beings and things that matter to us, and, given this, mutual value creation must consider how we pool risk to ease our fears and worries. This means extending mutual value to include the creation of common goods, recognising that sustaining lives we value depends upon all those affected by change being able to access such goods.

Public value and collective value—Public value has been proposed as a counterweight to the rise of new public management approaches to the production of welfare goods (see Moore, 1995). However, in response to expectations that all organisations will assume responsibilities for their impact upon society, the value logics of private enterprise have adopted aspects of publicness, thereby becoming increasingly hybrid. Public value creation can no longer be limited to public and civic organisations, leading Bozeman (2007) to propose that the concept of public values must be expanded to include the range of organisations and actors who have a responsibility for the public interest, or 'the outcomes best serving the long-run survival and well-being of the social collective construed as "public"' (Bozeman, 2007: 12). For Bozeman, all organisations are public organisations because they are subject to regulative public power. Indeed, Rutgers (2015) argues for a maximally expansive concept of public values, which broadens responsibilities to create publicness to a wide variety of collectives and organisations:

> Public values are enduring beliefs in the organization of and activities in a society that are regarded as crucial or desirable—positively or negatively—for the existence, functioning, and sustainability of that society—instant or distant—the well-being of its members—directly or indirectly, and present and/or future—in reference to an—implicit or explicit—encompassing normative ideal of human society—the Good Society, the Common Wealth, the General Interest—that give meaning, direction, and legitimation to collective action as they function as arguments in the formulation, legitimation, and evaluation of such—proposed or executed—collective actions. They may or may not be posed or embraced by either an individual, collectives, and/or the entire political community, thus create consensus, or be the object of debate and twist.
>
> (p. 40)

Being involved in producing life value goods imbues all organisations—public, private, civic, and governmental—with characteristics of publicness, and responsibilities to join with other organisations in associational ecosystems in order to create life value through collective endeavour. To sustain commitment to the provision of public goods, there is the additional requirement of a sense of publicness, or 'the moral sentiments that sustain the structures of cooperation and solidarity seen in society' (Gasper and Comim, 2017). From the perspective of business value creation, Donaldson and Walsh (2015) define collective value as 'the agglomeration of the Business Participants' Benefits, [. . .] net of any aversive Business outcomes' (p. 188). Busch et al. (2018) propose that collective value is broadened to include stakeholder and ecological impacts, where value tracks collective participation of all affected stakeholders in the creation of goods needed for sustainable transitions, or 'the general metamorphosis of the world' (p. 218, cf. Beck, 2016). Collective value creation implies mutual values of fairness, care and flourishing in production and distribution. Thus, value cannot be allowed to accrue to the most powerful players in an ecosystem, without regard for the welfare and contributions of others.

In examining the connection between social value creation and BoP business models, Sinkovics et al. (2014) define social value creation as 'an activity that leads to the realisation of any of the three core values of development, i.e. sustenance, self-esteem, and freedom from servitude' (p. 692). For people who are building businesses within the base-of-the-pyramid, social value creation is 'an organic part of the business model design' (p. 693). As inhabitants of the BoP, such entrepreneurs do not conceive of a separate category of social value. Rather, social value is the necessary requirement for commercial success when seeking to produce goods and services that meet the needs of their customers and beneficiaries. Nor do they limit social value creation to what occurs within the confines of an organisation; rather, social value creation is a multiple organisation endeavour that cuts across sectoral lines and 'can occur within or across the non-profit, business, or government sectors' (Austin et al., 2006: 2). Drawing from this multi-layered perspective, ethical organising is directed to life value creation when organisational models combine aspects of shared, mutual, collective, and public value, through processes and objectives that recognise morally valuable beings and things as the source and target of value.

Value Worth Creating

If we are to recast capitalism around the sustainability imperative, we will need to make ourselves into people who are equipped to build ethical worlds. Value is worth creating to the extent it enables valuers to lead meaningful lives in the Anthropocene, where the basis for such lives is a conception of ourselves as relational, interdependent, and vulnerable persons, who have responsibilities to care for ensembles of morally valuable objects. In my formulation of ethical organising, the possibility of life value lies in how the social architecture of meaningfulness and mutuality converts the general capacity for organising into the human capability for ethical world-building. This is undertaken in life value organisations, where 'the origin, subject and ultimate purpose of all institutions is and must be the human person' (Argandona, 1998: 1094). In a materialist conception of life value, this organisational purpose is concerned with how to connect people into relational ensembles of morally valuable beings and things, where common goods equip people to fulfil their responsibilities to care for those beings and things, as well as to influence the values, meanings, and rules of ethical worlds, and thus the kinds of lives that may be lived.

Worth

In my account of life value, values and value are integrated via normatively desirable collective action. Stark (2009) proposes the 'wonderful word' *worth* to repair the divide between values and value and to answer the question *what counts?* (2009: 18). He says that the moral (values) and economic (value) dimensions of worth overcome the Parson's Pact, or the division of intellectual labour in which economists study value and sociologists study values (Stark, 2009: 19). The etymology of 'worth' tracks two strands of meanings. Firstly, as an inherent characteristic of an entity that affords the capacity for exchange: 'that quality which renders a thing valuable' (*Chambers 20th Century Dictionary*, 1977). This is derived from Germanic *werbaz*, or something 'worthy or valuable', and *wert*, or 'equal in value to; deserving of, worthwhile, significant, valuable, making a fair equivalent of'. Secondly, as a process of coming into being, or coming into existence, derived from Latin *vertere* and Germanic *werden*, or 'to come about; happen; come into being; become'. Drawing from these strands of meaning, I take worth to be an integrative notion that combines the inherent value of a thing (status) with its generative potential to contribute to life value, or the value is created from assembling into ethical worlds morally worthy objects (development). Worth therefore combines our desire to sustain the beings and things we value, with change that increases the life value of those objects and of ourselves in relation to them.

In classical philosophy, Aristotle derives two senses of use from treating 'the thing as what it is', where the first sense refers to the needs that the thing has the capability to satisfy (worth), and the second sense refers to the capability of a thing to be exchanged (value) (Rodriguez-Herrera, 2014: 2; cf. Aristotle, *Politics*). Locke uses Aristotle's dual meaning of use to describe value as intrinsic natural worth and marketable value:

> That the intrinsick natural worth of any Thing, consists in its fitness to supply the Necessities or serve the Conveniencies of human Life; and the more necessary it is to our Being, or the more it contributes to our Wellbeing the greater is its Worth.
>
> (Locke, 1692 in Bowley, 1963: 131)[1]

Rodriguez-Herrera (2014) traces how Barbon (1696) sought to subsume use to price in order to establish utility theory at the core of value theory.

This move opened up conceptual space for the replacement of worth by value and established the pathway for construing value as purely subjective. The older understanding of use value kept inherent worth separate from exchange value. By setting the valuable thing apart from the person, valuers were afforded an independent standpoint to perceive 'more than a subjective valuation about the thing' (Rodriguez-Herrera, 2014: 2). Obscuring the intrinsic worth dimension in use value permitted Marx to conceptualise use value as the thing itself rather than the 'ability of the thing to satisfy human needs' (p. 1). For Marx, use was no longer a capacity but rather the entire material existence of the thing as a commodity: 'it is therefore the physical body of the commodity itself, for instance iron, corn, a diamond, which is the use value or useful thing'. Allowing the whole of a thing to be conceived as a commodity reduces use value to exchange. Consequently, the meaning of value no longer encompassed the significance of things understood as inherent worth, or, in life value terms, those objective qualities that provide the fundamental conditions for life to happen and to flourish. This loss of worth as an inherent property of things is echoed in Mazzucato's (2019) observation that, at the end of the nineteenth century, economic thinking moved from objective to subjective theories of value, or from 'value determining price to price determining value' (p. 7). Thus, contemporary meanings of value seek value not in objective conditions of production, such as labour, time, and resources, but in subjective individual preferences, where value is assessed by the extent of consumer utility.

By grounding the meaning of value in an integrative notion of worth that combines inherent qualities with developmental potential, I retrieve the objective dimension of value and hence the interaction between objective and subjective value, which I identify with the hybrid value of meaningfulness. Simmel (1907) describes the dialectical relationship between subjective and objective value, where inherent value is amplified through a developmental process of exchange, emotional engagement, and subjective experience:

> We invest economic objects with a quantity of value as if it were an inherent quality, and then hand them over to the process of exchange, to a mechanism determined by those quantities, to an impersonal confrontation between values, from which they return multiplied and more enjoyable to the final purpose, which was also their point of origin: subjective experience.
>
> ([1907] 1978: 78)

Integrative worth can be adopted into sustainability transitions by considering how the change processes involved in life value creation may be constructed to increase the inherent worth of beings and things, in line with their developmental potential. For this, valuers need normative tools to excavate positive meanings constituting worthy objects and to incorporate these meanings into evaluating what value is worth creating. Boltanski and Esquerre argue that, in economic relations, value is 'a device of justification or of the critique of the price of things' (Susen, 2018: 9), where value is a combination of objective, normative, and subjective dimensions, observable by its impacts upon social relations, the different meanings of value arising from diverse cultural settings, and the appropriation of these meanings by valuers into their imaginaries of the world and their conception of self. To engage with value, people need to be equipped with the capability for ethical world-building that enables them to exercise dialogic power in interactive processes of value-making: 'at the heart of power lies the power to develop a discourse about things' (p. 59).

The meaning of value shapes our self-conception and therefore our orientations to other valuable beings and things. To see ourselves as the source and target of life value, we require a sense of being persons who have responsibilities to consider how our activities affect other beings and things and the ways in which our entwinement with these makes us vulnerable to how well they are doing. Elson argues that Marx's theory of value was not concerned with price but with how economic production shapes labour and thereby our humanity: 'the object of Marx's theory of value is not price at all but rather of seeking an understanding of why labour takes the form it does and what the political consequences are' (Elson, 1979: 123). Under the sustainability imperative, our contributions to life value are the work that we do to take care of morally valuable objects, where use value is that which is worthy of investing in and contributing to, and exchange value is that which is worth giving something up for or paying for. Use value and exchange value are incorporated into life value to form an integrative notion of worth such that value is created when we are prepared to sacrifice something in order to invest in the inherent worth of a thing to which we are bound by affective ties and responsibilities to care. In life value, integrative worth combines inherent worth of a valuable being or thing with its developmental capacities to generate or contribute to goods of enduring significance.

Integrative Worth and Publicness

The integrative worth of relational ensembles is constituted by their life value; that is, how they contribute to the collective creation of necessary life supports. Such gatherings have an irreducible core of publicness because we all have an interest in how well objects within these ensembles are doing. Much of the organising that we do is therefore concerned with maintaining and caring for gatherings of beings and things that enable our common world to exist and to continue. Honig (2017) argues for a politics that attends to the things of our worldly existence, without which there would be nothing to value and therefore nothing to exchange (p. 1). World-building involves mobilising valuers as citizens and workers around *public things*, or those things that invest the human world with 'stability, adhesion, attachment, resilience, concern and care' (p. 2). Public things include, for example, infrastructure, schools, hospitals, libraries, parks, prisons, etc. They are the common goods or the facilities we need to lead lives that we judge to be worth living (Hussein, 2018: 5). As objects of common concern, they are characterised by publicness, even when produced and maintained by private enterprise. They do not just provide for our needs but also 'constitute us, complement us, limit us, thwart us, and interpellate us into democratic citizenship' (Honig, 2017: 5). Public things are meaning-making arenas for mobilising our attention and action; they 'press us into relations with others. They are sites of attachment and meaning that occasion the inaugurations, conflicts and contestations that underwrite everyday citizenships and democratic sovereignties' (p. 6). By orientating ourselves towards the publicness of things, we come to see ourselves as more than 'subjects reduced to human capital' (p. 26) and rather as 'humans crafting and controlling their fates together' (p. 26). This is a source of citizenship that draws us into collective action through our different roles as workers, family, community members, and citizens: 'At their best, in their public thingness, they may bring people together to act in concert. And even when they are divisive, they provide a basis around which to organize, contest, mobilize, defend, or reimagine various modes of collective being together in democracy' (p. 24).

I maintain that life value creation transcends public–private distinctions. All organisations have public responsibilities invested in them by public power, directing them to make their contribution to producing the life requirements for people, animals, the natural world, and the human world. Thus, world-building orchestrated around the public things outlined by Honig is relevant to all forms of production, distribution, consumption, and investment because all the things generated through these processes possess life value to at least a minimal extent. Constructing ethical worlds for life value creation connects individual and organisational responsibilities. Zheng (2018; cf. Young) argues that we are responsible for structural injustice through our various social roles but that by collectively pushing the boundaries of these roles, we set in train incremental changes that escalate to a radical reordering of 'an entire complex of interlocking structures' (p. 870). As part of our capability for ethical organising, role reframing engages valuers in what Escobar describes as 'ontological struggles' that produce different imaginaries of how to live (Escobar, 2017). At a world scale, the observable fact of plurality is captured by the concept of the *pluriverse* or 'a world where many worlds fit' (Escobar, 2017: 337). In examining the divergent ways in which two Chilean communities negotiated a conflict over a pulp mill,

Ehrnström-Fuentes (2016) makes 'the co-existence of different forms of life' (p. 436) part of a pluriversal world characterised by multiple legitimacies. Rural communities carried into dialogue meanings through which they understood themselves to be made vulnerable to harms visited upon their natural environment. The villagers saw a clean ocean and river as integral to their identities, but the inherent worth of their water system was put at risk by the pulp mill's manufacturing practices that degraded the intrinsic status of the ocean. People felt that the inherent worth of a core life requirement had been violated, constituting a severe challenge to a way of life they valued. By failing to connect with participants' values and identities, the dialogic processes were unable to produce a form of integrative worth that ensured the meanings associated with sustaining valued lives would be carried forward into change processes judged by those affected to be just and legitimate.

Ethical Worlds

Worlds can be small or large—intricate in local scale, densely connected into broader histories and cultures, and 'inextricably entangled with each other' (Escobar, 2017: 337). In order to counter the complaint that our worlds are limited by embodiment, cognition, and culture, the biologist Sharma (2015) explores our relational interdependence in a world full of 'small, vast worlds' (p. 104). Rather than being a limitation, our relational interdependence is the very thing we have available to use to 'produce a *world*, full stop' (p. 96). Instead of seeing constraints, Sharma says we should exclaim: 'thank goodness! Here are my body, my senses, my thoughts, my language, my culture, my society, my environment! And therefore, here I am, here it all is!' (p. 97). Without the constraints of being and things, there is no human world: 'human existence [. . .] would be impossible without things, and things would be a heap of unrelated articles, a non-world, if they were not the conditioners of human existence' (Arendt, HC: 9).

The normative characteristic shared by these worlds is that they are sufficiently rich in plural meanings to be 'the space in which things become public' (Arendt, in Zerilli, 2016: 35). The publicness of things is revealed through what Heidegger (1971b) calls 'presencing', or a public gathering for discourse and deliberation, through which we bring to 'nearness' (p. 164) the diversity and variety, richness and difference of the being and things with which we dwell. Heidegger (1971a) describes the activity of worlding as dwelling, or presencing things by bringing them into relationship to one another, thereby connecting micro to macro worlds through practices of attention, moral imagination, and care. Gathering things into worlds requires valuers to exercise vigilance, or the 'thinking that responses and recalls', in order to guard against 'the dominance of the distanceless', through which things are annihilated as independent sources of value. This means critically evaluating how organisations use devices of distancing and nearing to capture collectively created value; for example, by using surveillance technology to control employee activities, whilst maintaining distance from the needs and claims of suppliers and communities. Turning the stakeholder relationship into one of 'watching and being watched' (van Bommel and Spicer, 2017: 156) enables organisations to discount the value of their members as sources of inherent and developmental worth.

Creating Life Value

People make values and value. Creating life value requires people to engage in an evaluation of how values and value are connected and what changes to meanings, values, and norms this implies. But even under the logic of capital, values do not reduce entirely to value; rather, values and value are mutually implicated, or are 'dialogic, dependent and co-constituting' (Skeggs, 2014). Values and values are brought into relation through collective action, such that value is a way of 'evaluat[ing] [. . .] not things, but actions' (Graeber, 2005: 18). The market imperative and the normalising processes of capital have not succeeded in fully subsuming to capital the values that underpin different ways of being human. Remainders circulate in our social worlds, an excess ready to be taken up into meaning-making. When filtered through the value of meaningfulness in practical reasoning, these leftover meanings become available for ethical world-building. For example, Stewart (1996) shows how communities in West Virginia coal camps used 'just-talk', or values of fairness and kindness, to create social solidarity as a type of collective value grounded in an ethic of care.

In a materialist ethics, the circulation of meanings is potentially productive for life value creation when relations between self, others, and objects are characterised by mutual interdependence and shared vulnerabilities, as well as the potential to progress together in moral learning. For example, our interaction with new technologies can be recast as a relationship forged by mutual need. By conceiving of technology as malleable and susceptible to values and purposes, people can use meaning-making to insert human needs into machine processes that are dependent upon human acts of concern, attention, and improvisation. Pink et al. (2018) argue that the incomplete and fractured character of data generates meanings of data as lively, organic, entangled, and susceptible to 'breakage, decay and repair' (p. 2). Data needs us to engage in processes of meaning-making where data must be 'narrated' to make it serviceable by individuals and communities (Dourish and Cruz, 2018). Narrating helps stabilise data temporarily for use and development, particularly when meaning-making is incorporated into political practices of 'data activism' (Kennedy, 2018: 18), bringing multiple perspectives to bear upon claims of justice and recognition with respect to accessing, interpreting, and developing data. Such inclusive engagement with technology and data is needed particularly to understand life value creation from the perspective of just transitions, especially in communities vulnerable to consequences such as deindustrialisation.[2]

Live Worth Living in the Anthropocene

We must design life value organisations for the production of lives that reflect the kinds of people we need to be in the Anthropocene. In their report from the Commission on the Measurement of Economic Performance and Social Progress, Stiglitz et al. (2010) connect social value theory to 'people's evaluation of their lives as a whole or of its various domains' (p. 53). Under the sustainability imperative, the evaluation of lives across different domains of living is directed towards life value, or what is needed to maintain valuable beings and things within planetary boundaries. Noonan (2012) argues that intrinsic life value is grounded in the life-requirements needed for 'leading lives rich in expressed and enjoyed human capacities to feel and sense, think and imagine, and act and create' (loc. 962). The value of material and immaterial objects therefore depends upon 'the existence of living things who *care about being alive and maintaining their lives*' (loc. 962, italics in original). Creating value involves judging 'what value is worth creating'. Judging implies an ethical and political demand for all valuers to be entitled to access the natural and social life requirements needed for leading meaningful lives in the Anthropocene. I argue that this criterion specifies the ethical viability of the life value model, or model of organising, which targets people-making as the source and purpose of wealth creation.

Recent studies on sustainability transitions identify the need to bring a moral-spiritual dimension alongside socio-technical innovations. Creating viable sources of life meaning in the Anthropocene, such as contributing to life value organisations, motivates the social cooperation needed for deliberate social and environmental transformation. In examining prospects for maintaining global temperature rise within 1.5%, O'Brien (2018) shows how rapid deliberate transformation involves crafting three interacting spheres of the practical, political, and personal that represent the objective and subjective elements of change. The technical aspects of change cannot be achieved without considering the values through which problems are understood and solutions developed. O'Brien concludes that people need to be seen as moral agents who are capable of contributing to transition pathways and that change processes should be designed to engage people in all three spheres. Ives et al. (2019) argue that sustainability transitions, even those focussed on just transitioning, have failed to explain the importance of changes to our 'inner worlds', or the narratives, stories, and values that shape our internal motivations.

In order to guide just and inclusive change, motivations related to our need for meaning in life can be stimulated using the social architecture of meaningfulness and mutuality, where value that is worth creating involves crafting narratives rooted in ensuring each person has access to what they need for their lives to be worth living.

Flanagan (2007) argues for a materialist foundation to life meaning and describes how organic finite beings can craft lives that 'really matter, that make a positive and lasting contribution' (p. 1). Following Goodman's ways of world-making, Flanagan (2007) proposes spaces of meaning that incorporate six domains of making meaning, including—art, science, technology, ethics, politics, and spirituality. He summarises a meaningful life as 'being moral, having true friends, and having opportunities to express our talents, to find meaningful work, to create and live among beautiful things, and to live cooperatively in social environments where we trust each other' (p. 58). To this can be added the natural life requirements of a sustainable planetary ecosystem where a human life includes stewardship and care of other living beings and natural life supports. Flanagan (2007) says that a naturalistic grounding for life meaning requires a self-conception, or sense of ourselves as artful world-builders, through which we re-enchant the world with value and meaning. Sustainability transitions will transform our many 'socio-technical-ecological configurations', at the same time changing sources of life meaning and the range of lives these enable (Turnheim et al., 2015: 240). Meeting the demands of the sustainability imperative will provide us with new materials and immaterials from which to build ethical worlds, and these will make us into different kinds of people. An additional benefit to adopting a materialist ethics is that becoming involved in creating life value puts eco-anxiety to work upon existential threats, within a framework of collective action that eases fear and isolation, and provides people with sources of meanings for crafting a meaningful life.

Valuing in Life Value Organisations

As 'valuing creatures', valuing exposes us to emotional vulnerability, or the feelings that arise from how something that matters to us may be affected by changes in its condition (Scheffler, 2010: 15). Scheffler (2010) says that '[o]ur projects and relationships are among the primary things we value. They give purpose and meaning to our lives' (p. 47). However, a morality based upon direct interpersonal relations no longer reflects our complex reality in which much of our valuing is mediated, sometimes at great distance and across cultural divides, by multinational organisations, value chains, international institutions, and networks of cities, regions, and sectors. Increasingly, we must extend our valuing to how our activities, projects, and relationships impact valuable beings and things up to global scale, including recognising that other people have projects and relationships that are as important as our own.

Thus, life value organisations must mediate valuing between people who are separated by distance, culture, and power. At an organisational level, valuers are drawn into continual 'justification work' (Jagd, 2011: 343), in which they engage in valuations of beings and things across overlapping domains, characterised by conflicting value regimes. Justification work is undertaken in moments of exchange that crystallise worth, revealing what we are prepared to give up in order to acquire, invest, or contribute to something of independent significance. Stark (2017) describes these 'moments of valuation' as critical and attentive (p. 390): they constitute 'troubling and perplexing situations' (Dewey, [1933] 1998: 140), and involving conflicting 'orders of worth' (Boltanski and Thévenot, 2006). Boltanski and Thévenot (2006) make compromise the mechanism for stabilising critical moments of conflictual valuing, but this underspecifies the range of possible responses to tensions and paradoxes. Compromise fails to capture how diverse meanings remain latent and potentially fertile for further rounds of contestation and how conflictual moments accumulate into social worlds. Through valuing as a process of worlding, valuers make congregations of valuable things and beings for the sake of caring for matters of common concern. In my philosophy of ethical organising, social worlds become ethical worlds when the value of meaningfulness informs the practical reasoning that harnesses morally viable meanings into collective action.

In ethical organising, valuing what is worth creating involves bringing together multiple perspectives on what is worthy of engagement, involvement, and contribution. Stark (2009) argues that holding together dissonant conceptions of worth is necessary for social cooperation: 'our worth is increased when there is open disagreement about what is worthy' (p. xviii). Stark shows the importance of tensions, frictions, and diversity for cooperation and innovation. Indeed, cooperation is made possible 'when we do not agree about why our actions are valuable'. He finds that multiple orders of worth are present simultaneously in organisations and that the dissonances these generate are productive for value creation: 'Organizations create wealth when they support dissonant principles of worth' (Stark, 2017: 388). Misunderstandings, diverse interpretations of meanings, and productive tensions can be sources of 'innovative coordination'. This operates at a group level such that 'teams were held in tension: cognitive distance was pulling the groups apart while structural folding was binding them together' (p. 389). Cognitive distance stimulates interpretive variety in standard practices, whilst trust creates a holding environment which supports hospitable attentiveness to novelties. In order to expand their source of meanings regarding the worth of their activities, organisations might foster a cognitive ecology, expressed in 'the organised dissonance of rivalrous evaluative principles' (p. 395).

Valuing is an intersubjective process. Stark (2011) shows how worth is established by activities of *appraising* connected to becoming valuable, worthy, significant, and those of *prizing* connected to status as inherent worth. Stark proposes *performing* as an additional mode of valuation that is expressed through activity using socio-material technologies: 'there is no calculation apart from calculating devices, no judgments apart from judgment devices' (Stark, 2011). Performing value opens up ethical questions of how value is created, by whom, and for whom. Harvie and Milburn (2010) argue that value is related to the organisation of labour and emerges from relationships between people. Under the capitalist imperative, they describe how 'value organises' by establishing a regime of constant re-organisation by which organisational managers promote a language of value creation within organisations, based on measurement, driving performance, internal competition. However, the requirement of justice in sustainability transitions places demands upon organisations to work with dissonant principles and tensional meanings of worth. The sustainability imperative imposes a life value logic on organising, such that activities are ordered under valuations of integrative worth, thereby directing participants towards what ought to be valued, who does the valuing, and how power is distributed in valuation. The significance of life value therefore lies in how it tracks what matters to us when seeking to live meaningful lives in the Anthropocene—our priorities, needs, desires, intentions, hopes, and terrors, as well as our capabilities to understand, connect with, and act towards all these.

The Life Value Model

To create life value is to make people, as well as the worlds they inhabit with other beings, living things and objects. Arendt (1961) describes world-building as the 'human capacity for building, preserving, and caring for a world that can survive and remain a place fit to live in for those that come after us' (p. 95). However, neoliberalism has hollowed out our sense of being citizens and has undermined our capacity to take up responsibilities to care for things that matter: 'People are now trained to think of themselves as a resource to be invested in [. . .] not as subjects of integrity or [. . .] stewards of a shared future' (Honig, 2017: 13). Given this, we must respond with a new conception of ourselves as ethical worldbuilders, capable of gathering valuable beings and things into habitations of care. As world-builders, people identify what is important in life and therefore the forms of value that are 'worthy of pursuing, by humans and other creatures' (Graeber, 2013: 231). Value creation has at its core 'production as people-making', where world-building involves 'human beings as projects of mutual creation, value as the way such projects become meaningful to the actors, and the worlds we inhabit as emerging from those projects rather than the other way around' (p. 238). Ingold (2000) argues that dwelling is simultaneous with cultivating and constructing, and this demands an ethical consciousness that encompasses 'the whole manner in which one lives one's life on the earth' (p. 18). When this

ethical consciousness is shaped by the value of meaningfulness stewarding and caring for ensembles of valuable beings and things becomes central to value creation. In this way, we provide ourselves with an inner
resource of narratives, meanings, and values that is made available for
practical reasoning when we participate in the polyphonic moral spaces
of life value organisations ordered by the mutuality principle.

Materialist Ethics

Life value organisations require members to adopt a 'problem orientation' rather than an ideological orientation to troubling situations (Dietz,
1994). Since these situations often present with multiple economic, political, and social challenges, some group, organisation, or society of people must be called upon to work collectively on specifying the common
concerns they entail. This includes articulating how value worth creating is tied to what is needed for living together under the sustainability
imperative. Current and Metzger (2017) argue that living well requires
capabilities for sustainability, such as self-governance and participation,
which are exercised in fair systems of social cooperation. When enacted
through life value organisations, the human capability for ethical world-
building generates life value, or those resources by which we cultivate
the relational conditions for all beings and things to have their life needs
and concerns cared for. Noonan (2012) argues that the capacities of life
value are the 'life-ground of value', connecting the human being to the
natural and social worlds, where 'the good for each individual is to satisfy her life-requirements in ways that enable her to contribute back to
the fields of natural life-support and social life-development' (loc. 237).
A materialist ethics that draws up the values and principles for assessing
good and bad states of affairs in the production and distribution of the
material and immaterial objects is necessary for satisfying human needs:
'the comprehensive values made possible by the organic-social and finite
nature of human life' (loc. 162). In a life-grounded materialist ethics, the
natural grounding of values means that values are to be 'enjoyed as an
expression of our human capacities to feel, sense, think, imagine and create' (loc. 306).

Framing Life Value Organisations

Answering the question—*what is of worth*—is a strategic task for life value
organisations to find their place in associational ecosystems directed by
the sustainability imperative. In Chapter 4, I shall examine how life value
organisations are maintained as collective moral agents by the various
stakeholders who have an interest in the organisation's activities. Silver
(2018) argues that corporations may be worthy of moral consideration
as moral agents, distinct from their instrumental value to their members.

For example, a corporation demonstrates its capacity for moral agency through evaluative responses, such as regret or remorse, that are independent of the feelings of individual members. Organisations are 'interpretation systems' through which members 'interpret and elaborate values, symbols and meanings that exist at broader social levels' (Suddaby et al., 2010: 1239). In other words, they are 'conversable agents', who have the ability to speak for themselves, interpret their own purposes, communicate these interpretations to their members, and are therefore responsible for accounting for their actions (Pettit, 2017). In a life value model, collective moral agency is realised by incorporating the value of meaningfulness into practical reasoning, augmented by the meaning-generating processes and practices derived from mutuality as an organising principle. Such organisations possess an independent moral value, making them worthy of their members' contributions, and justifying legal protections and social legitimacy.

When an organisation conforms to the life value model, it is privileged with moral agency. In general terms, the business model is 'a description of an organization and how that organization functions in achieving its goals (e.g., profitability, growth, social impact)' (Massa et al., 2017: 73). As a cognitive schema, a discursive device, and a map for thinking, feeling, and acting, the business model is socially constructed from the interactions of its various stakeholders, including their meanings, values, purposes, and concerns. Magretta (2002) comments that business models 'are, at heart, stories—stories that explain how enterprises work' (p. 4). With respect to sustainable business models, Boons and Lüdeke-Freund (2013) identify that sustainability transitions rely upon socio-technical innovations and neglect how human agency acts as 'a conduit to facilitate problematic interactions between actors' (p. 11). This neglect weakens the prospects for sustainable innovation since 'without a successful diffusion in society, eco-innovations are meaningless' (p. 12). Boons and Lüdeke-Freund (2013) recommend that business models are extended to practices that co-create sustainable solutions with diverse stakeholders at multiple levels. In their review of the prospects for business model innovation to contribute to circular economy approaches, Pieroni et al. (2019) identify the lack of attention given to 'human-behaviour aspects' (p. 208), including normative dimensions of leadership and organisational culture.

Increasingly, organisations must collaborate to realise their value proposition, combining inter-organisational resources into collective value-creating activities, whereby each organisation establishes its position relative to other actors through a variety of value-appropriating mechanisms, such as capturing, devolving, and distributing (Fjeldstad and Snow, 2018: 34). Where the aim is life value creation, associational ecosystems are constituted by life value organisations, characterised by 'multiple forms of value creation', or types of hybridity (Davies and Chambers, 2018:

378). For example, 'integrated hybrids' and 'differentiated hybrids' represent different ways of managing values tensions and paradoxes, which themselves become a source of value because they motivate valuers to innovate novel responses when seeking to take care of valuable things and beings. Extensive hybridisation requires associational ecosystems to create whole system capabilities that connect individual, collective, and organisational capabilities to the shared, mutual, collective, and public value dimensions of life value creation (see Chapter 6).

At the level of associational ecosystems, practices of 'meta-organizing' (Berkowitz and Bor, 2018) orchestrate the cooperation of multiple participants assembled into regional clusters, industry sectors, supply chains, and other entities, often cutting across nation state boundaries. Ostrom (2005) shows how everyday life consists of navigating the rules and norms of collective behaviour in multilayered activities, organisations, and systems. She identifies the common building blocks that make up the structured contexts in which we act, feel, and think together with others. Using her Institutional Analysis and Development (IAD) framework, she draws out the 'nested subassemblies of part-whole units in complex adaptive systems' (p. 11), connecting individual behaviours, values, and capabilities to those of collective units of affiliation, production, and distribution. The common building block is the action arena, which is the interaction between the individual and an action situation. Life value creation is therefore connected to equipping people with the capability for ethical world-building by which they navigate the relevant action arenas. Diversity and plurality bring different perspectives into the appraisal of alternative pathways to sustainability, and are critical to designing system-level transition processes that integrate diverse action arenas. In such transitions, the generative potential of difference-making is activated by bringing the value of meaningfulness into practical reasoning, through mutual practices that foster liberal value pluralism.

Elements of the Life Value Model: Source, Target, Process, and Significance

Creating life value as a form of integrative worth resists reducing the status of value to either exchange value or use value and opens up new developmental processes by which value may be generated and dispersed, as well as the diversity of perspectives upon what value means and how it is to be evaluated. This requires new norms to guide organisational design. For example, Agafonow (2015) describe how social enterprises foster practices of value devolution, or 'mechanisms for value creation that forgoes value capture and engages in value devolution to serve a wider vulnerable clientele' (p. 1038). Where corporate restraint acts as a norm in associational ecosystems, focal organisations pool, share, or give away market power, enabling whole system change that produces collective value. Lepak et al. (2007) argue that value creation involves understanding the meaning and content of value, the processes of value generation, and the role of management, as well as other stakeholders. In the context of life value organisations, I consider the following aspects of value creation—*source* (valuers), *target* (ethical worlds), *process* of producing and distributing value (life capabilities), and moral *significance* of created value (values-based sustainability).

The *source* of value is valuers. McMurtry (2011) characterises a human being as 'a self-organizing unity capable of independent fields of life learning, sentience, affect and body action' (p. 3), for whom the human vocation is 'to be of living worth' and 'to do what is of value to others and meaningful to oneself' (p. 15). Ikaheimo (2007) identifies two dimensions of personhood we would want to recognise in social life: firstly, 'the interpersonal status of being respected as a co-authority' and 'psychological capacities for norm-administration' (p. 36) and, secondly, the values, relations, states of affairs such that 'caring about the happiness or good life of oneself/others is a structuring principle' (p. 36). Being involved in life value creation means seeing ourselves and others as interdependent, vulnerable, and embodied beings. Malleson (2018) says that we must recognise ourselves to be 'fundamentally social beings: fragile, vulnerable, variously disabled, and intrinsically dependent' (p. 161) and that 'all human beings are functionally dependent on the infrastructure and built environment of social life to accomplish their goals' (p. 165). Malleson (2018) emphases interdependency as an ontological fact rather than an ethical virtue (p. 167), where the relevant norms include 'empowerment, control, and self-determination' (ibid.). Control, for example, does not mean the ability to control a singular destiny as an independent individual but rather the ability to influence how we interact with others when we elicit their support for our projects. Accepting the fact of interdependency generates public values such as 'care and social support, enhanced concern for the needs of others, and mutual aid' (p. 168) and adopting these values will produce a cultural change in the form of a 'new sense of self' (ibid.).

The *target* of value is the ethical worlds through which we form objective ethical-moral and subjective cognitive-emotional orientations to the life ground, or 'the connection of life to life's requirement as a felt bond of being' (Noonan, 2012: loc. 231). A systematic materialist ethics for building ethical worlds demands 'comprehensive meaning and value across the spectrum of life-requirements and capacities' (loc. 256). Life value organisations offer their resources, capabilities, and stakeholders into ethical worlds, or assemblies of valuable beings and things, where the shared purpose is the transformation of the production system in order to create life goods. These life goods are social bases that are 'any and all social constructs which enable universal access to human life goods without which people's capacities are always reduced or destroyed' (McMurtry,

2011: 27). Civil commons includes not only natural resources but also 'all human-made goods that people need and to which community members have universal access by social regulation of production and use' (p. 44). In life value organisations, the value-adding combinations of material and immaterial assets may be evaluated by stakeholders to be more or less successful against the extent to which life-capabilities are fostered. Finitude, vulnerability, possibilities, constraints, and potentiality derive from interdependent relational beings and are the source of new forms of wealth or human richness. This includes the 'shared life requirements that link human beings to one another and to the natural world' (loc. 178), through which we make ourselves into beings capable of understanding the meanings that underpin what we value by engaging in 'materially rational judgements of what is and is not good' (loc. 235). In so doing, we become sensitised to what is of worth: 'human life is not just bread and sex but the self-conscious expression and enjoyment of capacities for creation and world-building which have no real analogues in the rest of nature' (loc. 277).

The *process* of producing and distributing life value requires all those affected by the activities of the organisation to become valuers by forming and exercising life capabilities. Frederick (1995) argues that human beings possess natural techno-symbolic capacities that we use to make culture. Boltanski and Esquerre address the power at work in meaning-making by arguing that people require 'socio-ontological competences' (Susen, 2018: 58) if they are to be successful in resisting exploitative value justifications. These competences are 'foundational capacities' (ibid.) for people to create ethical worlds and play a 'pivotal civilizational role' (ibid.) in stabilising the social order. Challenging and critiquing value justifications depends upon people being able to mobilise 'interpretive resources' (p. 16), as well as the linguistic capacities necessary to evaluate the objective, normative, and subjective dimensions manifested in their forms of life, thereby enabling them to 'attribute meaning to the world' (p. 56).

Reinecke et al. (2017) draw upon Boltanski and Thévenot's concept of orders of worth to explain how audiences, or stakeholder constituencies, contest and mobilise moral multiplexity in order to establish moral legitimacy and secure a sense of justice. In evaluating the consequences of commensuration, Reinecke et al. (2017) argue that the question becomes one of *whether* to commensurate rather than *how* to commensurate, where evaluation must establish what order of worth applies in a given situation (p. 13). Moral free spaces, constituted by liberal value pluralism, bring forth different ways of knowing that shape evaluation, thereby helping participants to work with conflict and ambiguity. Life value organisations will maintain such diverse sources of knowledge as a generative resource for interpretive difference-making. For example, in a study of private transnational regulation regimes that address global social and environmental challenges, such as the Forestry Stewardship Council and the Fair Labour Association, Bartley (2007) found that multi-vocal inscriptions, when taken up into participatory architectures, led to innovative institutional arrangements.

Finally, the *significance* of value, or value worth creating, is signalled by the integrative dimensions of worth: firstly, worth as a status derived from the quality of being valuable and, secondly, worth as a dynamic process of coming into being. McMurtry, asks: 'what exactly is worthwhile that is not an expression of enjoyment of a life capacity?' McMurtry (2011) specifies the 'primary axiom of life value' to be 'life is good, and is better the more coherently inclusive its life-fields and ranges in thought, felt being and action'. The significance of value lies in how it supports, on the basis of justice and dignity, the life capabilities of valuers who are vulnerable, interdependent, and embodied beings.

I have shown that life value creation involves making people, and through them, multiple worlds. In the context of provisioning, Narotzky and Besnier (2014) say '[m]aking a living is about "making people" in their physical, social, spiritual, affective, and intellectual dimensions. [. . .] It is about struggles and stabilization around the worth of people and how to make life worth living' (p. 14). The worth of the worlds we build consists in the opportunities they generate for the kinds of lives people lead, including how people can be enabled to contribute to activities, projects, and things of significance and worth. For this, we need to see ourselves as dwelling in a world that is susceptible to our involvement and our care. With this in mind, establishing organisations as life value organisations is both a political and a moral project—political because of the struggle to control the meanings and apparatus by which people and the worlds they inhabit are created, and moral because it involves creating people who have the 'equal power to determine for themselves what they believe to be important' (Graeber, 2005: 18). The significance of life value therefore resides in how it helps us to establish the relational and structural conditions for people to possess the status, capabilities, and resources for building worlds in which their lives count for something because these worlds equip them to fulfil their responsibilities to care for valuable beings and things. In Chapter 3, I outline the features of a social architecture of meaningfulness and mutuality that converts the general capacity for organising into a human capability for ethical world-building.

Notes

1. See Bowley's overview of seventeenth-century concepts of value that includes Locke's (1692) *Some Considerations of the Consequences of the Lowering of Interest and Raising the Value of Money*.
2. Jenkins et al. (2018) argue that energy transitions need to be supplemented by social justice frameworks that address 'contestations over what is just, equitable, and right' (p. 66).

Bibliography

Aakhus, M., & Bzdak, M. (2012). Revisiting the Role of "Shared Value" in the Business–Society Relationship. *Business & Professional Ethics Journal*, 31 (2): 231–246.

Agafonow, A. (2015). Value Creation, Value Capture, and Value Devolution: Where Do Social Enterprises Stand? *Administration & Society*, 47 (8): 1038–1060.

Alberti, M. (2017). Grand Challenges in Urban Science. *Frontiers in Built Environment*, 3 (March): 1–5.

Arendt, H. (1958). *The Human Condition*. Chicago & London: University of Chicago Press.

Arendt, H. (1961). *Between the Past and the Future*. London & New York: Penguin Books.

Argandona, A. (1998). The Stakeholder Theory and the Common Good. *Journal of Business Ethics*, 17: 1093–1102.

Austin, J. E., Stevenson, H., & Wei-Skillern, J. (2006). Social and Commercial Entrepreneurship: Same, Different, or Both? *Entrepreneurship: Theory & Practice*, 30 (1): 1–22.

Barbon, N. (1696). *A Discourse Concerning Coining the New Money Lighter. In Answer to Mr. Lock's Considerations About Raising the Value of Money*. Printed for Richard Chifwell at the Rose and Crown in St Paul's Church Yard.

Bartley, T. (2007). Institutional Emergence in an Era of Globalization: The Rise of Transnational Private Regulation of Labor and Environmental Conditions. *American Journal of Sociology*, 113: 297–351.

Beck, U. (2016). *The Metamorphosis of the World: How Climate Change is Tranforming our Concept of the World*. Cambridge & Malden, MA: Polity Press.

Berkowitz, H., & Bor, S. (2018). Why Meta-Organizations Matter: A Response to Lawton et al. and Spillman. *Journal of Management Inquiry*, 27 (2): 204–211.

Boltanski, L., & Esquerre, A. (2016). The Economic Life of Things: Commodities, Collectibles, Assets. *New Left Review*, 98 (March–April): 31–54.

Boltanski, L., & Thévenot, L. (2006). *On Justification: Economies of Worth*. Princeton, NJ: Princeton University Press.

Bonney, L., Clark, R., Collins, R., & Fearne, A. (2007). From Serendipity to Sustainable Competitive Advantage: Insights from Houston's Farm and Their Journey of Co-Innovation. *Supply Chain Management: An International Journal*, 12 (6): 395–399.

Boons, F., & Lüdeke-Freund, F. (2013). Business Models for Sustainable Innovation: State-of-the-Art and Steps Towards a Research Agenda. *Journal of Cleaner Production*, 45: 9–19.

Bowley, M. (1963). Some Seventeenth Century Contributions to the Theory of Value. *Economica, 30* (118), new series: 122–139.

Bozeman, B. (2007). *Public Values and Public Interest: Counterbalancing Economic Individualism*. Washington, DC: Georgetown University Press.

Busch, T., Hamprecht, J., & Waddock, S. (2018). Values(s) for Whom? Creating Value(s) for Stakeholders. *Organization & Environment*, 31 (3): 210–222.

Colquitt, J. A., & George, G. (2011). Publishing in AMJ: Topic Choice. *Academy of Management Journal*, 54: 432–435.

Crane, A., Palazzo, G., Spence, L. J., & Matten, D. (2014). Contesting the Value of "Creating Shared Value". *California Management Review*, 56 (2): 130–153.

Curren, R., & Metzger, E. (2017). Living Well Now and in the Future Why Sustainability Matters. *Ethics, Policy & Environment*, 20 (3): 227–239.

Davies, I. A., & Chambers, L. (2018). Integrating Hybridity and Business Model Theory in Sustainable Entrepreneurship. *Journal of Cleaner Production*, 177: 378–386.

de los Reyes, G., Scholz, M., & Smith, N. C. (2017). Beyond the "Win–Win". *California Management Review*, 59 (2): 142–167.

Dembek, K., York, J., & Singh, P. J. (2018). Creating Value for Multiple Stakeholders: Sustainable Business Models at the Base of the Pyramid. *Journal of Cleaner Production*, 196: 1600–1612.

Dewey, J. (1939). *Theory of Valuation*. Chicago: University of Chicago Press.

Dewey, J. ([1938] 1998). Analysis of Reflective Thinking. In Hickman & Alexander (eds.), *The Essential John Dewey, Volume 2: Ethics, Logic, Psychology*. Bloomington: Indiana University Press, 137–144.

Dietz, M. G. (1994). The Slow Boring of Hard Boards: Methodical Thinking and the Work of Politics. *American Political Science Association*, 88 (4): 873–886.

Donaldson, T., & Walsh, J. P. (2015). Toward a Theory of Business. *Research in Organizational Behavior*, 35: 181–207.

Dourish, P., & Gomez Cruz, E. (2018). Datafication and Data Fiction: Narrating Data and Narrating with Data. *Big Data & Society*, December: 1–10.

Ehrnström-Fuentes, M. (2016). Delinking Legitimacies: A Pluriversal Perspective on Political CSR. *Journal of Management Studies*, 53 (3): 433–462.

Elson, D. (1979). *The Value Theory of Labour. In Value: The Representation of Labour in Capitalism*. London: CSE Books.

Escobar, A. (2017). Complexity Theory and the Place of the Now. *Cultural Dynamics*, 29 (4): 333–339.

Fagioli, F. F., Rocchia, L., Paolottia, L., Słowińskib, R., & Boggia, A. (2017). From the Farm to the Agri-Food System: A Multiple Criteria Framework to Evaluate Extended Multi-Functional Value. *Ecological Indicators*, 79 (February): 91–102.

Farber, S. C., Costanza, R., & Wilson, M. A. (2002). Economic and Ecological Concepts for Valuing Ecosystem Services. *Ecological Economics*, 41 (3): 375–392.

Ferraro, F. (2018). Going Political? Towards Deliberative Corporate Governance. *Journal of Management and Governance* (0123456789).

Ferraro, F., Etzion, D., & Gehman, J. (2015). Tackling Grand Challenges Pragmatically: Robust Action Revisited. *Organization Studies*, 36 (3): 363–390.

Fineman, M. A. (2008). The Vulnerable Subject: Anchoring Equality in the Human Condition. *Yale Journal of Law & Feminism*, 20 (1): 1–23.

Fjeldstad, Ø. D., & Snow, C. C. (2018). Business Models and Organization Design. *Long Range Planning*, 51: 32–39.

Flanagan, O. (2007). *The Really Hard Problem: Meaning in a Material World*. Cambridge, MA: MIT Press.

Fourcade, M. (2010). *Cents and Sensibility: Economic Valuation and the Nature of "Nature"*. Unpublished manuscript. Berkeley: University of California.

Fraser, E. D. G., Mabee, W., & Slaymaker, O. (2003). Mutual Vulnerability, Mutual Dependence: The Reflexive Relationship Between Human Society and the Environment. *Global Environmental Change*, 13: 137–144.

Frederick, W. C. (1995). *Values, Nature, and Culture in the American Corporation*. New York: Oxford University Press.

Fullerton, J. (2013). *Regenerative Capitalism*. [Online] http://harvardworkshop.thenextsystem.org/RegenCap.pdf

Gasper, D. R., & Comim, F. (2017). Public Goods and Public Spirit. In: Keleher & Kosko (eds.). *Agency, Democracy and Participation in Global Development*. Cambridge: Cambridge University Press.

George, G., Howard-Grenville, J., Joshi, A., & Tihanyi, L. (2016). Understanding and Tackling Grand Challenges Through Management Research. *Academy of Management Journal*, 59 (6): 1880–1895.

Glassman, M. (2000). Mutual Aid Theory and Human Development: Sociability as Primary. *Journal for the Theory of Social Behaviour*, 30 (4): 391–412.

Goldfarb, K. E., & Schuster, C. E. (2016). Introduction: (De)materializing Kinship— Holding Together Mutuality and Difference. *Social Analysis*, 60 (2): 1–12.

Graeber, D. (2005). Value as the Importance of Action. *The Commoner 10*. www.commoner.org.uk

Graeber, D. (2013). It Is Value That Brings Universes into Being. *HAU: Journal of Ethnographic Theory*, 3 (2): 219–243.

Grand Challenge Canada (2011). *The Grand Challenges Approach*. Toronto, Canada: McLaughlin-Rotman Centre for Global Health.

Gronroos, C., & Helle, P. (2010). Adopting a Service Logic in Manufacturing: Conceptual Foundation and Metrics for Mutual Value Creation. *Journal of Service Management*, 21 (5): 564–590.

Harvie, D., & Milburn, K. (2010). Speaking Out: How Organizations Value and How Value Organizes. *Organization*, 17 (5): 631–636.

Hastings, G. (2012). Why Corporate Power Is a Public Health Priority. *BMJ*, 345: e5124.

Heidegger, M. (1971a). Building Dwelling Thinking. In: Hofstadter (trans.), *Poetry, Language, Thought*. New York: HarperCollins.

Heidegger, M. (1971b). The Thing. In: Hofstadter (trans.), *Poetry, Language, Thought*. New York: HarperCollins.

Herzog, L. (2017). No Company Is an Island: Sector-Related Responsibilities as Elements of Corporate Social Responsibility. *Journal of Business Ethics*, 146 (1): 135–148.

Hobbes, T. (1996). *Leviathan*. Tuck (ed.). Cambridge: Cambridge University Press.

Hollensbe, E., Wookey, C., Hickey, L., George, G., & Nichols, V. (2014). Organizations with Purpose. *Academy of Management Journal*, 57 (5): 1227–1234.

Honig, B. (2017). *Public Things: Democracy in Disrepair*. New York: Fordham University Press.

Hussein, W. (2018). The Common Good. In Edward N. Zalta (ed.), *The Stanford Encyclopedia of Philosophy* (Spring 2018 ed.), [Online] https://plato.stanford.edu/archives/spr2018/entries/common-good/

Ikaheimo, H. (2007). Recognizing Persons. *Journal of Consciousness Studies*, 14 (5–6): 224–247.

Ingold, T. (2000). *The Perception of the Environment: Essays on Livelihood, Dwelling and Skill*. London & New York: Routledge.

Ives, C. D., Freeth, R., & Fischer, J. (2019). Inside-Out Sustainability: The Neglect of Inner Worlds. *Ambio*, 24 April.

Jagd, S. (2011). Pragmatic Sociology and Competing Orders of Worth in Organizations. *European Journal of Social Theory*, 14 (3): 343–359.

Jenkins, K., Sovacool, B. K., & McCauley, D., (2018). Humanizing Sociotechnical Transitions Through Energy Justice: An Ethical Framework for Global Transformative Change. *Energy Policy*, 117: 66–74.

Jørgensen, T. B., & Bozeman, B. (2007). Public Values: An Inventory. *Administration & Society*, 39 (3): 354–382.

Kennedy, H. (2018). Living with Data: Aligning Data Studies and Data Activism Through a Focus on Everyday Experiences of Datafication. Krisis. *Journal for Contemporary Philosophy*, 1.

Kennedy, R. (1968). *Remarks at the University of Kansas, March 18, 1968*. John F. Kennedy Presidential Library and Museum. Boston, MA: Kennedy Library.

Knudsen, M. P., Lundø Tranekjer, T., & Bulathsinhala, N. (2019) Advancing Large-Scale R&D Projects Towards *Grand Challenges* Through Involvement of Organizational Knowledge Integrators. *Industry and Innovation*, 26 (1): 1–30.

Korsgaard, C. M. (1986). Aristotle and Kant on the Source of Value. *Ethics*, 96 (3): 486–505.

Kuhlmann, S., & Rip, A. (2018). Next Generation Innovation Policy and Grand Challenges. *Science and Public Policy*, 45 (August): 448–454.

Lepak, D. P., Smith, K. G., & Taylor, M. S. (2007). Introduction to Special Topic Forum: Value Creation and Value Capture: A Multilevel Perspective. *Source: The Academy of Management Review*, 32 (1): 180–194.

London, T., Anupindi, R., & Sheth, S. (2010). Creating Mutual Value: Lessons Learned from Ventures Serving Base of the Pyramid Producers. *Journal of Business Research*, 63 (6): 582–594.

Magretta, J. (2002). Why Business Model Matter. *Harvard Business Review*, 80 (5): 86–92.

Mäkinen, S., & Seppänen, M. (2007). Assessing Business Model Concepts with Taxonomical. *Management Research News*, 30 (10): 735–748.

Malleson, T. (2018). Interdependency: The Fourth Existential Insult to Humanity. *Contemporary Political Theory*, 17 (2): 160–186.

Massa, L., Tucci, C. L., & Afuah, A. (2017). A Critical Assessment of Business Model Research. *Academy of Management Annals*, 11 (1): 73–104.

Mazzucato, M. (2019). *The Value of Everything: Making and Taking in the Global Economy*. London: Penguin.

McMurtry, J. (2011). Human Rights Versus Corporate Rights: Life Value, the Civil Commons and Social Justice. *Studies in Social Justice*, 5 (1): 11–61.

Moore, M. (1995). *Creating Public Value: Strategic Management in Government*. Boston: Harvard University Press.

Narotzky, S., & Besnier, N. (2014). Crisis, Value, and Hope: An Introduction to Supplement 9. *Current Anthropology*, 55 (August): 4–16.

Noonan, J. (2012). *Materialist Ethics and Life-Value*. Montreal & London: McGill-Queen's University Press.

O'Brien, K. (2018). Is the 1.5 C Target Possible ? Exploring the Three Spheres of Transformation. *Current Opinion in Environmental Sustainability*, 31: 153–160.

Ostrom, E. (2005). *Understanding Institutional Diversity*. Princeton, NJ, and Oxford: Princeton University Press.

Pettit, P. (2017). The Conversable, Responsible Corporation. In Eric Orts & Craig Smith (eds.), *The Moral Responsibility of Firms*. Oxford: Oxford University Press, 15–35.

Pieroni, M. P. P., McAloone, T. C., & Pigosso, D. C. A. (2019). Business Model Innovation for Circular Economy and Sustainability: A Review of Approaches. *Journal of Cleaner Production*, 215: 198–216.

Pink, S., Ruckenstein, M., Willim, R., & Duque, M. (2018). Broken Data: Conceptualising Data in an Emerging World. *Big Data and Society*, June: 1–13.

Porter, M. E., & Kramer, M. R. (2011). Creating Shared Value. *Harvard Business Review*, 89: 1–17.

Ramaswamy, V. (2011). It's About Human Experiences . . . and Beyond, to Co-Creation. *Industrial Marketing Management*, 40: 195–196.

Reinecke, J., van Bommel, K., & Spicer, A. (2017). When Orders of Worth Clash: Negotiating Legitimacy in Situations of Moral Multiplexity. *Research in the Sociology of Organizations*, 52: 33–72.

Robinson, J. (1942). *Essay on Marxian Economics*. London: Macmillan.

Robinson, J. (1962). *Economic Philosophy*. London: Watts.

Rodriguez-Herrera, A. (2014). *Aristotle Versus Marx: Modes of Use, Use Value or Useful Object?* Working Paper No. 201402, Universidad de Costa Rica.

Runciman, D. (2018). *How Democracy Ends*. London: Profile Books.

Rutgers, M. R. (2015). As Good as It Gets ? On the Meaning of Public Value in the Study of Policy and Management. *The American Review of Public Administration*, 45 (1): 29–45.

Sahlins, M. D. (2011). What Kinship Is (Part One). *Journal of the Royal Anthropological Institute* (n.s.), 17 (1): 2–19.

Scheffler, S. (2010). *Equality and Tradition: Questions of Value in Moral and Political Theory*. Oxford: Oxford University Press.

Schneider, D. M. (1968). *American Kinship: A Cultural Account*. Chicago: University of Chicago Press.

Sharma, K. (2015). *Interdependence: Biology and Beyond*. New York: Fordham University Press.

Silver, K. (2018). Can a Corporation Be Worthy of Moral Consideration? *Journal of Business Ethics*. Published online 23 January, 2018.

Simanis, E., Hart, S., Enk, G., Duke, D., Gordon, M., & Lippert, A. (2005). *Strategic Initiatives at the Base of the Pyramid: A Protocol for Mutual Value Creation*. Base of the Pyramid Protocol Workshop Group Wingspread Conference Center, Racine, WI. 19–22 October, 2004.

Simmel, G. (1907 [1978]). *The Philosophy of Money*. Boston: Routledge.

Sinkovics, N., Sinkovics, R. R., & Yamin, M. (2014). The Role of Social Value Creation in Business Model Formulation at the Bottom of the Pyramid—Implications for MNEs? *International Business Review*, 23 (4): 692–707.

Skeggs, B., 2014. Values Beyond Value? Is Anything Beyond the Logic of Capital? *British Journal of Sociology*, 65 (1): 1–20.

Stark, D. (2009). *The Sense of Dissonance: Accounts of Worth in Economic Life*. Princeton, NJ, and Oxford: Princeton University Press.

Stark, D. (2011). What's Valuable? In: Patrik Aspers and Jens Beckert (eds.), *The Worth of Goods: Valuation and Pricing in the Economy*. Oxford: Oxford University Press, 19–42.

Stark, D. (2017). For What It's Worth. *Research in the Sociology of Organizations*, 52: 383–397.

Stewart, K. (1996). *A Space on the Side of the Road: Cultural Practices in an 'Other' America*. Princeton: Princeton University Press.

Stiglitz, J. E, Sen, A., & Fitoussi, J.-P. (2010). *Report by the Commission on the Measurement of Economic Performance and Social Progress*. [Online] https://ec.europa.eu/eurostat/documents/118025/118123/Fitoussi+Commission+report

Suddaby, R., Elsbach, K. D., Greenwood, R., Meyer, J. W., & Zilber, T. B. (2010). Organizations and Their Institutional Environments—Bringing Meaning, Values, and Culture Back In: Introduction to the Special Research Forum. *Academy of Management Journal*, 53 (6): 1234–1240.

Susen, S. (2018). The Economy of Enrichment: Towards a New Form of Capitalism? *Berlin Journal of Critical Theory*, 2 (2): 5–98.

Turnheim, B., Berkhouta, F., Geelsb, F. W., Hof, A., McMeekinb, A., Nykviste, B., & van Vuuren, D. P. (2015). Evaluating Sustainability Transitions Pathways: Bridging Analytical Approaches to Address Governance Challenges. *Global Environmental Change*, 35: 239–253.

Van Bommel, K. & Spicer, A. (2017). Critical Management Studies and Paradox. In: Smith, Lewis, Jarzabkowskin & Langley (eds.), *The Oxford Handbook of Organizational Paradox*. Oxford: OUP, 144–160.

van Tulder, R., & Keen, N. (2018). Capturing Collaborative Challenges: Designing Complexity-Sensitive Theories of Change for Cross-Sector Partnerships. *Journal of Business Ethics*, 150 (2): 315–332.

Virokannas, E., Liuski, S., & Kuronen, M. (2018). The Contested Concept of Vulnerability: A Literature Review. *European Journal of Social Work*, DOI: 10.1080/13691457.2018.1508001

Voltan, A., Hervieux, C., & Mills, A. (2017). Examining the Win–Win Proposition of Shared Value Across Contexts: Implications for Future Application. *Business Ethics*, 26 (4): 347–368.

von Mises, L. (1949). *Human Action: A Treatise on Economics*. Eastford, CT: Martino Fine Books.

Watts, M. J., & Bohle, H. G. (1993). The Space of Vulnerability: The Causal Structure of Hunger and Famine. *Progress in Human Geography*, 17: 43–67.

Yang, G. Z., Bellingham, J., Dupont, P. E., Fischer, P., Floridi, L., Full, R., Jacobstein, N., Kumar, V., McNutt, M., Merrifield, R., Nelson, B. J., Scassellati, B., Taddeo, M., Taylor, R. H., Veloso, M., Wang, Z. L., & Wood, R. (2018), The Grand Challenges of Science Robotics. Science Robotics, 3 (14).

Zerilli, L. M. G. (2016). *A Democratic Theory of Judgment*. Chicago & London: University of Chicago Press.

Zheng, R (2018). What is My Role in Changing the System? A New Model of Responsbility for Structural Injustice. *Ethical Theory and Moral Practice*, 21: 869–885.

3   Meaningfulness and Mutuality

In a philosophy of ethical organising, meaningfulness and mutuality are conceptualised as meta-values for structuring life value organisations, ranging from small-scale collectives to planetary-scale organising in associational ecosystems. Meta-values are values invested with diverse historical and cultural meanings and endowed with the capacity for architecting other values into value-systems. Using meaningfulness and mutuality as meta-values, I specify elements of a social architecture that operates as a normative technology for valuers to create life value organisations as collective moral agents. This establishes life value organisations as entities that are fit to be held responsible and are worthy of the contributions of their members (see Chapter 5).

The value of meaningfulness is taken up into practical reasoning by participants in collective action who must jointly determine what they ought to do. Mutuality as an organising principle activates the value of meaningfulness at the organisational level and also in the inter-organising and meta-organising needed for associational ecosystems. Mutual practices establish members as equal co-authorities in meaning-making, equipping them with capabilities for reflecting meaningfulness into practical reasoning. People are motivated to develop the relevant capabilities when they participate in action contexts structured by the goods of meaningfulness, specifically autonomy as non-alienation, freedom as domination, and experiencing oneself as a dignified person (Yeoman, 2014a). The social architecture of meaningfulness and mutuality (Figure 3.1) yields a number of design elements for life value organisations that are considered in subsequent chapters: *public meaningfulness* or a common-pool resource of positive meanings, bounded by a value-horizon (this chapter); *agonistic republicanism* to foster responsible difference-making and constructive conflict (Chapter 4); and membership of *the society of meaning-makers*, which invests people with collective capacities for world-building (Chapter 7).

The Value of Meaningfulness

Although scholars disagree whether meaningfulness is a final or instrumental, universal or personal value, there is general consensus that meaning in

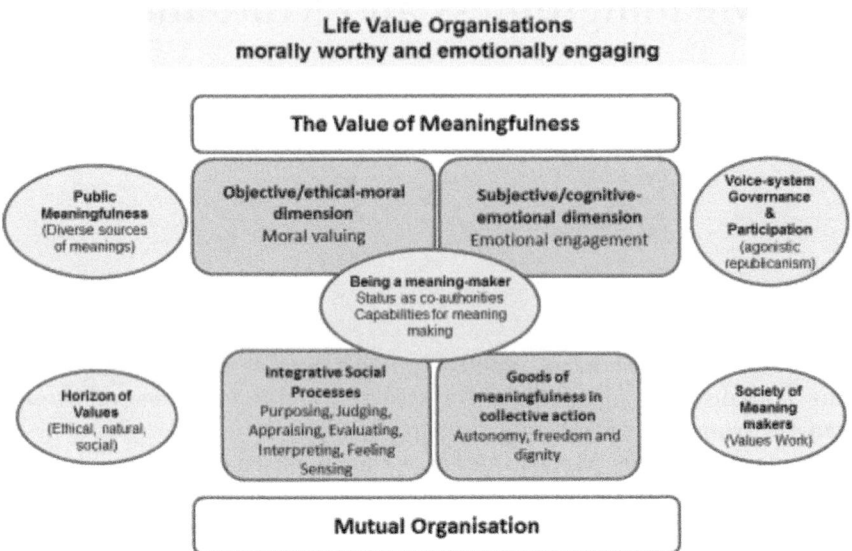

Figure 3.1 The Social Architecture of Meaningfulness and Mutuality (adapted from Yeoman, 2019)[1]

life matters to people and has been neglected as a source of human motivation. I situate the value of meaningfulness within naturalist theories of meaning in life and work, which proceed without reference to a supernatural being or commitments to an overarching view on the meaning of life. Meaning in life is a prudential value because it is valuable for the one who is living it, and a moral value, because it derives its significance from promoting the good for worthy objects. I take meaningfulness to be socially constructed by individuals and collectives from the materials of everyday living and argue that maintaining sources of positive meanings is a collective responsibility, and necessary for ethical organising.

Meaningfulness structures normatively desirable collective action when, firstly, collective action promotes the good for worthy objects that are independently valuable and, secondly, the activities involved in caring for worthy objects are structured by the goods of meaningfulness. When harnessed to the purpose of life value creation, such collective action enables people to develop life capabilities through complex contributions that underpin meaningful lives (Veltman, 2016), or as Susan Wolf puts it, a 'life well lived' or 'a life worth living' (Wolf, 2010: 10). By acting upon problems, we interpret, evaluate, and create meanings, taking them up into the meaningfulness of life and work in diverse ways, according to our conception of a good life: 'Life ultimately means taking the responsibility to find the right answer to its problems and to fulfil the tasks which it constantly sets for each individual. These tasks, and therefore the meaning of life, differ from man to man, and from moment to moment' (Frankl, 2004: 85). We evaluate the moral significance of our activities against how well we are doing to take care of those being and things we have incorporated into the meaningfulness of our lives. In other words, the moral viability of collective action involves caring for consequences (Dewey, 1927), where the work of care is enacted through mutual practices that foster the thinking and feeling of moral judgement.

Meaningfulness: Objective, Subjective, Hybrid[2]

In moral philosophy, meaningfulness is theorised using objective, subjective, and hybrid accounts of value, which take different approaches to the role that independent and personal value play in life meaning. *Objective accounts* make lives meaningful to the extent we are involved in projects and activities that have independent significance and that generate worthwhile outcomes. In his consequentialist approach that combines welfare and meaning into a theory of worth, Smuts (2018) outlines an objective list theory, where life is worth living to the extent that welfare outcomes are consistent with objectively valuable goods, such as pleasure, meaning, knowledge, and relationships. Metz (2011) maintains a non-consequentialist orientation to final value, categorising final value under 'the good, the true, and the beautiful', which are 'inherently worthwhile or finally valuable conditions that confer meaning for anyone' (Metz, 2013).

Subjective accounts consider how meaningfulness is experienced by the individual whose life it is. Subjective accounts of meaningfulness differentiate satisfaction that is assessed by an individual's own satisfaction and sense of fulfilment from aim-fulfilment that is realised through achievement of freely chosen ends (see Campbell and Nyholm, 2015). Axtell (2016) seeks a reconciliation between objectivity and subjectivity by arguing that objectivity cannot be captured by a 'single unified or 'core' meaning' (p. 7) and is characterised by 'irreducible complexity' (p. 8). Morally valuable objects are identified by and evaluated against different kinds of objective features that are manifested in varying combinations. Objectivity becomes a way of thinking about an object that constructs the object through 'objective world-talk' (p. 2), and brings the object of such talk in view as part of our world. In organisational life, objectivity interacts with subjectivity through social processes of meaning-making, involving many kinds of talk, including objective world-talk, that are directed towards making relational ensembles of beings and things visible for collective action.

Purely objectivist or purely subjectivist theories of meaningfulness break down when trying to maintain a clear dividing line between independent value and personal preferences. Svensson (2017) advances a desire-based account, such that a person's life is meaningful to the extent that she satisfies categorical desires or those desires constituting her practical identity. This leads Svensson to argue that we should take seriously the many mundane activities constituting meaningfulness, such as 'spending time with one's family, bird watching, cooking, collecting wrist watches, moral decency, singing, travelling, working as a teacher, and gliding' (p. 48). By so doing, Svensson incorporates an objective dimension into her account because categorical desires do not allow any kind of desire to count towards meaningfulness. This is because projects constituting our practical identities have an independent significance apart from how they fulfil our desires.[3] In other words, meaningfulness is related both to something of independent significance and value beyond ourselves as well as to what we personally enjoy and care about.

Wolf (2010) integrates objective and subjective dimensions, so that feelings of attachment and fulfilment are united to an assessment of the independent worth or significance of the object: 'meaning arises when subjective attraction meets objective attractiveness' (p. 9). The experience of meaningfulness is more likely to occur when a person becomes actively connected to a worthy object or something or someone of value, such that they are 'gripped, excited, involved by it' (Wolf, 2015: 109). Wolf (2010) distinguishes her bipartite value of meaningfulness from morality (duty) or happiness (feelings of goodness), where meaningfulness is 'a category of value that is not reducible to happiness or morality, and that is realized by loving objects worthy of love and engaging with them in a positive way' (p. 13). This helps to account for the special ties we feel towards our 'ground projects', which answer the question 'what reasons do we have for living?' (p. 56).

For Wolf (2010), meaningfulness is '*felt* to answer to a certain kind of human need' (Wolf, 2010: 26). This human need is the interest we have in being able to assess and justify our lives as worthwhile from some external standpoint: 'By engaging in projects of independent value, by protecting, preserving, creating, and realizing value the source of which lies outside of ourselves, we can satisfy these interests' (p. 31). Williams (1981) refers to ground projects as 'closely related to [one's] existence and [. . . that] to a significant degree give meaning to [one's] life' (p. 12). Ground projects organise our values, frame our practical identities, and direct us to the responsibilities we have to act appropriately towards those objects for the sake of which such projects exist. Such projects direct our attention to how meaningfulness derives not from the aggregation of individual goods but from long lasting commitments to promote the good for valuable beings and things.

In narrative theories of meaningfulness, the significance and value of a life derive from how the coherent progression of projects and relationships over time constitute a narrative arc, or 'shape of a life' (Kauppinen, 2008). MacIntyre (2007) comments that those who fear their life has lost meaning are expressing concern that 'the narrative of their life has become unintelligible to them, that it lacks any point, any movement towards a climax or *telos*' (p. 217). Although Strawson (2004) resists the proposal that we should judge our moral agency against the extent to which our lives have achieved a narrative structure, narratives play a role in practical and moral reasoning by operating as forms of arguments about our moral behaviour and its consequences (Benabou et al., 2018). When incorporated into practical reasoning, the value of meaningfulness provides normative tools for evaluating the objective ethical-moral and subjective cognitive-emotional aspects of narratives. The meaning content of narratives provides meaning-makers with the ethical resources to launch persuasion attempts or justifications as to why people should behave in morally desirable ways. Using the value of meaningfulness to judge the meaning content of narratives opens up behavioural pathways that direct people to attend to their responsibilities to care for morally worthy objects. Shiller (2017) describes narratives as stories that 'motivate and connect activities to deeply held values and needs' (p. 967). He characterises narratives as 'causative innovations' originating in the mind of an individual to serve their interests, and sometimes possess the contagious potential to 'go viral', in the form of 'mutated narratives' that generate unpredictable changes in collectives and societies. Some of these mutations provide new ways of thinking and feeling that support moral progress; others are morally regressive. The task of meaning-makers is to apply moral judgement to the meaning content of narratives and the process of their transmission, evaluating these against the dimensions of moral worth and affective engagement provided by the value of meaningfulness.

Judging the narrative content of work, organisations, societies, and lives involves consideration of the temporal and dynamic aspects of the narrative arc created from how people and organisations learn from failures and build the future up from the past. This is a process of creating coherence not as submission to a singular overarching goal but as a commitment to the messiness, diversity, and significance of lively things and beings that have interests and lives independent from our own (Kauppinen, 2008). Applying the value of meaningfulness to practical reasoning involves 'narrative understanding', which is an interactive process of adopting an empathetic orientation to the storied lives of others (Ritivoi, 2016: 54). When people engage with meaning and value through intersubjective encounters, moral agency and narratives become mutually implicated. Caracciolo (2012) says that narratives express societal values, such that recipients of stories interpret meanings depending upon the nature of their relationship with the authors of stories. The relational quality of intersubjective encounters shapes the content and transmission of meanings encapsulated by narratives. This means that the relational struggle to create and impose narratives is also the struggle to establish the value of beings and things and therefore to determine the kinds of lives that are judged to be meaningful (Plummer, 2019). This becomes a matter of justice when unequal access to the goods of meaningfulness, and the interactive processes of meaning-making means that 'some people's lives are often less meaningful than the lives of others through no fault or voluntary choice of their own. Under such conditions, it seems unfair or unjust that the former lead less meaningful lives than the latter' (Persson and Savulescu, 2012: 110).

Sources of Meaning and Public Meaningfulness

Psychological approaches to meaning describe how meaning systems are constituted by varieties of meaning-sources, clustered into meaning domains that operate between personal and public meaningfulness (see Schnell, 2009). Park (2017) identifies how meaning tensions, manifesting at various scales (micro, meso, and macro), are a source of differences that can be rendered productive, given the right relational conditions. In her global meaning system model, Park (2010) combines content, or beliefs about the world/identity and goals/values, with judgement, or a sense of comprehensibility, mattering, and purpose. To this, she adds subjective factors, such as 'positive affect, engagement, conscience, mindfulness, and spiritual resonance' (Park, 2017). Schnell (2011) describes meaningfulness as a 'fundamental sense of meaning, based on an appraisal of one's life as coherent, significant, directed and belonging' (p. 669). Where a life contains a diversity of meaning-sources, clustered across a density of meaning domains, meaningfulness is increased. Meaning domains include self-transcendence, self-actualisation, order, and well-being and relatedness, with generativity—the most important meaning-source—ordered under the other-regarding domain of self-transcendence.

Generativity is an integrative orientation, characterised by 'a concern for guiding, nurturing, and establishing the next generation through an act of care' (p. 671). In Erikson's (1982) life span theory, individuals must balance eight fundamental psychosocial tensions, related to life stage.[4] Erikson relates the adult stage of generativity versus stagnation to a concern for doing something of worth and significance that contributes to future generations. The psychological task is to find a balance between opposing poles, so that these poles become sources of positive meaning and creativity. But, the struggle to create an intra-psychological balance can also produce fears, anxieties, and potential breakdowns in meaning. Using self-determination theory, Bauer et al. (2017) incorporate generativity into a comprehensive model of internal motives for human flourishing, or eudaimonic accounts of lives well lived. However, SDT is a subjective model of fulfilment and as such cannot account for 'objectively more complex structures of interpretation' (p. 1), which underpin valuations of moral worth. When adjusting to the ebbs and flows of life, we require additional moral standpoints to reflect upon adverse events and amend personal meaning systems, which also contribute to the evolution of public meaning systems. Bauer et al. (2017) assign this moral task to '*wise* meaning-making' (p. 3).

The search for meaning is not solely a private endeavour. We share a public interest in how personal conceptions of meaningfulness influence our own and others' behaviour: 'others have an interest in, not only what we care about, but also what we do about our caring. And these interests are given voice through public meaning-making in the form of deliberative democratic evaluation of the worthiness of objects and the place they ought to have in our lives' (Yeoman, 2014a). Public meaningfulness is demarcated by our shared social horizon (Note, 2010), which is constrained by liberal value pluralism. To maintain the diversity of meaning-sources and domains in public meaningfulness, people must make their contribution to replenishing values, beliefs, norms, stories, concepts, and meanings. In so doing, public meaningfulness interacts with personal meaningfulness through processes of judging, evaluating, where meaning-makers bring temporal reflections upon the past and the future into 'symbolic systems of relevances' (Schutz, in Muzzetto, 2006: 15–17). As meaning-makers, people engage in meaning maintenance (Heine et al., 2006), which is how we 'strive to create and maintain order, certainty, and value in light of challenges and abruptions in their endeavours to do so' (p. 89). When people are threatened by a loss of personal meaning and breakdowns in meaning-systems, they are tempted to affirm 'any alternative framework of associations that is intact, coherent, compelling, and readily available' (p. 93). However, not all alternative frameworks are equally desirable. In the social architecture of meaningfulness and mutuality, the range of alternative frameworks is judged against the requirement for liberal value pluralism for liberal value pluralism to provide materials for objective valuing using an ethic of care.

Public interest in personal meaningfulness does not entail making it obligatory for people to contribute to activities judged to be worthy from a collective standpoint but towards which the persons themselves are indifferent or alienated. Wolf (2015) says that simply performing 'functions of worth' as judged by others is not enough for a person's life to be meaningful, if she is 'bored or alienated from most of what she spends her life doing' (p. 111). In other words, we cannot take lives to be meaningful or worth living, 'just in case one is contributing (in a Robust way) to good things' (Bramble, 2015: 453). Rather, public and personal meaningfulness emerge from a dynamic process between the individual and her society of discovering, claiming and struggling over meanings. This leads to an evolving public awareness of the connections between meaning-sources that contribute to the meaningfulness of lives in general, but which also specify the limits of collectives to impose meaning. Lives must be evaluated from the perspective not only of public value, but also from that of the person whose life it is. This includes examining how the social, environmental, and economic context promotes or inhibits a person's access to varieties of meaning-sources in crafting personal meaning, as well as their opportunity to influence the content of public meaningfulness.

Practical Reasoning

Giving meaningfulness a public dimension and using the value of meaningfulness in public reasoning are legitimate when people have the deliberative means to collectively determine the content of meaning-systems and the processes by which public meanings shape their personal meanings. Wolf situates objective valuing in a pluralistic framework 'against the background assumption that the facts about our value are likely to be highly pluralistic and complex and that in consequence our approach to questions of objective value should be tolerant and open-minded' (Wolf, 2002: 237). Ethical organising that harnesses the objective dimension of meaningfulness into practical reasoning requires valuers to have an active engagement with background assumptions. This involves public contestation and challenge as to what meanings constitute values and what these values imply for how we should act towards objects within our care. Višak (2017) says that meaning in life is best understood as 'normative reasons for action', where 'a normative reason for action' is 'a fact that counts, for the agent, in favour of his or her performing the action' (p. 517). Actions are performed in order to 'make an overall positive difference in terms of what grounds normative reasons for action' (p. 518). Višak ties objectivism to actions that promote some value and subjectivism to actions that fulfil a person's desires. In ethical organising, people are able to form reasons for action by combining the objective and subjective dimensions of meaningfulness into an internally complex moral value, when they participate in integrative social processes, such as judging, assessing, evaluating, caring, and attending. Multiple sources and domains of meaning become available to be integrated across work and lives when meaning-makers are participants in mutual organisations that establish voice practices as pathways for how 'people judge their work to matter and be meaningful' (Steger et al., 2012: 241; also van Heuvel et al. 2009).[5]

At an organisational level, practical reasoning that uses the value of meaningfulness helps to establish organisations as morally worthy (Ciulla, 2000). Life value organisations are potentially morally worthy when they proliferate moral free spaces constituting liberal value pluralism. In so doing, they make productive the paradoxes, dilemmas, and differences involved in the social construction of meaningfulness. In their examination of how sustainability professionals experience their work, Mitra and Buzzanell (2016) identify that meaningfulness arises from a tension-centred process of everyday negotiation in meaning-making, based on 'circumstances and factors that were both enabling and constraining, stemming from a variety of organizational, professional and political structures' (p. 19). Chen et al. (2011) show how controversy in task conflicts, when mediated by voice and personal control, can be harnessed for productive disagreement and generative meaning-making, which 'increases employees' tendency to consider task issues and different views deeply, which improves personal learning and growth' (p. 1012). Lips-Wiersma and Wright (2012) argue that tensions are unavoidable in the search for meaning and that these tensions are manifested in efforts to integrate doing/being and self/other. This involves interactive processes of discovering, prioritising, and balancing, leading to moments of choice and taking responsibility. In this way, tensions and differences become potential sources of learning and knowledge building. However, management efforts to deliver meaningfulness to their employees lack legitimacy in the absence of consent. To make meaningfulness part of practical reasoning requires a critical evaluation of power relations in interpersonal processes of meaning-making, as well how elite groups appropriate meaning-making through ideology or fail to provide organisational practices such as voice. Tourish (2013) has argued that, in transformational leadership models, employees too readily alienate their meaning-making capabilities to managers who are thereby afforded the opportunity to influence or close down meanings or to appropriate sense-making moments for corporate advantage. This concern extends beyond employees to all those affected by the organisation's activities.

Ethic of Care

Practical reasoning that integrates the objective and subjective dimensions of meaningfulness demands an 'active orientation of one's self to the particular value of worthy objects' (Yeoman, 2014a: 34). Frankl (1985) says that the meaningfulness is stitched together from ordinary, everyday experiences towards which we adopt positive and active orientations: 'The perception of meaning boils down to becoming aware of a possibility against the background of reality, or, more simply, becoming aware of what can be done about a given situation' (p. 260). In the social architecture of meaningfulness and mutuality, valuers use an ethic of care to evaluate how well they are doing to promote the good for worthy objects. Evers and van Smeden (2016) argue that 'many people who long for meaning do not simply long for doing good but also for a kind of connectedness to the good they do' (p. 369). Frankl makes this point:

> Human behaviour is really human to the extent to which it means acting into the world. This, in turn, implies being motivated by the world. In fact, the world toward which a human being transcends itself is a world replete with meanings that constitute reasons to act and full as well of other human beings to love.
>
> (Frankl, 1985: 269)

Frankfurt (1982) argues that loving is a powerful source of universal meaning, such that 'locating the source of meaning in the activity of loving renders opportunities for meaningful life much more readily accessible' (p. 250). He goes on to say that this requires us to find something we are capable of caring about. By engaging in acts of care towards whatever objects it is possible for us to care about, we establish the value of those objects—we make them worth caring about and in the process, we make ourselves into creators of value. Finding things to care about and acting appropriately towards such things are not things we leave purely to individual preference or even individual moral judgement. As a public activity, caring and the meaning-making associated with caring involve a politics of meaningfulness via collective struggles to secure recognition of meaning claims that justify our actions towards those beings and things we have incorporated into the meaning and purpose of our lives.

Domination and Alienation

Ethical organising directed by the sustainability imperative subjects meaning-making to moral evaluation using the value of meaningfulness. Rosenbloom (2017) describes sustainability 'pathways' as a framework for the 'theory and governance of low-carbon transitions' (p. 38). As a bridging concept, three types of pathways include biophysical, techno-economic, and socio-technical narratives. Rosenbloom (2017) argues that what is missing are the choices that must be made at critical junctures regarding how social practices should evolve. Ethical organising requires those affected by the consequences of such choices to be engaged in decision-making and problem-solving. Involving multiple voices in meaning-making demands 'polyphonic orchestration', since innovation is more likely to emerge when dialogic spaces manifest the relational dynamics for creative knowledge generation, include people representing diverse disciplines and roles, and stimulate imagination through voicing tension and difference (Ness, 2017). The value of meaningfulness enacted through mutual organisation provides the social basis for meaning-making that builds knowledge and understanding. But action contexts are less likely to be fruitful for collective problem-solving when they fail to provide people with the goods of meaningfulness (Yeoman, 2014a)—in other words, when their contributive activities are structured by alienation, domination, and lack of dignity.

In relations of oppression and domination, Scott (1990) identifies how domination involves symbolic structures of deference on the one side and dishonouring on the other. He distinguishes between hidden and public transcripts, where public transcripts are used as part of the structure of ideologies that aim to shape the subjectivity of one person to the advantage of another, thereby making it less costly for the dominant partner to extract the benefits of the relationship and hidden or behind-the-scenes transcripts express a critique of power by oppressed persons .[6] Objective structures and subjective formations can be made to work together to form a system of domination. Blaug (2007), for example, identifies how pathologies of cognition and subjective formations arise when dominating organisational structures foster the development of perverse capabilities such as obsequiousness, impression management, and co-dependency. He argues that strategies of objective and subjective domination deliberately exploit meaning-making capacities in order to support managerial ideologies, such as the natural superiority of hierarchical organisations, which means that 'any democratization of organisational life is seen to turn on the capacity of participants to selectively use and manage hierarchy and to minimise its cognitive costs' (p. 24).

In order to allow some to extract the advantages of a system of domination, objective conditions of domination are reinforced by subjective conditions of socialisation, adaptive preferences, and identity formations. McMahon (1994) shows, for example, how the directives of managers have the force of orders that are meant to pre-empt an employees' own judgement upon how to employ his or her time (p. 188) and that the internalisation of organisational rules through forms of socialisation reduce the need for managers to add coercive force to their directives; instead, 'subordinates are expected to be adept at reading the wishes of their bosses and putting them into effect without being told in so many words to do so' (p. 188). Such dominating relations are more likely to take root in 'conditions where people have to live at the mercy of another, have to live in such a way that leaves them vulnerable and exposed to the arbitrary interference and imposition of the will of another' (Alexander, 2008: 166). And these conditions pertain when the organisation of work thwarts capability formation by making workers dependent upon the coordinating capacities of others in order to be able to get their work done.

Dominating relations generate alienation of people from their core commitments. The negative impact of alienation upon meaningfulness means that, even if they recognise the objective good that they are doing, people may still experience emotional distance from their projects. This sense of alienation arises in social contexts where social relations tend towards indifference, misrecognition, and exclusion. Jaeggi (2014) argues that alienation can be understood as a sense of not having oneself at one's command, of being distanced from one's most important commitments, and particularly of not 'being able to understand oneself as the author of one's own actions' (p. 49). She describes alienation as an impaired relationship to the world or as 'a relation of relationlessness' (p. 1), arising from, firstly, meaninglessness as a distorted ability to 'meaningfully to *identify* with what one does and with those with whom one does it' (p. 12) and, secondly, powerlessness as 'the inability to exert *control* over what one does—that is, the inability to be, individually or collectively, the subject of one's actions' (ibid.). This can lead to an emotional condition whereby a person can feel himself to be 'a stranger in the world that he himself has made' (MacIntyre, 1953: 23). Jaeggi (2014) proposes that alienation may be overcome through a productive praxis, or 'way of relating practically to the world' (p. 38), which restores 'productive relations, as open processes in which appropriation always means both the integration and transformation of what is given' (p. 1). To avoid alienating people from the worlds they have had a share in making and have a continuing responsibility to maintain, we require a relational, pluralist, power-sharing conception of organisations, which I develop next by applying the mutuality principle to organising.

Mutuality as an Organising Principle

In my philosophy of ethical organising, the capacity of meaning-makers to apply the value of meaningfulness to the practical reasoning needed for building ethical worlds is dependent upon the extent to which mutuality is designed into organisational purpose, structures, and processes. Mutuality is concerned with questions of *synoikismos*, or how we are to live together. In general terms, mutuality as an organising principle describes the conditions under which we are prepared to join our efforts to those of others in order to secure together what one cannot secure alone. Mutuality becomes morally relevant when everyday constraints reflect Hume's (2000) circumstances of justice; that is, when social conditions and human interactions are characterised by moderate scarcity and limited altruism. Under such conditions, justice becomes possible, where justice is understood as: 'how the good and bad things in life should be distributed among the members of a human society' (Miller, 1999: 1). Throughout our lives, we suffer from, but are also nourished by, limits to our agency. As children, we require nurturing care from others to survive and grow; as adults, we rely upon one another for numerous services if our lives are to go well. We are mutually inter-dependent, bound up in the lives of others who provide us with not only goods and services through the division of labour, but also emotional connections and reasons for action that make our lives worth living. When faced with finite time, resources, talent, and motivation, we can be successful in our plans for living only when we elicit the support of others and, in turn, contribute to helping them thrive.

It is not only self-interest that motivates us to join in social cooperation. Just as important are other-regarding concerns for the welfare of valuable beings and things that constitute our lives and with whom we seek the shared benefits and intrinsic satisfactions of joint action. In life value organisations orchestrated by the social architecture of meaningfulness and mutuality, social cooperation is constituted by mutual relations that engender a sense of solidarity and sharing in a common fate. At the root of these mutual relations is our fundamental human condition of interdependence that reflects what we need to live a decent human life. Social justice requires inclusiveness, under terms of equality and freedom, of all those affected by particular forms of cooperation, where normatively desirable social cooperation is dependent upon legitimate coordinative authorities that incorporate into their practices human values of equality, fairness, care, respect, esteem, and dignity. With this in mind, the object of mutual organisation is to distribute among all affected members a fair share of the benefits and burdens arising from their joint activities. Fair shares are those contributions and distributions of social cooperation that are judged to be worthy and to have inherent value and developmental potential and that are determined through procedures in which all affected members have a voice, or joint control rights, in influencing the framing rules governing organisational purposes and actions.

Roots of Mutuality

Mutuality consists of a network of meanings and concepts describing how we are to live together, how we should treat one another, and what we owe to one another. The *Chambers 20th Century Dictionary* defines '*mutual*' as 'interchanged, reciprocal, given and received, common, joint, shared by two or more' and '*mutualism*' as the 'theory that mutual dependence is necessary for the welfare of the individual and society'. In the fifteenth century, the earliest usage of 'mutual' applies to the relationship between two or more people and equates the meaning of mutual to 'reciprocal'. From the sixteenth century onwards, this developed into 'having in common' or 'shared' (see Hogg, 2017). In another thread of meaning, mutuality derives from *mutare*, *mutuo*, and *mutates*, associated with 'modify', 'move', 'change', 'shift', and 'substitute'. This draws from the etymological root of mutuality as *mūtāre*, the Latin verb 'to change' or 'to change oneself into'. Furthermore, this change is interactive, involving something that is 'felt or done by each to the other' (*Oxford Concise Dictionary of English Etymology*). *Mutatis mutandis*, understood as 'the necessary changes having been made', is rooted in *mutuo*, or 'I alter, change, modify or transform'. However, the properties of *mutare* are unpredictable, uncontrollable, making us vulnerable to contingency and complexity, and this points to a 'dark side' of mutuality. Not all changes are desirable or judged to be good. The change that I bring about may be destructive when *mutare* is associated with 'I mutate, spoil' and 'I forsake'. *Mutare* takes '*essere*', or being as the auxiliary verb, from which we derive 'mutant', or risky changes-in-being that may be prolific with unexpected novelties, some monstrous, some generative, and therefore must be subject to moral judgement. From *mutus* and *muto*, we derive the word 'mute' or silent, unable to speak. To restore moral agency to *mutare* as 'to vary, diversify', meaning-makers need the power of utterance to influence change in things, people, and situations, as well as the capacity for judging as thinking and feeling into the consequences of change (Chapter 4).

Mutuality and Reciprocity

Mutuality is closely associated with conceptions of reciprocity that have influenced social exchange theories of human behaviour and have become incorporated into ethics, politics, and economics. Cicero comments: 'there is no duty more indispensable than that of returning a kindness' and that 'all men distrust one forgetful of a benefit' (in Gouldner, 1960: 161). As the basis of social cooperation, Hobhouse (1906) claims that reciprocity is 'the vital principle of society', and Simmel (1950) observes that social cohesion depends upon 'the reciprocity of service and return service'. Bruni (2008) describes reciprocity as the 'bond of society', or plural bond that provides social relationships with a general 'mutual interpersonal structure' of 'giving-and-receiving, taking-and-giving, going-and-returning' (p. ix). Moral norms and rules derived from reciprocity range from *lex talionis* or 'an eye for an eye', to the Golden rule, or 'Do unto others as you would have them do unto you' (Gewirth, 1978: 133). However, as Gewirth (1986) points out, reciprocity is a recipient-centred principle, which privileges the needs, wants, and desires of the receiver, so that 'the criterion of the rightness of actions consists in the agent's wishes for himself *qua* recipient—that is, a right or a morally obligatory action is one that the agent would want to have done to himself' (p. 31). Consequently, those with a taste in loud music might interpret the rule as meaning they are authorised to distribute similar experiences to others. Strict reciprocal exchanges, based upon giving like for like, ignore other kinds of mutual exchanges, such as solidarity, cooperation, care, and flourishing. As Goodin (2002) observes:

> [G]iving you back the same Christmas gift that you gave me earlier in the day may constitute a paradigm case of lock step reciprocity—but it is definitely not a friendly gesture. If what we want norms of reciprocity to do for us, in part, is to bind us together in a 'community of shared fate' then that form of reciprocity is actually contra-indicated.
> (Goodin, 2002)[7]

Reciprocity, understood as mutual gain, underpins notions of agent-centred justice, where gains are defined by the needs and interests of the recipient (Buchanan, 1990). Any person who is unable to participate in creating mutual gains cannot be 'contributors to the cooperative surplus' and are excluded from the scope of justice (p. 228). Gewirth (1996) counters this blind spot by arguing that we should judge our actions towards one another against certain invariant features of the human condition. He describes people as purposive agents who need freedom and well-being if they are to act and embeds purposive agency in a community of rights that is maintained by the ethos and practices of mutuality. Gouldner (1960) seeks to go beyond reciprocity as an interlocking exchange of benefits, and the obligations these entail, to understanding that there exists a 'whole reciprocities complex' which contributes to the 'maintenance of social systems' (p. 173). The normative ambition of 'win–win' constituting the shared value creation proposal can be viewed as an attempt to create a temporally and spatially extended system of reciprocities.

In examining what justice requires towards the disabled, Becker (2005) develops a more complete understanding of reciprocity as 'a fully reciprocal response' (p. 31), where reciprocity is 'a matter of making a fitting and proportional return for the good or ill we receive' (p. 18). He develops an 'unrestricted conception of reciprocity' (p. 31) based on a two-part expression of the standards needed for fittingness and proportionality. *Fittingness* comes from 'the range of things that count as goods for recipients', and in the case of bads, how to 'return corrective good for bad received' (p. 23). *Proportionality* demands that we respond 'with an equal marginal sacrifice' to the good we receive and craft corrective responses aimed at 'restoring and sustaining productive reciprocal relationships' to the bad we receive (p. 23). The overall objective is to recognise that people occupying marginal social and economic positions may not have the resources to reciprocate in kind to more advantaged individuals. If people are prevented from forming stable reciprocal relationships that are 'psychologically and sociologically necessary for creating and sustaining the social conditions in which human beings can flourish' (p. 32), they may be forced to withdraw from cooperative exchanges. A corrective response to the burdens of disability, for example, includes distributing the capabilities for health, and these capabilities are a concern for everyone because most of us expect to need care during vulnerable periods of our lives. Indeed, Becker (2005) footnotes Eva Kittay's (1999) alternative concept of reciprocity as *doulia*, or 'just as we are required care to survive and thrive, so we need to provide conditions that allow others—including those who do the work of caring—to receive the care they need to survive and thrive' (Kittay, in Becker, 2005: 18).

Cultural anthropology uses the concept of reciprocity to describe non-market exchanges, including immediate exchange, such as direct barter and delayed exchange, such as gifting. Sahlins (1972) outlines three forms of reciprocal exchange between two distinct actors occupying different social positions, who bring into exchange their separate interests and needs. These three forms are: *generalised*, or altruistic/'weak reciprocity' where the obligations to reciprocate are unclear; *balanced*, or symmetrical reciprocity involving direct exchange of things of equivalent worth and with no delay; and *negative*, or trying to get 'something for nothing with impunity' (p. 195). Reciprocity also operates in pooling, or a 'system of reciprocities', involving the collection and distribution of goods and services via an organised centre and recognised leadership.

Using social exchange theory, Molm et al. (2010) show that different types of reciprocity impart different kinds of sociality, with negative reciprocity being the least social and generalised reciprocity the most social. Reciprocity, as 'the act of giving benefits to another in return for benefits received' (Molm et al., 2007: 200), consists of two dimensions: the *instrumental or utilitarian* value of 'the value of the actual benefits received from exchange' (p. 199) and the *communicative or symbolic* value or 'the expressive and uncertainty reduction value conveyed by features of the act of reciprocity itself' (p. 199). Whereas symbolic value is associated with the development of mutual trust that underpins social capital, 'expressive value' is a more recent, new source of value, associated with social norms of equality, and generating expectations that others should respond to us in ways that make us feel 'valued, respected, and treated well' (p. 201). These affective orientations are 'process benefits', in which 'the act of reciprocity itself becomes a good', thereby enabling the formation of valuable relationships. With this in mind, Molm et al. (2007) show that different types of exchange produce different affective outcomes. For example, negotiated exchange, involving procedural fairness and voice, does not produce the anticipated benefits of trust and affective bonds unless exchanges are judged by participants to be reciprocal and constitutive of what is valued in the relationship. In mutual organisation, directed towards life value creation, I am concerned with those forms of mutuality capable of promoting expressive value and fostering reciprocal exchanges that accrue relational benefits upon organisational members.

Constrained and Expansive Mutuality

Mutuality encompasses reciprocal exchanges, but goes beyond these to a concern for the general relational and structural conditions that characterise the ways we live together. Baumard et al. (2013) identify altruism and mutualism to be two kinds of cooperative relations, where altruism is more costly for the recipient than for the actor, and mutualism is beneficial to both the actor and the recipient. However, not all mutual relationships, even if superfically benefical to both parties, are normatively desirable. Mutuality can also encompass a form of interaction where one party sacrifices advantage to ensure the fuller development of the other party. To see how this works, I distinguish constrained mutualism from expansive mutualism. In constrained mutualism, the benefits to the recipient are so minimal that she remains in a condition of permanent dependence, gaining little opportunity for capacity development or even a minimally decent life. The fear of being left outside of social interactions renders a recipient vulnerable to exploitative exchanges, especially if her society is unable to offer a sufficiently enriching alternative choice set. This means that expansive mutualism must be attentive to how the background framing rules and structural conditions shape exchanges to advantage one party at the expense of the other. Where the collective aim is the mutual flourishing of all within an ecosystem, this may require decentring more powerful parties in the interests of creating whole system relational value.

Constrained mutualism can produce enduring and stable systems of cooperation, even when distributive outcomes are unfairly skewed towards one party. When considering distributive justice in international trade, De Bres (2011) argues that there is no automatic connection between fairness, cooperation, and welfare outcomes, concluding that fairness is not essential to stable cooperative systems. However, we may consider there to be more or less desirable systems of social cooperation, from which we will select in order to promote certain moral or efficiency objectives. For example, a stable system of social cooperation could be a 'poverty trap' (Sindzingre, 2010), which institutionalises dependence, exploitation, silence, and minimal benefits. Exploitation is characterised by 'interacting with another person in a way that generates for oneself an unfairly large share of the gains from interaction' (Arneson, 2013: 405). Exploitative exchanges are fundamentally disrespectful and undignified, damaging the possibility of interactions between equals or persons of intrinsic human worth (Sample, 2003). Goodin (2002) argues that the problem of exploitation lies in 'reinforcing relations of social subordination' (p. 592), which act to the permanent advantage of one party over another. When people freely enter into relations which bring them benefits but where those relations are selected from a choice set so impoverished that the chooser cannot experience adequate human development, then the recipient's participation in the interaction has a 'demeaning quality, creating a form of 'surface endorsement' of the treatment she receives (Snyder, 2013: 353). This should lead us to an assessment of the relational contexts that treat people with disrespect and unconcern, where the expressive features of exchange are examined as one aspect of a system of reciprocities or dimensions of mutuality.

Despite moral concerns regarding exploitation, Arneson (2013) argues against strict prioritisation of fairness that forbids the good that might be done. Joan Robinson (1962) famously comments that 'the misery of being exploited by capitalists is nothing compared to the misery of not being exploited at all' (p. 45). Arneson (2013) points out that strict fairness may lead us to disengage from exploited persons, thereby depriving them not only of vital resources but also of a place in our social world. What we owe to another human being is not only the degree of gain or loss in exchanges but also seeing them as part of our life world, and therefore a person with whom we must have an ongoing relationship. One way through this dilemma is to consider how voluntary but exploitative exchanges can be embedded into long-term relationships of

mutual obligation, where the aim is to shift the system to greater productivity and complex contribution using mutual practices of voice and
power-sharing. This suggests a role for substantive mutuality in moral
learning and social development, where substantive mutuality is understood to be established within networks of enduring obligations. In his
application of justice theory to strategic alliances, Luo (2008) identifies
how fair treatment must operate at both the individual level (self-esteem,
social identity, team spirit) and the organisational level (commitment,
trust, and social harmony), if alliances are to produce cooperative outcomes: 'Fair treatment creates cooperative value by removing fears of
exploitation and by demonstrating respect for the rights and dignity of
the other party' (p. 29).

Mutuality involves seeing vulnerable, marginalised, and exploited others as part of our social world. This means that organisations cannot
sidestep their responsibilities for those, such as factory workers in global
value chains, who may not be in a position to engage on equal terms in
bargaining games framed by the multinational businesses they supply.
Cushing and Lewis (2002) suggest that whilst both mutuality and reciprocity refer to 'relationships in which something is given and something
is received', reciprocity is not identical with mutuality because 'reciprocity emphasises the instrumental value of a relationship, and has generally been used to describe temporally united, contractual relationships'
(p. 179). Consequently, those who are not in a position to return what
is given in kind, such as the physically and mentally disabled, are 'not
'due' anything in a reciprocity model' (ibid.). In win–win exchanges, this
includes those who have little to offer in bargaining. Cushing and Lewis
argue that the mutuality between the disabled and their carers 'implies
a wider range of gifts (often intangible) that are considered in exchange
[. . .] and is something which is universally "due" to all people, not just
those who can reciprocate' (p. 179). These gifts involve mutual care
and learning from each other regarding the situations in which they are
bound together. Given how we are all, to some degree, vulnerable to powerful others but still bear responsibilities to care for valuable beings and
things, then mutuality must do more than capture reciprocal exchanges
and must extend mutual organising to those values of caring and flourishing that yield positive meanings conducive to practical reasoning that
enables us to construct a life of meaning and purpose.

Dimensions of Mutuality

I use resources from John Rawls's Theory of Justice to expand the concept
of mutuality. Becker (2005) observes that Rawls hints at a 'a deeper idea
of reciprocity' when he says that the difference principle applied to basic
structures ought to recognise how institutions can take account of misfortune, bad luck, and the need to maintain free and equal relationships

between citizens (p. 19). In the Rawlsian schema, the basic structure of society is just when it is organised to the mutual advantage of all. If the basic structure embodies values of equality and freedom to the maximal degree, people will be free to live according their own ideas of the good, where individual conceptions of living interlock into a social union through association, sociability, and the enjoyment of one another's excellences. Rawls (1999 [1971]) describes a progressive *modus vivendi*, or a way of living with diversity and difference, which we can interpret as moving from bargaining to cooperating to flourishing. Society advances from *bargaining* behind the veil of ignorance, where people who are ignorant of their eventual position in the future society reason together under conditions of impartiality and fairness in order to create the social contract that will govern the future society, to *cooperating* in the social system that produces the primary goods that 'every rational man is presumed to want' (p. 54), to *becoming* in a 'social union' (p. 459) that is the 'shared final end' of the 'successful carrying out of just institutions' (p. 461–462). The social union is always in a process of becoming, such that each person's development is necessary for the development of all, giving rise to a mutuality of increasing and enriching excellences and mutual flourishing that forms the basis for self-respect, which is Rawls's most important primary good.

With this in mind, I propose that mutuality operates in three dimensions, associated with three core ethical orientations and principles: bargaining (associated with fairness and reciprocity), cooperating (associated with care and contribution), and becoming (associated with flourishing and world-building). In social organisation, these dimensions are manifested to a greater or lesser degree depending upon how the institutional framework and social practices mitigate moral concerns in each dimension of mutuality. These moral concerns are exploitation, alienation, and capability malformation. In bargaining, the rules of the game can operate to the advantage of some who are able to appropriate the benefits of bargaining with no regard for the welfare of the disadvantaged (exploitation); in cooperating, people can be disengaged or disaffected in relations vital to their well-being such as their work, their colleagues, their sense of self, their organisation (alienation); in becoming, people can find that domination and alienation distort their abilities to meet their fundamental needs for agency and self-determination, making them vulnerable to exploitation (capability malformation). In life value organisations, practices of bargaining, cooperating, and becoming are cumulative. An organisation can operate principally in the dimension of bargaining, with weak practices of cooperating and becoming. However, strengthening practices of cooperating and becoming adds robustness and integrity to the life value model. Together, these three dimensions imply the need for a reinforcing bundle of organisational practices, which have the potential to generate outcomes responsive to the sustainability imperative. (See Table 3.1.)

Table 3.1 Dimensions of Mutuality

Degree	Ethical Orientation	Moral Concern	Key Principle	Guiding Question
Bargaining	Fairness	Exploitation	Reciprocity	What do I lack that you can provide?
Cooperating	Care	Alienation	Contribution	What can I contribute to promote our shared interests?
Becoming	Flourishing	Capability Malformation	World-Building	What do I need for acting and being that I recognise you need also?

Ethical Orientations: Fairness, Care, and Flourishing

By invoking fairness, we indicate our moral concern for how people ought to be treated. Justice draws upon fairness as a notion of equivalences that must be modified under certain conditions. The formal principle of distributive justice can be found in Aristotle's statement of equality that equals should be treated equally and unequals unequally. In his analysis of the etymological origins of 'fair', Cupit (2011) traces the links between fairness and social order. Perceptions of fairness indicate what our moral sensibilities find to be pleasing and attractive. In particular, fairness picks out the kinds of reasons that should guide our interactions: 'To be partial and biased is to be moved by the wrong sorts of reasons' (p. 398). Arrangements may be judged to be orderly and therefore fair when allocations are 'in accordance with what is due' (p. 399) and subject to allocative procedures that are guided by the correct reasons of impartiality and efficiency according to some publicly recognised feature of the recipient, such as need or desert. Thus, it is fair to treat participants equally, but this does not imply that they must be treated the same. Rather, equal treatment means that all participants should have their claims satisfied in proportion to relevant public criteria, such as their contribution or their need. Furthermore, fairness practices, such as giving participants a role in determining the rules restricting their liberties, reduce the anxieties of participants that they will be exploited or be subject to unpredictable, arbitrary treatment. Hence, fairness practices encompass procedures as well as outcomes, where associated interactions provide opportunities for expressive variety in dialogic exchange, including narratives, as well as impartial reason-giving. Finally, acceptance by participants of the benefits of cooperation generates obligations upon them to make their contribution, and to take part in shaping the rules governing social cooperation. Phillips (1997) describes the principle of fairness in stakeholder relations as:

> Whenever persons or groups of persons voluntarily accept the benefits of a mutually beneficial scheme of co-operation requiring sacrifice or contribution on the parts of the participants and there exists the possibility of free-riding obligations of fairness are created among the participants in the co-operative scheme in proportion to the benefits accepted.
>
> (Phillips, 1997: 57)

Although a sense of fairness may be universal, interpretations of fairness are contextual and socially constructed by background norms, values, and cultural expectations. Empirical studies of fairness principles indicate that people often favour collections of fairness principles, prioritising or combining them according to their circumstances. Konow (2003) argues that the following principles can be excavated from the empirical literature: the need principle, aimed at the 'equal satisfaction of basic needs'; the efficiency principle, aimed at maximising the surplus; the equity (accountability) principle, based on 'proportionality and individual responsibility'; and the context family of principles, derived from 'dependence of the justice evaluation on the context, such as the choice of persons and variables, framing effects and issues of process' (p. 1189). In grappling with the tensions between these principles, people's perspectives upon fairness are affected by scope effects, competing forces, weighting of justice principles, and procedural justice. They arrive at pluralistic combinations of fairness principles, depending on the context. For example, Ordonez and Mellers (1993) find that 'people value equity but prefer to live in societies that sacrifice some equity in order to provide for higher minimum and mean earnings' (Konow, 2003: 1234). Harrison and Wicks (2013) argue that it is in the interests of firms to go beyond the just-enough principle in stakeholder management. The just-enough principle optimises value creation when managers aim for distributions in which stakeholders believe the value they receive is better than what they would receive elsewhere by just enough to make a difference to them. But if people want to live in societies that provide some resources for everyone, this suggests the need for a more expansive conception of mutuality directed towards whole-system flourishing rather than strict adherence to a penny-pinching reciprocity that calculates mutual gain as maximal returns for the dominant player and minimal returns for everyone else.

Positive fairness perceptions depend upon organisational practices for conciliating difference, such as voice and participation in the decision-making needed for world-building. Christiano (2013) argues that fairness exists to the extent that 'each person [has] a voice in how to construct the social world they live in' (p. 370.). Christiano (2013) picks out two core human interests that are met by such a notion of fairness. Firstly, our interest in avoiding alienation, which is met by 'being at home in the world' (p. 375). Secondly, our interest in having our particular concerns, needs, and plans for living recognised in circumstances that protect us against the cognitive biases of others. This is met by 'participating in shaping my world' (ibid.). World-building draws upon other values than fairness, including care and flourishing. Care ethicists argue that standard theories of justice are limited by their requirement for impartiality in reason giving and the adoption of a hyper-individualist ontology. Consequently, they are not able to account for the particularity of our commitments, the importance of our relationships, and the manner in which relations of power determine the distribution of benefits and burdens. Conversely, an ethical orientation of care, based upon a relational ontology, 'conceives agents as mutually interconnected, vulnerable and dependent, often in asymmetrical ways' (Pettersen, 2011: 52) where moral agents are understood to be 'entrenched in a web of relationships' (ibid.: 55). Bargaining initiates a system of social cooperation, and cooperating stabilises collective action, but neither alone produce the transformations required to elevate a cooperative system to a new equilibrium capable of generating care and flourishing across a whole ecosystem. For this, we require the additional dimension of becoming, which Tsoukas and Chia (2002) describe as 'an attempt to order the intrinsic flux of human action, to channel it towards certain ends, to give it a particular shape, through generalizing and institutionalizing particular meanings and rules' (p. 570). At an individual level, becoming is the search for meaning, involving a quest for wholeness and unity; at an organisational level, it is the manifestation of a morally worthy organisation that is capable of providing the goods of meaningfulness and necessary life-supports, as part of its contribution to the planetary-scale social cooperation required to address the sustainability imperative.

Sherman (1993) argues that 'it is in the act of relating and being reflected in the opinions and judgements of others whom we respect that we refine our sense of who we are and how worthwhile our lives have been' (p. 278).[8] This suggests that mutuality is not concerned solely with reciprocity or even with cooperation, but also with the equal participation of each person in building a world-in-common that provides for the flourishing of all the beings and things assembled within its dispensation. Indeed, one of the reasons we engage with others in common pursuit is that 'we simply value doing things together, for its own sake' (p. 276). This is because 'we value creating a shared world and the mutuality that is defined by our interactions' (p. 276). The intrinsic satisfactions of mutual interaction in joint action stimulate the experience of an expanded self that contributes to collective flourishing. Interrelating through shared endeavour helps to create 'a sense of tracking something with one another, of creating a sense of unity through attunement to each other other's moves' (p. 282). The mutual joining of mind, feeling, and effort creates a temporary sense of unity between those engaged in a common purpose. As such, mutuality in joint action becomes an outworking of coactive, relational power, in which participants are open to be influenced by the differences of others and to share in the production and enjoyment of the outcome.

Voice: Democratic World-Building

To be human is to be an inhabitant of worlds that we have collectively created and that we share with other beings and things. The task given to us by the sustainability imperative is not to create any kind of world but to direct our will to organise towards making all worlds into ethical worlds. This means converting the general capacity to organise into a human capability for ethical world-building, using conversation factors provided by the social architecture of meaningfulness and mutuality. I argue that mutuality as an organising principle implies that associational ecosystems must be arranged into systems of democracy, in order to address what Fraser (2007) calls 'the problem of the frame' (p. 193), or the terms under which world-builders participate in deciding 'what should count as a just ordering of social relations within a society' (p. 194). I explore next the role of voice in democratic world-building, in particular drawing upon the idea of *mêtis* to invoke the practical skills that meaning-makers need to build ethical worlds.

Structures and Institutions

In its general form, mutual organisation requires a power-sharing voice-system, capable of activating the value of meaningfulness in practical reasoning and providing channels for meanings to be adopted into narratives that carry into collective action the human values needed to expand social cooperation. In life value organisations, this implies organisational practices that proliferate moral free spaces constituted by liberal value pluralism, framed by considerations of who is entitled to participate in these spaces and how they will do so. Modern organisational practices of shared leadership, joint knowledge creation, and self-managed teams derive from the expectation that employees will take up responsibilities to care for outcomes, as well as the pragmatic understanding that, if employees are going to fulfil such responsibilities, they require the tools for collaborative working in the form of an organisational system of democratic participation (Knoll et al., 2016; see Johnson, 2006). Voice practices are essential to forming multi-level associational ecosystems that incorporate multiple perspectives into problem-solving, and use meaning-making to motivate social cooperation. In essence, to address the sustainability imperative, we need an ecological democracy, constituted by life value organisations that are internally democratic and interconnected in associational ecosystems through deliberative forms of governance, where 'ecological civilisation is based on diverse lifeways sustaining linked natural and social ecologies' (Morrison, 1995: 11).

Voice presents a critical challenge to distributions of corporate power that allow private governance regimes to subject employees to domination, interference, and control (Anderson, 2017). Assumptions that organisations are entitled to do what they like to their employees and to other stakeholders are legitimated when ideological formations, such as market freedom construed as non-interference, come to be seen as natural and inevitable. Anderson (2017) describes ideologies as simplifying representations, that are necessary for maintaining social life:

> An ideology is good if it helps us navigate [the world] successfully. To help us, it must identify the normatively important features of the world, and the main causal connections between these features to which people can respond, enabling them to discover effective means to promoting their goals. Ideologies also help us orient our current evaluations of the world, highlighting what we think is already good or bad in it. [. . .] [T]hey are vehicles for our hopes and dreams.
>
> (Anderson, 2017: xx)

Ideologies can operate for good or for ill. When harnessed into ethical world-building, they can generate sustainability narratives capable of carrying positive meanings and values into the identity formation needed for expansive social cooperation. But when appropriated to serve the interests of the powerful, they can corrupt public meaningfulness, and therefore the meaning-sources we have to create morally worthy organisations. In ethical world-building, ideologies and narratives establish a sense of collective psychological ownership, or 'the collectively held sense (feeling) that this target of ownership (or a piece of that target) is collectively 'ours'' (Pierce and Jussila, 2010: 812). When guided by a value-system based upon our responsibilities to steward and care for ensembles of morally valuable beings and things, collective psychological ownership helps to mobilise normatively desirable collective action through the construction of shared mental models, and the 'emergence of a personal feeling of our-ness' at the level of the group (p. 818). Group members invest their own selves into 'the target of ownership' through 'intimate knowing' (p. 823). In ethical organising, experiences of jointness are supported by positive narratives—collectively created and shared—that aim at the moral expansiveness needed to include all those affected by the organisation's activities. Routes to collective psychological owner-ship include self-governing teams, being well-informed, doing 'whole and identifiable' jobs (p. 823), increasing the number of skills and abilities in the team, fostering greater integration through task interdependence, and increasing task significance through recognition of one's impact upon other team members.

In ethical organising, all those affected by the activities of the organisa-tion are entitled to shape the ideologies and narratives influencing the meaning-sources that underpin their joint activities. Organisations seek-ing a positive and inclusive ideology to ground organisational integrity must establish practices of narrative justice, using voice practices to draw upon the interpretive variety of meanings latent in the society of meaning-makers, and which cluster around their organisational challenges. The social architecture of meaningfulness and mutuality specifies moral free spaces of dialogic encounter where such spaces draw upon diverse meaning-sources to create liberal value pluralism as a common good of the organisation. When orchestrated by a system of deliberative representative governance, such moral free spaces become productive of ideological formations, mak-ing these ideologies available to be endorsed by members who will draw upon the meanings and values embedded in them.

In characterising firms as political entities, analogous to states, Fer-raras (2017) proposes accountability mechanisms based upon economic bicameralism in which governance becomes a joint responsibility of capi-tal and labour. She says, '[T]he firm is not the capital investors' *res*'. Given employee contributions to creating the organisation, investors are not 'free to dispose of it as they wish' (p. 13). The complexity of an organisation's interactions with multiple stakeholders, including, for example, integra-tion of suppliers' purposes and practices into corporate-defined objectives, makes this argument relevant to all members of the associational ecosys-tem of which an organisation is a part. Participatory multi-stakeholder initiatives are increasingly incorporated into private governance regimes that have the potential to become representative and deliberative at the level of meta-organising, but which risk becoming exploitative, if stable forms of social cooperation. Furthermore, these moves could result in democratic deficits opening up between employees and external stake-holders, since organisations can develop voice systems for suppliers, cus-tomers, and communities, whilst maintaining their employees in a 'black hole' of voicelessness (Wilkinson et al., 2018).

Democratic deficits between member constituencies are addressed by developing an equal capability for ethical world-building, instituted by a multi-scalar voice system. This system consists of internally democratic organisations, inter-organisational voice processes, and meta-governance of the associational ecosystem, where diverse members can find a place within a 'collective intelligence model' focussed on shared prob-lems (Landemore and Ferreras, 2016: 70). Beirne (2008) characterises participatory practices as 'negotiated, contested and precarious' (p. 682), which means that establishing mini publics within associational ecosystems requires a 'consolidated, independent source of influence and continuity' (Brogger, 2010: 491), or a system of independent institutions that can provide checks and balances within a pluralised system of democratic accountability. At an organisational level, Wegge et al. (2010) identify the importance of 'structurally anchored organisational democracy', including 'broad-based and institutionalised employee influence processes that are not ad hoc or occasional in nature' (p. 162). In a multichannelled voice system, representative mechanisms run vertically through the organisation, intersecting with horizontal layers of participatory practices. Representation includes democratic authorisation of managerial power to coordinate, as well as individual entitlements to participate in task- and practice-based organising (Pyman et al., 2006).

At the level of the associational ecosystem, Mansbridge et al. (2012) recommend establishing deliberative democracy as a distributed system, such that 'most democracies are complex entities in which a wide variety of institutions, associations and sites of contestation accomplish political work' (pp. 1–2). However, Owen and Smith (2015) worry that Mansbridge et al. (2012) lose sight of how people generate 'perspectives, claims, narratives and reasons' (p. 221) through social and political institutions and practices and how this perspective formation is connected to the deliberative capabilities of citizens and decision-makers. They propose an 'expansive approach' (p. 228) to deliberative systems, in which deliberation is extended to an evaluation of the structural context and background conditions enabling or disabling discursive action (p. 228). Ast (2019) recommends drawing on the idea of democracy as a system to add to Integrative Social Contracts Theory a test of 'Deliberative Capacity' (p. 207), or the deliberative procedures by which hypernorms can be identified and legitimated and hence incorporated into ethical decision-making. Ast (2019) describes deliberative capacity as operating in three dimensions of socio-economic, cultural, and institutional capacity that encompass resources, values, and rights. To this must be added an understanding of the intersubjective dimensions of meaning-making and narrative formation. Holdo (2018) argues that deliberative systems require a relational perspective, in which participants critically evaluate sites of intersubjective encounter for their capacity to foster 'deep learning of social meaning and practice' (p. 2). In the implementation of worker engagement technology, for example, the WEST principles, aimed at identifying worker exploitation in global supply chains seek to ensure that dialogic spaces are equipped with digital tools to support worker voice. In a separate example, the Coalition of Immokalee Workers' 'Fair Food Program' turns corporate social responsibility into worker-driven social responsibility, using worker education and field monitoring of their human rights.[9] Such practical cases suggest how a human capability for ethical world-building can be activated using voice-systems and more broadly to institute deliberative democracy in associational ecosystems.

Mêtis: Overcoming Muteness and Harnessing Mutancy

The social architecture of meaningfulness and mutuality provides the design elements for generating varieties of organising that are responsive to changing human needs and responsibilities in the Anthropocene. But organising under conditions of complexity is also a source of unpredictable mutancy, throwing up monstrous creations, such as surveillance capitalism (Zuboff, 2019), that colonise democratic and regulatory voids. Yet at the same time, mutancy is an abundant resource of fertile novelties, containing an excess of the organisational possibilities we need for innovating new organisational models. Exploring these edges of human organising is valuable for learning what we are prepared to accept for our lives and the lives of others, and what we reject. But to make such ethical decisions, we need to guard against radical distortions of voice as silencing or muting that shut down evaluations of the mutant products of world-building. With this in mind, ethical organising may sometimes need to be done subversively, and a candidate capacity for such organising is *mêtis*, which, although associated with cunning and trickery, also indicates productive ways of acting that can overcome muteness and harness mutancy into collective action.

Drawing from Michel de Certeau, who connects *mêtis* to the tactics of 'making do' in difficult, complex, and ambiguous situations, Dolmage (2009) describes *mêtis* as 'cunning, adaptive, embodied intelligence' (p. 6). When contrasted with *phronesis*, which is ordered by wisdom, ethics, and scientific knowledge, *mêtis* is often dismissed as just 'bad *phronesis*' (p. 11): a form of thinking and feeling that is chaotic, ill-disciplined, and amoral. But when allied with the value of meaningfulness in practical reasoning, *mêtis* suggests tactical ways for world-builders to use the third dimension of mutuality as becoming, in order to act into moments of complex, power-laden, voiceless organising. Newswander and Newswander (2013) describe *mêtis* as 'a form of practical knowledge that is rooted in experimentation, inquiry, and cunning' (p. 2) and argue for a type of 'bounded metis', where 'crafty ethos is bound within a proper sphere'. In applying *mêtis* to public administration, they propose that 'a modified test like intermediate scrutiny provides conditions that allow metis to be properly contained and legitimated' (p. 12). In ethical organising, the products of mutancy that emerge from the polyphony of mutual organisation must be submitted to public reasoning, where the value of meaningfulness is used to evaluate organisational novelties.

Guided by the value of meaningfulness in practical reasoning, the craftiness of *mêtis* is lent normative direction and content, especially when organisations impose muteness upon their members. At an organisational level, silencing can produce a 'climate of silence' (Wilkinson et al., 2018), where single instances of silencing become, through repeated interactions, an established norm (Perlow and Repennings, 2009). Some choose muteness as a form of resistance against corporate extraction of their knowledge, information, and skill. *Mêtis* combined with the value of meaningfulness helps to overcome muteness by tapping into mutuality as mutability. Here, mutability can take the form of transformative change that can distort latent organisational potentials into exploitative hybrids and bureaucracies of indifference and systemic humiliation, or can act as a stimulant of organisational novelties needed to produce the structural and processual elements of life value models. Letiche and Statler (2005) show how using *mêtis* takes people into the territory of the intuitive and uncodified: 'With metis, there is something outside of sense-making that takes over when unforeseen and unforeseeable events gain control' (p. 8), or, as Bachelard puts it, 'we must head there [. . .] where reason likes to be in danger' (p. 8). *Mêtis* can challenge our acceptance that some groups should remain mute. Muteness includes missing voices of subalterns, such as children, who are both 'subject to and object of organisation' but who are voiceless because there is no social space in organisations for genuine exchange (Kavanagh, 2013: 1489). For example, the spectacle of children protesting climate change by striking from school and bringing lawsuits to compel governments to meet carbon emission targets has disrupted our assumptions that it is natural for adults to speak in their place.[10]

Mêtis represents surplus meaning and excess that escapes self-knowledge—potentially, fickle, unpredictable, reckless, and even violent. However, in judging how to act in situations characterised by uncertainty, this mode of thinking and feeling is potentially generative. In the context of change, *mêtis* is associated with the unexpected and emergent rather than with incremental gradual changes: 'metis appears to be a mode of intelligent action that involves responsiveness to changing circumstances' (Letiche and Statler, 2005: 20). *Mêtis* has a role when there is confusion in unresolved circumstances and a lack of clear direction. In this way it is suited to the constituent power of agonistic republicanism. Letiche and Statler (2005) connect *mêtis* to system-level shifts as emergent properties unexpectedly and unpredictably manifest at higher levels of aggregation. Employees use *mêtis* to resist the purposes of their employers and to co-opt organisational means to do things that they value: 'Employers' purposes are thwarted and the organizational technology is (momentarily) not used to make money, but to do what the employees think is worthwhile' (p. 12). Brady (2003) explores a case study of *mêtis* and boundary working, where *mêtis* is an 'agile intelligence' akin to the responsive expertise of a midwife during a difficult labour. Such a situation cannot be resolved through the formal application of rules laid down by technological determinism. Brady (2003) describes Virginia, who was tasked with writing computer instructions in a move to a paperless office and who engaged in problem-solving to help workers understand and use new technologies. This problem-solving activity was unrecognised by the organisation which saw work as 'seamless, a series of routines carried out by a homogenous workforce' (p. 232). Virginia says:

> Problem-solving is different for each problem. It's my angle on how I'm going to solve a particular problem [. . .]. I have a little bag of tricks that I always use over and over again. Strategic ambiguity is one of them.
>
> (p. 228)

Virginia's managerial colleagues would disapprove of her preparatory work—exploring employees' files to retain information that the user might need—as costly and inefficient. Given this, Virginia used strategic ambiguity to inform her supervisor of what needed looking at without explaining why. She gained access to the files without requiring supervisory permission because she reframed this step with her supervisor as necessary for deleting files and therefore in the interests of the organisation. Such vignettes are repeated daily in countless organisations. Employees, such as Virginia, use *mêtis* to respond to needs with resourcefulness and attention, so as to have a care for the anxieties of workers caught up in confusing change, where the worth of that change has not been evaluated from their perspective by the organisation.

In sum, the core object of ethical world-building is to expand social cooperation to planetary scale. To achieve this, we must activate in collective action those motivations necessary for our civilisational survival, such as our fundamental need for meaning, harnessing this need to narratives that carry forward into our social relations values consistent with a cosmopolitan consciousness. Heine et al. (2006) argue that the tradition of Western existentialism ties the pursuit of meaning to a 'fundamentally relational mode of being' (p. 89). In combining independent and personal value, the value of meaningfulness gives us scope to explore our own selves in the abundance of our relations to other beings and things. This relational entwinement is an 'interspace', described by Cooper (2005) as a 'prime mover of human agency in the continuous work of cultivating its world' (p. 1690). Mutual organisation supplies organisational practices for proliferating the polyphonic moral spaces through which world-building takes place, thereby activating the possibility of incorporating the value of meaningfulness into practical reasoning. In Chapter 4, I shall argue that these organisations are worthy of the interactions of their members when they are collective moral agents, but that collective moral agents depend upon their members being willing to create organisational integrity, emotions, and purposes.

Notes

1. Adapted from Figure 27.1 in Yeoman (2019: 469). Reproduced by permission of Oxford University Press.

2. Danaher (2016) identifies four main theoretical descriptions of the value of meaningfulness: simple subjectivist, simple objective, aim-achievement, and fitting-fulfillment.

3. Veltman argues that Wolf's account of objective value is incomplete and needs to be supplemented by 'Aristotelian approaches to human well-being which provide ground for a claim that meaningful work is integral to living well' (p. 114). Veltman identifies four eudaimonistic dimensions by which meaningful work may be considered to be objectively valuable (p. 117), including (1) development of human capabilities; (2) supporting virtues; (3) providing purpose and producing something of enduring value; (4) integrating elements of a worker's life (for example, relationships, values, or connection). Veltman does not making work meaningful just because it develops or exercises such capabilities. Rather, work may be considered to be meaningful in a variety of ways, such as the sense of purpose and usefulness experienced by the unskilled worker who is contributing necessary work to his or her community

4. Erikson's stages are Trust vs. Mistrust (infancy); Autonomy versus Shame and Doubt (toddlerhood); Initiative versus Guilt (early childhood); Industry versus Inferiority (middle childhood); Identity versus Role Confusion (adolescence and emerging adulthood); Intimacy versus Isolation (emerging adulthood and adulthood); Generativity versus Stagnation (adulthood); Integrity versus Despair (old age).

5. van Heuvel et al (2009) define meaning-making as 'the ability to integrate challenging or ambiguous situations into a framework of personal meaning using value-based reflection' (p. 510).

6. Section adapted from Yeoman (2014a: pp. 101–102). Reproduced by permission of Palgrave Macmillan.

7. Proudhon recognised the connection between mutuality and association: 'In cases in which production requires great division of labour, it is necessary to form an association among the workers [. . .] because without that they would remain isolated as subordinates and superiors, and there would ensue two industrial castes of masters and wage workers, which is repugnant in a free and democratic society'. He argues that mutualism requires a system of industrial democracy.

8. Nineteenth-century mutualism can be considered a form of libertarian socialism. For example, derived from Proudhon's anarchism, mutualists adopted cooperation as a core principle for economic interactions, whilst also supporting the development of free markets. This can be traced in the associational democracy of Paul Hirst. Mikhail Bakunin critiques anarchist mutualism for assuming that people join together in collective action only through contracts between individuals: 'As if these men had dropped from the skies, bringing with them speech, will, original thought, and as if they were alien to anything of the earth, that is, anything having social origin'.

9. See FairFood Program, www.fairfoodprogram.org/

10. Children are bringing legal claims against governments, arguing that they have 'violated their constitutional rights to life, liberty and property by failing to prevent dangerous climate change'. See: US Supreme Court Allows Historic Kid's Climate Lawsuit to Go Forward. *Nature*, 563, 163–164 (2018). www.nature.com/articles/d41586-018-07214-2

Bibliography

Agle, R. A., Donaldson, T., Freeman, R. E., Jensen, M. C., Mitchell, R. K., & Wood, D. J. (2008). Towards a Superior Stakeholder Theory. *Business Ethics Quarterly*, 18 (2): 153–190.

Alexander, J. M. (2008). *Capabilities and Social Justice: The Political Philosophy of Amartya Sen and Martha Nussbaum*. Aldershot: Ashgate.

Anderson, A. (2017). *Private Government: How Employers Rule Our Lives (and Why We Don't Talk About It)*. Princeton, NJ: Princeton University Press.

Arneson, R. (2013). Exploitation and Outcome. *Politics, Philosophy, and Economics*, 12: 392–412.

Ast, F. J. (2019). The Deliberative Test, a New Procedural Method for Ethical Decision Making in Integrative Contracts Theory. *Journal of Business Ethics*, 155 (1): 207–221.

Axtell, G. (2016). *Objectivity*. Cambridge & Malden, MA: Polity Press.

Bauer, J. J., King, L. A., & Steger, M. F. (2018). Meaning Making, Self-Determination Theory, and the Question of Wisdom in Personality. *Journal of Personality*, (June 2017): 1–20.

Baumard, N., André, J. B., & Sperber, D. (2013). A Mutualistic Approach to Morality: The Evolution of Fairness by Partner Choice. *Behavioral and Brain Sciences*, 36 (1): 59–78.

Becker, L. C. (2005). Reciprocity, Justice, and Disability. *Ethics*, 116 (1), Symposium on Disability (October 2005): 9–39.

Beirne, M. (2008). Idealism and the Applied Relevance of Research on Employee Participation. *Work, Employment and Society*, 22 (4): 675–693.

Benabou, R., Falk, A., & Tirole, J. (2018). *Narratives, Imperatives and Moral Reasoning*. IZA Discussion Papers 11665. Bonn: Institute of Labor Economics (IZA).

Blaug, R. (2007). Cognition in a Hierarchy. *Contemporary Political Theory*, 6: 24–44.

Brady, A. (2003). Interrupting Gender as Usual: Mêtis Goes to Work. *Women's Studies: An Inter-Disciplinary Journal*, 32 (2): 211–233.

Bramble, B. (2015). Consequentialism About Meaning in Life. *Utilitas*, 27 (4): 445–459.

Brogger, B. (2010). An Innovative Approach to Employee Participation in a Norwegian Retail Chain. *Economic and Industrial Democracy*, 31 (4): 477–495.

Bruni, L. (2008). *Reciprocity, Altruism and the Civil Society: In Praise of Heterogeneity*. London & New York: Routledge.

Buchanan, A. (1990). Justice as Reciprocity Versus Subject-Centered Justice. *Philosophy & Public Affairs*, 19 (3): 227–252.

Campbell, S. M., & Nyholm, S. (2015). Anti-Meaning and Why It Matters. *Journal of the American Philosophical Association*, 1 (4): 694–71.

Caracciolo, M. (2012). Narrative, Meaning, Interpretation: An Enactivist Approach. *Phenomenology and the Cognitive Sciences*, 11 (3): 367–384.

Chen, Z., Zhang, X., & Vogel, D. (2011). Exploring the Underlying Processes Between Conflict and Knowledge Sharing: A Work Engagement Perspective. *Journal of Applied Social Psychology*, 41: 1005–1033.

Christiano, T. (2005). An Argument for Egalitarian Justice and Against the Levelling-Down Objection. In: Campbell, O'Rourke & Shier (eds.), *Law & Social Justice*. Cambridge, MA, & London: MIT Press.

Christiano, T. (2013). Equality, Fairness and Agreements. *Journal of Social Philosophy*, 44 (4): 370–391.

Ciulla, J. B. (2000). *The Working Life: The Promise and Betrayal of Modern Work*. New York: Random House.

Cooper, R. (2005). Relationality. *Organization Studies*, 26 (11): 688–1710.

Cuguero-Escofet, N., & Fortin, M. (2014). One Justice or Two? A Model of Reconciliation of Normative Justice Theories and Empirical Research on Organizational Justice. *Journal of Business Ethics*, 124: 435–451.

Cupit, G. (2011). Fairness as Order: A Grammatical and Etymological Prolegomenon. *Journal of Value Inquiry*, 45: 389–401.

Cushing, P., & Lewis, T. (2002). Negotiating Mutuality and Agency in Care-Giving Relationships with Women with Intellectual Disabilities. *Hypatia*, 17 (3): 173–193.

Danaher, J., (2016). Will Life Be Worth Living in a World Without Work? Technological Unemployment and the Meaning of Life. *Science and Engineering Ethics*, 23 (1), 41–64.

De Bres, H. (2011). The Cooperation Argument for Fairness in International Trade. *Journal of Social Philosophy*, 42: 192–218.

Dewey, J. (1927). *The Public and Its Problems*. Athens: Ohio University Press.

Dolmage, J. (2009). Metis, Metis, Mestiza, Medusa: Rhetorical Bodies Across Rhetorical Traditions. *Rhetoric Review*, 28 (March 2015): 1–28.

Erikson, E. H. (1982). *Childhood and Society*. New York: W. W. Norton.

Evers, D., & van Smeden, G. E. (2016). Meaning in Life: In Defense of the Hybrid View. *Southern Journal of Philosophy*, 54 (3): 355–371.

Ferraras, I. (2017). *Firms as Political Entities: Saving Democracy Through Economic Bicameralism*. Cambridge: Cambridge University Press.

Frankfurt, H. (1982). The Importance of What We Care About. *Synthese*, 53: 257–272.

Frankl, V. E. (1988). *The Will to Meaning*. New York: New American Library.

Frankl, V. E. (1985). Logos, Paradox, and the Search for Meaning. In: Freeman, Mahoney, & DeVito (eds.), *Cognition and Psychotherapy*. New York: Springer Publishing Company.

Frankl, V. E. (2004). *Man's Search for Meaning*. London: Random House.

Fraser, N. (2007). Democratic Justice in a Globalizing Age: Thematizing the Problem of the Frame. In: Karagiannis & Wagner (Eds.), *Globalization or World-Making?* Liverpool: Liverpool University Press, 193–215.

Gewirth, A. (1978). The Golden Rule Rationalized. *Midwest Studies in Philosophy*, 3: 133–147.

Gewirth, A. (1986). Human Rights and the Workplace. *American Journal of Industrial Medicine*, 9: 31–40.

Gewirth, A. (1996). *The Community of Rights*. Chicago: University of Chicago Press.

Goodin, R. E. (2002). Structures of Mutual Obligation. *Social Policy and Society*, 31: 579–596.

Gouldner, A. W. (1960). The Norm of Reciprocity: A Preliminary Statement. *American Sociological Review*, 25: 161–178.

Harlos, K. P. (2001). When Organizational Voice Systems Fail: More on the Deaf-Ear Syndrome and Frustration Effects. *The Journal of Applied Behavioral Science*, 37 (3): 324–342.

Harrison, J. S., & Wicks, A. C. (2013). Stakeholder Theory, Value, and Firm Performance. *Business Ethics Quarterly*, 23 (1): 97–124.

Heine, S. J., Proulx, T., & Vohs, K. D. (2006). The Meaning Maintenance Model: On the Coherence of Social Motivations. *Personality and Social Psychology Review*, 10 (2): 88–110.

Hobhouse, L. T. (1906). *Morals in Evolution: A Study in Comparative Ethics*. London: Chapman and Hall.

Hogg, M. (2017). *Obligations: Law and Language*. Cambridge: Cambridge University Press.

Holdo, M. (2018). A Relational Perspective on Deliberative Systems: Combining Interpretive and Structural Analysis. *Critical Policy Studies*, DOI: 10.1080/19460171.2018.1506349

Hume, D. (2000), *A Treatise of Human Nature*. David Fate Norton and Mary J. Norton (ed.). New York: Oxford University Press.

Jaeggi, R. (2014). *Alienation*. New York: Columbia University Press.

Johnson, P. (2006). Whence Democracy? A Review and Critique of the Conceptual Dimensions of the Business Case for Organizational Democracy. *Organization*, 13 (2): 245–274.

Kauppinen, A. (2008). *Why the Shape of a Life Matters*. [Online] www.philosophy.northwestern.edu/conferences/moralpolitical/08/papers/Kauppinen.pdf

Kavanagh, D. (2013). Children: Their Place in Organization Studies. *Organization Studies*, 34 (10): 1487–1503.

Kittay, E. (1999). *Love's Labor: Essays on Women, Equality, and Dependency*. New York: Routledge.

Knoll, M. D., Wegge, J., Unterrainer, C., Silva, S., & Jønsson, T. F. (2016). Is Our Knowledge of Voice and Silence in Organizations Growing? Building Bridges and (Re)discovering Opportunities. *German Journal of Human Resource Management*, 30 (3–4): 161–194.

Konow, J. (2003). Which Is the Fairest One of All? A Positive Analysis of Justice Theories. *Journal of Economic Literature*, 41: 1188–1239.

Landemore, H., & Ferreras, I. (2016). In Defense of Workplace Democracy: Towards a Justification of the Firm: State Analogy. *Political Theory*, 44 (1): 53–81.

Letiche, H., & Statler, M. (2005). Evoking Metis: Questioning the Logics of Change, Responsiveness, Meaning and Action in Organizations. *Culture and Organization*, 11 (1): 1–16.

Lips-Wiersma, M., & Morris, L. (2009). Discriminating Between "Meaningful Work" and the "Management of Meaning." *Journal of Business Ethics*, 88 (3): 491–511.

Lips-Wiersma, M., & Wright, S. (2012). Measuring the Meaning of Meaningful Work: Development and Validation of the Comprehensive Meaningful Work Scale (CMWS). *Group & Organization Management*, 37 (5): 655–685.

Luo, Y. (2008). Procedural Fairness and Interfirm Cooperation in Strategic Alliances. *Strategic Management Journal*, 29: 27–46.

MacIntyre, A. (1953). *Marxism: An Interpretation*. London: SCM.

MacIntyre, A. (2007). *After Virtue: A Study in Moral Philosophy*, 3rd edition. London: Duckworth.

Mansbridge, J., Bohman, J., Chambers, S., Christiano, T., Fung, A., Parkinson, P., Thompson, D. F., & Warren, M. E. (2012). A Systemic Approach to Deliberative Democracy. In: J. Parkinson & J. Mansbridge (eds.), *Deliberative Systems*. Cambridge: Cambridge University Press, 1–26.

McMahon, C. (1994). *Authority and Democracy: A General Theory of Government and Management*. Princeton, NJ: Princeton University Press.

Metz, T. (2011). The Good, The True and The Beautiful: Toward A Unified Account of Great Meaning in Life. *Religious Studies*, 47: 389–409.

Metz, T. (2013). "The Meaning of Life". *The Stanford Encyclopedia of Philosophy*. https://plato.stanford.edu/entries/life-meaning/ [accessed 5 December 2018].

Miller, D. (1999). *Principles of Social Justice*. Cambridge, MA, & London: Harvard University Press.

Miller, D. (2007). *National Responsibility and Global Justice*. New York: Oxford University Press.

Mitra, R., & Buzzanell, P. M. (2016). Communicative Tensions of Meaningful Work: The Case of Sustainability Practitioners. *Human Relations*: 1–23.

Molm, L. D. (2010). The Structure of Reciprocity. *Social Psychology Quarterly*, 73 (2): 119–131.

Molm, L. D., Schaefer, D. R., & Collett, J. L., (2007). The Value of Reciprocity. *Social Psychology Quarterly*. 70 (2): 199–217.

Morrison, R. (1995). *Ecological Democracy*. Boston: South End Press.

Muzzetto, L. (2006). Time and Meaning in Alfred Schutz. *Time & Society*, 15 (1): 5–31.

Ness, I. J. (2017). Polyphonic Orchestration: Facilitating Creative Knowledge Processes for Innovation. *European Journal of Innovation Management*, 20 (4): 557–577.

Newswander, C. B., & Newswander, L. K. (2013). Metis: Using Wile and Wisdom to Inform Administrative Discretion. *The American Review of Public Administration*, 45 (2): 153–166.

Note, N. (2010). Reflections on Meaningfulness and Its Social Relevance. *Kritike: An Online Journal of Philosophy*, 4 (1): 138–149.

Nozick, R. (1981). *Philosophical Explanations*. Cambridge, MA: Belknap Press.

Ordonez, L. D., & Mellers, B. A. (1993). Trade-Offs in Fairness and Preference Judgments. In: Mellers & Baron (eds.), *Psychological Perspectives on Justice*. Cambridge: Cambridge University Press, 138–154.

Owen, D., & Smith, G. (2015). Survey Article: Deliberation, Democracy, and the Systemic Turn. *Journal of Political Philosophy*, 23 (2), 213–234.

Park, C. L. (2010). Making Sense of the Meaning Literature: An Integrative Review of Meaning Making and Its Effects on Adjustment to Stressful Life Events. *Psychological Bulletin*, 136 (2), 257–301.

Park, C. L. (2017). Unresolved Tensions in the Study of Meaning in Life. *Journal of Constructivist Psychology*, 30, 1, 69–73.

Perlow, L., & Repennings, N. (2009). The Dynamics of Silencing Conflict. *Research in Organizational Behaviour*, 29, 195–223.

Persson, I., & Savulescu, J. (2012). The Meaning of Life: Science, Equality and Eternity. *Proceedings of the 2012 Uehiro-Carnegie-Oxford Ethics Conference, "Ethics for the Future of Life"*, 109–124. http://media.philosophy.ox.ac.uk/docs/uehiro/2012_UC/Persson-Savulescu-iPad.pdf [accessed 20 April 2018]

Pettersen, T. (2011). The Ethics of Care: Normative Structures and Empirical Implications. *Health Care Analysis: HCA: Journal of Health Philosophy and Policy*, 19 (1): 51–64.

Phillips, R. A. (1997). Stakeholder Theory and a Principle of Fairness. *Business Ethics Quarterly*, 7: 51–66.

Pierce, J. L., & Jussila, I. (2010). Collective Psychological Ownership Within the Work and Organizational Context: Construct Introduction and Elaboration. *Journal of Organizational Behavior*, 31, 810–834.

Plummer, K. (2019). *Narrative Power: The Struggle for Human Value*. London: Polity Press.

Pyman, A., Cooper, B., Teicher, J., & Holland, P. (2006). A Comparison of the Effectiveness of Employee Voice Arrangements in Australia. *Industrial Relations Journal*, 37 (5): 543–559.

Rawls, J. (1999 [1971]). *Theory of Justice*. Oxford: Oxford University Press.

Ritivoi, A. D. (2016). Reading Stories, Reading (Others') Lives: Empathy, Intersubjectivity, and Narrative Understanding. *Storyworlds: A Journal of Narrative Studies*, 8 (1): 51–75.

Robinson, J. (1962). *Economic Philosophy*. London & New York: Routledge.

Sahlins, M. (1972). *Stone Age Economics*. New York: Aldine De Gruyter.

Sample, R. J. (2003). *Exploitation: What It Is and Why It's Wrong*. New York & Oxford: Rowman & Littlefield.

Schnell, T. (2009). The Sources of Meaning and Meaning in Life Questionnaire (SoMe): Relations to Demographics and Well-Being. *The Journal of Positive Psychology*, 4 (6): 483–499.

Schnell, T. (2011). Individual Differences in Meaning-Making: Considering the Variety of Sources of Meaning, Their Density and Diversity. *Personality and Individual Differences*, 51 (5): 667–673.

Scott, J. C. (1990). *Domination and the Arts of Resistance: Hidden Transcripts*. New Haven: Yale University Press.

Sherman, N. (1993). The Virtues of Common Pursuit. *Philosophical and Phenomenological Research*, 53 (2): 227–299.

Shiller, R. J. (2017). Narrative Economics. *American Economic Review*, 107 (4): 967–1004.

Simmel, G. (1950). *The Sociology of Georg Simmel*, Wolff (trans. and ed.). Glencoe, IL: Free Press.

Sindzingre, A. (2007). *Poverty Traps: A Perspective from Development Economics*. Working Paper 2007–26, Paris, University Paris 10, Economix.

Sindzingre, A. (2010). *Is the Poverty Trap a Relevant Concept ? Sub-Saharan African Countries Growth Trajectories and Their Constraints*. Background Paper, Development Research Seminar, Institute of Social Studies (ISS), The Hague, 14 June.

Smuts, A. (2018). *Welfare, Meaning and Worth*. New York & London: Routledge.

Snyder, J. (2013). Exploitation and Demeaning Choices. *Politics, Philosophy and Economics*, 12: 345.

Steger, M. F., Dik, B. J., & Duffy, R. D. (2012). Measuring Meaningful Work: The Work and Meaning Inventory (WAMI). *Journal of Career Assessment*, 20 (3): 239–241.

Strawson, G. (2004). Against Narrativity. *Ratio*, 17 (4): 428–452.

Svensson, F. (2017). A Subjectivist Account of Life's Meaning. *De Ethica*, 4 (3): 45–66.

Thaddeus, M. (2013). *The Meaning of Life: The Stanford Encyclopedia of Philosophy*, Summer 2013 edition, E. N. Zalta (ed.), https://plato.stanford.edu/archives/sum2013/entries/life-meaning/.

Tourish, D. (2013). *The Dark Side of Transformational Leadership: A Critical Perspective*. London & New York: Routledge.

Tsoukas, H., & Chia, R. (2002). On Organizational Becoming: Rethinking Organizational Change. *Organization Science*, 13 (5): 567–582.

van den Heuvel, M., Demerouti, E., Schreurs, B. H., Bakker, A. B., & Schaufeli, W. B. (2009). Does meaning-making help during organizational change? Development and validation of a new scale. *Career Development International*, 14 (6): 508–533.

Veltman, A. (2016). *Meaningful Work*. Oxford: Oxford University Press.

Višak, T. (2017). Understanding "Meaning of Life" in Terms of Reasons for Action. *Journal of Value Inquiry*, 51 (3): 507–530.

Wegge, J, Jeppesen, H. J., Weber, W. G., et al. (2010). Promoting Work Motivation in Organisations: Should Employee Involvement in Organisational Leadership Become a New Tool in the Organisational Psychologist's Kit? *Journal of Personnel Psychology*, 9 (4): 154–171.

Weil, S. (1977 [1946]). Factory Work. In: Panichas (ed.), *The Simone Weil Reader*. New York: David McKay Company.

Wilkinson, A., Gollan, P. J., Kalfa, S., & Xu, Y. (2018). Voices Unheard: Employee Voice in the New Century. *The International Journal of Human Resource Management*, DOI: 10.1080/09585192.2018.1427347.

Williams, B. (1981). Persons, Character and Morality. In: Williams (ed.), *Moral Luck*. Cambridge: Cambridge University Press.

Wolf, S. (2002). The True, the Good, and the Lovable: Frankfurt's Avoidance of Objectivity. In: Buss & Overton (eds.). *Contours of Agency: Essays on Themes from Harry Frankfurt*. Cambridge, MA, & London: MIT Press.

Wolf, S. (2010). *Meaning in Life and Why It Matters*. Princeton, NJ: Princeton University Press.

Wolf, S. (2015). Happiness and Meaning: Two Aspects of the Good Life. In: Wolf (ed.), *The Variety of Values: Essays on Morality, Meaning and Love*. Oxford: Oxford University Press.

Yeoman, R. (2014a). *Meaningful Work and Workplace Democracy: A Philosophy of Work and a Politics of Meaningfulness*. London: Palgrave Macmillan.

Yeoman, R. (2014b). Conceptualising Meaningful Work as a Fundamental Human Need. *Journal of Business Ethics*, 125 (2): 235–251.

Yeoman, R. (2019). The Meaningful City. In: Yeoman, Bailey, Madden, & Thompson (eds.), *Oxford Handbook of Meaningful Work*. Oxford: Oxford University Press.

Zuboff, S. (2019). *The Age of Surveillance Capitalism*. London: Profile Book.

4 Collective Action
Integrity, Purpose, Work

An adequate response to the sustainability imperative necessitates reorientating local, national, and international social cooperation to the task of life value creation. Adam Smith says that each member in society 'stands at all times in need of the cooperation and assistance of great multitudes' (WN I.ii.2: 26). In my proposed philosophy of ethical organising, collective action conforms to normatively desirable characteristics, derived from the social architecture of meaningfulness and mutuality, where the ends and means of joint activities promote human emancipation and ecological repair. Such normatively desirable collective action is created and maintained by 'morally worthy work undertaken in a morally worthy organization' (Ciulla, 2000: 226), or in my terms, life value organisations. Morally worthy work is meaningful work and is realised when people are able to exercise their human capability for ethical world-building to form life value organisations. Such organisations are collective moral agents that are worthy of their members' contributions when they bring the objective/ethical-moral and subjective/cognitive-emotional dimensions of meaningfulness into their purposes and activities, Yeoman (2014).

Ensembles of life value organisations constitute the varieties of associational ecosystems upon which expansive social cooperation depends. Associational ecosystems derive their purposes from the problems that they have been established to solve. In a philosophy of ethical organising, collective action is undertaken through associational ecosystems that pursue morally worthy purposes, such as caring for valuable beings and things, through morally viable means, or meaningful work. Life value organisations accumulate the value of meaningfulness to an associational level by establishing purposes that are objectively valuable and subjectively attractive, consistent with the requirement to generate life value. When building associational ecosystems, 'we become participants in constructing purposes consistent with the interests of worthy objects, through activities that are characterised by autonomy, freedom and dignity' (Yeoman, 2014).

In morally worthy organisations, the value of meaningfulness is activated through practices of collective purposing and voice, where all affected members use their capability for ethical world-building to construct the organisation as a collective moral agent. The life value organisation that emerges from this process of world-building is equipped with organisational capabilities for sensitising members to moral concerns and cultivating in them the relevant moral emotions. Life value organisations derive their public status as collective moral agents from their organisational integrity, where integrity grounds their public presence as collective entities, possessing durable ethical characteristics that make them worthy of the emotional commitment of their members. Life value organisations therefore provide an enriched action context for people to become involved with co-constructing morally valuable purposes, to find those purposes emotionally engaging, and to take these up into the meaningfulness of their work and lives. In this chapter, I shall examine how the social architecture of meaningfulness and mutuality supplies mutual organisation with a voice system that uses agonistic republicanism as a conversion factor to create a human capability for ethical world building.

Normatively Desirable Collective Action

Expanding social cooperation requires institutional mechanisms for risk-pooling and social trust (Heath, 2016).[1] Historically, the development of cultural technologies enabled many more people to be included in widening circles of moral awareness, thereby making possible the shift from small-scale egalitarian to large-scale hierarchically organised cooperation. Boyd and Richer son (2009) define cooperation as 'costly behaviour performed by one individual that increases the payoff of others' (p. 3283). They observe that '[s]ometime during the last two million years, important changes occurred in human psychology that support larger, more cooperative societies' (p. 3281). They suggest that natural climate change created a rapidly changing and uncertain world, and that under this environmental pressure, cultural supports and moral systems were invented which directed emotions such as empathy and shame into moral learning. Specifically, cultural evolution produced moral systems of rewards and sanctions that aided the genetic selection of individuals exhibiting prosocial behaviours and motivated the social evolution of a moral psychology. Spurred by new agricultural technologies and technical-material advances in the cultural realm, this moral psychology was reinforced by social institutions capable of coordinating the efforts of large numbers of individuals (Powers and Lehman, 2013). Mullins et al. (2012) show how record keeping and a shared writing system facilitated empathy and a common group identity. These cultural technologies enabled more diverse and distant groups to be incorporated into social cooperation, using a store of memory into a group identity, and a store of memory in the form of literature with which to 'transmit group identities across increasingly large numbers of individuals' (p. 147).

Today, the pressures of human-induced climate change demand planetary-scale cooperation, supported by new narrative formations describing how we are to live together. The value of meaningfulness, allied to mutuality as an organising principle, provides a motivational basis for people to conceive of life value in terms of making enduring contributions to sustaining and developing beings and things of moral worth, and to do so by creating ethical worlds that enable them to fulfil their responsibilities to take care of these things. An important aspect of ethical organising is the entitlement of all those affected to contribute to the narratives that influence the formation of collective intentions and social cooperation. Human beings possess a cognitive armoury for 'participating in collaborative problem-solving and cooperative communication', consisting of prosocial, cultural, and cognitive skills that enable us to create with others 'joint goals, joint intentions and joint attention' (Moll and Tomasello, 2007: 645). Moll and Tomasello (2007) argue that when we participate in joint activities involving shared intentions, we create 'new forms of cognitive representation, specifically, perspectival or dialogic cognitive representations' (p. 645), by which we come to see the situation from the perspective of others. This shared cognitive and emotional perspective, expressed through culture and values, is an important outcome of the human capability for ethical world-building.

However, the cognitive-affective capabilities for making culture are not evenly distributed. A recent Royal Society (2018) study of narratives and artificial intelligence technologies shows how human behaviour is influenced by the 'narrative ecosystem' of such technologies but that narrative formation is impeded by 'narrative injustice', which excludes marginalised groups and individuals from authoring narratives or having their narratives taken up as the accepted version (p. 15). Depriving narrative formation of the full spectrum of meaning-makers has real-world effects on life value creation. In the context of transforming the global food and agricultural system, Dentoni et al. (2017) argue that multiple change strategies are needed, directing multiple perspectives towards *depth* of change in the redistribution of power and resources, and *breadth* of change across interconnected subsystems. Potential strategies include the unilateral action of powerful actors, the self-motivated small-scale innovations of local people, the co-creative collaborative initiatives of diverse public, private, and civic organisations, and the mobilisation of confrontation and resistance. Dentoni et al. (2017) propose a mix of change approaches integrated under 'a compelling narrative and set of supporting memes around sustainable agriculture' (p. 11), where such narratives seek to cohere the values, purposes, and actions of all the actors of a system. To build ethical worlds, we must therefore be concerned with inclusive processes of narrative formation that are directed towards supporting the expansive social cooperation needed for sustainability transitions. The kinds of narratives relevant to this endeavour are those related to forming collective moral agents that are recognised by their members as possessing integrity. Collective moral agents develop integrity to the extent that they are successful in fulfilling their responsibilities to achieve objectively valuable purposes, whilst generating subjective appeal by stimulating the moral emotions of their members.

Collective Moral Agents

A philosophy of ethical organising forbids collective entities that do not have the capacity for moral agency and makes becoming a collective moral agent a core purpose for all organisations. List and Pettit (2011) argue that collective moral agency is necessary if an organisation is to be held responsible for its actions.

> It would seem to be a serious design fault, at least from the perspective of society as a whole, to allow any group agents to avoid making judgments of this kind. Why should any group of individuals be allowed to incorporate under an organizational structure that deprives the group of the ability to assess its options normatively, thereby making it unfit to be held responsible for its choices?
>
> (List and Pettit, 2011: 159)

Wallace (2006) describes moral agency as 'the capacity to grasp and apply the justifications that support moral demands, as well as the general capacity to comply with moral demands' (p. 125). As collective moral agents, life value organisations manifest capacities for organisational moral agency through their members. In other words, they are created and maintained by the ethical organising of their members and develop ethical capacities for responding to moral requirements by instituting structures, processes, and systems of normatively desirable collective action. Collective action is normatively desirable when it is characterised by non-coercion, commitments to joint action, and mutual support: 'shared cooperative activity involves appropriately interlocking and reflexive systems of mutually uncoerced intentions concerning the joint activity' (Bratman, 1992: 336). Pettit and Schweikard (2006) describe 'unforced cooperation' (p. 20) in joint action in terms of joining our agency to that of others in order to produce a shared outcome: 'There can be nothing underhanded or overbearing involved in unforced joint action; people must voluntarily contribute whatever is required for the desired performance' (p. 22).

A critical evaluation of collective action involves being alert to how people experience their joint involvements, or 'what it is like to be jointly engaged' (Seemann, 2009b: 639). Pacherie (2008) talks about having a 'sense of control and a sense of agency' in collective action (p. 180). In ethical organising, this sense of control includes both the ability to justify decisions against the accepted rules and the ability to reflect upon and influence the rules themselves (Hedahl, 2013). In organisations, Weick and Roberts (1993) conceptualise 'collective mind' as 'a pattern of heedful interrelations of actions in a social system' (p. 357). Organisations are made up of individuals who act as if they are a group, and in doing so 'interrelate their actions with more or less care' (p. 360). With respect to moral agency in collective action, more care directs members towards creating collective moral agents; less care can result in cognitive dysfunctions, such as impression management, wilful blindness, and narcissism. Pettit and Schweikard (2006) says it is possible to imagine ourselves to be the only genuine agent in the group: 'It might just be that we each thought that others were zombies who would automatically, as if under hypnotism, do what was required of them. It might be, in other words, that we thought of ourselves as the only properly intentional agent involved' (p. 22). Collective agents are collective *moral* agents when they foster collective ethical capacities for moral awareness, attention, and learning that mitigate such organisational dysfunctions. This requires voluntary curtailment of personal autonomy, or 'coordination by mutual constraint' (Weick and Roberts, 1993: 360), for the sake of the joint outcome. We permit such interference in our autonomy when it furthers our interests and helps us experience the satisfactions of joint endeavour. In life value organisations, constraints on autonomy are legitimate when organisational features include: morally worthy purposes aimed at life value creation, discursive control over framing rules, status and capabilities for meaning-making, mutual relations, and action contexts structured by the goods of meaningfulness.

Integrity

An organisation's independent moral presence in society is signalled by its integrity, thereby communicating the extent to which the organisation is worthy of our interactions and contributions. Integrity is publically manifested when the organisation refuses to allow its people and assets to be used for morally objectionable purposes. As reported by *The Guardian*, this is well understood by Google employees who have demanded that Google refrain from providing the U.S. immigration agencies with support: 'In working with CBP, ICE or ORR, Google would be trading its integrity for a bit of profit, and joining a shameful lineage' (employee).[2] Bernard Williams expresses integrity as a form of agential capacity in his declaration 'Not through me'. Honig (2017) interprets Williams's statement as a requirement upon moral agents not to be the means for unworthy ends: 'I may be morally bound to refuse to be a vehicle through which such ends are pursued' (p. 32). Such agential capacity interacts with the presence or absence of organisational integrity, understood as an enduring normative feature, derived from the history, culture, and character of the organisation and communicating the quality of organisational relationships with those who care about how well it is doing.

Palazzo (2007) argues that 'organizational integrity refers to the ethical integrity of the individual actors, the ethical quality of their interaction as well as that of the dominating norms, activities, decision making procedures and results within a given organization' (p. 113). Palazzo links integrity to unified agency, a coherence of conduct, and a commitment to purposes, values, and principles that is long lasting and identity forming. This means that, in order to maintain their integrity, a moral agent may adopt fixed commitments consistent with an uncompromising and inflexible character. Moreover, if integrity is associated with authenticity, this may fail to mark out integrity as a moral characteristic because evil persons can be authentic (Moseley, 2014). But rather than being marked by a fixed set of principles, integrity can be understood as a 'sophisticated, reflective, constant state of awareness that results in an attitude that encompasses moral creativity' (Verhezen, 2008: p. 137). Verhezen (2008) makes organisational integrity a relational value, as well as a standard of moral excellence, that bridges personal and organisational integrity through 'institutionalised bonding' (p. 134), or a culture of interaction between members and stakeholders of the organisation. Maak (2008) argues that corporate integrity can operate as a master virtue to make whole the 'divided corporate self' that has been fragmented by the expectation that organisations will adopt multiple social, environmental, and financial objectives. Integrity therefore emerges from moral agency operating within a process of integration, extending into associational ecosystems where organisations will 'synchronise the integrities of all moral agents' (p. 361). In globally extended supply chains, for example, Maak (2008) says that companies, such as Nike, must 'close all potential integrity gaps' (p. 363) that fracture the wholeness of the organisation as a system of values and solidarity. Brown (2005) connects organisational integrity to being committed to pursuing a worthwhile purpose, where purpose is realised through structured practices involving multiple valuers, who are alert to 'the relationships in which they live' (p. 6).

Organisational integrity enables collective moral agents to achieve a stable public presence when they open themselves up to stakeholder evaluation. In associational ecosystems, this requires decentring the focal organisation, by adopting self-restraint in value-creating and value-taking (Calton et al., 2013). As Verhezen (2008) puts it, 'integrity needs to emphasise the well-being of the other at the organisational level' (p. 139), a collective attitude which requires 'a process-oriented approach that implements ethical principles and taps into a broader vision rather than a formalistic rule-based compliance approach' (p. 142). Ethical world-building, which makes integrity a core characteristic of life value organisations, implies that organisational members have collective duties to maintain the social processes that tie morally desirable ends to morally viable means. This is a form of ethical work that is more likely to be experienced as meaningful when the activities involved are structured by the value of meaningfulness.

Emotions and Reasons

Collective moral agency is developed when organisations become sensitised to values by augmenting the moral emotions of their members. The proposal that collectives can be considered to be moral agent when they display moral emotions is contested. Cheng-Guajardo (2018) says that organisations cannot be moral entities because they lack 'the capacity for feeling affects or phenomenally-conscious states' (p. 14; see also Thompson, 2018). They are not the kind of experiential beings capable of ethical participation, and so they cannot be admitted as members of the moral community. However, Collins (2018) argues that, although organisations lack emotions, they have 'duties over their emotions' (p. 813) and duties to foster emotions in their members, appropriate to the roles they occupy. In other words, organisations possess a capacity for moral emotions via the moral emotions of their members. Hindriks (2018) proposes that collective moral agency is accompanied by a normative perspective, such that 'a properly designed moral collective agent systematically enables its members to put forward normative propositions as input to corporate deliberation' (p. 8). A normative perspective influences corporate behaviour through 'commitments that are functionally equivalent' (p. 15) to moral emotions. These commitments are forged when organisations enable members to draw upon positive meaning-sources and bring these meanings into emotion-tracking procedures and practices that are conducive to social cooperation. Members are more likely to manifest moral emotions when the organisations they belong to, and are responsible for maintaining, develop an organisational character based upon integrity. Public recognition of integrity identifies an organisation with ethical capabilities for moral awareness, attentiveness, and learning. Such an organisation interacts with its members to develop a normative perspective that is expressed in its range of policies promoting other-regarding attitudes and in its contributions to life value creation across its associational ecosystem.

Collective moral agents that seek to sensitise their members to the values inhering in morally worthy beings and things will create moral spaces for intersubjective encounters that encourage thinking and feeling in expressive reason-giving.[3] By so doing, collective moral agents will establish pathways for organisational emotions that direct members to the duties they have to create life value. Emotions are forms of thinking that alert us to what we care about and why we care about it; they are 'concerned with value, they see their object as invested with value or importance' (Nussbaum, 2001: 30). They provide us with information about how we need to respond in order to have a care for how well the target of our emotions is doing. The possibility of organisational integrity relies upon a culture of public emotions that combines principles and institutions with moral sentiments: 'a society that is held together only by adherence to a temporary compromise, viewed as instrumentally useful, is not likely to remain stable for long' (Nussbaum, 2013: 10). For Nussbaum, 'all the major emotions are 'eudaimonistic', meaning that they appraise the world from the person's own viewpoint and the viewpoint, therefore, of a worthwhile life' (2013: 11). Evaluative emotions are public emotions when they are linked to 'a definite set of normative goals' (p. 16). In ethical organising, the relevant target for public emotions are evaluations concerning how well we are doing to look after morally valuable objects and what this implies for life value creation. Nussbaum (2013) identifies two capacities needed to cultivate public emotions: 'the capacity of concern for others and its relationship to the capacity for imaginative play' (p. 21). Collective moral agents can establish practices that replicate concern and imagination and encourage members to respond with the appropriate emotions.

The organisational emotions of life value organisations must extend to the variety of members who constitute the society of meaning-makers. Nussbaum (2013) argues that the circle of humanity is too remote and that the correct level for public emotions is the nation state. However, emotional connections are achievable in associational ecosystems that cut across national state boundaries, such as supply chains, especially when these are constituted by life value organisations. Applying Nussbaum's concept of public emotions to transnational social and economic entities involves envisioning how a meaningful life can be shared with distant others, by using empathetic narrative formation to stimulate imaginative perspective-taking: 'emotions necessarily involve cognitive appraisals, forms of value-laden perception and/or thought directed at an object or objects' (p. 17). This is a form of intensive attachment or love because 'all the core emotions that sustain a decent society have their roots in, or are forms of, love' (p. 15). Morally worthy organisations will manufacture the functional equivalent of such public emotions through policies and practices that are co-created by members exercising their human capability for ethical world-building. I shall discuss how dialogic mechanisms, consistent with collective moral agency, can usefully draw upon the principles of agonistic republicanism. Before doing so, however, I outline the nature of purpose and purposing in morally worthy organisations.

Morally Worthy Organisations

Purposing is a core process in creating the life value organisation as a collective moral agent, characterised by integrity. To arrive at morally worthy purposes, purposing as a social process must conform to the requirements of the value of meaningfulness. In practical reasoning, meaningfulness has both ends and means in view, such that 'the purposes of work are concerned both with the object and the activity. The object is constructed through interpretive sense-making, and the activity is both a mediator for self-realisation and a means to attend to the needs of worthy objects' (Yeoman, 2014: 246). Anscombe (1969) argues that 'the description of something as a human action could not occur prior to the existence of the question "Why?"' (p. 32). The question of 'why' is dynamically related to the question of 'how'. Being able to say 'why' we are doing something is influenced by evaluations of 'how' we do things. Intentions to do something are 'psychological devices' for revealing to ourselves aspects of our mental life and making our actions intelligible to ourselves and to others (Seemann, 2009a: 645). Jointly held intentions express shared goals that we intend to bring about by cooperating with others. Follett (1949) argues that purpose is perpetually created and recreated through integrative social processes that engage all those involved in acting together. She critiques the 'teleological psychology' (p. 33) that fixes purpose prior to action and seeks to submit relational process to its predetermined ends: 'no more fatally disastrous conception has ever dominated us than the conception of static ends' (Follett, 1919: 578). There are no already existing purposes waiting to be discovered, since 'purpose is not 'preexistent, but involved in the unifying act which is the life process. It is man's part to create purpose and to actualize it' (Follett, 1998 [1918]: 58). If we are to fulfil our responsibilities to make purposes, then we must engage in meaning-making from inside the processes of action, since 'ends and meanings truly and literally make each other' (Follett, 1919: 579). Purpose is always evolving, internal to the relational process of its own production, and made by people from the material of their interpretive differences. Purpose is more likely to be morally worthy when it is forged through constructive conflict in an organisation that is a collective moral agent. Finally, common purpose enables cooperation that 'begins at the very bottom', is distinct from bargaining, and relates people to one another through their interests in mutual excellence and accountability (Follett, 1942: 223).

Philosophy of Purpose

The philosophical roots of purpose lie in Aristotelian teleology, or the tendency of a being to develop towards its *telos*, or final cause, for the sake of which the being exists. From this, Aristotle derives the idea of 'eudaimonia', which is generally translated as human flourishing. Cameron (2010) describes teleology as 'the study of *ends* and *goals*, things whose existence or occurrence is *purposive*' (p. 1096). The teleological approach has been highly influential on the function, design and objectives of organisations. For example, Christensen (1996) develops the idea of the cybernetic organisation in which 'teleology is a property of certain types of complex cybernetic systems' (p. 302), where the teleological process is goal directed and intentional. This makes teleological behaviours functional for self-organisation. However, functional cybernetic perspectives on teleology as goal-directed behaviour do not account for other motivations and ways of responding that matter to people, such as the acting out of values, as opposed to acting for goals, and their need for meaning. Indeed, Bedau (2012) notes that such perspectives do not recognise how teleology is constitutively normative, implying a notion of the good, and that a 'value-centred theory of teleology' (p. 793) requires 'evaluative involvement' (p. 787) in judging the normative status of purpose. Some scholars of teleology have sought a conjunction of objective and subjective dimensions that is useful for linking organisational meaning and purpose. For example, Hofstadter (1941) distinguishes subjective teleology (experience) and objective teleology (independent of the agent), where objectivity lies in how 'the end entertained is possessed in an act of meaning or intent' (p. 39), where meaning-making informs the dynamic interaction between conditions (processes and actions) and ends.

From the perspective of materialist philosophy, Midgley (2011) characterises Aristotelian teleology as an inquiry into 'what particular things are for—what they do for the organism that owns them, what is their telos, their end or aim in the context where they belong' (p. 556). Countering Richard Dawkin's interpretation of Darwin's theory of evolution as containing 'no purpose', she says that 'our own planet—which is certainly part of the universe—is riddled with purpose' (p. 558). In other words, we inhabit a world of living things that exhibit manifold purposes or 'things that are done for their own sake because they fulfil our nature' (p. 555), where such purposes have meaning for the creatures who are acting. Creatures, such as human beings, are complex beings 'whose faculties all grow out of their nature as a whole' (p. 561), and their development is a source of value, where value is 'a real emergent property of situations in the world' (p. 559), and 'what evolves is an emotional constitution that shapes our lives as a whole' (p. 546). Teleology evolves or emerges from the social construction of ends and purpose. Ross (2013) argues that some objectivity can be derived from mind-dependent things, arising through 'collective intentionality' (p. 376) and making possible normative assessments. Objectivity is a product of judgements in social practices; for example, novel writing involves writing a good novel against the terms and standards of novel writing as a social practice. Commenting upon problems where cooperative solutions depend on participants subscribing to a shared system of norms and standards, Copp (2009) argues for a 'pluralist-teleology' (p. 21) in which people pursue diverse ends in a normative system of rules and standards. According to Copp (2009), this system addresses the problem of the sociality needed to reduce the risk of breakdowns in cooperation. Johnson (2005) proposes to reinterpret

Aristotle as referring to ends not as final causes but rather as ways to make things comprehensible and achievable, positioning them within limits 'for the sake of which' they exist. Johnson (2005) separates the aim and the beneficiary into a symbiotic relationship, where the pursuit of the aim changes the nature of the beneficiary. Taking the organisation to be the target: organisational purpose, as a type of *telos*, arises from the collective intentions of multiple participants who are more likely to maintain the social conditions for cooperation when joint purpose provides space for them to also pursue their diverse ends that contribute to the meaningfulness of their work and lives.

Such an understanding of organisational purpose as an accumulation of streams of personal meanings and purposes connects the process of purposing to flourishing.Norton (1992) seeks to recover the *telos* in teleology by describing *telos* as 'an intimate end whose actualization through a process of development constitutes the "flourishing" or "fulfillment" of the entity whose end it is' (p. 3). His concern is that, when we eliminate *telos* from our conception of the human being, we make room for attempts to control meaning-making by promoting monovocal ideological formations that dim the 'dazzling diversity' of human values and the 'value actualizing course of life that individuals experience as intrinsically rewarding' (p. 9). Desirably, in our practical reasoning regarding what forms of living we should pursue, and what projects we should dedicate ourselves to, *telos* provides an internal criterion for judging the rightness or wrongness of our actions and choices. Norton argues that this inwardly constituted *telos* or purpose has both objective and subjective characteristics because it 'projects a process of self-actualization which is the objectivizing of the self into the world' (p. 11). Norton (1992) goes on to say that our autonomy over our choice of what projects to pursue is context specific and limited by 'grounding individual choice among socially acceptable possibilities. (Meanwhile one measure of a good society is that it maximizes the possibilities that it leaves open.)' (p. 11). Norton (1992) understands autonomy as a type of relational, interdependent autonomy, such that autonomy means 'deciding for oneself what values to contribute to the lives of others and what use to make of the values provided by the self-fulfilling lives of others' (p. 11).

Norton (1992) links moral development to a division of ethical labour over the creation and actualisation of values: firstly, 'each person requires more values, of different kinds, than he or she personally actualizes, and is dependent upon others for these values', and, secondly, 'each self-fulfilling life contributes values to others—specifically to those others who fulfil the conditions for recognizing, appreciating, and utilizing worth of the distinctive kind that the given individual manifests' (p. 12). Purpose or *telos* is afforded moral character when structured by the objective and subjective dimensions of meaningfulness. Meaning and purpose evolve together through processes of moral learning in which moral agents contribute values to the lives of others and in return receive their actualised values. Meaningfulness enriches purpose with a diversity of meanings and values and, via an ethic of care, provides a moral basis for evaluating the worth of purpose. Collective moral agency is constructed when organisations provide moral free spaces for members to encounter difference and variety, as well as the policies and practices consistent with being able to experience the relevant moral emotions. This constitutes an offer, or invitation, to members that they become willing to be influenced by difference and diversity when taking up their responsibilities to create the organisation as a life value organisation. Such an invitation is more likely to be welcomed when organisational purpose provides room for the multiple dimensions of life value creation, into which members can enfold their own ends.

Organisational Purpose

In order to connect meaning and purpose at an organisational level, we require a richer model of human behaviour than can be found in management practices rooted in ideologies of the self-regarding individual (see Ghoshal's, 2005 critique). Ghoshal (2005) argues that management research incorporates a narrow conception of human beings as utility maximisers and assumes a functional role for management, separate from ethical or moral considerations. This has led to harmful management practices being recommended and implemented, including justifying managerial monopoly over organisational purposing. Ghoshal (2005) quotes Herbert Simon:

> Nothing is more fundamental in setting our research agenda and informing our research methods than our view of the nature of human beings whose behaviours we are studying. [. . .] It makes a difference to research, but it also makes a difference for the proper design of [. . .] institutions.
>
> (Simon, 1985: 293)

Shareholder primacy as the purpose of the firm is grounded in agency theory, which assumes moral hazard for managers who, without the disciplining effect of profit maximisation, will capture organisational assets for personal benefit. Although this view of corporate purpose is no longer dominant, there is no settled agreement regarding what concept of organisational purpose may serve instead. Henderson and Van Den Steen (2015) note the instrumental reasons firms have for claiming to have a purpose beyond shareholder value, including reputation management and identity formation. They define purpose as 'a concrete goal or objective for the firm that reaches beyond profit maximization; a person's "reputation" as others' beliefs about that person, i.e., about her type; and a person's "identity" as her own beliefs about herself and her type' (p. 2).

Purpose helps to create social as well as economic value by connecting purpose to employees' personal identity and reputation. Hollensbe et al. (2014) state that purpose involves 'redefining organizations as purposeful, with purpose defining the remit and scope of business activity', and they propose six values that could 'help organizations achieve purpose: (1) dignity, (2) solidarity, (3) plurality, (4) subsidiarity, (5) reciprocity, and (6) sustainability' (p. 1229).

Despite such promising theoretical moves, as well as significant shifts by business leaders to adopt a long-term stakeholder perspective, the assumption that the interests of owners require protection from management opportunism continues to influence corporate decision-making.[4] In order to reflect the diverse goals an organisation may have with respect to different stakeholders, Mohr (1973) distinguishes between reflexive goals and transitive goals, where reflexive goals aim to impact beneficiaries internally located within the company, and transitive goals aim to impact those outside the organisation, within its environment and society as a whole.[5] Finally, there is a tendency towards a division of ethical labour, such that purpose or mission is attached to ethically motivated organisations, leaving other kinds of organisations free to pursue profit-oriented goals through conventional means. Organisational hybridity has challenged this division of ethical labour, and we may be seeing even hybridity itself overcome as organisations become conscious of the urgent need under the sustainability imperative for fundamentally reordered organisational models that transcend traditional public/private distinctions.

Aspects of Purpose and Purposing

In life value organisations, a holistic approach to purpose incorporates means and ends through an integration of objective and subjective dimensions of meaningfulness. This is collectively achieved by using the practices of mutual organisation to activate liberal value pluralism as a resource for adaptation, innovation, and change. Consequently, properly constructed whole purpose—encompassing local and ultimate goods—provides us with compelling reasons to act, provided that we have opportunities to become actively involved with objects of independent value. Active involvement includes sharing with others the responsibility for shaping purposes, maintaining values, and adopting correct orientations: 'to value something is to have a complex of positive attitudes towards it, governed by distinct standards for perception, emotion, deliberation, desire, and conduct' (Anderson, 1995: 2). Hence, morally worthy organisations contain morally worthy purposes when they direct their activities towards those objects that are the source and target of life value. Such purposes may be local or transcendent, enduring or transient, but they may not be futile, trivial, or pointless.

   The aspects of organisational purpose that I consider to be relevant for connecting purpose to collective moral agency, via the incorporation of the value of meaningfulness into practical reasoning, are: the purpose of purpose, the structure of purpose, the agents and beneficiaries of purpose, the practices of purpose, and the impact of purpose. (See Figure 4.1.)

   The purpose of purpose—Purpose provides legitimating reasons that all can understand for why an organisation exists and why it should be allowed to continue to exist. Relevant reasons for claiming an organisational purpose to be morally worthy include: motivating the morally viable collective action needed to solve complex problems; addressing critiques of the relationship of business and society; supplying goods and services to meet needs of humans, animals, and other valuable objects; producing and distributing human goods, such as meaningful work; and enabling people to express their human faculties, values, desires, and aspirations. The purpose of purpose in a collective moral agent is to provide moral spaces that are capacious in their content and scope, where content is specified by the diverse meanings and values afforded by liberal value pluralism, and scope expands moral circles of concern to include all those who have an interest in helping to solve a specific problem.

   The structure of purpose—Organisational purpose is frequently evoked without explicating its normative basis. This is remedied by using the value of meaningfulness to supply practical reasoning about 'we ought to do' with the means to assess purpose claims. Drawing upon the hybrid value of meaningfulness, purpose has a specific structure, such that purposes may be judged to be morally worthwhile, significant, or in some other way valuable (objectively valuable) and also emotionally engaging

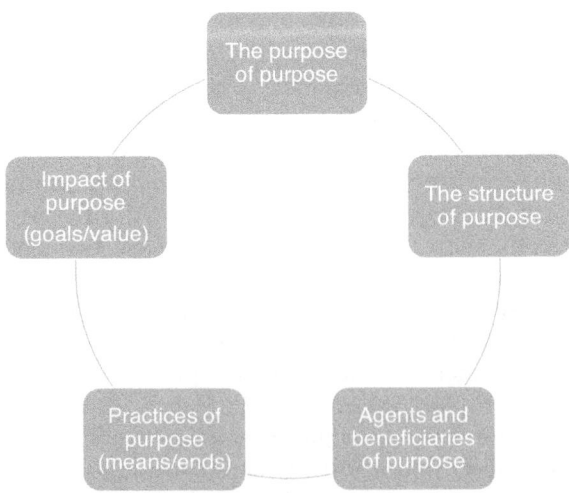

Figure 4.1 Aspects of Organisational Purpose

and satisfying (subjectively attractive). Ethical values that imbue purpose with objective value and subjective appeal include: refraining from doing harm, engaging in repair, caring for the common world and valuable things, meeting needs, promoting flourishing, and creating enduring worth. In the objective dimension, organisations that lack the capacity for objective valuing can fail to evaluate their purpose and mission against morally desirable means and ends. In the subjective dimension, organisations can appropriate the meaning-making capacities of their members, inhibiting the development of the moral emotions needed for collective moral agency. For example, Facebook's corruption of the objective dimension of purpose is illustrated by the ambivalent soul-searching in the internal memo called 'The Ugly'.[6] In the subjective dimension, Mark Zuckerberg overidentified the organisation with his own interests by evoking a collective 'we'.[7] Not all purposes, even when strategically significant, clearly specified, or fervently pursued, can be judged to be good. Therefore the identification and pursuit of purpose must be allied to the development of moral judgement and associated ethical capabilities such as moral imagination, as well as organisational practices of deliberation and collective decision-making.

Agents and beneficiaries of purpose—Purposing is an organisational practice that enables people to exercise their capability for ethical world-building and is a feature of morally viable collective action. This requires a pluralist perspective of organisations as multi-stakeholder and embedded in associational ecosystems, where organisational purpose is an integration of different parts that must be continually adjusted, conciliated, traded off, and synthesised. Rather than conceptualising the organisation as a bargaining game, even when conducted under conditions of pluralised stakeholder management and mutual gains, the organisation is re-imagined as a polyvocal, dispersed-power entity, characterised by an organisational pattern of entitlements and obligations that shares influence among diverse stakeholder constituencies. Purposing requires a voice-system, not as a gift from enlightened managers but as an entitlement that managers are obliged to provide. The life value organisation as a collective moral agent calls upon all members to make their contribution to life value creation. This requires stakeholder constituencies to be related to one another through joint endeavour, underpinned by a system of organisational democracy, where each constituency benefits from and derives enjoyment from the increased excellences of the other.

Purposing as a social practice—Local and ultimate organisational purposes are socially constructed through *purposing* which connects all affected stakeholders to independently valuable objects that are also emotionally attractive. Purposeful action is often described as goal oriented (Rosso et al., 2010; May et al., 2004). However, Stocker (1981) argues that not all action is goal directed, since we also act 'from or out of' some particular source of values or meanings. Thorpe (2008) describes such non-teleological action as 'values-driven' wherein a person acts because he or she judges the action to be 'good, right, required by duty or supported by reasons' (p. 158). Values-driven behaviour means acting out of values, as distinct from fitting values to goal-directed activity, and collective actions to further whole purpose will often be both goal directed and values driven. In a pluralist organisation, the simultaneous presence of values and goals means that creating purpose involves deliberation and contestation, where people wrestle together with objectively valuable purposes, turning them into meanings, values, goals, activities, tasks, feelings, judgements, and outcomes.

Impacts of purpose—Purposing is a practical and ethical undertaking that takes place inside joint action. In general terms, life value organisations aim to create and maintain the many public and private goods we need to lead lives we have reason to value. Increasingly, hybrid organisations combine social, environmental, and financial purposes to produce goods that are neither purely public nor purely private. As hybridity spreads into mainstream shareholder and public organisations, with businesses being urged to take on public responsibilities and public organisations required to adopt market-based practices, the goods they produce in associational ecosystems take on a public character. Drawing upon Kaul's public goods approach, Khoo (2013) identifies features of the 'publicness' of public goods, specifically publicness in consultation, publicness in decision-making, and publicness in benefits. With this in mind, associational ecosystems, which assemble private enterprise and public organisations in order to produce the goods needed in specific situations, can use the concept of integrative worth to enrich organisational purpose with elements of publicness and privateness, and therefore expand their sources of meanings.

Work: Complex Contribution

Purposing in ethical world-building is a form of work. In ethical organising, such work must benefit not only the organisation but also the person doing the work. The relevant benefits are those associated with members being able to exercise their human capability for ethical world-building, through contributive activities that are structured by the goods of meaningfulness. Veltman (2016) claims that, in the absence of complex contribution, we cannot have meaningful work, and this inhibits prospects for flourishing lives. In a study of agro-ecological farming in Cuba, Costa Rica, and elsewhere, Timmerman and Félix (2015) argue for a fairer provision of meaningful work in agriculture and not merely decent work. In this case, meaningful work fosters human development through complex capability formation by incorporating understandings of how craft and tacit knowledge in sustainable farming practices arise from an intimate connection to the land. However, many economies lack sufficient opportunities to provide all their people with complex contribution. Hausmann et al. (2014) point out that 'poorly connected communities, such as petroleum, cotton, rice and soy beans, tend to be low in complexity' (p. 54). The poverty of opportunities for meaningful work undermines social cooperation and transgresses social justice. Rawls (1999 [1971]) recognises this by making participation in complex activity generative of mutual respect, where the sentimental basis of the social union is enjoyment in one another's achievements and excellences. He outlines an Aristotelian Principle that captures our desire for complex activity, motivating us to seek excellence through increasing mastery of complex skills, carried out in social unions where we receive recognition through the public display of our capabilities and where we can recognise the accomplishments of others. Thus, we cannot enjoy the spectacle of somebody labouring under demeaning and meaningless work—to do so would be to do harm to ourselves as well as to others. Using a Kantian framework, Arnold and Bowie (2003) argue that humiliating institutions, such as sweatshops, are not good for any person who belongs to them because they violate the dignity of both managers and workers. This is because engaging in the practices of coercive, hierarchical authority necessary for maintaining such enterprises undermines managers' own interest in their personhood and distorts their capacity to respect their fellow workers as equal co-authorities, with entitlements to a life a worth living.

Keynes (1930) argues that the equal enjoyment of economic abundance—particularly if technology eliminates paid work—will require the setting aside of historically useful norms derived from 'intense, unsatisfied purposiveness' (p. 199). Rather, we will need new values tied to 'the art of living itself' (p. 198), and this will generate new forms of work. Méda (2016) links new work to the objective of 'ecological conversion' (p. 19) and a process of creating jobs without growth that secures fair transitioning 'by pooling the gains and losses and developing real solidarity among all the members of society involved, so that the cost of the transition should be equitably shared by everybody' (p. 22). Such a shift of economic values demands that we concentrate upon the quality and durability of products, and not only the distribution of productivity gains, such that we 'obligatorily *care for and care about* our natural heritage, social cohesiveness and human labour' (p. 24). The protection and enhancement of life value will require us to revalue forms of work, such as repair and reproduction. Repair, as Spelman (2003) reminds us, brings into focus the mutability of our world; its changefulness that makes repair an uncertain engagement with the meanings and value of things. Repair as an activity necessitates judging 'what is possible and desirable to repair' (p. 8), where 'such judgments disclose in an intimate way what we do and do not value about ourselves and the people and things around us' (p. 8). Acts of repair may mutate the world in unforeseen ways, as repair efforts on one object shifts and reorders its relationship with other objects in a complex system of interconnected things. With such forms of work in mind, together with a materialist ethics of care, I understand contribution in very broad terms as the ability of a valuable being or thing, uniquely placed in a relational ensemble, to generate a positive influence by acting towards and interacting with those other beings and things with which it exists in interdependency. This wide definition of contribution allows us to count in those people who may be disadvantaged in some way, as a consequence of ill health or disability, but who nonetheless contribute to making our lives worth living. It also extends to the contributions of animals and natural systems and even artificial entities, from which we benefit but which may also be harmed by our actions and must therefore be afforded caring concern. Clearly, not all such entities are moral agents, so they depend upon those who are to harness their beneficent influence into acts of moral care. This also includes organisational entities which rely upon their members to design an infrastructure of care into the organisation's procedures and identity, and thereby establish them as collective moral agents.

Associational ecosystems are sites of complex contribution and potential systems of social cooperation. Thus, capability justice applies to all members of associational ecosystems, who are entitled to the complex contribution that constitutes meaningful work and develops their human capabilities. Castro (2014) defines a stakeholder as 'a person who stands to be benefitted or harmed through the causality of an organisation in a morally evaluable way' (p. 604). This means that organisational members are not just employed workers but any whose lives are significantly impacted by their proximity to the firm, including contractors, suppliers, communities, and associations, such as NGOs and unions. Ha-Brookshire (2015) argues for a symmetry of concern for internal and external stakeholders, such that, for a supply chain to be 'truly sustainable, each member of the supply chain must also be sustainable. For each member of the supply chain to be truly sustainable, the individuals who work in a corporation must be truly sustainable as well' (p. 228). Sustaining personhood means developing those capabilities for becoming a self-determining being that we need to fulfil our responsibilities to care for valuable beings and things. This involves being able to do meaningful work or 'intrinsically life-valuable work' that Noonan describes as 'an individually meaningful human vocation that consciously contributes something that others' lives require' (loc. 1385). Sison and Fontrodona (2013) connects the common good of the firm to collaborative work, which they describe as 'first, an opportunity to develop knowledge, skills, virtues, and meaning (work as praxis), and second, inasmuch as it produces goods and services to satisfy society's needs and wants (work as poiesis)' (p. 611). Such work enriches our being, cultivating our internal resources and equipping us to fulfil our responsibilities to make ethical worlds, constituted by collective moral agents.

Agonistic Republicanism

In the context of technological development, William Gibson said 'the future is already here—it's just not evenly distributed'. In the same spirit, the elements for ethical organising ethical organising directed at the purpose of life value creation are scattered throughout the system, ready to be combined and scaled up by life value organisations. Re-purposing already existing organisational elements accesses a repository of system-level emancipatory potentials, making these available to be activated by organisational forms with the capacity to multiply moral free spaces, constituted by liberal value pluralism, and to instil in their members the human capability for ethical world-building. These spaces provide ethical resources for all affected members involved in organisational purposing to grapple with diversity, difference, and contestation. I frame intersubjective encounters between people using the principles of agonistic republicanism derived from the social architecture of meaningfulness and mutuality. Agonism and republicanism can be brought together to describe a system of democracy that incorporates organisations and associational ecosystems. Bell characterises Tully's (2014) account of cosmopolitanism as a form of agonistic republican:

> [Tully's] orientation is *agonistic* insofar as it stresses the irreducibility and inevitability of conflict and struggle in the negotiation of political life. It is *republican* insofar as it seeks to harness the powers of active virtuous citizenship in enacting democratic freedom [emphasis added].
>
> (Bell in *On Global Citizenship*, Tully, 2014)

Stakeholder theory is an underdeveloped, or 'weak', theory (Lépineux, 2005). Agonistic republicanism provides a critical dimension to stakeholder theory by specifying normative resources for evaluating organisations and associational ecosystems for 'the unjustified use of power' Scherer (2009: 30). The aim is to amend organisational conditions that trap individuals into relationships of 'dependency, subordination and suppression' (Scherer, 2009: 30), thereby inhibiting their human capability for ethical world-building. Agonistic republicanism connects contestation to: firstly, republican concerns for the common good and, secondly, agonistic concerns for the relational and institutional conditions that will allow cooperation to continue even where there is difference and dissent (Westphal, 2019). Khan (2013) identifies three features of critical republicanism that recognise the importance of civic accord, the value of conflict, and the value of collective self-government. In an agonistic perspective on stakeholder relations, Dawkins (2015) bases a fair fight between opposing interests on prizing discordant perspectives, advancing countervailing voices, and augmenting input legitimacy. However, the co-creation of collective moral agents through purposing and integrity formation means that dialogic encounter must go beyond 'having it out' or 'getting it all out on the table'. Rather, all those affected by the organisation's activities must be involved in a critical examination of the framing rules governing their participation, specifically who is included, how they are included, what benefits and burdens they share, and how procedures promote common good outcomes.

Consensus and Conflict

Ends and means are mutually implicated. Purposing takes place in the midst of acting together on common problems. The dilemmas, tensions, and paradoxes of collective action, even when directed at matters of shared concern, places us in 'an agonistic relationship' to others (Tully, 2014: 237). People are increasingly connected below the state level in associational ecosystems that cut across national boundaries. These connections include, for example, alliances of cities, globally extended supply chains, and private or hybrid governance initiatives for natural resources or vulnerable sectors. The prospects of collective moral agency depends upon the dual participation of members in the co-creation of organisational practices and in the collective self-determination of framing rules. Mansbridge (1994) argues that solving collective action problems in order to get things done requires more democratically organised collective power, which combines coactive power (power with) and coercive power (power over). Collective power requires deliberation to move away from 'a consensus-centred teleology-contestation', which shuts down on generative difference-making, leaving 'precious little space for initiatory or expressive modes of political action' (Villa, 1999: 108). Deliberative procedures that aim for strong consensus encourage the 'self-reinforcing tendencies of deliberation' (Beste, 2013), leading to stagnation, forgetfulness, and conformism. Rather, deliberation should provide each party with the same opportunity to influence the outcome, to contribute their understandings of the common good, and to play their part in clarifying conflict for the benefit of all. Alternatives to strong consensus that make room for difference include plural agreement (Bohman, 1996), meta-consensus (Niemeyer and Dryzek, 2007), and apparent consensus (Moore and O'Doherty, 2012). Procedures based on difference-generating outcomes are hospitable to persuasion attempts that use alternative modes of expression and emotional engagement, such as storytelling, passionate articulation of concerns or polarised positions (Mansbridge et al., 2012). However, it is not enough simply to encourage a diversity of views. Rather, it is the contact between opposing 'views and reasons that is necessary for deliberation, not just their diversity' (Manin, 2005). Difference is not eliminated by perspective formation that tames and suppresses conflict.

Unheeded and uncared for, difference marginalisation erupts further down the line into frustrations, resentment, and resistance.

But whilst guarding against premature closure on differences, we must at the same time be alert to the harms of permanent openness. The capacity of people to absorb variety and difference is not boundless. Van Leeuwen (2014) counsels against the use of agonistic practices in fragile contexts, arguing that people can be made unacceptably 'vulnerable to psychological injury as a consequence of attempts by others to "de-centre" their identity' (p. 797), which can disrupt stable social patterns of routine civility and getting by. Rather, 'the moment of antagonistic conflict is not constantly and everywhere expressed, and in that sense remains a momentary expression of the political' (p. 800). Given this, we may need to give up some of what we consider to be our entitled differences and exercise restraint for the sake of the other and of the whole. This means finding a form of inclusion that maintains the diversity of people's legitimate and sincerely held values and identities as a common resource for meaning-making. Organisational framing rules often mediate subjectivity through interactions that freeze meanings rather than fostering mutual development and endorsement of the kinds of people we could be. For this, agonistic practices are a partial remedy. In multi-stakeholder contexts of disagreement and conflict, Dawkins (2015) recommends an agonistic framework that 'emphasizes reframing the rules and conventions of conflict such that legitimate stakeholders have a viable opportunity to prevail' (p. 12). When combined with republicanism, agonistic practices can help to reframe conflict by directing contestation into a collective moral inquiry concerning common good outcomes. I develop the idea of agonistic republicanism by considering how the constituent power of agonism in constructive conflict can be combined with the responsible difference-making of republicanism.[8]

Agonism: Constructive Conflict

Ethical organising requires capability justice for all those affected by the activities of the organisation and who are members of the society of meaning-makers. These members include employees, customers, suppliers, and shareholders and extend to community members and civil society groups, such as NGOs. Agonism acknowledges the often unavoidable aspects of power and conflict in stakeholder interactions, which frequently involve 'manipulations of discourse, and entail aspects of passion and identity' (Dawkins, 2015: 11). Agonistic organisational practices seek to provide all affected members with the opportunity to exercise constituent power in constructive conflict. Constituent power consists in the unexpected interruption of the genuinely novel and revolutionary that is carried forward through innovation and democratic augmentation into new standards and practices for ordering the human world. Wenman

(2013) identifies agonism with two dimensions of constituent power: firstly, *augmentation* which describes 'a (re)foundation that simultaneously expands and preserves an existing system of authority' and, secondly, *revolution* which 'is characterised by an absolute beginning [. . .] that brings a new principle or set of norms and values into the world, as it were ex nihilo' (p. 9). Wenman (2013) describes how moments of radical eruption, emerging from struggles of multiple actors against structural domination, enter into a world marked by plurality, tragedy, and conflict and are therefore fragile and uncertain. But these innovations can be strengthened when linked to 'a politics of open-ended judgement' (p. 26), involving diverse publics in an evaluation of their significance. When allied to republicanism in a philosophy of ethical organising, the significance of such innovations are assessed against the common good, or the extent to which they promote life value.

Wenman (2013) hopes that a militant cosmopolitanism will emerge from social movements or alternative forms of economic organising such as cooperatives. These new formations will resist neo-liberal capitalism by birthing novelties sufficiently robust and persuasive to be grown into a new organising principle. However, this overburdens oppressed and struggling fringes of our economic and political world. We cannot rely upon these being able to produce scalable innovations capable of addressing the socio-technical challenges of the sustainability imperative. And even if something does emerge, we do not have enough time for a militant cosmopolitanism to forge a new principle suitable for universal adoption out of oppositional struggles between capitalism (presumed to be homogeneous and monist) and the alternatives (presumed to be heterogeneous and pluralist). Rather, we need to activate the immanent potential already present in all organisational forms—whether shareholder, private equity, family, co-owned, public, charitable, or civic. Clegg et al. (2006) argue that power structures may be challenged by an 'insurgent consciousness' (p. 389), generated by workers and managers in alliance with new types of professional groups, to be found, for example, in ethical trading teams focussed on procurement and supply chains. When broadened out to all affected members of associational ecosystems, an insurgent consciousness could be used to create new narratives that underpin agonistic republicanism and connect innovations arising from within organisations to those originating from the economic fringes.

Republicanism: Responsible Difference-Making

Agonism lacks an account of the moral purpose of contestation. In ethical organising, this is amended by incorporating a republican concern for self-government that is directed at the common good. In a social architecture of meaningfulness and mutuality, difference-making is valuable to the extent that it helps us fulfil our responsibilities to take care of the morally valuable beings and things that constitute life value organisations. In

Cicero's (2017) words, the commonwealth [*res publica*] is the concern of a people, but a people is not any group of men assembled in any way, but an assemblage of some size associated with one another through agreement on law and community of interest' (p. 18). Khan (2013) says that republicanism is guided by 'the duty to participate in the public life of the community [as] a precondition of the enjoyment of personal liberty' (p. 333). Laborde (2008) describes critical republicanism as an 'immanent critique of existing institutions that identifies forms of domination and oppressive practices in order to transform them' (Khan, 2013: 321). What constitutes the common good will be viewed from a plurality of often conflicting perspectives, and these can be harnessed into difference-making when each person is recognised as a co-authority in meaning-making. This requires a 'contestatory' (Pettit, 1997) form of democracy, where interactions are non-dominating because they do not put one at the mercy of another. Rather, people experience themselves as free persons, when they are invested with a standing in relation to others such that 'they are fit to be held responsible; they do not act under pressure or duress or coercion or whatever' (Pettit, 2001: 65). Such persons possess a particular kind of freedom as 'discursive control' (Pettit, 2001), or the ability to take part in rational discourse combined with the 'relational capacity that goes with enjoying relationships that are discourse-friendly' (p. 70).

Understanding freedom as discursive control addresses the alienation that arises from not feeling ourselves to be the authors of our actions. This depends, however, upon people being able to voice their differences through expressive means that may be at odds with consensus-driven deliberation. Republicanism provides a responsibility framework for agonist encounter in which we show mutual concern for all those involved in interaction. In this way, agonistic republicanism can be used by life value organisations to create moral free spaces that manifest organisational emotions of respect, care, and empathy.

In sum, collective moral agents become alert to the plurality of their members when they use agonistic republicanism to incorporate the equivalent of organisational moral emotions into collective purposing. When invested with the tools of constructive conflict and responsible difference-making, participants are equipped to evaluate how constituent power shapes acting and being, and to propose framing rules within which constituent power will be exercised for the common good. In the multi-stakeholder context of ethical organising, this extends even to a concern for competitors, since the associational ecosystem consists of life value organisations that are simultaneously rivals and collaborators. For example, pre-competitive agreements among retail brands who share apparel manufacturing factories reset background conditions in order to improve human rights and working conditions. In Chapter 5, I will elaborate upon an ethic of care as a moral standpoint for making judgements regarding the ethical significance of collective action at an organisation and system level.

Notes

1. Messner et al (2013) argue that human beings are good at and enjoy co-operating. They identify seven behavioural mechanisms for successful cooperation that are applicable to international institutions: reciprocity, trust, communication, reputation, fairness, enforcement, and we-identity.
2. Helmore, E. (2019). *Hundreds of Google Employees Urge Company to Resist Support for Ice*. www.theguardian.com/technology/2019/aug/16/hundreds-of-google-employees-urge-company-to-resist-support-for-ice
3. Section adapted from Yeoman (2019: 482). Reproduced by permission of Oxford University Press
4. The Business Roundtable Advocates Organisational Purpose Grounded in Stakeholder Value, Rather Than Shareholder Value (Monday 19, 2019). www.ft.com/content/3732eb04-c28a-11e9-a8e9-296ca66511c9
5. Singleton (2014) reviews the historical evolution of the concept of purpose and identifies a number of dichotomies: instrumental/intrinsic—organisational purpose should capture consequences only, or those things that are valuable in themselves, irrespective of consequences; unitary/plural—organisation should follow single or multiple purposes; individual/collective—only individuals have purpose and there is no such thing as group purpose; function/intention—purpose had no separate function apart from process.
6. "Maybe someone finds love. Maybe it even saves the life of someone on the brink of suicide. So we connect more people. That can be bad if they make it negative. Maybe it costs a life by exposing someone to bullies. Maybe someone dies in a terrorist attack coordinated on our tools. And still we connect people. The ugly truth is that we believe in connecting people so deeply that anything that allows us to connect more people more often is *de facto* good. [. . .] We connect people. Period. That's why all the work we do in growth is justified. All the questionable contact importing practices. All the subtle language that helps people stay searchable by friends. All of the work we do to bring more communication in. The work we will likely have to do in China some day. All of it". Bosworth (2016). *The Ugly*. www.buzzfeednews.com/article/ryanmac/growth-at-any-cost-top-facebook-executive-defended-data#.xt4mkokxx
7. "We didn't focus enough on preventing abuse and thinking through how people could use these tools to do harm as well", he finally conceded. "That goes for fake news, foreign interference in elections, hate speech, in addition to developers and data privacy. We didn't take a broad enough view of what our responsibility is, and that was a huge mistake. It was my mistake". Mark Zuckerberg in Naughton, J. (2018). www.theguardian.com/technology/2018/apr/07/facebookgot-into-mess-cant-get-out-of-it-mark-zuckerberg-surveil lance-capitalism
8. The *agon* can be viewed as a struggle for mutual excellence and, in the context of friendly contestation, a way for us to explore our humanity and to experience one another's human richness—the distinctiveness of each person's contribution to the human and natural world.

Bibliography

Aas, S. (2014). Distributing Collective Obligation. *Journal of Ethics & Social Philosophy*, 9 (3): 1–22.

Anderson, E. S. (1995). *Value and Ethics in Economic Theory*. Cambridge, MA: Harvard University Press.

Anscombe, E. (1969). *Intention*. Ithaca, NY: Cornell University Press.

Arnold, D. G., & Bowie, N. E. (2003) Sweatshops and Respect for Persons. *Business Ethics Quarterly*, 13 (2): 221–242.

Bedau, M. (2012). Where's the Good in Teleology. *Philosophy and Phenomenological Research*, 24 (1): 106–116.

Beste, S. (2013). Contemporary Trends of Deliberative Research: Synthesizing a New Study Agenda. *Journal of Public Deliberation*, 9 (2).

Bohman, J. (1996). *Public Deliberation: Pluralism, Complexity, and Democracy*. Cambridge, MA: MIT Press.

Bowie, N. E. (1998). A Kantian Theory of Meaningful Work. *Journal of Business Ethics*, 17: 1083–1092.

Boyd, R., & Richerson, P. J. (2009). Culture and the Evolution of Human Cooperation. *Philosophical Transactions of the Royal Society B*, 364: 3281–3288.

Bratman, M. E. (1992). Shared Cooperative Activity. *The Philosophical Review*, 101 (2): 327–341.

Brown, M. T. (2005). *Corporate Integrity*. Cambridge & New York: Cambridge University Press.

Calton, J. M., Werhane, P. H., Hartman, L. P., & Bevan, D. (2013). Building Partnerships to Create Social and Economic Value at the Base of the Global Development Pyramid. *Journal of Business Ethics*, 117 (4): 721–733.

Cameron, R. (2010). Aristotle's Teleology. *Philosophy Compass*, 5 (12): 1096–1106.

Castro, S. V. H. (2014). The Morality of Unequal Autonomy: Reviving Kant's Concept of Status for Stakeholders. *Journal of Business Ethics*, 121 (4): 593–606.

Cheng-Guajardo, L. (2018). Responsibility Unincorporated: Corporate Agency and Moral Responsibility. *The Philosophical Quarterly*, 69 (275): 294–314.

Christensen, W. (1996). A Complex Systems Theory of Teleology. *Biology and Philosophy*, 11 (3): 301–320.

Cicero (2017). *On the Commonwealth and On the Laws*. Zetzel (trans.). Cambridge: Cambridge University Press.

Ciulla, J. B. (2000). *The Working Life: The Promise and Betrayal of Modern Work*. New York: Random House.

Clegg, S., Courpasson, D., & Phillips, N. (2006). *Power and Organizations*. London: Sage Publications.

Collins, S. (2018). 'The Government Should Be Ashamed': On the Possibility of Organisations' Emotional Duties. *Political Studies*, 66 (4): 813–829.

Cooper, D. (2003). *Meaning*. Montreal: McGill-Queen's University Press.

Copp, D. (2009). Towards a Pluralist and Teleological Theory of Normativity. *Philosophical Issues*, 19 (1): 21–37.

Dawkins, C. (2015). Agonistic Pluralism and Stakeholder Engagement. *Business Ethics Quarterly*, 25 (1): 1–28.

Dentoni, D., Bitzer, V. & Schouten, G. (2018). Harnessing Wicked Problems in Multi-Stakeholder Partnerships. *Journal of Business Ethics*, 150 (2): 1–24.

Dentoni, D., Waddell, S., & Waddock, S. (2017). Pathways of Transformation in Global Food and Agricultural Systems: Implications from a Large Systems Change Theory Perspective. *Current Opinion in Environmental Sustainability*, 29: 8–13.

Follett, M. P. (1919). Community Is a Process. *Philosophical Review*, 28 (6): 576–588.

Follett, M. P. (1942). The Psychology of Consent and Participation. In: Metcalf & Urwick (eds.). *Dynamic Administration: The Collected Papers of Mary Parker Follett*. New York: Routledge.

Follett, M. P. (1949). *Creative Experience*. Peabody, MA: Martino Fine Books.

Follett, M. P. (1998 [1918]). *The New State: Group Organization the Solution of Popular Government*. Pennsylvania: Pennsylvania State University Press.

Ghoshal, S. (2005). Bad Management Theories are Destroying Good Management Practices. *Academy of Management Learning & Education*, 4 (1): 75–91.

Ha-Brookshire, J. (2015). Toward Moral Responsibility Theories of Corporate Sustainability and Sustainable Supply Chain. *Journal of Business Ethics*, 145 (2): 227–237.

Hausmann, R., Hidalgo, C. A., Bustos, S., Coscia, M., Simoes, A., & Yildirim, M. A. (2014). *The Atlas of Economic Complexity: Mapping Paths to Prosperity*. Cambridge, MA: MIT Press.

Heath, J. (2016). The Benefits of Cooperation. *Philosophy & Public Affairs*, 34 (4): 313–351.

Hedahl, M. (2013). The Collective Fallacy: The Possibility of Irreducibly Collective Action Without Corresponding Collective Moral Responsibility. *Philosophy of the Social Sciences*, 43 (3): 283–300.

Henderson, R., & Van Den Steen, E. (2015). Why Do Firms Have "Purpose"? The Firm's Role as a Carrier of Identity and Reputation. *American Economic Review: Papers & Proceedings*, 105 (5): 326–330.

Hindriks, F. (2018). Collective Agency: Moral And Amoral. *Dialectica*, 72 (1): 3–23.

Hofstadter, A. (1941). Objective Teleology. *The Journal of Philosophy*, 38 (2): 29–39.

Hollensbe, E., Wookey, C., Hickey, L, George, G., & Nichols, V. (2014). Organizations with Purpose. *Academy of Management Journal*, 57 (5): 1227–1234.

Honig, B. (2017). *Public Things: Democracy in Disrepair*. New York: Fordham University Press.

Isaacs, T. (2011). *Moral Responsibility in Collective Contexts*. New York: Oxford University Press.

Isaacs, T. (2017). Responsibility, Obligation, and Climate Change. In: Goldberg (ed.), *Reflections on Ethics and Responsibility*. New York: Springer International Publishing.

Johnson, M. (2005). *Aristotle on Teleology*. Oxford: Clarendon Press.

Keohane, R. O., & Victor, D. G. (2011). The Regime Complex for Climate Change. *Perspectives on Politics*, 9: 7–23.

Keynes, J. M. (1930). Economic Possibilities for Our Grandchildren. In: *Essays in Persuasion* [1963]. New York: W.W. Norton, 358–373.

Khan, G. (2013). Critical Republicanism: Jürgen Habermas and Chantal Mouffe. *Contemporary Political Theory*, 12 (4): 318–337.

Khoo, S. (2013). Public Goods : From Market Efficiency to Democratic Effectiveness. In: Robertson (ed.), *Commonwealth Governance Handbook 2013/14*. London: Commonwealth Secretariat, 97–100.

Kraft, M. (1982). Kant's Theory of Teleology. *International Philosophical Quarterly*, 22: 42–49.

Laborde, C. (2008). *Critical Republicanism: The Hijab Controversy and Political Philosophy*. Oxford: Oxford University Press.

Lépineux, F. (2005). Stakeholder Theory, Society and Social Cohesion. *Corporate Governance: The International Journal of Business and Society*: 1–20.

List, C., & Pettit, P. (2011). *Group Agency: The Possibility, Design, and Status of Corporate Agents*. Oxford: Oxford University Press.

Maak, T. (2008). Undivided Corporate Responsibility: Towards a Theory of Corporate Integrity. *Journal of Business Ethics*, 82: 353–368.

Manin, B. (2005). *Democratic Deliberation: Why Should We Promote Debate Rather Than Discussion?* Program in Ethics and Public Affairs Seminar, Princeton University Press, Princeton, NJ, 13 October.

Mansbridge, J. (1994). Using Power/Fighting Power. *Constellations*, 1 (1): 53–73.

Mansbridge, J., Bohman, J., Chambers, S., Christiano, T., Fung, A., Parkinson, P., Thompson, D. F., & Warren, M. E. (2012). A Systemic Approach to Deliberative Democracy. In: J. Parkinson & J. Mansbridge (eds.), *Deliberative Systems*. Cambridge: Cambridge University Press, 1–26.

May, D. R., Gilson, R. L., & Harter, L. M. (2004). The Psychological Conditions of Meaningfulness, Safety and Availability and the Engagement of the Human Spirit at Work. *Journal of Occupational and Organizational Psychology*, 77: 11–37.

Messner, D., Guarín, A., & Haun, D. (2013). *The Behavioural Dimensions of International Cooperation*. Global Cooperation Research Papers 1 Global Cooperation Research Papers 1 Käte Hamburger Kolleg/Centre for Global Cooperation Research (KHK/GCR21). https://www.die-gdi.de/uploads/media/Messner-Guarin-Haun_Behavioural-dimensions_GCRP-1-WEB.pdf [accessed 5 September 2019]

Méda, D. (2016). *The Future of Work: The Meaning and Value of Work in Europe*. ILO Research Paper, No. 18. International Labour Office.

Midgley, M. (2011). Why the Idea of Purpose Won't Go Away. *Philosophy*, 86 (4): 545–561.

Mohr, L. B. (1973). The Concept of Organizational Goal. *The American Political Science Review*, 67 (2): 470–481.

Moll, H., & Tomasello, M. (2007). Cooperation and Human Cognition: The Vygotskian Intelligence Hypothesis. *Philosophical Transactions of the Royal Society B: Biological Sciences*, 362 (1480): 639–648.

Moore, A., & O'Doherty, K. (2012). *Deliberative Voting: Operationalizing Consensus in a Deliberative Minipublic*. SSRN eLibrary. http://ssrn.com/paper=2104573.

Moseley, D. D. (2014). Revisiting Williams on Integrity. *Journal of Value Inquiry*, 48: 53–68.

Mullins, D. A., Whitehouse, H., & Atkinson, Q. D. (2012). The Role of Writing and Recordkeeping in the Cultural Evolution of Human Cooperation. *Journal of Economic Behaviour & Organization*, 90S: S141–151.

Niemeyer, S., & Dryzek, J. S. (2007). The Ends of Deliberation: Meta-Consensus and Inter-Subjective Rationality as Ideal Outcomes. *Swiss Political Science Review*, 13 (4): 497–526.

Norton, D. L. (1992). On Recovering the Telos in Teleology, or, "Where's the Beef?" *The Monist*, 75 (1): 3–13.

Nussbaum, M. C. (2001). *Upheavals of Thought: The Intelligence of Emotions*. Cambridge: Cambridge University Press.

Nussbaum, M. C. (2013). *Political Emotions: Why Love Matters for Justice*. Cambridge, MA, & London: Harvard University Press.

Pacherie, E. (2008). The Phenomenology of Action: A Conceptual Framework. *Cognition*, 107 (1): 179–217.

Palazzo, G. (2007). Organizational Integrity: Understanding the Dimensions of Ethical and Unethical Behavior in Corporations. *Corporate Ethics and Corporate Governance*: 113–128.

Pettit, P. (1997). *Republicanism: A Theory of Freedom and Government*. Oxford: Oxford University Press.

Pettit, P. (2001). *A Theory of Freedom: From the Psychology to the Politics of Agency*. Cambridge: Polity Press.

Pettit, P. (2007). Responsibility Incorporated. *Ethics*, 117: 171–201.

Pettit, P., & Schweikard, D. (2006). Joint Actions and Group Agents. *Philosophy of the Social Sciences*, 36 (18): 18–39.

Powers, S. T., & Lehmann, L. (2013). The Co-Evolution of Social Institutions, Demography, and Large-Scale Human Cooperation. *Ecology Letters*, 16: 1356–1364.

Rawls, J. (1999 [1971]). *Theory of Justice*. Oxford: Oxford University Press.

Ross, S. (2013). Morality, Teleology, Objectivity, Authority. *The Philosophical Forum*: 373–393.

Rosso, B. D., Dekas, K. H., & Wrzesniewski, A. (2010). On the Meaning of Work: A Theoretical Integration and Review. *Research in Organizational Behavior*, 30: 91–127.

The Royal Society. (2018). *Portrayals and Perceptions of AI and Why They Matter*. https://royalsociety.org/topics-policy/projects/ai-narratives/

Scherer, A. G. (2009). *Critical Theory and Its Contribution to Critical Management Studies*. Oxford Handbook of Critical Management Studies. Oxford: Oxford University Press.

Seemann, A. (2009a). Joint Agency: Intersubjectivity, Sense of Control, and the Feeling of Trust. *Inquiry*, 52 (5): 500–515.

Seemann, A. (2009b). Why We Did It: An Anscombian Account of Collective Action. *International Journal of Philosophical Studies*, 17 (5): 637–655.

Singleton, L. G., (2014). Understanding the Evolution of Theoretical Constructs in Organization Studies: Examining "Purpose." *Academy of Management Annual Meeting Proceedings*: 1132–1137.

Simon, H. (1964). On the Concept of Organizational Goal. *Administrative Science Quarterly*, 9 (1): 1–22.

Simon, H. (1985). Human Nature in Politics: The Dialogue of Psychology with Political Science. *American Political Science Review*, 79: 293–304.

Sison, A., & Fontrodona, J. (2013). Participating in the Common Good of the Firm. *Journal of Business Ethics*, 113 (4): 611–625.

Spelman, E. V. (2003). *Repair: The Impulse to Restore in a Fragile World*. Boston: Beacon Press.

Stocker, M. (1981). Values and Purpose: The Limits of Teleology and the Ends of Friendship. *Journal of Philosophy*, 78 (12): 747–765.

Thompson, C. (2018). The Moral Agency of Group Agents. *Erkenntis*, 83 (3): 517–538.

Thorpe, C. (2008). The Limits of Teleology. In: Chan (ed.), *Moral Psychology Today: Essays on Values, Rational Choice and the Will*. Philosophical Studies Series (Book 110). New York: Springer.

Timmermann, C., & Félix, G. F. (2015). Agroecology as a Vehicle for Contributive Justice. *Agriculture and Human Values*, 32 (3): 523–538.

Tully, J. (2014). *On Global Citizenship: James Tully in Dialogue*. London & New York: Bloomsbury Academic.

Van Leeuwen, B. (2014). Absorbing the Agony of Agonism? The Limits of Cultural Questioning and Alternative Variations of Intercultural Civility. *Urban Studies*, 52 (4): 793–808.

Veltman, A. (2016). *Meaningful Work*. Oxford: Oxford University Press.

Verhezen, P. (2008). The (Ir)relevance of Integrity in Organizations. *Public Integrity*, 10 (2): 133–149.

Villa, D. R. (1999). *Politics, Philosophy, Terror: Essays on the Thought of Hannah Arendt*. Princeton, NJ: Princeton University Press.

Wallace, R. J. (2006). *Normativity and the Will: Selected Essays on Moral Psychology and Practical Reason*. Oxford: Oxford University Press.

Wallace, R. J. (2019). *The Moral Nexus*. Princeton, NJ, & Oxford: Princeton University Press.

Weick, K. E., & Roberts, K. H. (1993). Collective Mind in Organizations: Heedful Interrelating on Flight Decks. *Administrative Science Quarterly*, 38: 357–381.

Wenman, M. (2013). *Agonistic Democracy: Constituent Power in the Era of Globalisation*. Cambridge: Cambridge University Press.

Westphal, M. (2019). Overcoming the Institutional Deficit of Agonistic Democracy. *Res Publica*. 25 (2): 187–210.

Yeoman, R. (2014). Conceptualising Meaningful Work as a Fundamental Human Need. *Journal of Business Ethics*, 125 (2): 235–251.

Yeoman, R. (2019). The Meaningful City. In: Yeoman, Bailey, Madden, & Thompson (eds.), *Oxford Handbook of Meaningful Work*. Oxford: Oxford University Press.

5   Judging, Responsibility, and an Ethic of Care

In my proposed philosophy of ethical organising, values connect collective action to value creation through multi-perspective evaluations of what is worth creating. In this chapter, I shall explore questions related to moral judgement and responsibility in ethical organising by applying a materialist ethic of care to the question of 'how well we are doing' in looking after those beings and things that we judge to be morally valuable. Care involves determining what activities constitute looking after such valuable beings and things, requiring us to exercise ethical capabilities for judging as thinking and feeling. In ethical organising, judging is a relational activity, undertaken with others in collective action contexts, such as practices, professions, projects, specialisms, supply chains, sectors, platforms, associations, networks, families, communities, cities, states, and international institutions. As moral agents, we cannot do anything we like to valuable objects. A materialist ethic of care in a social architecture of meaningfulness and mutuality helps to establish legitimate connections to things that matter to us, where care is concerned with 'the compelling moral salience of attending to and meeting the needs of the particular others for whom we take responsibility' (Held, 2006: 10). Care is a way to acquire moral knowledge of valuable beings and things, and enable people to overcome the separations of distance, power, and culture that inhibit the expansion of social cooperation.

Judging as Thinking and Feeling

Judging implies an intention to choose and act well. In the social architecture of meaningfulness and mutuality, judging is an interactive process that facilitates the integration of the objective ethical-moral and subjective cognitive-emotional dimensions of meaningfulness. As such, judging is an ethical capability for thinking and feeling in action contexts: many of which will be intractable, paradoxical, and characterised by contestation, difference, and resource scarcity. In other words, judging involves us in all kinds of troubling situations that are abundant with emancipatory potentials but which need activating via hospitable institutional conditions. When troubling situations are viewed through the lens of meaningfulness and mutuality, judging is directed at the welfare of valuable objects, with an ethic of care providing a standpoint for assessing the objective ethical-moral worth of objects, as well as the legitimacy of our subjective cognitive-emotional engagements with these objects. Attending to objects, however, is not one-way: objects act upon us, even as we act upon them. In her analysis of the global trade in matsutake mushrooms, Tsing (2015) shows how production and exchange changes the value of the mushrooms, so that they acquire meanings reflecting the social relationships between traders and customers. Wholesalers select grades of mushrooms to meet the needs of customers with whom they want to maintain particular kinds of relationships. In so doing, they invest the mushrooms with 'relation-making powers' (p. 123). The mushrooms take on 'relational qualities' (p. 124) as they pass through exchange processes that combine gift and profit, such that 'things are extensions of persons, and persons are extensions of things' (p. 122). In his ethnographic studies of manufacturing work, Dejours (2006) describes how subjectivity is forged through a dynamic intersubjectivity between self, others, and object. Such relations are a source of tensions and dilemmas, often involving struggle, which is experienced by workers as a form of suffering as they confront themselves, organisational rules, and material realities. Intersubjective encounters between self, material objects, and others give rise to interpretive differences in meanings and values that shape identities. These meanings can lie fallow, or be activated for practical reasoning when meaning-makers are afforded voice as members of life value organisations that adopt mutuality as an organising principle.

World-building involves gathering material and immaterial objects into ethical worlds, structured by a social architecture of meaningfulness and mutuality, and where we use an ethic of care to judge how well we are doing in looking after valuable objects. Thus, the source of value is not singular, separated objects but rather the relational web of entangled beings and things—human and non-human, material and immaterial, natural and artificial. Such ensembles form 'more than human worlds' (Puig de la Bellacasa, 2017: loc. 50), binding us into a relational nexus of obligations, through which we come to see others as having interests, projects and lives that are just as important as ours. I describe judging as an intersubjective process, through which we transform things and, in turn, are transformed by them. Transformations are judged to be ethically desirable when they generate mutual relations, consistent with fairness, care, and flourishing, and direct those relations into morally viable collective action that is structured by the value of meaningfulness. Judging therefore involves becoming committed to relational values, using attentiveness and empathetic imagination to sensitise ourselves to the responsibilities we have to care for valuable beings and things.

Judging requires thinking and feeling. In an ethic of care, judging harnesses emotion and reason into a concern for the object under consideration. This augments our awareness of the object and its embeddedness in networks of relations. In her reconstruction of Arendt's concept of judging, Zerilli (2016) describes 'the capacity to judge [as] a specifically political ability' (p. 8), where *judging* is an ordinary human facility of evaluation, and judging *politically* is political because it invites multiple perspectives into a collective appreciation, understanding, and knowledge of objects of common concern. Judging is 'a democratic world-building practice' (p. ix), operating in social spaces that enable the shared objects of judgement to appear. As a cognitive and emotional activity, judging helps us to attend to how we create a common world by bringing into view 'relevant "objects" for judgment', so that they are collectively seen as 'matters of common concern' rather than as targets of preferences (p. 10). In organisations, judging is assumed to be a strategic activity located in managerial hierarchies and practices, where managers are privileged with a helicopter view of the object landscape. However, this narrow range of observers causes many relevant objects to become invisible or excluded from the organisation's care-scape. Consequently, judging is constrained by 'the shrinkage of the common world in which plural perspectives can be voiced' (p. 280). In collective moral agents, this can be countered by creating moral free spaces as relationally rich and processual action arenas for responsible difference-making and constructive conflict.

In such dialogic spaces, the knowledge and expertise people acquire through their diverse social roles equip them for meaning-making, enabling them to expand the meanings constituting the objects of their attention and situating them in relational networks. Zerilli (2016) identifies how the 'space of relation' (p. 279) structures our distance and proximity to one another, thereby enabling or disabling our capacity to mobilise meanings, understanding, and knowledge around the objects that make up our common world. When dialogic spaces are steeped in history, culture and values, meaning-makers can introduce meanings into processes of judging as thinking and feeling to render objects vivid and present, even those that are spatially or culturally distant. An intriguing imaginary of socio-technical practices, rich in meaning and social value, can be found in Ursula LeGuin's story, 'the fisherman of the inner most sea', where 'deep planning' of farm management integrates a 'complexity of factors [. . .] ecology, politics, profit, tradition, aesthetics, honor, and spirit all functioning in an intensely practical and practically invisible balance of preservation and renewal, like the homeostasis of a vigorous organism' (Le Guin: 156). On the sustainability front line, deep planning characterises emerging practices that are aimed at curating, repairing and maintaining vital life requirements, such as forests, water, and clean air. We also find it in public services grappling with the tension between public values and values of efficiency under the market logic. Both natural resource management and public service provision provide examples of integrated multi-stakeholder, multi-agency workings that enlarge collective understanding and appreciation of the object through inter-organisational capability formation, such as shared knowledge building and joint expertise.

Objects

Objects worthy of shared concern draw the moral gaze of people who are vulnerable to negative changes in that object's condition. How we see such objects shapes our relationship to them and also how we see ourselves. Drawing upon Vygotskian psychology and Leont'ev's concept of activity, Engeström (1987) developed the concept of the activity system that is 'a collective, artefact-mediated, object-oriented activity system, seen in its network relations to other activity systems' (Engeström, 2001: 136). Participants use the activity system to harness multiple perspectives and plural meanings upon the object, thereby stimulating collective knowledge building and learning. When participants in an activity system recognise a shared need that an object can satisfy, they are motivated to engage with that object. However, Smolka et al. (1995, in Nicolini, 2012) argue that object-oriented activity overemphasises teleological collaborative activity at the expense of other modes of interaction with objects, such as acting out of intrinsic values inhering in objects or acting for the needs of objects themselves.

Thus, our needs are not the only consideration when evaluating how to relate to and act towards objects. By becoming involved in objects, we acquire moral responsibilities to consider how well they are doing, promote their welfare, and make caring for their good part of our good. However, objects do not appear in our world ready formed for care efforts or other uses. Objects are emergent, fragmented, and evolving (Nicolini, 2012: 112). They are mutable, slip from our control, become broken and lost, and require repair and maintenance. Given this, one of our responsibilities is to create the object as an object in the first place: 'For things exist as objects for us only as they have been previously determined as outcomes of enquiries' (Dewey, 1991 [1938]: 122). This means making efforts to acquire knowledge about the contextual embeddedness of particular objects, bringing them into view in their vulnerabilities and complexities and thereby giving them a moral presence in our ethical worlds.

Concern for Objects

Sayer (2011) argues that our fundamental relation to the world is an orientation of concern (p. 1) and that how our lives are going is partially determined by 'how they are', where 'they' are the many objects that give our lives meaning and purpose. Attending to things we care about calls out our capacities for practical reasoning, through which we assess 'what is good or bad about what is happening, including how others are treating them, and of how to act, and what to do for the best' (ibid.). Sayer says that our everyday experience of 'lay normativity' is related to our being 'evaluative beings' (p. 19) or the kinds of social creatures for whom things matter: 'We don't just do things and interpret one another. Things matter to us' (p. 19). Because we live with others, mattering is a collective undertaking, through which we seek to connect our values to those of others and to understand how values and valuing steer collective actions with good or bad consequences.

The sense of something mattering is signalled by the urgency we feel when the context in which valuable objects are embedded changes, making them vulnerable to harm and motivating us to call upon others to join with us in mitigating damage and instituting protections. For joint action to be possible, we must assume the presence of a shared objectivity: 'we act in ways that imply that they are about something that goes beyond our subjective experience' (p. 34). Objective presence is captured by the sense that what you feel subjectively about your situation has objective presence for me, even if I do not possess full knowledge of what you are experiencing. Our knowledge about objects is contingent, incomplete, and fallible, and we must be ready to revise our understanding of objects as new knowledge becomes available. However, the assumption that we can revise our provisional knowledge about objects implies that objects are separate from us; that there is an objective realm where things exist 'independently of our knowledge of them' (p. 47). This objective realm mediates our interactive encounters with objects, through which we amend provisional knowledge, using diverse sources of meanings to bring objects into view and give them presence in our world.

Bringing Objects into View

With this in mind, how do we bring forward valuable objects as matters of common concern, so that we can make them susceptible to collective action? Or, as Zerilli (2016) puts it, how do we get 'certain objects into view as objects of judgment at all' (p. 9)? Gathering objects into assemblages of beings and things is how we act collectively in troubling situations. Sabeel Rahman (2016) draws upon Dewey to argue that bringing objects into view as targets of collective action depends upon public institutions whose 'ultimate purpose [. . .] is to create practices and help organise collective action that would render these kinds of concentrated power and diffuse systemic injustices actionable' (p. 87). In life value creation, this involves not only public institutions but also the varieties of life value organisations that make up associational ecosystems. As members of life value organisations, we assess *what is worth creating*; viewing objects through the multi-perspectival lenses of shared, mutual, collective, and public value: 'when we think from the angle of public things, we are switched to questions of orientation and receptivity, from subjectivity to objectivity, from identity to infrastructure, from membership to worldliness' (Honig, 2017: 28). What we learn from these different perspectives changes our motivations and makes us available for developing new orientations to valuable beings and things, based upon an ethic of care: 'the world endures not through the durability of the objects alone, but through the willingness of citizens to care for them: to replace those that have broken [. . .] and replace those that have worn out' (Kiess, in Honig, 2017: 52). When we share a common world with objects in life value organisations, we come to see valuable beings and things as 'candidates for judgment' (Zerilli, 2016: 267) In life value organisations, we are equipped to use our capability for ethical world-building to gather selves, others, and objects into a normative nexus of ethical relations. Such organisations are moral agents when they foster the relevant organisational emotions, establish a public presence grounded in organisational integrity and morally viable purposes, and develop organisational capabilities for sensitising members in thinking and feeling towards valuable beings and things. This is achieved through structures, practices, and processes such as, for example, governance practices informed by agonistic republicanism; mechanisms of data gathering and reporting against ESG or SDGs, multi-stakeholder engagement initiatives; and ensuring that collective action is structured by the goods of meaningfulness. Such mechanisms provide a sensitising environment for members of collective moral agents to see other beings and things more distinctly and concretely, so that 'they emerge into view *as* 'objects' in need of our judgment' (Zerilli, 2016: 8). Zerilli (2016) argues that this requires joining divergent ways of seeing and understanding the object to 'sustaining, renewing and expanding the network of tangible and intangible relations, of what counts as an object of shared concern' (p. 274).

Ways of knowing travel through reasons and emotions.[1] In her cognitive theory of emotions, Nussbaum (2001) characterises emotions as 'forms of judgement' (p. 22) that, in their intensity and particularity, are 'acknowledgements of neediness and lack of self-sufficiency'. What we value is derived from those beings and things that give our lives meaning, in the sense provided by the value of meaningfulness where objective independent significance and worth is joined to subjective feelings of attachment and engagement. This means that emotions are 'concerned with value, they see their object as invested with value or importance' (Nussbaum, 2001: 30). Emotions bring knowledge and reasons into evaluations of worth and significance. When they are directed at objects (goals, projects, persons) constituting our vital interests in our conception of the good life, such evaluative emotions indicate where we are vulnerable to reversion, loss, or harm. Our sense of meaning, our place in the world, is dependent upon the flourishing of the valuable beings and things we have appropriated to the meaning and purpose of our lives. The type and intensity of our emotions indicate the relative importance of various objects and how they structure our lives as a whole. Nussbaum specifies the normative dimensions of the relevant emotions in relation to their objects that explains also the nature of our vulnerability: Firstly, our emotions have an object (and in the value of meaningfulness, it is a worthy object). Secondly, the kind of emotion that it is appropriate for us to experience is 'internal' to the object (Nussbaum, 2001: 27) because the nature of the object specifies the correct emotional orientation. Thirdly, our beliefs about the object generate types of emotions, for example, the anger we experience if a loved one is threatened (p. 29). And fourthly, the kind and intensity of our emotions signals the value of the object; they are 'concerned with value, they see their object as invested with value or importance' (p. 30). In practical reasoning, the intensity and persistence of our emotions alert us to what is important and direct us to how the judgements we make are legitimate when they are structured by what is good for the worthy objects to which we are affectively engaged. Life value organisations as collective moral agents provide us with a context for educating and socialising our emotions, making them available for interactive processes of judging, and directing these processes towards caring for valuable beings and things.

Responsibility to Create Collective Moral Agents

In order to bring forth objects as the target of appropriate cognitive emotions, we must create the collective moral agents by which the object acquires presence and identity in common worlds and through which we fulfil our responsibilities to care for such objects. Collective responsibility therefore consists in the dynamic interaction between the responsibilities of organisations as collective agents and the responsibilities of individual members to create and maintain the organisation as a moral agent. Sciaraffa (2011) argues that we have an obligation not merely to belong, but to participate in institutional maintenance, thereby ensuring that there are social roles that are 'sufficiently rich and complex to sustain the goods of meaning and self-determination' (p. 123). In life value organisations, such social roles provide us with specific positions, perspectives, and expertise for adding our difference to the practical reasoning needed to create and maintain collective moral agents.

In the terms outlined by List and Pettit (2011), collective moral agents are 'fit to be held responsible' when their design is ordered by 'the normative status they ought to be accorded' (p. 2). List and Pettit's (2011) functionalist theory of group agency conceives of corporations as 'real entities' with an independent existence rather than aggregates of individuals: 'let a collection of individuals form and act on a single, robustly rational body of attitudes, whether by dint of a joint intention or on some other basis, and it will be an agent; let it function or perform in the role of an agent, and it will indeed be an agent' (p. 75). However, organisations are dependent upon their members to establish and maintain them as collective moral agents, and members can be held responsible for moral breakdowns as an element of their organisational roles. This means that group members have responsibilities to contribute to the design and generation of group agency: 'individuals may be held responsible for what a group does as designers of a group agent, as members of the group, or as those who enact its wishes' (Pettit, 2007: 193). In the context of the 2008 financial crisis, Admati (2016) comments: 'it takes many collaborating individuals, each responding to their own incentives and roles, to enable a dangerous financial system' (p. 9). He says that the financial system's collective failure lay in how participants eschewed their responsibilities to act upon their knowledge about the system's problems and thereby prevent harm. People reinforced narratives in which they wanted to believe and supported a culture of silence and collective blindness where meanings of significance for collective behaviour, such as a safe level of capital, were interpreted in ways that were deliberately confusing and misleading. This led to a breakdown in ethical organising at scale—the failure of participants to create collective moral agents in an associational ecosystem upon which we all depend for life goods.

This, and other less dramatic examples of breakdowns in moral agency, have important implications for investing life value organisations with morally valuable purposes and morally viable collective action. Organisations are processual: they emerge from and are maintained by ongoing social interactions with their members and their environment. However, as emergent entities, they are more than simply aggregates of their members' interests, values, and claims. Indeed, we might even say that it is disrespectful of the labour, craft, and skill of members to conceive of them as such. We contribute to building organisations as ethical worlds because we believe we are creating something of enduring value, possessing independent significance beyond ourselves. Thus, part of the moral status of organisations lies in their capacity to be carriers of valuable purposes and worthy objects, imbuing them with temporal value. When creating an enduring positive legacy, members draw upon the meaning-source of generativity to connect their activities to a shared history and hopeful future. In this way, morally worthy organisations, as creations of human skill, knowledge, and labour and as consumers of natural and human resources, assume a moral status in society that establishes what we owe to them and what they owe to us, who have brought them into being and for whom they exist. Social regulation can assist in making morally worthy organisations present in society. Organisations acquire ethical status when they adhere to rules, such as Article 14 of the Basic Law for the Federal Republic of Germany, which says, '[P]roperty entails obligations. Its use shall also serve the public good'. The moral status of an organisation can be projected through its public reputation, but I am arguing that we ground the moral presence of an organisation in its integrity. Organisations judged to possess integrity are evaluated as collective moral agents, privileged with an independent presence in society, and provided with legal supports and cultural legitimacy.

To be awarded status as collective moral agents, organisations must be worthy of our interactions with them and the contributions we make to their existence. Organisations contribute value to our lives when they afford us opportunities to 'interact with it, criticize it, and make demands on it, in a manner not possible with a non-agential system' (List and Pettit, 2011: 5). This sets up a social bond between members of the organisation who care about its integrity and moral status in society, and the organisation itself. The morally worthy organisation demonstrates caring concern for its members by providing them with 'humanising duties' that oblige them to take care of morally valuable beings and things (Raz, 1989). Humanising duties are specific to the nature of the beings and things members have made part of their lives. In other words, duties 'make activities and relationships such as friendship into the goods they are' because 'the duty is (an element of) a good in itself' (p. 19). Having such duties enriches lives with opportunities for complex contribution. Indeed Raz (1989) says of them, '[B]ut for their presence our lives would be considerably impoverished' (p. 21). Humanising duties are elements of institutional 'infrastructures of responsibility' (Williams, 2006) that must be subject to justification and the consent of members. Using Rainer Forst's right to justification, Budderberg and Hecker (2018) argue for a 'discursive conception of responsibility' (p. 456), where collective moral agents are obliged to justify their actions to those affected by them. This requires organisations to develop an 'internal justification structure' (p. 473) in order to bring multiple perspectives to bear upon evaluating the worth of their activities, which implies that they need to become a 'community of discourse' (p. 474). In turn, organisational members are required to judge the extent to which the organisation's activities are consistent with its stated purposes and to contribute to the practices that constitute the organisation as a collective moral agent.

Duties to Organise

Given that none of us can now evade knowledge of climate change, this yields 'duties of adaptation' (Caney, 2010: 204), including obligations to create and support the collective agents capable of addressing such duties. However, Isaacs (2017) worries that we cannot rely upon already existing organisations being sufficient for the necessary response to climate change and other grand challenges. Organisational voids, for example, in problems such as antibiotic development, requires world-building to not only repurpose existing organisations but also to create new organisations, especially at the level of meta-governance. Collins (2013) argues that acts over which collectives bear duties generate 'individual duties to be responsive to others with a view to there being a group that meets the Agency and Can Conditions' (p. 242). In other words, individuals have duties to form organisations that are equipped with collective capabilities to fulfil the 'can' condition when the situation demands that they do so and when others are willing to play their part. Some of these groups do not yet exist. French (in Isaacs, 2017) says that 'fictive groups' cannot be intentional moral agents and therefore cannot be held responsible for problems such as hunger or poverty. However, Isaacs (2017) argues that this ignores the capacity of even 'putative groups' (Isaacs, 2011)—unformed or only imagined or otherwise loosely structured, temporary and emergent—to help us solve complex problems. If people who are invested with the capability for ethical organising are willing to take up their collectivisation duties, then putative collective moral agents have a realistic possibility of being formed, and Isaacs (2011) says that we should do so because it is not likely that all the organisations needed to address the sustainability imperative are already in existence.

Expansive social cooperation demands an associational revolution, or the equivalent of a Cambrian explosion in associational variety, and indeed one is already becoming evident in the proliferating bottom-up initiatives and transnational institutions accumulating around climate governance (Keohane and Victor, 2011). Horton Smith (2017)points towards the growth of associational life in the nineteenth century that accompanied the Industrial Revolution, arguing that we have an abundance of associational 'dark matter', or informal organisations that are available to be harnessed into world-building. Isaacs (2017) says that the duty to bring new collectives into being provides individuals with 'valuable moral opportunities' to contribute to worthwhile goals. People want to make such contributions for the sake of things that matter to them and for the experience of meaningfulness this engenders. In a T20 policy brief (Stewart, 2017), a 2009 survey of 140,000 business people found that over two-thirds thought the economic crisis was also a values crisis and that they wanted to practice the same values at work as they did at home: 'Humans don't mind hardship; in fact, they thrive on it; what they mind is not feeling necessary. Modern society has perfected the art of making people not feel necessary. It's time for that to end' (Junger, 2016: xxi).

Whether putative collectives will be formed depends on the extent to which we can equip one another with the human capability for ethical world-building. Aas (2014) argues that an obligation to be willing to help, if others are also willing to help, is prior to an obligation to organise. How do we stimulate willingness to form intentions to act collectively? We do so through awareness and knowledge building about others in our circles of concern and forming the basic competences for experiencing appropriate emotions such as empathy and concern—that is, through moral learning. At a global scale, Aas (2014) claims that, whilst committing to the global application of Rawls's different principle does not tell us 'who should be ready to do what' (p. 22), it does suggest that '*we should want to know this*' (p. 22), which implies obligations to acquire knowledge regarding how we act together to create collectives capable of instituting justice. Collectivisation duties are linked to global moral obligations, such that we have duties to create organisations and associational ecosystems systems with the structural and cultural capacities for moral reflection, deliberation, and collection action directed to planet-spanning problems. When organisations manifest incomplete moral agency, our first response is to reach for judicial controls and regulations (Hedahl, 2013: 297). However, to change collective corporate behaviour, we need to change motivational structures, and especially create the 'background institutions' (De George, 1993: 26) that enable the operation of ethical norms, values, and principles. This means that we need to go beyond regulatory compliance and extend deliberative engagement of all affected members in moral free space to collective self-determination of the institutional framing rules. Thus, collective moral agents that are worthy of their members' contributions sustain two core types of interactions: firstly, deliberative engagement and mutual learning in order to co-create morally worthy purposes and collective action and, secondly, legislative entitlements to influence the framing rules governing collective action at multiple levels from the organisation to the associational ecosystem. Such interactions augment the moral capacity of organisational members to see objects across separations of power, culture, and distance, bringing them into view as valuable beings and things who share with those members a common world

Responsibility to See Others

Jonas (1985) articulates the moral imperative of responsibility to 'act so that the effects of your actions are compatible with the permanence of genuine human life' (p. 11). Accepting our responsibilities as members of a collective moral agent means being willing to act in ways that promote life value. To take up such responsibilities, we need to become sensitised to how other beings and things are affected by our activities, and this requires us to see them as members with us of a shared world. Using the example of textile and garment supply chains, Young (2011) outlines a social connection model of responsibility that identifies how structural injustice arises from the cumulative decisions and actions of individuals. Structural injustice is 'produced and reproduced by thousands or millions of people usually acting with institutional rules and according to practices that most people regard as morally acceptable' (p. 95).[2] Although we are not engaged in a collective determination to harm others or put them at a severe disadvantage, we nonetheless contribute indirectly to cumulative harms:

> [I]ndividuals bear responsibility for structural injustice because they contribute by their actions to the processes that produce unjust

outcomes. Our responsibility derives from belonging together with others in a system of interdependent processes of cooperation and competition through which we seek benefits and aim to realize projects.

(2011: 105)

Specifically, contributing to justice-inhibiting processes obliges us to cooperate with others to amend the norms, rules, and practices by which the structural conditions of domination and exploitation are maintained. When socio-structural processes are systemically unjust, they reduce opportunities for the disadvantaged to make the kinds of complex contributions that develop human capabilities. Gomberg (2007) argues that we should make it possible for everyone to contribute to creating shared social worlds: 'it is unfair to deprive so many of the opportunity to contribute complex abilities' (p. 42). The fear of capability deprivation can hinder the equal distribution of the human capability for ethical world-building. Those who occupy advantageous positions in economic exchange or in the division of labour will be tempted to maintain their advantage by using their general capacity for organising to reproduce the structural conditions that enhance their lives, even though this may diminish the lives of others. The worlds they create are not ethical worlds. Indeed, contributing to structural injustice constrains their own, as well as others', opportunities to convert the capacity for organising into a capability for ethical world-building. One way forward is to sensitise people to others in the associational ecosystems to which they jointly belong through their various social roles. We need to acquire 'a certain *way of looking* at the whole of society' (Young, 2011: 70) that makes visible the divergent positions of people and other valuable objects. Young leans on solidarity to overcome the 'vertigo of political responsibility' (p. 124) and to show that we do not bear responsibilities alone: rather, 'I bear it in awareness that others bear it with me' (p. 109). At a minimum, this involves us in looking at the whole so that we come to see how others are positioned in the shared worlds made up of entities, such as transnational corporations and globally extended supply chains. By focussing our moral vision on the relational nexus of self, other, and object, we learn to see one another as members together of systems of social cooperation.

Responsibilities for structural injustice are discharged by joining with others to create life value organisations as collective moral agents. Dempsey (2015) argues that when we join organisations, we do so in order to gain benefits associated with committing to the aims of the organisation. These commitments entail obligations that give us reasons to act in certain ways, where joint commitments are forms of shared values. By sharing in the values and culture of the organisations we belong to, we contribute to maintaining them as collective agents, and this makes us complicit in the actions of the organisation. To turn these organisations into moral agents, we need to join with others to exercise what Young (2011) calls 'collective ability' (p. 146), through which we 'enable one another and share responsibility by treating one another as responsible agents' (Williams, 2019: 990). This collective ability permits organisational members to generate reasons and justifications for collective action, or as Edmundson (2018) put it: 'collectivities can be moral agents if they appreciate and act upon moral reasons' (p. 2). Moral reasons are generated when organisational members acquire knowledge of how others are affected in their work and lives as a consequence of the positions they occupy in associational ecosystems: 'the purpose is to make social connections between individuals in a structural process visible' (Larrère, 2018: 435).

To summarise, shared responsibility for structural injustice includes a number of elements: firstly, we are responsible for maintaining the collective moral agents that extend our individual moral agency into systems of social cooperation; secondly, to fulfil our responsibilities, we must use our occupational and social roles to press our organisations into action; thirdly, we need to recognise that responsibility entails resisting wilful blindness by cultivating practices of awareness, attentiveness, and moral imagination. This will include organisational members helping each another to become aware of how their connections to others and other valuable objects may impact the welfare of those objects, encouraging them to assess how their actions impact those others and what joint efforts are required to mitigate those in mitigating harms. In Chapter 6, I shall argue that, to make their contribution, moral agents need multi-scalar capabilities that connect individual, collective, and organisational capabilities. Such capabilities enable people to make complex contributions to ethical organising, and are therefore constitutive of meaningfulness in life, work, and organisations.

Ethic of Care

I consider two ways of thinking about an ethic of care: firstly, as a scaffolding of practices, institutions, and processes, through which we reconceive extended social and economic entities, such as supply chains, as systems of social cooperation; and secondly, as a social bond and cognitive-emotional connection grounded in imaginative empathy. In this chapter, I concentrate on the first in the context of our responsibilities towards others in associational ecosystems, such as transnational corporations and value chains. I argue for the second in Chapter 7, where I show how imaginative empathy plays an important role in establishing the society of meaning-makers.

An ethic of care is concerned with 'the compelling moral salience of attending to and meeting the needs of the particular others for whom we take responsibility' (Held, 2006: 10). I use care as the vantage point from which to apply judging as thinking and feeling to the evaluation of ethical worlds: 'The ethics also extends beyond the activities from which it arises, generating a stance (or standpoint) towards 'nature', human relationships and social institutions' (Ruddick, 1998: 4). Fisher and Tronto (1990) define taking care as including 'everything that we do to maintain, continue and repair our world, so that we can live in it as well as possible' (p. 40). Care practices are not mere repetitive reproductions but involve judging as thinking and feeling, where the knowledge we acquire through care is potentially transformative of people and societies. In developing a political perspective on care, Tronto (2010) argues that we need to create 'caring institutions' (Tronto, 2010). With this in mind, a public ethic of care must be relational, contextual, and processual, encouraging us to expand our circles of moral concern to reveal all those beings and things to whom we are systemically connected. By so doing, we acknowledge our mutual dependence, create shared knowledge of the lives and circumstances of others, and evaluate what responsibilities this knowledge entails.

In remedying structural injustice, an ethic of care provides a promising route for understanding our relational responsibilities, especially, for example, in value chains where dominant organisations use practices of coproduction and collective governance to integrate marginalised participants under corporate-defined purposes. Slote (2007) argues that an ethics of care does not say we have an obligation to 'have or act from caring motives' but rather that we have an obligation 'not to act from uncaring motives; not to act in ways that reflect a lack of empathetic concern for others' (p. 33). In any troubling situation, to act with care involves becoming alert to the particular needs of valuable objects through empathetic awareness. Care implies a form of practical reasoning, which Hawk (2011) describes as 'where the individual uses all of his/her capabilities, including affective, intuitional, and imaginative, to arrive at a reasonably defensible assessment of the uniqueness of the context and a reasonable action to care in collaboration with those who are part of the relationship' (p. 12). In becoming alert to how matters stand for others with whom we are indirectly connected, we acquire responsibilities to act. Held (2018) argues that applying ethics of care to Young's social connection theory of responsibility calls 'on persons and groups into which they are organised to take responsibility for what needs to be done' (p. 393) and to do so by 'exercising what capacities we have for moving groups to act' (p. 398). Held (2018) says that care must often be practised through conflict and tension, where 'the underlying relations and aims are ones of mutuality' (p. 404) or 'mutual commitment to mutual well-being' (p. 405). Care ethics will therefore care for tensions and conflicts as sources of knowledge about those others who are members with us of associational ecosystems. This means that an essential element of collective action which uses an ethic of care is understanding how acting is a form of 'doing together' rather than 'doing to', where acting together with care requires all those who act to become capable of experiencing themselves as self-determining beings with needs to be met through joint capability formation. With this in mind, collective moral agents enact an ethic of care by adopting policies, processes, and practices that sensitise members to one another across separations of culture, distance, and power, thereby facilitating the manifestation of caring emotions at an organisational level.

Materialist Ethics of Care

Problematic situations, such as climate change, entangle persons, animals, natural ecosystems, resources, and other objects into mutually dependent relationships, simultaneously connecting and separating them through space, time, and culture. A materialist ethics of care helps us to evaluate the processes by which we gather together and bring into view those objects of common concern that constitute our shared worlds. Puig de la Bellacasa (2017) describes a materialist ethics of care in terms of a 'force distributed across a multiplicity of agencies and materials and supports our world as a thick mesh of relational obligation' (loc. 394). In differentiating between care and concern, Puig de la Bellacasa (2017) argues that, whilst we can be concerned about something, care conveys an imperative that demands action, both ethical and political. Echoing Wallace's normative nexus of moral relations, to act with care means to hold disparate objects in mutual relation through their tensions and differences, thus forming the relational basis for responsible collective acting into the world. To make visible, or to bring beings and things that matter to us into view, depends upon developing knowledge and understanding that cannot be separated from the intersubjective materiality of our shared existence. Creating knowledge out of material relations between ourselves and other beings and things requires us to exercise our 'material-semiotic agency in the mattering of worlds' (loc. 335), and especially when creating knowledge involves applying an ethic of care to 'an ethical reorganization of human–nonhuman relations' (loc. 465). When we build knowledge regarding morally valuable beings and things that matter to us, we are accessing knowledge and understanding through evaluative pathways of care and concern: 'knowledge is involved in making things matter and caring is a way of knowing' (loc. 335). Puig de la Bellacasa (2017) draws upon Natasha Myers' (2015) observations of how molecular scientists relate to their object by 'giving life' to molecules through care as affective labour, resulting in a 'human-molecule gathering' laden with passionate connections (loc. 1120). Meaning-makers imbue care-knowledge with meanings and values using 'semiotic technologies' (Haraway, 1991: 197) or 'practices and arts of fabricating meaning with sign, words, ideas, descriptions, theories' (Puig de la Bellacasa, 2017: loc. 1241). In this way, meaning-makers create ethical worlds as congregations of beings and things, bound by mutual 'immanent obligations' (loc. 2715) that represent the specific intersubjective materiality of each relational context.

In Young's social connection theory of responsibility, we pool individual responsibilities for structural injustice. These are discharged when each person makes the contribution that is theirs to make to amending unjust, or in some other way harmful, socio-technical processes that impede the flourishing of gathered congregations of people, animals, artefacts, natural ecosystems, and other valuable things. The ethic of care, with its relational underpinnings, provides a moral resource for evaluating gatherings of beings and things as complex systems, in which agents are understood to be 'mutually connected, vulnerable and dependent, often in asymmetric ways' (Pettersen, 2011: 52). This sets up a dynamic interaction between people and social structures because whilst people experience social structures as an objective reality that resists their efforts, they are also the agents who are responsible for amending social structures.

People experience unequal constraints upon their world-building agency. In ethical organising, this demands an evaluation of the asymmetrical ways in which social structures act as conversion factors for translating abilities and capacities into capabilities for functioning. Among the relevant conversion factors to be assessed are the roles and positions that people occupy in social practices, and which supply them with duties, resources, knowledge, and relationships. These practices include materiality and technology. Oosterlaken (2011) argues we must incorporate technology into a relational ontology, and that this involves recognising the role of technological artefacts in human capabilities. Our need for capability development drives social and technological change and motivates us to 'invest in particular networks of interdependencies (Lawson, 2010: 220). Lawson (2010) says that the entanglement of human capabilities with technology requires us to evaluate 'what kinds of things we wish to be capable of and, of course, are we happy with others being capable of' (p. 219). This is addressed by deliberating upon the candidate capabilities that capability justice should ensure are available to each person in order to achieve a threshold standard of human flourishing. Since ethical worlds are constructed by people located in every part of an associational ecosystem, capability justice demands that their contributions are structured by the goods of meaningfulness. Capability justice also requires that world-builders see themselves and others as self-determining beings, both capable and vulnerable, who are bound together by mutual obligations to help one another develop the relevant capabilities for fulfilling their responsibilities of care.

Becoming a Self-Determining Being

Clark Miller (2010) argues that care ethics requires us to attend to 'the moral significance of human vulnerability, dependence and need' (p. 150). Clark Miller develops a cosmopolitan ethics of care that responds to the needs of distant others by generating obligations based upon meeting needs or avoiding creating needs in others, so that each person can develop as a self-determining being: 'Fundamental needs occur when a person's agency, or potential agency, is under significant threat. When people fail to have their fundamental needs met, the result can be significant harm and a curtailment of their powers of self-determination' (p. 150). We have responsibilities to help one another form capabilities as self-determining beings who are equipped to fulfil caring obligations, not just by providing humanitarian aid but also by supporting caring practices that empower people in their own efforts to care. Clark Miller argues that although responding to the needs of distant others in order to improve their ability to meet their caring obligations is less direct than simply providing humanitarian aid, it is nonetheless formative for human development, provided people are supported with caring practices and empowered in their own efforts to care. Threats to our agency arise when our fundamental needs are ignored, misunderstood, or produced through structural injustice. A duty of care requires us to refrain from creating fundamental needs in others but instead to repair their self-determination as active agents (p. 151). This involves not just a concern for the welfare of others but also respect for them as moral agents, such that 'moral agents develop a critical awareness of where they are situated in terms of global power structures' (p. 155).

Applying care ethics to cosmopolitanism yields an informationally rich and context-sensitive morality, rooted in a relational ontology and responding to actually existing persons as whole human beings, who are invested with dignity as particular persons with interests and lives of their own. In acquiring an understanding of ourselves and others as self-determining beings, we learn about the responsible share we have in constructing the social worlds that frame our lives and what we must do to populate those worlds with things of value: 'The humanity of a person is that person's capacity to recognise, appreciate, engage with, harmonise with, and produce intrinsic goods. It is in virtue of this feature of human beings that they bring something unique and distinctive to the world' (Christiano, 2005: 47–48). As self-determining beings, each of us has a distinctive contribution to make to the projects of world-building that construct systems of social cooperation. Expansive social cooperation relies upon our being able to bridge separations of power, distance, and culture by seeing others as equal contributors who collectivise their efforts to amend the socio-technical processes that institute structural domination.

Ethic of Care and Systems of Social Cooperation

If they are to thrive, people have no choice but to engage in social cooperation. Cooperation is therefore accompanied by an element of coercion, and this means that the terms under which cooperation takes place must be accepted by all as reasonable and just. Rawls (1971) specifies the principles of justice needed to maintain society as a fair, stable, and enduring system of cooperation. He confines these principles of social cooperation to the level of the nation state, arguing that, since nations enter into trading or political relationships voluntarily, international cooperation lacks the element of coercion that necessitates justice. However, although global value chains are not nation states, neither are they mere bundles of voluntary trading relations. Rather, they are sustained social practices governed by shared organising purpose and characterised by varying degrees of coercion and compliance (James, 2012). This means that when their work and lives are intertwined with such economic entities, people frequently have little option but to participate. Even when they are stable systems of social cooperation, global value chains may be 'poverty traps' (Sindzingre, 2010), characterised by dependence, exploitation, silence, and minimal benefits to weakly positioned participants.

Separations of Distance, Power, and Culture

Living in systemic structural relations with others is often an attenuated experience. Separations of distance, power, and culture are frequently evoked as being relevant criteria for behaving differently towards distant beings and things. A philosophy of ethical organising rejects this, proposing instead that we use judging as a form of thinking and feeling to foster 'seeing' as an ethical orientation of care, by which we become sensitised to the presence of distant others and attentive to how our good is partly dependent upon how well they are doing. An ethic of care sharpens our vision, bringing distant others into clear relief and complexly detailed in the particularity of their lives. This moral attentiveness is aided by envisaging associational ecosystems, such as supply chains, cities, sectors, clusters, as systems of social cooperation. For example, the interconnectedness of supply chain structures, processes, and people means that 'the complex moral judgements that must be made need to—in the spirit of supply chain analysis—entail some consideration of the whole system' (New, 2004: 272).

As organisations acquire knowledge and understanding of how they are bound to others through ties generated by the requirements of collective action, remoteness is becoming harder to maintain. Increasing levels of mutual dependency are accompanied by vulnerability and risk, with potentially high impacts on dimensions of sustainability, including organisational survival. Multi-level and multi-domain interdependence makes it likely that organisational members will be 'involved in high impact activities over which they have no control' (Castro, 2014). At the same time, the ability of those affected to respond to the vulnerabilities that accompany their organisational connections are limited, because '[w]e

are all effectively reduced to minor parties in relation to such large organizations, or potentially so' (p. 602). Castro (2014) uses an ethic of care
to establish the obligations that corporations have to those affected by
their activities. With respect to employees, a corporation has a primary
duty to support an ethical or caring corporate culture, such that 'I am not
merely someone who happens to work there, I am someone in its care to
whom it has duties that go beyond whatever is specified in our employment contract' (p. 605). Culture, however, is just one piece of scaffolding in an infrastructure of care. In collective moral agents, stakeholder
integration requires an ethic of care that combines a culture of care with
practices of self-determination, where stakeholders join together to agree
on the framing rules governing the system of social cooperation in which
they are implicated.

Supply Chains as Systems of Social Cooperation

I use the example of global value chains to examine prospects for conceiving of such entities as associational ecosystems, constituted by collective moral agents, where practices of social cooperation aim to overcome
the separations of distance, power, and culture that license the different treatment of other beings and things (Yeoman and Mueller Santos,
2019). O'Neill (2000) says:

> [I]f we owe justice (or other forms of moral concern) to all whose
> capacities to act, experience and suffer we take for granted in act-
> ing, we will owe it to strangers as well as to familiars, and to distant
> strangers as well as to those who are near at hand.
>
> (p. 196)

In considering the morally relevant features of persons embedded in
supply chains, we tend to marshal three registers of response to distant
others: firstly, they are vulnerable and needy and therefore require aid
and compassion; secondly, they are universal types and therefore require
rights and respect; thirdly, they are contributors to social cooperation
and therefore require capabilities and care. Freeman (in Agle et al., 2008)
captures the third sense when he says that business theory must move
away from partial accounts of what it means to being a person to ones
that understand people to be 'whole, fully integrated human beings, with
names, faces, families and pasts' (p. 163), and who therefore require caring concern, as well as human capabilities to join their efforts with ours
in building ethical worlds. I argue that concentrating on the third register
in social and economic entities such as supply chains helps us to overcome the separations of culture, power, and distance that weaken the
solidarity needed for capability justice.

Supply chains are de facto systems of social cooperation that shape the
work and lives of their members in morally significant ways. Corporations

have increasingly adopted high integration strategies that cohere their employees, suppliers, and producers around purpose, identity and values, binding them into a shared fate through means that benefit the focal organisation. In functional terms, supply chains integrate information, technologies, processes, and relationships, making them into entities that are characterised by 'cooperation, collaboration, information sharing, trust, partnerships, shared technology' (Power, 2005). Unified supply chains oblige supply chain members to prioritise 'the common interest' (p. 256), which is generally described from the standpoint of the most powerful participants. Suppliers are required to adopt a partnership approach involving enhanced relationships (Beske et al., 2014), pooled interdependent tasks (Thompson, 1967), reciprocal interdependence (Crook and Combs, 2007), and mutual dependence and coordination (Tolhurst, 2001). Focal organisations align practices across boundaries to meet standards, certifications, and assessments, and to help them to do so, members are socialised to share knowledge, information, commitment and purpose. In other words, focal organisations have the power to reach inside supplier organisations to influence the purpose of that organisation, the development of their business practices, the organisation of their work, the identity and belonging of their employees, and hence the meaningfulness of their lives.

Power imbalances tempt focal organisations to keep weaker partners in situations of permanent dependency, making it easier to appropriate the gains of social cooperation. Efforts to amend exploitative relations have focussed on filling regulatory vacuums through voluntary codes, certification schemes, participatory initiatives, and private governance arrangements (Fayet and Vermeulen, 2014). However, remedial attempts to foster inclusion through communicative methods, such as multi-stakeholder roundtables (Schouten et al., 2012; Ponte and Daugbjerg, 2015) often fail to produce the expected ethical outcomes. This is because deliberation privileges modes of reasoning based upon values of rationality and impartiality, thereby de-valuing expressive reason-giving, characterised by emotion, storytelling, and particularity (Reinecke and Ansari, 2015). Emotional responses, stemming from the particularity of lives, are silenced or downgraded. But communicative practices that forbid moral intuition and affect from ethical judgement can result in unfair, disrespecting, or excluding outcomes. This weakens the ability of organisations to sensitise their members to valuable persons and objects, inhibiting their ability as members of collective moral agents to have a care for how well valuable objects within their circle of concern are doing (Milligan and Wiles, 2010). Rather than suppressing or sublimating tensions, practices involving constructive conflict and responsible difference-making surface rich experiential information, using interpretive difference in meanings to stimulate moral attention and moral imagination.

Seeing others across separations of distance, power, and culture can be partially achieved by envisioning associational ecosystems as systems of social cooperation, mapped out as care-scapes, or those 'spatial manifestations of the interplay between the sociostructural processes and structures that shape experiences and practices of care' (Milligan and Wiles, 2010: 739). Massey (2004: 10) argues that imagining distance as spatial can stimulate a sense of mutual connectedness. By translating distant places into interrelated and mutually constitutive spaces, we can sensitise supply chain participants to one another as whole human beings, each with a life of her own to lead, thereby enabling people to 'see' one another as equal members of a cooperative system. This consciousness-raising is developmental, requiring people to reach out to one another using empathetic imagination to foster a rich appreciation of other lives, as well as cultivating an openness towards the different ways of knowing that people bring into collective action.

As I have discussed, when an ethic of care is used to incorporate the value of meaningfulness into ethical organising, this enables world-builders to apply judging as thinking and feeling to the question of how well they are doing to look after morally valuable objects. By bringing beings and things into view as objects of caring concern, members develop the mutual awareness, interest, and respect for one another that grounds sociality and solidarity. Burton and Dunn (1996) concentrate on poorly placed members to make the case for a care-based stakeholder approach to organisations. Palmer and Stoll (2011) argue that caring for stakeholders involves 'becoming emotionally attuned to their situation, and responding in a manner that reflects an appreciation of the particularities of their situation. By treating them as autonomous and reason understanding beings, we respect their humanity' (Palmer and Stoll, 2011: 124). Engster (2011) limits an organisation's caring responsibility to those with whom it has a direct relationship, where stakeholders are 'any groups or individuals whose ability to care for themselves or others is directly dependent upon a firm's actions or decisions' (p. 107). This includes employees, shareholders, and customers but excludes suppliers. However, Engster picks out the importance of complex contribution for an ethic of care. Caring firms will create productive work that equips people with the skills and resources they require to fulfil their caring obligations. This involves fostering 'a work environment that allows workers to exercise their basic capabilities for reason, imagination, communication, and sociability and avoids assigning mind-numbing or back-breaking work that erodes workers' basic capabilities" (p. 102). The need for complex contribution applies also to suppliers and producers, and collective moral agents as participants in associational ecosystems have responsibilities to ensure that all members have opportunities to make complex contributions that foster meaningfulness in their work and lives.

In an interdependent world, even marginalised members of associational ecosystems are being called upon to contribute their knowledge, skill, and craft into collaborations to look after natural resources, respond to initiatives aimed at remedying social inequalities, and work with state and non-state actors to co-create new organisational models that address multiple objectives. This often means working with people whose values and ways of knowing may be very different from our own. Nonetheless, in ethical organising, we are 'tasked with the challenge of recognizing in practices not our own the interests, purposes, and desires that make them humanly intelligible' (Zerilli, 2016: 270). To reinforce ordinary capacities for judging in ethical world-building, we need to draw upon material-semiotic technologies, such as multi-stakeholder initiatives, using values-work, joint knowledge-building, and face-to-face encounter to foster the empathetic encounter and moral learning needed for joint problem-solving. Mena and Palazzo (2012) define multi-stakeholder initiatives (MSIs) as 'private governance mechanisms involving corporations, civil society organizations, and sometimes other actors, such as governments, academia or unions, to cope with social and environmental challenges across industries and on a global scale' (p. 528). Participation in MSIs fosters capability development and critical consciousness through complex collective action that expands knowledge, awareness, and learning.

Planetary-scale social cooperation will depend upon ethical world-building to create the collective ability that enables people to work with one another across multiple separations and ways of knowing. The weakening of national authority and the difficulties of replicating representative democratic institutions on a global scale require new modes of governance that combine public and private power. For multi-level systems in which MSIs play a part, collaborative governance offers a viable institutional mechanism for harnessing the contributions of self-determining beings into collective action. A 'collaborative governance regime' includes governance relationships such as collaborative public management, multi-partner governance, joined-up or network governance, hybrid arrangements, and participatory governance incorporating civic engagement (Emerson et al., 2012). In circumstances requiring collective action, Ostrom (1990) considers 'governance as a dimension of jointly determined norms and rules designed to regulate individual and group behaviour' (Emerson et al., 2012: 2). However, such approaches risk creating a less critical stakeholder culture and threatening the independence of organisations, such as NGOs. In other words, governance must guard against 'wilful blindness', or the denial of 'uncomfortable truths that cry out for acknowledgement, debate, action and change' (Heffernan, 2011: loc. 55). To avoid weakly positioned stakeholders being ignored or rendered invisible, associational ecosystems must be constituted by life value organisations that have the features for collective moral agency, such as integrity and moral sensitivity. In Chapter 6, I discuss what justice requires in the processes of social construction by which collective moral agents are created and maintained.

Notes

1. Section adapted from Yeoman (2014). Reproduced by permission of Palgrave Macmillan.
2. See the 1987 Brundtland Report, "Our Common Future". https://sustainable development.un.org/content/documents/5987our-common-future.pdf

Bibliography

Aas, S. (2014). Distributing Collective Obligation. *Journal of Ethics & Social Philosophy*, 9 (3): 1–22.

Admati, A. R. (2016). *It Takes a Village to Maintain a Dangerous Financial System*. Stanford University Graduate School of Business, Working Paper No. 3426, 31 May.

Agle, R. A., Donaldson, T., Freeman, R. E., Jensen, M. C., Mitchell, R. K. & Wood, D. J. (2008). Towards a Superior Stakeholder Theory. *Business Ethics Quarterly*. 18 (2): 153–190.

Bailey, C., & Madden, A. (2015). Time Reclaimed: Temporality and the Experience of Meaningful Work. *Work, Employment & Society*, 31 (1): 3–18.

Ballou, R. H., Gilbert, S. M., & Mukherjee, A. (2000). New Managerial Challenges from Supply Chain Opportunities. *Industrial Marketing Management*, 29 (1): 7–18.

Baur, D., & Schmitz, H. P. (2012). Corporations and NGOs: When Accountability Leads to Co-Optation. *Journal of Business Ethics*, 106 (1): 9–21.

Beske, P., Land, A., & Seuring, S. (2014). Sustainable Supply Chain Management Practices and Dynamic Capabilities in the Food Industry: A Critical Analysis of the Literature. *International Journal of Production Economics*, 152: 131–143.

Budderberg, E., & Hecker, A. (2018). Justification Incorporated: A Discursive Approach to Corporate Responsibility. *Ethical Theory and Moral Practice*, 21: 465–475.

Burton, B. K., & Dunn, C. P. (1996). Feminist Ethics as Moral Grounding for Stakeholder Theory. *Business Ethics Quarterly*, 6: 133–147.

Caney, S. (2018). Justice and Future Generations. *Annual Review of Political Science*, 21 (1): 475–493.

Caney, S. (2010). Climate Change and the Duties of the Advantaged. *Critical Review of International and Political Philosophy*, 13 (1): 203–228.

Castro, S. V. H. (2014). The Morality of Unequal Autonomy: Reviving Kant's Concept of Status for Stakeholders. *Journal of Business Ethics*, 121: 593–606.

Christiano, T. (2005). An Argument for Egalitarian Justice and Against the Levelling-Down Objection. In: Campbell, O'Rourke & Shier (eds.), *Law & Social Justice*. Cambridge, MA, & London: MIT Press.

Clark Miller, S. (2010). Cosmopolitan Care. *Ethics and Social Welfare*, 4 (2): 145–157.

Collins, S. (2013). Collectives' Duties and Collectivization Duties. *Australasian Journal of Philosophy*, 91 (2): 231–248.

Collins, S. (2018). "The Government Should Be Ashamed": On the Possibility of Organisations' Emotional Duties. *Political Studies*, 66 (4): 813–829.

Crook, T. R., & Combs, J. G. (2007). Sources and Consequences of Bargaining Power in Supply Chains. *Journal of Operations Management*, 25 (2): 546–555.

De George, R. T. (1993). *Competing with Integrity in International Business.* New York: Oxford University Press.

Dejours, C. (2006). Subjectivity, Work and Action. *Critical Horizons*, 7 (1): 45–62.

Dempsey, J. (2015). Moral Responsibility, Shared Values, and Corporate Culture. *Business Ethics Quarterly*, 25 (3): 319–340.

Dewey, J. (1991 [1938]). Logic: The Theory of Inquiry. In: Boydston (ed.), *John Dewey: The Later Works, 1925–1953*, Vol. 12. Carbondale: Southern Illinois University Press.

Edmundson, W. A. (2018). Distributive Justice and Distributed Obligations. *Journal of Moral Philosophy*, 15 (1): 1–19.

Emerson, K., Nabatchi, T., & Balogh, S. (2012). An Integrative Framework for Collaborative Governance. *Journal of Public Administration Research and Theory*, 22 (1): 1–29.

Engeström, Y. (1987). *Learning by Expanding: An Activity-Theoretical Approach to Developmental Research.* Helsinki: Orienta-Konsultit.

Engeström, Y. (2001). Expansive Learning at Work: Towards an Activity Theoretical Re-Conceptualisation. *Journal of Education and Work*, 14 (1): 133–156.

Engster, D. (2011). Care Ethics and Stakeholder Theory. In: M. Hamington & M. Sander-Staudt (eds.), *Applying Care Ethics to Business: Issues in Business Ethics*, Vol. 34. Dordrecht: Springer, 93–110.

Fayet, L., & Vermeulen, W. J. V. (2014). Supporting Smallholders to Access Sustainable Supply Chains: Lessons from the Indian Cotton Supply Chain. *Sustainable Development*, 22 (5): 289–310

Fisher, B., & Tronto, J. (1990). Toward a Feminist Theory of Caring. In: Abel & Nelson (eds.), *Circles of Care: Work and Identity in Women's Lives.* Albany: State University of New York Press.

French, P. (1979). The Corporation as a Moral Person. *American Philosophical Quarterly*, 16: 207–215.

Gaventa, J., & Cornwall, A. (2008). Power and Knowledge. *The Sage Handbook of Action Research: Participative Inquiry and Practice*, 2: 172–189.

Gilbert, M. (2008). Two Approaches to Shared Intention: An Essay in the Philosophy of Social Phenomena. *Analyse & Kritik*, 30: 483–514.

Gilligan, C. (1982). *In a Different Voice.* Cambridge: Harvard University Press.

Gomberg, P. (2007). *How to Make Opportunity Equal: Race and Contributive Justice.* Malden, MA: Blackwell Publishing.

Haraway, D. (1991). In the Beginning Was the Word: The Genesis of Biological Theory. In: *Simians, Cyborgs, and Women.* New York: Routledge.

Hawk, T. F. (2011). An Ethic of Care: A Relational Ethic for the Relational Characteristics of Organizations. In: Hamington & Sander-Staudt (eds.), *Applying Care Ethics to Business.* Netherlands: Springer, 3–34.

Hedahl, M. (2013). The Collective Fallacy: The Possibility of Irreducibly Collective Action Without Corresponding Collective Moral Responsibility. *Philosophy of the Social Sciences*, 43 (3): 283–300.

Heffernan, B. (2011). *Wilful Blindness: Why We Ignore the Obvious at Our Peril.* London & New York: Simon & Schuster UK Ltd.

Held, V. (1970). Can a Random Collection of Individuals Be Morally Responsible? *The Journal of Philosophy*, 67 (14): 471–481.

Held, V. (2006). *The Ethics of Care: Personal, Political and Global.* Oxford: Oxford University Press.

Held, V. (2018). Taking Responsibility for Global Justice. *Journal of Social Philosophy*, 49 (3): 393–414.

Hindriks, F. (2018). Collective Agency: Moral and Amoral. *Dialectica*, 72 (1): 3–23.

Honig, B. (2017). *Public Things: Democracy in Disrepair*. New York: Fordham University Press.

Horton Smith, D. (2017). The Global Historical and Contemporary Impacts of Voluntary Membership Associations on Human Societies. *Voluntaristics Review*, 2 (5–6): 1–125.

Isaacs, T. (2011). *Moral Responsibility in Collective Contexts*. New York: Oxford University Press.

Isaacs, T. (2017). Responsibility, Obligation, and Climate Change. In: Goldberg (ed.), *Reflections on Ethics and Responsibility: Essays in Honor of Peter A. French*. Springer International Publishing, 101–116.

James, A. (2012). *Fairness in Practice: A Social Contract for a Global Economy*. Oxford: Oxford University Press.

Jonas, H. (1985). *The Imperative of Responsibility: In Search of an Ethics for a Technological Age*. Chicago: University of Chicago Press.

Junger, S. (2016). *Tribe: On Homecoming and Belonging*. London: 4th Estate, HarperCollins.

Keohane, R. O., & Victor, D. G. (2011). The Regime Complex for Climate Change. *Perspectives on Politics*, 9: 7–23.

Larrère, C. (2018). Responsibility in a Global Context: Climate Change, Complexity, and the "Social Connection Model of Responsibility". *Journal of Social Philosophy*, 49 (3): 426–438.

Lawson, C. (2010). Technology and the Extension of Human Capabilities. *Journal for the Theory of Social Behaviour*, 40 (2): 207–223.

List, C., & Pettit, P. (2011). *Group Agency: The Possiblity, Design, and Status of Corporate Agents*. Oxford: Oxford University Press.

Macdonald, K., & Macdonald, T. (2010). Democracy in a Pluralist Global Order: Corporate Power and Stakeholder Representation. *Ethics & International Affairs*, 24 (1): 19–43.

Massey, D. (2004). Geographies of Responsibility. *Geografiska Annaler*, 86 B (1): 5–18.

Mena, S., & Palazzo, G. (2012). Input and Output Legitimacy of Multi-Stakeholder Initiatives. *Business Ethics Quarterly*, 22 (3): 527–556.

Milligan, C., & Wiles, J. (2010). Landscapes of care. *Progress in Human Geography*, 34 (6): 736–754.

Myers, N. (2015). *Rendering Life Molecular: Modeling Proteins and Making Scientists in the Twenty-First Century Life Sciences*. Durham: Duke University Press.

New, S. (2004). The Ethical Supply Chain. New & Westbrook (eds.). *Understanding Supply Chains: Concepts, Critiques, & Futures*. Oxford: Oxford University Press, 253–280.

Nicolini, D. (2012). *Practice Theory, Work & Organization: An Introduction*. Oxford: Oxford University Press.

Nussbaum, M. C. (2001). *Upheavals of Thought: The Intelligence of Emotions*. Cambridge: Cambridge University Press.

O'Neill, O. (2000). *Bounds of Justice*. Cambridge: Cambridge University Press.

Oosterlaken, I. (2011). Inserting Technology in the Relational Ontology of Sen's Capability Approach. *Journal of Human Development and Capabilities*, 12 (3): 425–432.

Ostrom, E. (1990). *Governing the Commons: The Evolution of Institutions for Collective Action*. New York: Cambridge University Press.

Palmer, D. E. & Stoll, M. L. (2011). Moving toward a More Caring Stakeholder Theory: Global Business Ethics in Dialogue with the Feminist Ethics of Care. In: M. Hamington & M. Sander-Staudt (eds.), *Applying Care Ethics to Business: Issues in Business Ethics*, Vol. 34. Dordrecht: Springer, 93–110.

Pettersen, T. (2011). The Ethics of Care: Normative Structures and Empirical Implications. *Health Care Analysis: HCA: Journal of Health Philosophy and Policy*, 19 (1): 51–64.

Pettit, P. (2007). Responsibility Incorporated. *Ethics*, 117: 171–201.

Ponte, S., & Daugbjerg, C. (2015). Biofuel Sustainability and the Formation of Transnational Hybrid Governance. *Environmental Politics*, 24 (1): 96–114.

Power, D. (2005). Supply Chain Management Integration and Implementation: A Literature Review. *Supply Chain Management: An International Journal*, 10 (4): 252–263.

Puig de la Bellacasa, M. (2017). *Matters of Care: Speculative Ethics in More Than Human Worlds*. Minneapolis & London: University of Minnesota Press.

Rawls, J. (1999 [1971]). *Theory of Justice*. Oxford: Oxford University Press.

Raz, J. (1989). Liberating Duties. *Law and Philosophy*, 8 (1): 3–21.

Reinecke, J., & Ansari, S. (2015). What Is a "Fair" Price? Ethics as Sensemaking. *Organization Science*, 26 (3): 867–888.

Ruddick, S. (1998). Care as Labor and Relationship. In: Halfon & Haber (eds.), *Norms and Values: Essays on the Work of Virginia Held*. Lanham, MD: Rowman & Littlefield.

Sabeel Rahman, K. (2016). *Democracy against Domination*. Oxford: Oxford University Press.

Sayer, A. (2011). *Why Things Matter to People: Social Science, Values and Ethical Life*. Cambridge: Cambridge University Press.

Scheffler, S. (2006). Projects, Relationships and Reasons. In: Wallace, Pettit, Scheffler & Smith (eds.), *Reason and Value: Themes from the Moral Philosophy of Joseph Raz*. Oxford: Oxford University Press.

Schouten, G., Leroy, P., & Glasbergen, P. (2012). On the Deliberative Capacity of Private Multi-Stakeholder Governance: The Roundtables on Responsible Soy and Sustainable Palm Oil. *Ecological Economics*, 83: 42–50.

Sciaraffa, S. (2011). Identification, Meaning, and the Normativity of Social Roles. *European Journal of Philosophy*, 19 (1): 107–128.

Sindzingre, A. (2010). *Is the Poverty Trap a Relevant Concept? Sub-Saharan African Countries Growth Trajectories and Their Constraints*. Background Paper, Development Research Seminar, Institute of Social Studies (ISS), The Hague, 14 June.

Slote, M. (2007). *Ethics of Care and Empathy*. Abingdon & New York: Routledge.

Smith, D. H. (2017). The Global Historical and Contemporary Impacts of Voluntary Membership Associations on Human Societies. *Voluntaristics Review*, 2 (5–6): 1–125.

Smolka, A. L., De Goes, M. C., & Pino, A. (1995). The Construction of the Subject: A Persistent Question. In: Wertsch, del Rio, & Alvarez (eds.), *Sociocultural Studies of the Mind*. Cambridge: Cambridge University Press, 1–46.

Stewart, W. (2017). *Creating a Future Where All Are Valuable: A New Narrative for the Richer Countries in the World*. T20 Vision Brief, 8 May. www.g20-insights.org/policy_briefs/creating-future-valuablenew-narrative-richer-countries-world/

Thompson, J. D. (1967). *Organizations in Action*. New York: McGraw-Hill.

Timmermann, C., & Félix, G. F. (2015). Agroecology as a Vehicle for Contributive Justice. *Agriculture and Human Values*, 32 (3): 523–538.

Tolhurst, C. (2001). It All Gets Down to Saving the Bottom Line. *The Australian Financial Review*, Special Report on Supply Chain Management, 2: 10.

Tronto, J. (2010). Creating Caring Institutions: Politics, Plurality, and Purpose. *Ethics and Social Welfare*, 4 (2): 158–171.

Tsing, A. L. (2015). *The Mushroom at the End of the World*. Princeton, NJ, & Oxford: Princeton University Press.

Utting, P. (2002). Regulating Business Via Multistakeholder Initiatives: A Preliminary Assessment. In: NGLS Development Dossier (ed.), *Voluntary Approaches to Corporate Responsibility: Readings and a Resource Guide*. New York: UN Non-Governmental Liaison Service 61–130.

Williams, G. (2006) 'Infrastructures of Responsibility': The Moral Tasks of Institutions. *Journal of Applied Philosophy*, 23 (2): 207–221.

Williams, G. J. (2019). Regulation Enables: Corporate Agency and Practices of Responsibility. *Journal of Business Ethics*, 154: 989–1002.

Yeoman, R. (2014). Conceptualising Meaningful Work as a Fundamental Human Need. *Journal of Business Ethics*, 125 (2): 235–251.

Yeoman, R., & Mueller Santos, M. (2019). Global Value Chains, Reputation, and Social Cooperation. In. Deephouse, Gardberg & Newburry (eds.). *Global Aspects of Reputation and Strategic Management. Research in Global Strategic Management*, Vol. 18. Emerald Publishing, 69–91.

Young, I. M. (2011). *Responsibility for Justice*. Oxford: Oxford University Press.

Zerilli, L. M. G. (2016). *A Democratic Theory of Judgment*. Chicago & London: University of Chicago Press.

6 A Philosophy of Ethical Organising

Justice, Capabilities, Meaningfulness

Capability Justice

People make organisations to fulfil the abundant purposes that imbue their lives and work with a sense of meaning and significance. When motivated by the sustainability imperative, people use their capability for ethical world-building to congregate beings and things into relational ensembles for the purpose of life value creation. As constituent elements of associational ecosystems, these ensembles are located at multiple scales, often significantly impacting the lives of participants and the condition of the beings and things that matter to them. I develop a social constructivist account of organising, in which the capability for ethical world-building is subject to capability justice. Capability justice requires that each person, as a self-determining, interdependent, and vulnerable being, be entitled to a contributive share in determining the means and ends of ethical world-building, and securing them the status as co-authorities in judging between constructed worlds.[1]

The social architecture of meaningfulness and mutuality provides the relational underpinnings, institutional patterning, interactive processes, and ethical standpoint for converting a general capacity for organising into a human capability for ethical world-building: 'organisations are sites of continuously changing human action and organization is the making of form, the patterned unfolding of human action' (Tsoukas and Chia, 2002: 577). Social constructivism, consistent with ethical organising, involves maintaining organisations as collective moral agents, where such organisations are invested with the organisational capabilities for life value creation. Young's (2011) account of structural injustice specifies our responsibility to contribute to the social processes that construct life value organisations that are capable of reforming background conditions and advance organisational models for production, distribution, and investment, consistent with the sustainability imperative. Capability justice therefore involves evaluating the distribution of individual capabilities for functioning, for example, using Nussbaum's (2011) list of central human capabilities, which she describes as entitlements. An ethical assessment of capability distribution also requires an evaluation of the structural and processual circumstances under which organisations connect individual and collective capabilities to organisational capabilities. Two conditions must be met if such connections are to be consistent with the meta-values of meaningfulness and mutuality: firstly, collective action is structured by the necessary goods of autonomy, freedom, and dignity, and, secondly, participation contributes to the development of life capabilities, specifically to the human capabilities for meaning-making and our status as co-authorities as meaning-makers, upon which prospects for experiencing meaningfulness depend (Yeoman, 2014).

I examine what this implies for justice in the social construction of ethical worlds, understood as habitations for relational ensembles of morally valuable beings and things, or those people, other beings, natural ecosystems, artefacts, organisations, practices, concepts, narratives, and more that pattern lives with meaning and purpose. A synthesis of meaningfulness and mutuality supplies people engaged in the social construction of collective moral agents with normative design elements, including a self-identity as co-authorities in meaning-making, processes for ethically desirable social interactions, and relational values of fairness, care, and flourishing. In comparing worlds, the value of meaningfulness provides practical reasoning with a basis for judging what value is worth creating and how well we are doing to take care of morally valuable beings and things.

Worlds, constructed as ethical worlds, are built through the work of care, involving collaborative work that is a common good of the life value organisation. Such work extends beyond the boundaries of single organisations and demands whole system capabilities operating intra- and inter-organisationally. This makes the capability for ethical world-building a type of meta-capability, connecting individual, collective, and organisational capabilities into a multi-scalar system of capabilities. In Sen's and Nussbaum's capability approaches, capabilities are features of the individual that she chooses to activate or not, depending upon the functionings she considers necessary for a life worth living.[2] To these, scholars have added collective capabilities in order to capture how our individual capabilities are dependent upon social belongings and groups. In organisational theory, organisational capabilities are derived from resource-based theories of the firm (Nelson and Winter, 1982), which describe the micro-level elements of distinctive strategic capabilities that provide organisations with competitive advantage. More recently, organisational capabilities have become identified with the general features of sustainable business models and include the cultural and deliberative capabilities needed to organise multi-stakeholder partnerships and collaborative governance systems.

People construct organisational capabilities using their individual and collective capabilities. But how their capability agency is activated and for what purpose must meet an ethical threshold, described by Sen (2009) as those beings and doings constituting a life we have reason to value. A life worth living, or a meaningful life, specifies the terms under which it is legitimate for life value organisations to ask their members to bring their individual and collective capabilities to bear upon the formation of organisational capabilities. Furthermore, organisational capabilities (dynamic, operational, integrative) are not simply aggregations of individual capabilities, where people can be treated as interchangeable units of human capital. Rather, people have interests in contributing their capabilities to creating organisations as collective moral agents that are fit to be held responsible and to do so in non-alienating and non-dominating ways that are expressive of their dignity as particular persons with lives of their own to lead. This means that a philosophy of ethical organising requires an account of justice in the social interactions through which people contribute to constructing the capabilities of life value organisations.

Justice demands that we are afforded agency freedom to join our capabilities to organisations that are worthy of our attachments and contributions because they are collective moral agents. The relevant agency freedom involved in our freedom to connect individual to organisational capabilities is captured by 'navigational agency', or what Claassen describes as 'the ability to move freely between social practices' (Claassen, 2018, loc. 349), which he distinguishes from 'participational agency', or 'the ability of an agent to make a move within a social practice'. Claassen says that navigational agency includes being able to enter and exit, resolve conflicts and tensions, reform, and create social practices (loc. 349). We require justice to protect our entitlements to navigational agency. We need both navigational and participational agency freedom if we are to realise our human capability for ethical world-building. When creating life value organisations, these two kinds of agency enable us to gather ensembles of beings and things into a multi-scalar system of capabilities and to live ourselves among such congregations—revising, repairing, and renewing these, according to what is needed to fulfil our responsibilities of care.

Social Constructivism and Justice

Ethical world-building implicates people and other valuable things in the collaborative work of creating and maintaining organisations over their life course. I draw upon social constructivism to develop a theoretical account of what is involved when people build ethical worlds. Constructivism is a general meta-ethical theory about the nature of value in the world. I adapt Street's (2010) distinction between a 'proceduralist characterization' of constructivism, and a 'practical standpoint characterization' (p. 363). Street (2010) argues that what lies at the core of constructivism is 'the point of view of a valuing creature' (p. 366), who possesses an 'evaluative standpoint on the world' (p. 366). In developing an account of ethical organising, I take the practical standpoint of the valuing creature but also recognise that their standpoint is enabled by their participation in procedures and practices, which must be judged by participants as conforming to normative criteria, such as fairness, care, and flourishing. Valuing creatures must be equipped with the normative tools for developing a practical standpoint, and these are provided by the social architecture of meaningfulness and mutuality.

In the development of organisations, Buckley (2013) argues that constructivism can be used as an ethical tool for bringing normative resources to bear upon concrete action contexts: 'humans construct normative principles to solve problems we collectively face' (p. 698). Life value organisations are constructed as collective moral agents by people who enjoy the 'free association of free human beings' (Marx and Engels, Communist Manifesto).[3] In creating life value organisations, the social architecture of meaningfulness and mutuality specifies the organisational design elements necessary for ensuring that, in the social processes of meaning-making, people experience the status and capabilities for being meaning-makers, exercised in constructivist activities that are structured by the goods of meaningfulness, or freedom as non-domination, autonomy as non-alienation, and being treated as dignified persons. These goods of meaningfulness render interpretive differences productive when people engage in the collaborative work needed to address matters of common concern, making it more likely that people experience collaborative work as meaningful work. The normative features of mutual organisation, such as voice and purposing, facilitate the take-up of collectively endorsed meanings into judging as thinking and feeling, thereby providing the interactive pathways by which the value of meaningfulness can be incorporated into practical reasoning at different scales of organising, from the group to the system.

In order to activate their capability for ethical world-building, the interactions, practices, and processes that people use to construct life organisations must be just. Justice in the social construction of a system of multi-scalar capabilities is concerned with questions of: *for what*—organising is directed at producing the common goods we need to lead lives we have reason to value, within planetary boundaries; *by whom*—organising is inclusive of all self-determining beings with moral agency; and *by what means*—organising requires normatively desirable collective action, structured by the goods of meaningfulness. O'Neill (1996) says that practical reasoning, in the midst of acting, involves seeing people as 'the 'agents of construction' or 'builders', whose abilities determine what they can build out of the ethical materials available to them (p. 62). In constructivist practical reasoning, reasons must be followable by those who collaborate to build a plan of reason, which harnesses available ethical materials towards collectively determined ends: 'To construct is only to reason with all the possible solidity from available beginnings, using available and followable methods to reach attainable and sustainable conclusions for relevant audiences' (p. 63). Agents of construction must be meaning-makers, bringing meanings, values, and reasons into collective deliberations concerning what must be done to solve the problems implicated in particular action contexts. Thus, constructivist practical reasoning is a form of ethical work to which capability justice applies, so that all those who have a responsibility and entitlement to contribute to world-building are equipped to be agents of construction, capable of bringing reason to bear upon specific problems, where reasoning involves judging as thinking and feeling.

O'Neill (1996) argues that world-builders must attend to the intelligibility of the ends of action, as well as the virtues that are the sources of action (pp. 66–67). Specific considerations include the 'scope of ethical consideration' (p. 64) or 'whom or what do particular agents have grounds to include within the scope of their practical reasoning and of their ethical consideration?' (p. 65). World-builders must decide who is involved in construction, how they will construct, what construction aims at, and what values organise the change involved in construction. Hay (2016) describes social construction as 'a profoundly normative mode of political inquiry that seeks to discern, interrogate and elucidate the contingency of social, political and economic change' (p. 520). Such an inquiry must elicit a critical evaluation of how corporate power interprets the meanings of values and concepts that construct background conditions. Koch Industries, for example, grounds its world-building in Charles Koch's philosophy of Market Based Management that adapts Deming's continuous improvement and personal autonomy under a set of principles, the first of which is integrity (Leonard, 2019). However, integrity is understand by Koch as the projection of individual reputation, incentivising people to prioritise their reputational status ahead of adherence to regulations. Although Koch Industries demands total compliance with regulations, Leonard (2019) argues that the private power of Koch Industries has enabled the organisation to influence government and shape the regulatory background to its advantage.

We create a collective moral agent by using the relational processes of social construction to maintain an independent normative reality, with which we interact as self-determining beings, who are simultaneously vulnerable and capable. The sustainability imperative requires that an organisation's independent normative reality must be directed to the achievement of morally desirable ends that are consistent with life value creation, through means that involve all those affected by the organisation's activities. A collective moral agent is worthy of the interactions of its members. Koch Industries transgresses this core feature of collective moral agency, because it excludes those who are affected by its activities from having an influence upon the social construction of its normative reality and admits no accountability structures and procedures that would sensitise the organisation to its social responsibilities.

What is missing in cases such as Koch Industries is a concept of life value creation, understood as provisioning societies with common goods that benefit all members and produced by those members through the complex contributions they make to building ethical worlds. A commitment to caring about the common good entails a 'political bond' whereby 'we give the interests of our fellow citizens a certain status in our practical reasoning' (Hussein, 2018). The common good indicates a particular kind of obligation to care that is derived from a certain relationship we have to others because of our shared concern for something that matters to both of us.

To solve problems associated with looking after the objects implicated in matters of shared concern, people must be invested with constructivist agency, and become world-builders who are equipped to harness meanings, understanding, and knowledge in intelligible, inclusive, and actionable purposes and plans. This also allows them to have a share in defining the background rules, structures, and processes that determine how they do their world-building, under what constraints and opportunities, through what kinds of relational encounters, and directed at what purposes. Buckley (2013) argues that the behaviour of organisational members are channelled by the organisation's teleological structure, represented by its purposes. Onuf (2016) says that constructivism involves three cognitive operations: simplifying sensory inputs into parts and then reconstructing them into wholes; using judgement and imagination to relate ideas, meanings, symbols to one another, and then representing them as objects; and adjusting these objects to human scale, so that they can be put into use. Where objectives are derived from the sustainability imperative and incorporated in a life value model, the organisation establishes a normative reality in which these cognitive capacities facilitate ethical world-building, ensuring that social construction is purposed for living meaningful lives in the Anthropocene.

In ethical organising, social construction includes moral evaluation of the normative reality emerging from processes of world-building. LeBar (2008) describes a form of Aristotelian constructivism, in which procedures of construction are allied to objective normative judgements on the kinds of good lives that procedures ought to produce: 'the truth about what we have reason to do is established in the light of the aim of *living well*' (p. 12). LeBar says that this satisfies our need for objectivity by providing us with an 'objectivity worth having' (p. 26), or one that provides normative content to questions of what is good for self, others, and objects. By participating in social cooperation, we become part of the good for others, and they become part of our good: 'stakeholders, human groups or individuals or institutions, are interdependent directly or indirectly in pursuing their complex of purposes even though their ethical convictions of a good or a meaningful life may differ' (Nathan, 2014: 13). Social construction of good lives therefore involves a dynamic interaction between self and others, in which 'the person blossoms through the recognition of the other as a whole' (Tzitzis, 1999). In ethical organising, this relational dynamic is instituted through the policies, practices, and culture of the organisation's normative reality that is manifested at vertical levels from the individual to the group to the system, and at horizontal levels in circles of moral concern that expand to include even those distant communities and marginalised participants whose lives are impacted by the activities of the organisation.

Seeing Ourselves as World-Builders

Justice is achieved in social constructivism when all those who are affected by the activities of the organisation are entitled to contribute to its organising and are equipped with the relevant status and capabilities for realising their entitlement. The contributions of individual moral agents to the practical reasoning needed for ethical world-building are mediated through a normative nexus of self, others, and objects. Bagnoli (2013) specifies an objectivist account of practical reasoning, in which 'practical reason is both discursive and emotional' (p. 155). Two aspects of Bagnoli's (2013) account are relevant to a constructivist account of ethical world-building: firstly, how we see ourselves as moral agents and, secondly, how knowledge is mediated by our encounters with others and objects in practical situations.

With respect to self-conception, the emotional dimension of practical reasoning directs us to moral self-regard, where we see ourselves as a moral agent with the capacity for self-legislation, and extend this to others similarly endowed. With respect to knowledge, Bagnoli (2013) identifies the objective dimension of practical knowledge with 'knowledge by principles', where the moral task is 'to establish a constitutive relation between knowledge of oneself as a practical subject and knowledge about what one ought to do' (p. 154). This implies that knowledge is dependent upon our self-conception, or 'an emotional mode of practical knowledge of oneself as an agent' (p. 155), where such knowledge 'arises out of the practical problems of coordination that face agents as such' (p. 1). This connection between self and coordinated action is mediated by objects, such that the goodness of objects is not just discovered but is generated through practical reasoning between self-legislating agents who jointly make 'the ends of action worthy of choice' (p. 6).

Bagnoli (2013) argues that a dialogical interpretation of self-legislation requires a moral sensibility, linking the agent and her action via an emotional orientation to herself, others, and objects that is marked by mutual respect. The result is practical knowledge constituted by a 'complex sort of objectivity' (p. 155), in which moral agents are judged to be capable of authorising action, provided that they are not 'manipulated, interfered with, obstructed, compelled, coerced or impeded' (p. 163).

When these conditions are in place, our agential capacity to authorise actions provides a justificatory basis for responsibility: 'the authority one exercises in one's actions in so far as one claims responsibility for it' (p. 164). Thus, an action becomes our own to the extent that we are prepared to acknowledge our responsibility for its origins, processes, and consequences. Where our concern is structural injustice, responsibilities extend to those with whom our connection is indirect and mediated by distance, time, culture, power, and materiality. This means that collective moral agents are tasked with increasing our moral sensitivity to those with whom we are indirectly connected in systems of social cooperation, thereby making us more willing to accept responsibility for how our actions affect their lives.

Constructing Basic Structures

Ethical organising requires justice in the processes of social construction that create the institutional infrastructure for social cooperation. This includes creating associational ecosystems of collective moral agents at multiple scales of organising, depending on the nature of the problem. Given the proliferation of boundary-transgressing, interconnected challenges, but also the fragmented organisational and governance tools at our disposal, planetary-scale social cooperation can be thought of as constructed from varieties of basic structures. These emerge from the ground up and are interlinked at transnational scales of organising (see Macdonald and Macdonald, 2010). In this way, each associational ecosystem is underpinned by a basic structure specific to its particular requirements, which interacts with other basic structures operating at the national and international levels. In these interlocking associational ecosystems, life value organisations, such as transnational corporations, can be considered to be agents of justice or collective moral agents that are capable of being administrators of justice. O'Neill (2004) argues that, especially when states are weak, transnational corporations and non-governmental organisations are agents of justice and their agency depends upon their members investing them with institutional capabilities: 'the fact that institutional capabilities exist only with the support and participation of individuals does not mean that institutions have no moral obligations' (p. 249).

In specifying the principles of justice to be applied to the basic structure, Rawls (1999 [1971]) argues that the fabric of international institutions does not constitute a basic structure because it has a limited impact upon opportunities to shape conceptions of living. However, given the known facts regarding climate change, biodiversity collapse, inequalities engendered by globalisation, and technological shifts, the absence of a global basic structure poses a severe risk to being able to form viable forms of life, consistent with capability justice. In developing a republican view of global governance, Thomas (2015) applies the concern for *res publica*, or the commonwealth, to the global common good, understood as 'particular substantive standards or values, pointing to specific ideals of justice or the realisation of political community' (p. 573). He argues that the potential for domination in the international sphere makes producing a global common good a precondition for achieving freedom as non-domination. The relevant responsible organisations include states, corporations, international institutions, civil society organisations, and informal collectives.

Efforts to construct just social cooperation from this organisational diversity, especially in the present times of economic nationalism and resistance to neo-liberal forms of globalisation, have yielded inconsistent outcomes. Given this, I am not proposing that we underpin planetary-scale social cooperation with a planet-spanning basic structure. Rather, we can draw from the idea of a pluriversal world (Escobar, 2017) by adopting a pluriversal perspective upon diverse basic structures, using ethical social construction to surface from within diverse worlds their latent potentials and emergent properties of social cooperation, such as sources of meanings, values, knowledge, learning, and trust. Indeed, undertaking such a critical audit is vital. James (2009) argues that when we degrade value-creating assets, such as social trust, values are subject to catastrophic collapse, leading to the decline of social and economic systems. Moral features of capitalist economies depend upon 'a delicate social infrastructure', which are 'intrinsically related to a capacity for empathy or sympathy, the capacity to put oneself in the perspective of another when contemplating a business transaction' (loc. 1888). We can establish reserves of trust and empathy across worlds by encouraging pluriversal diversity of economic organisation that enables people to express the meanings and values of what matters to them. For this, people need to experience themselves as world-builders, authorised and equipped with the capability for ethical world-building and make their contribution to creating the pluriverse (see Ehrnström-Fuentes, 2016).

A pluriversal perspective imagines how assemblies of beings and things may be gathered into life value organisations, with basic structures interconnecting them into particular associational ecosystems, depending upon what problems they have responsibilities to solve. The social cooperation this implies must be unforced. Unforced cooperation is characterised by fair terms of exchange and reciprocity to which people consent, as well as other features of a moral psychology associated with the mutuality of social relations. With this in mind, Rawls (1999) identifies the importance of ethical constraints upon collective action, such as human rights: 'What have come to be called human rights are recognized as necessary conditions of any system of social cooperation. When they are regularly violated, we have command by force, a slave system, and no cooperation of any kind' (p. 68). But where there is no basic structure, social cooperation is vulnerable to injustice, coercion, domination, and other harms. In other words, a basic structure must be established, if justice in social cooperation is to be realised. However, if it is to be just, the social interactions by which people construct such a basic structure must themselves be just. Abizadeh (2007) argues that social cooperation is fair when it is 'a fair or just system of social interaction' (p. 330). Social interactions marked by domination, fear, alienation, distrust, and exploitation cannot produce fair social cooperation.

Abizadeh (2007) makes the basic structure 'the indispensable means by which a system of social coordination or interaction could become a fair system of social cooperation' (p. 329). Hence, justice applies not merely to social interaction per se but more precisely to the *processes* of unfolding collective action that exist prior to the basic structure, through which the basic structure comes into being. We are responsible for making the social processes through which we interact to ensure social cooperation is just. Fulfilling such responsibilities depends upon inclusive practices and capability justice that equip each person to become involved in the articulation, interpretation, assessment, and selection of meanings and values, from which we construct the institutions and practices of basic structures that make ethical worlds possible.

Meaning-making and the translation of meanings into narratives for motivating ethical world-building is a fragile undertaking. Meanings can be manipulated or appropriated by powerful elites; people can voluntarily alienate their meaning-making capacities to avoid the personal efforts demanded by public meaning-making; relationships based on domination can result in meanings being exploited or silenced. Thus, the social interactions needed for organisational meaning-making can be marked by unfairness, even before a basic structure has been established. The institutions of the basic structure are fair when they foster inclusive participation procedures in which people, in their role as meaning-makers, are able to amend and authorize the values, meaning, and rules governing collective action. The social processes for world-building are also those by which people integrate the objective and subjective dimensions of meaningfulness. However, consistent with the value of meaningfulness, requiring people to engage in such processes is legitimate only when the activities involved pass the tests of autonomy, dignity, and freedom. When social interaction is just, we will have established the legitimate basis for requiring us to make our contribution to social cooperation because, by so doing, we enhance not only the diverse sources of meanings needed for world-building but also the common-pool resource of public meanings that we draw upon to craft meaningful lives and work.

Contesting Ethical Worlds

The philosophy of ethical organising applies the social architecture of meaningfulness and mutuality to the collective action needed for ethical world-building. Social cooperation consists of a moral community, or society of meaning-makers (Chapter 7) that incorporates public meaningfulness into deliberation, framed by agonistic republicanism as responsible difference-making and constructive conflict. Havercroft and Duvall (2017) describe *agonistic constructivists* as those 'who see norms as principles and standards constantly open to generation, critique, and renewal through practices of contestation at all scales of human life from the local to the global' (p. 157). By incorporating responsible difference-making and constructive conflict into ethical constructivism, people can use their normative agency to critically evaluate justice in the social processes of world-building. In ethical organising, world-builders situated in public, private, and civic organisations join together to act upon their concern for valuable beings and things and to create the common goods needed for life value. This generates a significant degree of hybrid organising that highlights the fundamental question posed by *synoikismos*, or how should we live together?

Answering this question involves adopting an ethical constructivist approach to processes of organising that produce a pluriverse of ethical worlds, through which all can express their status as co-authorities in the realm of value, become invested with meaning-making capabilities, and therefore acquire the resources for crafting meaningful lives that are a source of life value. This includes participating in the collective self-determination of the framing rules and social practices of the ethical worlds in which they are members together. Karagiannis and Wagner (2008) develop the concept of synagonism, arguing that agonistic pluralism needs to be formulated using 'considerations in economics about enhancing the common good, and from the implications about the socially structured nature of conflict in the antagonist strand of thinking' (p. 332).

Synagonism is 'the respectful struggle of one against another, bound by rules larger than the struggle, in view of excellence winning for the benefit of the city' (p. 324), but can refer to any social entity where struggle and cooperation coexist. *Syn* refers to co-/with/acting or considered together, indicating a form of co-struggle that makes conflict beneficial by joining it to some substantive notion of the good. Thus, the objective of synagonism is to stimulate 'conflict oriented thought', whilst maintaining 'a substantive orientation that is seen as identifiable in the meanings the actors attach to the conflict' (p. 333). People engaged in this kind of competition foster a shared striving for mutual excellence. Synagonism provides a way to think about how to construct planetary-scale social cooperation, where respectful struggle, constructive conflict, and desire for mutual excellence provide the relational basis for interconnecting pluriversal worlds through the creation of ground-up narratives, institutions, and procedures. As gatherings of morally valuable beings and things, pluriversal worlds can be brought to bear upon matters of common concern, using a struggle for mutual excellence to make productive the tensions between co-operation and competition.

Taking a multi-level view of global organising, Wiener (2016) develops a critical constructivist approach to international relations that uses contestation as a meaning-generating tool to close legitimacy gaps. Wiener (2016) describes a cycle of contestation in which three phases of norm constituting, negotiating, and implementing operate over three scales of global governance (micro, meso, and macro). Three normative practices of habitual, cultural, and formal validation, or 'legal validity, social recognition and cultural validation', operate within this cycle (p. 22). However, normative agency, or the capability to engage in the contestation and negotiation of governing norms, is unevenly distributed across these norm implementation phases, as well as at different scales. This means that nested scales of collective action constrain or enable the normative agency by which people construct the meanings that they carry into contestation over normative practices. In her examination of the 1965 Turbot War between Canadian and European actors, Wiener shows that contestation and conflict provided the basis for the normative work needed to establish 'fairer fisheries governance' ('right to fish' versus 'sustainable fisheries') (p. 33). Canadian actors focussed on the validity of sustainability norms, and this clashed with the emphasis that European actors put on regulatory norms and quotas. However, the European emphasis on justification by legal validity using international law was moderated by the need to reflect more local, culturally grounded concerns: 'this justification was informed by the individual background experience of the Galician fishing folk losing out on European quotas as a result of Spanish EU accession in 1986' (p. 31). Conflict settlement required an interrelational process of norm-change that drew upon shared meaning-sources created from within the process of conflict itself.

In a different example of contestation and difference, Wallis and Richmond (2017) use constructivism to engage critically with peacebuilding, by tracking the benefits of moving from the construction of a liberal peace to the construction of a hybrid peace. Liberal peacebuilding relies upon 'constructivist models of normative diffusion or norm cascades from a liberal and metropolitan core to dependent peripheries' (p. 423). This kind of peace is accused of being elite-driven, technocratic, and institution-focussed, and thereby failing to establish an inclusive and legitimate basis for sustainable peace at the local level. By contrast, hybrid peace-building is 'an intersubjective mediation between local and international scales and norms, institutions, law, right, needs and interests, depending on both power and legitimacy' (p. 426). It focusses on the everyday experiences of those who live with conflict, including how peace/conflict is interpreted and communicated through narratives, meanings, identities, and practices, where processes of communication are often prescribed by states, NGOs, and international agencies. For example, a Timor-Leste case of liberal peace-building failed to address women's rights and domestic abuse because the language of domestic abuse did not resonate with communities where there was no distinction between the public/private and no concept of human rights. When Timorese partners were recruited to help design peace-building, liberal peace-builders were advised to refocus their campaign on local meanings that connected women and the land: 'women give life; you should respect them; they guarantee your fertility and prosperity' (p. 431). However, Wallis and Richmond (2017) warn against critical peace-builders using instrumental extraction of local knowledge, including using concepts, such as 'local resilience', to displace the responsibility for peace-building work onto local communities. Hybrid peace-building views peace-building from the perspective of people in marginalised, subaltern positions and can be brought into ground-up world-building to illuminate how power disables vulnerable populations and to sensitise world-builders to diverse understandings of human well-being and meaning.

A Capability for Ethical World-Building

People need capabilities to realise their normative agency in world-building and to engage in ethical social constructivism that permits a wide variety of organising, at multiple scales and involving productive contestation and difference-making. Organisations that are worthy of being recognised as collective moral agents depend upon the collaborative work of their members to maintain their moral status and invest them with organisational capabilities to act responsibly. To undertake such work, people need to be equipped with the capability for ethical world-building that has the structure of a human capability for functioning. This is secured by using the social architecture of meaningfulness and mutuality to convert the general capacity for organising into the human capability for ethical world-building.

To create a pluriverse of ethical worlds, mutually intertwined through diverse basic structures expressing different conceptions of living, people must have the ability to partake of whole system capabilities, or of an infrastructure of multi-scalar capabilities operating at the individual, collective, and organisational levels. I draw upon the human capabilities for functioning literature and the organisational capabilities literature to specify the connections between individual, collective, and organisational capabilities. Collective moral agents depend upon people who are equipped with individual and collective human capabilities for functioning, and who can therefore create the organisational capabilities needed for ethical organising. Sen (1987) critiques behavioural models in economics that focus upon value monism, or the view that there is only one fundamental (intrinsic) value, resulting in an 'engineering approach' to economics dominating over approaches based upon 'the ethics-related view of motivation' (p. 4). Van Staveren (2001) argues that this results in economic rationality 'missing ethical capabilities' (p. 20) of 'commitment, emotional attachment, deliberation and human interaction' (p. 40). I argue for a system of multi-scalar capabilities that connects individual, collective, and organisational capabilities to what capability justice requires to realise a human capability for ethical world-building, where world-building involves just processes of social construction. The relevant kinds of organisational capabilities for ethical organising include: the strategic search for models of sustainable organising; designing practices to involve stakeholders in shaping the framing rules of collective action; creating an ethos of respect for difference and diversity; structuring common work for the goods of meaningfulness; and fostering evaluative mechanisms to track mutuality as fairness, care, and flourishing. These elements constitute a collective moral agent that is worthy of its members' interactions and contributions because it possesses organisational capabilities for sensitising people to one another as members of a moral community, where they come to see others as equally real, with interests and claims of their own (cf. Wallace, 2019).

Individual Capabilities

Ethical organising gathers together valuable objects—both human and non-human—into associational ecosystems, using a synthesis of meaningfulness and mutuality to create these as collective moral agents. The social cooperation in associational ecosystems requires joint purposes, values-sharing, boundary-crossing roles, and collaboration practices instituted through a division of labour into which members are integrated and brought into relation with one another. A whole system approach to multi-scalar capabilities starts with the person whose prospects of a life worth living are bound up with their capabilities. Sen (1999) develops a multidimensional approach to evaluating personal advantage, whereas Nussbaum (2000, 2011) provides a normative basis for evaluating the attributes of human flourishing. Sen argues that being human consists of both agency (what we can do) and well-being (what we can be) but that welfarism neglects the agency dimensions of persons who think, feel, evaluate, and act. Sen (1999) brings agency back into evaluations of what makes our lives go well, by making freedom dependent upon our ability to choose between the functionings, the doings and beings we want our lives to express.

This means that capabilities rather than commodities express the extent of the effective freedom (in a positive sense) that a person possesses, or 'the things a person may value doing or being' (Sen, 1999: 75). Sen (1999) specifies two aspects of freedom relevant to developing any particular capability: opportunity and process, where *opportunity* refers to the ability of the individual to achieve valued functionings, and *process* refers to the ability of individuals to demonstrate their agency in influencing processes and rules. Well-being freedom and agency freedom play a role in the value of meaningfulness, where meaningfulness depends upon moral agents having access to voice practices in order to make public claims regarding the integrations of objective value and subjective attachment that constitute the particular pattern of their life. Nussbaum (2000, 2011) develops a thicker notion of capabilities, or partial theory of capability justice. She specifies a list of human capabilities that she argues constitute the basic entitlements for a decent human life. Her normative framework arises from her concern that our freedom to choose which capabilities to turn into functionings is influenced by adaptive preferences. These preferences reflect how the ability of vulnerable people to choose is constrained by the restrictive social norms and options available to them. Converting abilities and capabilities into functionings depends upon mediating institutions and varieties of conversion factors, both individual and collective. Esquith (2010) argues that the capability approach needs to be more concerned with institutional power, involving moral assessment of the lives that people seek to lead by activating capabilities.

Nussbaum (1987) says that the task of societies is not to simply keep people alive by providing food, shelter, or paid work but to secure their capabilities for living a life worthy of a human being. Thus we do not fulfil 'perceptual needs in a mechanical way, producing a seeing eye, a hearing ear, etc' but rather 'make it possible for people to use their bodies and their senses in a truly human way' (p. 183). Giovanola (2005) argues that human beings need to be understood as '*pluralistic* entities, in whom a multiplicity of capabilities is at stake' (p. 250). Our ability to form and exercise capabilities depends on our relational connection with others, including our roles and responsibilities in structured action contexts. This means that each person is 'intrinsically related to the other members of a society' (p. 251) through an 'anthropological richness' that is echoed in the 'intrinsic diversity' of each person (p. 260). Our agency to choose between valuable modes of acting and being is related to the 'constitutive plurality', or pluri-potentiality of each person (p. 261). Our relational nature means that not only do human beings depend upon one another for cultivating innate richness, activated in lives we consider to be meaningful, but also 'the highest richness for each human being is *other human beings* and that such richness is felt in the form of a *need*' (p. 263; cf. Marx, 1844). The need we feel for relational connections to other beings and things fosters an internal variety of potential capability formation and stimulates the demand for full participation in group life. In ground-up ethical world-building, people will draw such internal resources into meaning-making and reason-giving. We must therefore attend to how members of different worlds understand their needs and aspirations and what priorities they place on wealth, happiness, and other aspects of a good life, such as respect and belonging.

Collective Capabilities

Sen makes individual capabilities for functioning, expressed in a person's capability set, necessary for leading a life we have reason to value. However, in the context of sustainability transitions, the range of lives we value and therefore the capabilities required to live them must be re-imagined, so that we are better equipped for living together in the Anthropocene. In particular, successful negotiation of the necessary system change depends upon our collective ability to construct life value organisations, using our ethical capability for world-building to connect individual, collective, and organisational capabilities. Collective capabilities operate as a bridge between individual and organisational capabilities by providing the social factors and relational ontology by which people realise their individual capabilities for functioning (Robeyns, 2005). On their own, individual capabilities do not account for the role of collectivities (Stewart, 2005), or the relationship between individuals and social structures (Ibrahim, 2006). Drawing upon Martins's (2006, 2007) examination of the meta-theoretical assumptions grounding Sen's capability approach, Smith and Seward (2009) argue for an extension of Sen's notion of capabilities and freedoms to 'an ontology of a relational society' (p. 214), where capabilities are 'the outcome of the interaction of an individual's capacities and the individual's position relative to others in society' (p. 214). We experience social structures as having an independent reality, but that are nonetheless susceptible to change and transformation through the application of human capabilities. A key link between agency and social structure are the social roles we occupy, which Smith and Seward (2009) describe as 'positioned practices', where positions include occupations, roles, tasks, duties, and practices include activities (p. 223; cf. Bhaskar, 1998). Individual capabilities are thus the product of a person's relational position in collectivities and their occupation of social roles as sets of 'sets of social relationships' (p. 232). These create the conditions for the emergence of social structures that, through a person's involvement in collective action and participation in a group, foster or inhibit capability formation.

Stewart (2005) describes group capabilities as aggregations of individual capabilities that are 'made up of individual capabilities—indeed they are the average of the capabilities (and sources of capabilities) of all the individuals in the selected groups' (p. 192). However, for Comim and Carey (2001), collective capabilities are not simply aggregations of individual capabilities but are 'those capabilities that can only be achieved socially [. . .] as a result of social interaction' (p. 17). Individual and collective capabilities exist in dynamic relationship, such that individuals depend on the social interactions of their collective belongings for expanding their capability set, and in turn collectives depend upon individuals using their human capabilities to maintain and develop the collective.

In this vein, Murphy (2014) argues that collective capabilities enable forms of freedom, such as self-determination, when such capabilities are 'exercised by individual human agents working together as part of a group or collective' (p. 323). Ibrahim (2006) defines collective capabilities as 'the newly generated functioning bundles a person obtains by virtue of his/her engagement in a collectivity that help her/him achieve the life he/she has reason to value' (p. 398). Stewart (2005) argues that the quality of the groups we belong to is an important dimension of our well-being: they shape our choices and our values, distribute resources, extend or constrain our capabilities, and therefore afford us opportunities to lead lives we have reason to value. She notes the importance of groups for the poor who need efficient organisation of collective action for provisioning in a manner that also respects their status and self-respect. Groups that generate collective capabilities include producer groups in the form of cooperatives, such as the Indian sugar mills; credit and savings groups; and self-organisation to take care of natural resources. For example, a cluster of large and small tanneries in Tamil Nadu addressed a pollution crisis by constructing collectively owned treatment plants. This associational ecosystem of tanneries realised a collective capability for world-building by creating inter-organisational capabilities for institutional design, values, and processes for cooperation and market development (see Stewart, 2005). The individual partakes in a form of 'communal well-being', or 'the whole network of social conditions that enable human individuals and groups to flourish and live a fully, genuinely human life' (Deneulin, 2004: 7). However, Deneulin (2004) points out that whether agency can be judged to be good or beneficial depends upon the values that are pursued (p. 2). Our individual agency freedom is enhanced when collective capabilities are structured to foster moral learning and the 'awakening of critical consciousness through the investigation of "generative themes"' (Freire, 1996), but not when we are compelled to maintain collective capabilities that advantage some individual members at great cost to others.

Agency freedom, realised through the interaction between individual and collective capabilities, is particularly relevant for understanding system-level sustainability transitions. The Multi-Level Perspective (MLP) approach to sustainability transitions is 'shot through with agency, because the trajectories and multi-level alignments are always enacted by social groups' (Fischer and Newig, 2016: 474). Sustainability transitions demand that we combine individual and collective capabilities to create capabilities for joint agency, enacted between diverse actors and intermediaries and operating at multiple scales. The dependence of human well-being on ecosystem services invites an incorporation of the capabilities approach into sustainability frameworks that brings sustainable development together with sustainable freedoms (Ballet et al., 2018). Ecosystems are conversion factors for realising human capabilities, but some realised capabilities are not consistent with sustainable development, so a critical standpoint is needed to evaluate the consequences of capability formation.

This standpoint is provided by the value of meaningfulness. A meaningful life that is richly endowed with human capabilities for functioning incorporates the practical identity of seeing oneself as an interdependent and relational person, sustained within networks of care, and in turn a person who is responsible for caring for those beings and things that constitute the life she values. The Millennium Ecosystem Assessment defines ecosystem services as 'the benefit people obtain from ecosystems' (Millennium Ecosystem Assessment, 2005: 26). As well as benefits, a capability approach highlights negative effects of degraded ecosystem services that are weakened in their ability to act as conversion factors for capability formation and realisation of functionings. Ballet et al. (2018) argue that strong sustainability requires a dynamic capability approach that takes into account how constitutively relational contextual factors shape capabilities as causal powers. Drawing upon Sen (2006), they connect capabilities to sustainable ecosystem services via identity and aspirations. Sen argues that people have multiple identities and that, even though social relations act as a constraint on identity formation, people still possess considerable freedom to choose their identities. When people highly value ecosystem services, they incorporate these into their identities in ways that motivate how they treat ecosystems. Having an identity rooted in valuable beings and things is therefore an important element of the capabilities by which we realise our agency freedom to act responsibly towards what we value. However, limits to individual agency means that we need to join with others in accessing collective capabilities and using them to create the organisational capabilities necessary for sustainable transitions.

Organisational Capabilities

In a philosophy of ethical organising, capability justice is concerned with our equal access to the capability for ethical world-building. We build worlds through intrinsically life-valuable, or meaningful, work by which we contribute to the creation of life goods, and among those life goods are the interior abundance of human capabilities that is consistent with living a good life within planetary boundaries. O' Neill et al. (2018) quantify the challenges of securing basic human development for all, concluding that we have insufficient resources for such an objective, and that the sustainable development goals (SDGs) will have to move away from economic growth towards an 'economic model where the goal is sustainable and equitable human well-being' (p. 93). In a review of responses to climate change, Gillard et al. (2016) argue that incremental adjustments are no longer sufficient for effective climate change mitigation and that transformative approaches to climate change governance require interconnected personal, practical, and political processes. Drawing upon a complex systems view, they show that transitioning of socio-technical systems demands a governance toolkit, consisting of strategic, tactical, operational, and reflexive elements which enable people to combine *what* the transition is towards (business model approach) with *who* determines the framing rules and parameters for transition pathways (democratic system approach). Gillard et al. (2016) argue that this means turning away from 'managerialist forms of governance' to democratic engagement, such as deliberative collaborative governance, by incorporating into just transitioning the experience, knowledge, and craft of multiple participants, taking into consideration their capacity to promote or resist transformational change.

In the Anthropocene, we need to construct new meanings for our beings and doings in lives we have reason to value that will also inform pathways for connecting our individual and collective capabilities to organisational capabilities. Derived from the resource-based view of the firm, organisational capabilities 'entail the capacity to carry out activities in a practised and patterned manner' (Schilke et al., 2018: 398; see Teece, 2007). Organisational capabilities are a general 'capacity to undertake activities' that remain latent until activated (Helfat and Raubitschek, 2018: 1393). If organisations choose to make use of them, they generate organisational competences, becoming the basis of value creation. Teece (2018) argues that organisations use dynamic capabilities to create innovative ecosystems and business models that facilitate value creation and capture. Helfat and Raubitschek (2018) show that platform leaders develop interlinked platform capabilities or 'externally-oriented integrative capabilities' to support organisational activities of 'sensing, seizing, and transforming' (p. 1392). This extends organisational capabilities beyond the organisation to inter-organisational capabilities, including innovation, environmental scanning and sensing, and integrative ecosystem orchestration. Schilke et al. (2018) proposes three types of organisational capabilities: *operational* capabilities maintain the business status quo; *dynamic* capabilities arise from innovative adaptations of the resource base; and *integrative* capabilities address the need to orchestrate system-level governance of organisational ecosystems including multiple partners. Herzog (2017) argues that inter-organisational capabilities are a kind of common good that, for the sake of the whole system, organisations have responsibilities to create and maintain.

The prospects for creating organisations as collective moral agents depends upon organisational capabilities for collective moral learning that sensitise members to values and equip them to create life value (Zollo and Winter, 2002). Organisational learning is a general-purpose dynamic capability necessary for integrative knowledge, or 'knowledge of how to integrate, different activities, capabilities, and products within a vertical chain or across vertical chains' (Helfat and Raubitschek, 2019: 964).

Beyond the organisation, members create inter-organisational capabilities (Fawcett et al., 2011) in the form of 'relational embeddedness' (Zheng et al., 2011), collective knowledge building, and joint problem-solving. At a societal level, societies advance economically when organisations are encouraged to adopt 'critical organizational capabilities', such as quality control and inventory and cost management (Khan, 2018: 47). Khan (2018) draws upon the Indian textile industry to illustrate how being able to manage different kinds of knowledge depends upon designing collective learning into organisational routines and capabilities and that the failure to do so explains the differences in productivity between firms which use similar machinery and comparable human capital to produce the same products.

The development of inter-organisational capabilities depends upon members creating common goods in associational ecosystems which convert organisational capabilities into system-level competences. This is a joint undertaking between private enterprise, public organisations, governmental institutions, and others. In ethical organising, inter-organisational capability development demands that people use their capability for ethical world-building to assemble beings and things into collective moral agents, operating at different scales and levels. Often, world-builders must draw upon the available set of co-creative, multi-stakeholder methods to generate the shared meanings, knowledge, and understanding that mobilises collective action across associational ecosystems, for the sake of caring for morally valuable purposes. Gray and Stites (2013) map business–NGO partnerships from the transactional to the transformative, ranging from short-term dyadic initiatives through to industry standard setting, policy dialogue, base-of-the-pyramid projects, and collaborative governance, involving multiple organisations. Gray and Purdy (2018) extend partnerships to communities and governments, where interdependent and interactive processes, based on shared rules, norms, and structures, constructive difference-making, mutual respect for expertise and knowledge, and joint ownership of outcomes, are necessary design features for long-term partnerships that generate collaborative governance at the system level.

However, as conceived by the mainstream management literature, processes of organisational and inter-organisational capability formation leave little room for the agency of organisational members, who are rarely afforded an opportunity to appear to one another as capable, interdependent, self-determining beings, and who are richly endowed with interior capabilities, enabling them to bring meanings and purposes into collective organising. Ethical organising seeks to account for the agency of world-builders, who construct organisations using cognitive structures or frames for imagining what is possible, where framing as 'an interaction process is a source of agency that is embedded in the everyday activities of individuals, groups, and organizations' (Purdy et al., 2019: 409).

Framing depends on meaning-making activities that originate in how participants relate to what is valuable in their lives, where values are constituted by webs of meanings. In ethical organising, these become available to be activated, augmented, and scaled through integrative social processes that participants consider to be just. Watson et al. (2017) discuss stakeholder engagement as a dynamic organisational capability that is made available for management use. They introduce value framing and systemized learning into organisational capacities that enable managers 'to navigate and harness the differences in the ways of seeing the world that exist between them and their stakeholder groups' (p. 256). However, in ethical organising, eliciting differences is legitimate only when all those affected have an opportunity to contribute their differences, to be involved in interpretation, and to have a say in how these differences and interpretations will be employed. Follett (1998 [1918]) says: 'Each must discover and contribute that which distinguishes him from others, his difference. The only use for my difference is to join it with other differences' (p. 29). Indeed, for Follett, producing and expressing our difference is almost a duty laid upon those who find themselves involved in joint activity, when she urges participants in group process to '[g]ive me your difference' (p. 33). She adds 'no member of a group which is to create can be passive. All must be active and constructively active' (p. 29) and that, in order to 'think together', then 'each man must contribute what is in him to contribute' (p. 29).

In collective moral agents, however, the duty to contribute our differences is a qualified duty that depends upon people making judgements on whether offering their difference will enable them to fulfil their responsibility to take care of valuable beings and things, or whether doing so will make them vulnerable to extraction of their knowledge or to censure of their different ways of looking at things. Managerial efforts to understand stakeholder differences must therefore include an evaluation of the extent to which those who contribute their differences have a share in determining how their differences will be used. Organisational capability development must therefore provide an ethical response to the question of, 'How do individual-level factors (such as traits, abilities or emotions) aggregate to create collective capabilities?' (Winter, 2012: 1403).

In answering this question, we need to make visible the dynamic interaction between individual, collective, and organisational capabilities that is essential for ethical organising. The organisation is dependent upon its members for maintaining its status as a morally worthy entity, and members depend upon organisational capabilities to fulfil their responsibilities for caring for valuable beings and things they have incorporated into the meaningfulness of their lives. In organisational capability formation, people appear as 'human capital' inputs (Schilke et al., 2018) or bundles of capacities to be moulded and orchestrated by managers, who are cast as the cognitive and strategic agents in processes of organising.

For example, in a study of platform-based ecosystems, Helfat and Raubitschek (2018) argue that it is platform leaders who are the architects of ecosystem design and therefore the prime responsible agents in forming organisational and inter-organisational capabilities. Neglecting the agency of employees and other stakeholders is increasingly understood to be a gaping hole in the theory, leading Schilke et al. (2018) to ask, '[W]hat is the role of employees at different levels in the organizational hierarchy for strategic change?' In a study of new product development at an Italian design firm, Salvato (2009) reveals the contribution of the mindful micro activities of individuals to the capability for product development. To understand how individual actions help form organisational capabilities, Salvato and Rerup (2011) open up the organisational black box of 'the fine-grained, multi-layered nature of routines and capabilities' (p. 469) to investigate their constituent elements, showing that organisational capabilities for managing change and innovation are created from the intentional actions of employees. Organisations harness this human agency by integrating their employees into 'high-quality relationships' and constructive dialogue that connects individual-level emotions, cognitions, and learning to the activities needed to generate dynamic capabilities (Salvato and Vassolo, 2018: 1738).

Applying the social architecture of meaningfulness and mutuality to the processes of social constructivism yields a number of ethical design features, including the society of meaning-makers (Chapter 7). This is a type of moral community that provides the relational conditions for connecting individual and collective capabilities for functioning to organisational capabilities for ethical competence. When mutual learning takes place between the organisation and the members of its moral community, this establishes the connective space for integrating individual and organisational capabilities. Tran et al. (2018) describe an interactive learning process whereby group interactions and cognitive perceptions and interpretations institutionalise new dynamic capabilities. Using a micro foundations perspective on 'capability emergence', they show that organisational capabilities are constructed from learning-by-doing, process improvements, and problem-solving over time. For example, in a study of firm–supplier relations of a European fashion company, they find that the emergence and maturation of dynamic capabilities depend upon individuals and units using conflict and difference to establish common ground. Although this 'conflict-triggered learning process' (p. 9) was destabilising, it also stimulated new capabilities as people sought solutions by bringing competing interests into social cooperation. In order to foster joint learning and collective responsiveness, participants at multiple levels deliberately selected a cooperative style to create a form of self-governance that used cooperative values as well as bargaining power to secure psychological lock-in of suppliers.

The creation of inter-organisational capabilities, grounded in the conflictual character of firm–supplier relations, stimulated managers and employees to develop new individual capabilities for dialogic engagement, in the form of a dynamic interpersonal capability (Salvato and Vassolo, 2018). This relational capability roots social cooperation in multiple perspectives through candour, inclusion, confirmation, and presentness (p. 1738). It also illuminates how the social, relational and ethical resources that people need to create organisational capabilities are frequently distributed—hidden and unrecognised—among individuals and teams, as well as externally among partners, suppliers, communities, competitors. Mutual practices that proliferate moral free spaces throughout an associational ecosystem provide relational contexts for multi-perspective formation that enables world-builders to surface and evaluate these resources. Sah and Stiglitz (1986) show how polyarchies give authority to those with knowledge who are close to the action, thereby reducing the possibility that valuable projects will be rejected as a result of social biases, wilful blindness, and other aspects of capability dysfunctions. I argue that the moral free spaces of agonistic republicanism provide the structural interconnectedness for individuals to connect their capabilities to collective and organisational capabilities. The organisation as a collective moral agent renders such resources and abilities visible through legitimate means when it institutes policies, practices, and procedures for collective determination, under relational conditions that are non-alienating, non-dominating, and dignifying.

Life Capabilities

People are not just resources to be inserted into processes of organisational capability formation but are moral and practical agents with responsibilities to co-create life value organisations as collective moral agents. When establishing the ethical resources for meaningful work and lives in the Anthropocene, this includes determining what organisational capabilities ought to be formed and what kinds of lives such organisational capabilities should support. Martins (2013) argues that the sustainability imperative requires us to define those capabilities that will enable us to prioritise 'a circular process of sustainability reproduction' over maximising utility (p. 230). McMurtry (2011) critiques Sen's capability approach for failing to specify a moral principle for distinguishing realised functionings that promote life from those that degrade life. Ethical organising requires a moral evaluation of what capabilities people should develop in themselves, others, and organisations and also of the purposes at which those capabilities should be directed. Warner (2018) argues that the capability approach needs a substantive 'orienting principle that transcends agency', such as those morally desirable capabilities that direct people towards achieving a meaningful life as 'the kind of life that one should value; and not just any life that one can produce good reasons for valuing' (p. 63). He offers the common good as a principle that will enable people to 'coordinate the flourishing of one person or group with that of others' (p. 54). A materialist ethics in a synthesis of meaningfulness and mutuality takes this further by extending flourishing to all those morally worthy beings and things for which we have responsibilities of care. To fulfil such responsibilities, people need life capabilities, or what McMurtry (2001) describes as those 'life ranges of capability' (p. 837) that map the landscape 'of thinking, of acting, and of feeling with all the very rich and complex parameters of each of these fields of being human' (p. 837–838).

Life capabilities are rooted in a motivational structure that is stimulated when we experience revulsion at the violation of natural ecosystems for profit, the appropriation of social resources for competitive advantage, or the humiliation of people for efficiency. When we stir such deeply held human values, we activate fertile sources of meanings by which we experience a shift in our practical identities, leading to the spread of 'a unifying life ethos that can arise across national and cultural divisions and move entire societies and people into action' (p. 851). McMurtry (2001) makes emotional responses against the destruction of our natural world the driver for a cosmopolitan consciousness that changes our motivational structure. He argues that the description and dispersion of such an ethos depends upon language as signs, symbols, meanings and concepts that represent 'a moving margin of life range' (p. 829), where the concept of life value articulates 'social meaning shared by all cultures' (p. 828), thereby refreshing our sources of public meaningfulness with the values of preserving and repairing our civilisational life ground.

In life value organisations, strategic search shifts to an evaluation of the contributions the organisation ought to make to the care-scape of valuable things, with operational practices derived from organisational life value models based upon the production of life goods and cultivation of life capabilities. In such a normative-cognitive framing of collective moral agency, life value organisations will see themselves as assemblages of valuable beings and things, invested with multi-scalar life capabilities, and tasked with using these life capabilities to create civic commons. Using McMurtry's materialist ethics, Sumner (2005) links sustainability to creating civil commons, where ethical capabilities enable us to contribute as self-determining beings to overcoming structural injustice in the processes that produce and distribute civil commons. The civil commons is 'any cooperative human construction that protects and/or enables the universal access to life goods' (p. 307) and as such signals that we are mutually dependent upon others for the formation of our capabilities and therefore on the agency freedom these afford us. The only purpose for organisational capabilities is to enable us to fulfil our responsibilities to contribute to ever more 'inclusive ranges of capability realization' across the domains of human and other natural life (Noonan, 2012: loc. 2892). Furthermore, the pattern of our responsibilities announces who we are as persons, marking out our dignity as particular persons who draw our practical identities from being stewards of valuable beings and things. To realise life capabilities, we must engage in multi-scalar capability formation, which involves making moral judgements on what capabilities are needed in particular contexts and what this implies for our responsibilities to care for the valuable beings and things that must be assembled to address matters of common concern.

Ethical Organising at the Base of the Pyramid

The social construction of worlds is frequently appropriated to benefit some at the expense of others. I examine base-of-the-pyramid (BoP) initiatives that are claimed by corporate sponsors to represent a win–win response to poverty alleviation. Corporations use BoP initiatives to establish new markets among the poorest in the world, simultaneously providing social welfare and stimulating corporate profit. They do so by uniting private power to public and not-for-profit resources for the purpose of opening up sales and distribution channels for the corporation's products. Proponents argue that these projects result in improved livelihoods and life opportunities for distributors and producers, as well as bringing benefits to a class of consumers who have been denied access to valued goods. However, such projects suffer from a number of problems, raising ethical concerns regarding how BoP interventions create and distribute value and who benefits from the created value (Arora and Romijn, 2012). Often, the poor are recruited into franchise or micro entrepreneur business models that exploit the social capital of the informal economy, whilst maintaining a convenient distance between the organisation and its workers. This generates low-skilled, precarious work; displaces locally produced, traditional goods; and stimulates frivolous and unnecessary consumer desires, whilst neglecting more urgent needs. Corporate benefit is secured by using the labour of already vulnerable groups, and degrading the social capital upon which the poorest depend for their survival. In a review of the evidence regarding the shared value impact of BoP style initiatives, Quak (2018) sums up:

> From a development perspective, there is evidence that BoP and shared value approaches are not lifting micro-business actors out of poverty and informal economies, but rather keeping them in poverty, as BoP strategies are based on copying from the informal economy, free-riding on informal community and economic networks,

bypassing informal intermediaries in favour of NGOs and social entrepreneurs, and ultimately shifting most of the risks and costs to the poor micro-enterprises, for example through franchising.

(Quak, 2018: 3)

To assess the impact of BoP initiatives, Ansari et al. (2012) argue for the capabilities approach to be united to an examination of social capital, whereby capabilities are produced, transferred, and retained through enhanced bonding and bridging social capital. However, they caution that the use of social capital to establish capability formation may be problematic because 'social capital can be exclusionary, [and] certain members of the BoP may receive more benefits than others, depending on their degree of engagement' (p. 835). From a capability perspective, social capital can constrain the navigational agency, or the collective self-determination involved in shaping, reforming, and creating social practices, including the social identities these entail. Navigational agency is stunted when corporations construct participants as micro entrepreneurs, with the consequence that the provisional and precarious nature of the worker–organisation relationship is obscured and glossed over. Such workers are obliged to form a practical identity constrained to the economic values that inhere in the entrepreneurial self. This subjective formation maintains people in a condition of dependence, where the poor quality of the work they are required to do stunts capability formation, underlining their inability to control the terms of their engagement with the corporation and inhibiting their capacity to develop a conception of living consistent with lives they have reason to value. A relationship in which the benefits to the participant are below what is needed for flourishing is exploitative. This includes projects that offer training limited to socialising participants into the corporate brand, as well as the personal habits and values of seeing themselves as an entrepreneur.

When development is assessed in terms of income and sales performance, there is little opportunity to form a capability set sufficient for agency freedom, particularly for women who have caring responsibilities. If workers attempt to advance claims that they are organisational members, these are ignored, thereby limiting prospects of a fully responsible relationship between the organisation and its workers. This harms not only BoP workers but also employees of the organisation who are denied an opportunity to see BoP workers as members with them of a moral community, which is a condition for them to construct together the organisation as a collective moral agent. Ultimately, this harms the moral development of the organisation by limiting the collective learning needed to create the ethical capabilities upon which the organisation depends if it is to become a life value organisation.

What is required is a perspective upon the associational ecosystem as a moral community, or society of meaning-makers. In the absence of such a social basis for cooperation, workers involved with corporations through BoP initiatives are frustrated in their ability to form and exercise a capability for ethical world-building and to join with other members of the associational ecosystem to generate life value. Workers do not see their relationship to the corporation simply in transactional terms. Their repeated interactions with the organisation generates expectations of mutual obligations beyond reciprocity and contractual fairness, causing them to seek, or at least hope for, substantive normative engagements based on care and flourishing. The remedy is the extension of the capability for voice to all internal and external members of the organisation. A distinctive design feature of mutual organisation is voice, or the ability of participants to have a share in shaping the decisions that affect their lives. The 2004 BoP Protocol 2.0 sets out best practice for engaging participants in the co-creation of solutions to poverty through 'interactive learning in close dialogue and partnership with the poor and other stakeholders'.[4] Voice is a precondition for the high trust, perceptions of fairness, and sense of psychological ownership upon which increasingly complex, interdependent organisations and systems rely for sustainable performance (Heckscher and Adler, 2006). Voice is important across associational ecosystems such as supply chains, as well as within organisations. In practice, however, co-creation of this order is rare, or at least limited to passive consultation and forms of participation that are not inclusive.

BoP projects have the capacity to manifest all three dimensions of mutuality by promoting reflection upon the purpose, strategy, and operational practices of the corporation itself. When participants of a BoP project, including for example a corporation, NGO, trade union, cooperative, government agency, and community, are invested with the ethical capability for world-building, their social interactions are informed by procedural, interactive, and outcome justice, and they are well placed to co-create their collective action as a system of social cooperation. If such projects are attentive to ethical goals of human flourishing and the common good, they foster dynamic feedback into the organisation in the form of new knowledge for innovation and the promotion of novel organisational practices, thereby simulating fresh cycles of 'organisational becoming'. When mutuality is applied as an organising principle, members are not mere stakeholders to be mobilised into interest groups and incorporated through negotiation, socialisation, or suppression into management-defined strategy but are rather vitally related to one another in joint endeavour, where each group benefits from and derives enjoyment from the increased excellences of the other.

Thus, when participants in a BoP acquire more complex capabilities, these may be combined in collective action with the capabilities of employees to create the organisational capabilities needed to establish life value organisations that are worthy of the moral status afforded them by society. In particular, such projects can be redesigned to incorporate the creation of public services and common goods that benefit everyone, rather than being reduced to marginal income-based returns to individuals. Finally, as well as providing the basis for using the capability for ethical world-building in social construction, such solidarity between internal and external stakeholders provides members with a generative meaning-source to assign significance and meaning to their work. In Chapter 7, I consider what this implies for creating the society of meaning-makers as that body of members who have interests in establishing life value organisations as collective moral agents.

Notes

1. McCauley and Heffron (2018) argue that injustices in climate mitigation transition can be evaluated using an understanding of justice as distributional, procedural and restorative. I highlight the importance of capability justice for just transition, and especially our capabilities for organising as a part of lives that we have reason to value in the Anthropocene.
2. See Nussbaum & Sen (1993) (eds.), *The Quality of Life*. Oxford: Clarendon Press.
3. The Ethical Trading Initiative recognises the importance of freedom of association in supply chains. See www.ethicaltrade.org/sites/default/files/shared_resources/foa_in_company_supply_chains.pdf
4. See BoP Learning Labs at www.bopglobalnetwork.org/bop-labs

Bibliography

Aaron, J. (2012). *Fairness in Practice: A Social Contract for a Global Economy*. Oxford: Oxford University Press.

Abizadeh, A. (2007). Cooperation, Pervasive Impact, and Coercion: On the Scope (Not Site) of Distributive Justice. *Philosophy and Public Affairs*, 35 (4): 318–358.

Ansari, S., Munir, K., & Gregg, T. (2012). Impact at the "Bottom of the Pyramid": The Role of Social Capital in Capability Development and Community Empowerment. *Journal of Management Studies*, 49 (June): 813–842.

Arora, S., & Romijn, H. (2012). The Empty Rhetoric of Poverty Reduction at the Base of the Pyramid. *Organization*, 19 (July 2011): 481–505.

Bagnoli, C. (2013). Constructivism About Practical Knowledge. In: Bagnoli (ed.), *Constructivism in Ethics*. Cambridge: Cambridge University Press.

Ballet, J., Marchanda, L., Pelencb, J., & Vosa, R. (2018). Capabilities, Identity, Aspirations and Ecosystem Services: An Integrated Framework. *Ecological Economics*, 147 (April 2017): 21–28.

Bhaskar, R. (1998). *The Possibility of Naturalism: A Philosophical Critique of the Contemporary Human Sciences*, 3rd edition. London: Routledge.

Buckley, M. (2013). A Constructivist Approach to Business Ethics. *Journal of Business Ethics*, 117 (4): 695–706.

Claassen, R. (2018). *Capabilities in a Just Society: A Theory of Navigational Agency*. Cambridge & New York: Cambridge University Press.

Comim, F., & Carey, F. (2001). *Social Capital and the Capability Approach: Are Putnam and Sen Incompatible Bedfellows?* Paper delivered at the EAEPE Conference "Comparing Economic Institutions", Siena, November.

Deneulin, S. (2004). *Freedom and the Common Good: Which Individual Agency for Development?* Paper presented at the 4th International Conference on the Capability Approach: Enhancing Human Security, Pavia, 5–7 September.

Ehrnström-Fuentes, M. (2016). Delinking Legitimacies: A Pluriversal Perspective on Political CSR. *Journal of Management Studies*, 53 (3): 433–462.

Escobar, A. (2017). Complexity Theory and the Place of the Now. *Cultural Dynamics*, 29 (4): 333–339.

Esquith, S. L. (2010). Introduction: Institutions and Urgency. In: Esquith & Gifford (eds.), *Capabilities, Power, and Institutions.* University Park: Pennsylvania State University Press, 1–17.

Fawcett, S. E., Wallin, C., Allred, C., Fawcett, A. M., & Magnan, G. M. (2011). Information Technology as an Enabler of Supply Chain Collaboration: A Dynamic-Capabilities Perspective. *Journal of Supply Chain Management*, 47 (1): 38–59.

Fischer, L., & Newig, J. (2016). Importance of Actors and Agency in Sustainability Transitions: A Systematic Exploration of the Literature. *Sustainability*, 8: 476.

Follett, M. P. (1998 [1918]). *The New State: Group Organization the Solution of Popular Government.* Pennsylvania: The Pennsylvania State University Press.

Freire, P. (1996). *Pedagogy of the Oppressed.* London: Penguin Books.1

Gillard, R., Gouldson, A., Paavola, J., & van Alstine, J. (2016). Transformational Responses to Climate Change: Beyond a Systems Perspective of Social Change in Mitigation and Adaptation. *WIREs Climate Change*, 7: 251–265.

Giovanola, B. (2005). Personhood and Human Richness: Good and Well-Being in the Capability Approach and Beyond. *Review of Social Economy*, 63 (2): 249–267.

Giovanola, B. (2009). Re-Thinking the Anthropological and Ethical Foundation of Economics and Business: Human Richness and Capabilities Enhancement. *Journal of Business Ethics*, 88: 431–444.

Gray, B., & Purdy, J. (2018). *Collaborating for Our Future: Multistakeholder Partnerships for Solving Complex Problems.* Oxford: Oxford University Press.

Gray, B., & Stites, J. (2013). Sustainability Through Partnerships: Capitalizing on Collaboration. *Wageningenportals.Nl*, 109. nbs.net/knowledge

Guillen-Royo, M., Velazco, J., & Camfield, L. (2013). Basic Needs and Wealth as Independent Determinants of Happiness: An Illustration from Thailand. *Social Indicators Research*, 110: 517–536.

Havercroft, J., & Duvall, R. (2017). Challenges of an Agonistic Constructivism for International Relations. *Polity*, 49 (1): 156–164.

Hay, C. (2016). Good in a Crisis: The Ontological Institutionalism of Social Constructivism. *New Political Economy*, 21 (6): 520–535.

Hayes, J. (2017). Reclaiming Constructivism: Identity and the Practice of the Study of International Relations. *PS: Political Science & Politics*, 50 (1): 89–92.

Heckscher, C., & Adler, P. (2006). *The Firm as a Collaborative Community: Reconstructing Trust in the Knowledge Economy.* New York: Oxford University Press.

Helfat, C. E., & Raubitschek, R. S. (2018). Dynamic and Integrative Capabilities for Profiting from Innovation in Digital Platform-Based Ecosystems. *Research Policy*, 47 (8).

Herzog, L. (2017). No Company Is an Island: Sector-Related Responsibilities as Elements of Corporate Social Responsibility. *Journal of Business Ethics*, 146 (1): 135–148.

Hussein, W. (2018). The Common Good. *The Stanford Encyclopedia of Philosophy,* Spring 2018 edition, E. N. Zalta (ed.). https://plato.stanford.edu/archives/spr2018/entries/common-good/

Ibrahim, S. S. (2006). From Individual to Collective Capabilities : The Capability Approach as a Conceptual Framework for Self-Help. *Journal of Human Development,* 7 (3): 397–416.

James, H. (2009). *The Creation and Destruction of Value: The Globalization Cycle.* Cambridge, MA, and London: Harvard University Press.

Karagiannis, N., & Wagner, P. (2008). Varieties of Agonism: Conflict, the Common Good, and the Need for Synagonism. *Journal of Social Philosophy,* 39 (3): 323–339.

Khan, M. H. (2018). Knowledge, Skills and Organizational Capabilities for Structural Transformation. *Structural Change and Economic Dynamics,* 48: 42–52.

LeBar, M. (2008). Aristotelian Constructivism. *Social Philosophy and Policy,* 25: 182–213.

Leonard, C. (2019). *Kochland: The Secret History of Koch Industries and Corporate Power in America.* London & New York: Simon & Schuster.

Macdonald, K., & Macdonald, T. (2010). Democracy in a Pluralist Global Order: Corporate Power and Stakeholder Representation. *Ethics & International Affairs,* 24 (1): 19–43.

Martins, N. O. (2006). Capabilities as Causal Powers. *Cambridge Journal of Economics,* 30 (5): 671–685.

Martins, N. O. (2007). Ethics, Ontology and Capabilities. *Review of Political Economy,* 19 (1): 37–53.

Martins, N. O. (2013). The Place of the Capability Approach Within Sustainability Economics. *Ecological Economics,* 95: 226–230.

Marx, K. (1978 [1844]). Economic and Philosophical Manuscripts. In: Tucker (ed.) *The Marx-Engels Reader* (2nd Edition). New York & London: W. W. Norton & Company.

McCauley, D., & Heffron, R. (2018). Just Transition: Integrating Climate, Energy and Environmental Justice. *Energy Policy,* 119: 1–7.

McMurtry, J. (2001). The Life-Ground, the Civil Commons and the Corporate Male Gang. *Canadian Journal of Development Studies,* 22 (4): 819–854.

McMurtry, J. (2011). Human Rights versus Corporate Rights: Life Value, the Civil Commons and Social Justice. *Studies in Social Justice,* 5 (1): 11–61.

Millennium Ecosystem Assessment. (2005). Ecosystems and Human Well-Being: Opportunities and Challenges for Business and Industry. Retrieved from http://www.millenniumassessment.org/en/index.html

Murphy, M. (2014). Self-Determination as a Collective Capability: The Case of Indigenous Peoples. *Journal of Human Development and Capabilities,* 15 (4): 320–334.

Nathan, G. (2014). Multi-Stakeholder Deliberation for (Global) Justice: An Approach from Modern Civic Republicanism. In: Schepers & Kakabadse (eds.), *Rethinking the Future of Europe.* London: Palgrave Macmillan.

Nelson, R., & Winter, S. (1982). *An Evolutionary Theory of Economic Change.* Cambridge, MA: Bellknap.

Noonan, J. (2012). *Materialist Ethics and Life-Value.* Montreal & London: McGill-Queen's University Press.

Nussbaum, M. C. (1987). *Nature, Function, and Capability: Aristotle on Political Distribution*. World Institute for Development Economics Research, WP 31.

Nussbaum, M. C. (2000). Aristotle, Politics, and Human Capabilities: A Response to Antony, Arneson, Charlesworth, and Mulgan. *Ethics*, 111 (1): 102–140.

Nussbaum, M. C. (2011). *Creating Capabilities: The Human Development Approach*. Cambridge, MA & London: The Belknap Press of Harvard University Press.

Nussbaum, M. C., & Sen, A. (eds.) (1993). *The Quality of Life*. Oxford: Clarendon Press.

O'Neill, D. W., Fanning, A. L., Lamb, W. F., & Steinberger, J. K. (2018). A Good Life for All Within Planetary Boundaries. *Nature Sustainability*, 88 (95).

O'Neill, O. (1996). *Towards Justice and Virtue: A Constructive Account of Practical Reasoning*. Cambridge: Cambridge University Press.

O'Neill, O. (2004). Global Justice. In: Chatterjee (ed.), *The Ethics of Moral Assistance: Morality and the Distant Needy*. Cambridge: Cambridge University Press, 242–259.

Onuf, N. (2016). Constructivism at the Crossroads; or, the Problem of Moderate-Sized Dry Goods. *International Political Sociology*, 10: 115–132.

Purdy, J., Ansari, S., & Gray, B. (2019). Are Logics Enough? Framing as an Alternative Tool for Understanding Institutional Meaning Making. *Journal of Management Inquiry*, 28 (4): 409–419.

Quak, E.-J. (2018). *Balancing Profit-Making with Social Value Creation: Challenges, Opportunities and Lessons Learned*. K4D Helpdesk Report. Brighton, UK: Institute of Development Studies.

Rawls, J. (1999 [1971]). *Theory of Justice*. Oxford: Oxford University Press.

Rawls, J. (1999). *The Law of Peoples*. Cambridge, MA: Harvard University Press.

Robeyns, I. (2005). The Capability Approach: A Theoretical Survey. *Journal of Human Development*, 6 (1): 93–117.

Sah, R., & Stiglitz, J. (1986). The Architecture of Economic Systems: Hierarchies and Polyarchies. *The American Economic Review*, 76 (4): 716–727.

Salvato, C. (2009). Capabilities Unveiled. The Role of Ordinary Activities in the Evolution of Product Development Processes. *Organizational Science*, 20 (2): 384-409.

Salvato, C., & Rerup, C. (2011). Beyond Collective Entities: Multilevel Research on Organizational Routines and Capabilities. *Journal of Management*, 37 (2): 468–490.

Salvato, C., & Vassolo, R. (2018). The Sources of Dynamism in Dynamic Capabilities. *Strategic Management Journal*, 39: 1728–1752.

Schilke, O., Hu, S., & Helfat, C. E. (2018). Quo Vadis, Dynamic Capabilities? A Content-Analytic Review of the Current State of Knowledge and Recommendations for Future Research. *Academy of Management Annals*, 2 (1): 390–439.

Scott, J. C. (1990). *Domination and the Arts of Resistance: Hidden Transcripts*. New Haven, CT: Yale University Press.

Sen, A. K. (1987). *On Ethics and Economics*. Oxford: Blackwell.

Sen, A. K. (1999). *Development as Freedom*. New York: Oxford University Press.

Sen, A. K. (2006). *Identity and Violence: The Illusion of Destiny*. New York: Norton.

Sen, A. K. (2009). *The Idea of Justice*. London: Penguin.

Smith, M. L., & Seward, C. (2009). The Relational Ontology of Amartya Sen's Capability Approach: Incorporating Social and Individual Causes. *Journal of Human Development and Capabilities*, 10 (2): 213–235.

Stewart, F. (2005). Groups and Capabilities. *Journal of Human Development*, 6 (2): 185–204.

Street, S. (2010). What Is Constructivism in Ethics and Metaethics? *Philosophy Compass*, 5 (5): 363–384.

Sumner, J. (2005). Value Wars in the New Periphery: Sustainability, Rural Communities and Agriculture. *Agriculture and Human Values*, 22 (3): 303–312.

Teece, D. J. (2007). Explicating Dynamic Capabilities: The Nature and Micro-foundations of (Sustainable) Enterprise Performance. *Strategic Management Journal*, 28 (13): 1319–1350.

Teece, D. J. (2018). Profiting from Innovation in the Digital Economy: Standards, Complementary Assets, and Business Models in the Wireless World. *Research Policy*, 47 (8): 1367–1387.

Thomas, C. A. (2015). Globalising Sovereignty? Pettit's Neo-Republicanism, International Law and International Institutions. *The Cambridge Law Journal*, 74 (3): 568–591.

Tran, Y., Zahra, S., & Hughes, M. (2018). A Process Model of the Maturation of a New Dynamic Capability. *Industrial Marketing Management*, in press.

Tsoukas, H., & Chia, R. (2002). On Organizational Becoming: Rethinking Organizational Change. *Organization Science*, 13 (5): 567–582.

Tzitzis, S. (1999). *Qu'Est ce que la Personnel?* Paris: Armand Colin.

Van Staveren, I. (2001). *The Values of Economics: An Aristotelian Perspective*. London & New York: Routledge.

Wallace, J. (2006). The Rightness of Acts and the Goodness of Lives. In: Wallace, Pettit, Scheffler, & Smith (eds.), *Reason and Value: Themes from the Moral Philosophy of Joseph Raz*. Oxford: Oxford University Press, 385–411.

Wallace, R. J. (2019). *The Moral Nexus*. Princeton, NJ, & Oxford: Princeton University Press.

Wallis, J., & Richmond, O. (2017). From Constructivist to Critical Engagements with Peacebuilding: Implications for Hybrid Peace. *Third World Thematics: A TWQ Journal*, 2 (4): 422–445.

Warner, J. (2018). Capabilities and the Common Good. In: Comim, Fennell, & Anand (eds.), *New Frontiers of the Capability Approach*. Cambridge: Cambridge University Press, 53–81.

Watson, R., Wilson, H. N., Smart, P., & Macdonald, E. K. (2017). Harnessing Difference: A Capability-Based Framework for Stakeholder Engagement in Environmental Innovation. *Journal of Product Innovation Management*, 35 (2): 254–279.

Wiener, A. (2016). Contested Norms in Inter-National Encounters: The 'Turbot War' as a Prelude to Fairer Fisheries Governance. *Politics and Governance*, 4 (3): 20–36.

Wiener, A. (2018). *Constitution and Contestation of Norms in Global International Relations*. Cambridge: Cambridge University Press.

Winter, S. G. (2012). Capabilities: Their Origins and Ancestry. *Journal of Management Studies*, 49 (8): 1402–1406.

Yeoman, R. (2014). Conceptualising Meaningful Work as a Fundamental Human Need. *Journal of Business Ethics*, 125 (2): 235–251.

Young, I. M. (2011). *Responsibility for Justice*. Oxford: Oxford University Press.

Zheng, S., Zhang, W., & Du, J. (2011). Knowledge-Based Dynamic Capabilities and Innovation in Networked Environments. *Journal of Knowledge Management*, 15 (6): 1035–1051.

Zollo, M., & Winter, S. G. (2002). Deliberate Learning and the Evolution of Dynamic Capabilities. *Organization Science*, 13 (3): 339–351.

7   The Society of Meaning-Makers
Dignity, Empathy, Power

The society of meaning-makers is a normative design element for ethical organising. Derived from the social architecture of meaningfulness and mutuality, the society of meaning-makers operates as one of the conversion factors that translate the general capacity for organising into the human capability for ethical world-building. Robeyns (2005) identifies three kinds of conversion factors influencing the transformation of resources into capabilities and functionings—personal, social, and environmental. The conversion of capacities into capabilities and of capabilities into functionings depends upon people being able to access resources and favourable background conditions, such as mediating institutions and the social basis for collective action. With respect to the latter, seeing one another as fellow meaning-makers provides the relational conditions for people to construct together life value organisations as collective moral agents.

In order to become meaning-makers, people need to acquire the relevant individual capabilities and status associated with meaning-making, which is reliably achieved in action contexts structured by the goods of meaningfulness. I have described these goods elsewhere as freedom as non-domination, autonomy as non-alienation, and dignity as being recognised as a particular person (see Yeoman, 2014b). In collective moral agents, the goods of meaningfulness are realised through *freedom* as 'practical freedom' or discursive power; *autonomy* as feeling that the world is susceptible to one's involvement and influence; and *dignity* as the 'capacity to dignify', or the ability to confer independent objective value on beings and things that inhabit ethical worlds. The goods of meaningfulness are interconnected, such that coming to see oneself as a dignified person depends upon not being undermined in one's core commitments due to arbitrary interference, where the possession of relational power protects us from feeling alienated from the world, others, our work, and ourselves. We create such goods using the normative materials to be found in social settings structured by the social architecture of meaningfulness and mutuality. The practices of mutual organisation include purposing, voice, and power-sharing, and these augment and transmit the positive meanings that inform the organisational frames needed for creating collective moral agents. In the society of meaning-makers, voice is generative of interpretive variety in meaning-making when it is underpinned by a system of power, particularly the *relational* power to be influenced by valuable beings and things and the *justificatory* power to advance claims regarding the meanings people want taken up into organisational and public meaningfulness.

The Society of Meaning-Makers

A major task given to organisations is to surface and attend to problems. Life value organisations, as collective moral agents, evaluate problems by applying the value of meaningfulness into practical reasoning and using the practices of mutual organisation to proliferate the moral free spaces through which meaning-makers can contribute their difference to problem-solving. Life value organisations are maintained as collective moral agents and equipped with organisational ethical capabilities by their members, who are related to one another through their status as co-authorities and capabilities for meaning-making (see Yeoman, 2014b). The relational conditions of the society of meaning-makers augments other-regarding orientations, such as empathetic perspective-taking and collective knowledge-building, enabling life value organisations to convert latent ethical capabilities into organisational competence for the purpose of life value creation.

The society of meaning-makers is that moral community of persons who possess meaning-making authority in particular situations by virtue of how they are affected by problems arising in that situation and the knowledge they possess of the relevant ensembles of valuable beings and things. We belong to many societies of meaning-makers gathered within—and dispersed between—organisations, associations, institutions, communities, and more. The society of meaning-makers mobilises the interests, needs, and concerns of organisational members, thereby augmenting their collective ability to ensure that the collective moral agents with which they interact are equipped with organisational capabilities for life value creation. I examine how we establish the society of meaning-makers as a moral community, using the capacity to dignify and empathy in moral expansiveness to open up the moral availability of organisations to its members. The capacity to dignify establishes the relational orientation that each member of the society of meaning-makers has to every other member. Empathy in moral expansiveness enriches the space of justifications by using interpretive differences in meaning-making to amplify reasons for action. This requires relational power, which provides people with the confidence to be open to the influence of others (Loomer, 1976), and discursive authority, which enables them to resist the kinds of dominating relationships that suppress difference-making and channel meaning-making towards goals and purposes benefiting some at the expense of others (Pettit, 2001). Dominating relationships interfere with the integrative social processes facilitating meaning take-up by ignoring, marginalising, appropriating, or misinterpreting meanings. These effects are mitigated when collective moral agents are democratically authorised authorities; that is, they institute governance systems in which people have a share in the collective self-determination of the rules coordinating their collective action, as well as the social norms and values that shape the subjectivities constituting their identities (Thompson, 2018). When moral free spaces, constituted by liberal value pluralism, afford non-dominating relationships, societies of meaning-makers become repositories of narratives regarding real or imaginary ways of living that are judged collectively to be worth living.

In Chapter 6, I explored the concern of justice in the social processes of organising, where justice directs our attention to the legitimate basis for organisations to call upon the contributions of their members. In ethical organising, organisations are entitled to the contributive effort of their members when they are morally worthy organisations that establish morally viable pathways for members to interact with them. Life value organisations meet the requirements of collective moral agency when they are high in moral availability; that is, they are open to the influence and collective self-determination of all affected members. The openness that characterises life value organisations can be distinguished from that which characterises what Watkins and Stark (2018) call the möbius organisational form. Watkins and Stark (2018) describe this as a boundary-less organisation that extracts and consumes public, private, and civic assets from its environment, including knowledge, information, and data. To create life value, the direction of openness needs to be reversed. Instead of 'opening up' to extract resources and absorb society, life value organisations 'open out' by inviting contributive connections from diverse groups and individuals who have a concern for the well-being of the organisation, thereby making the organisation available for moral development.

This openness constitutes a type of open-source publicness, where *open-source* describes the readiness of the organisation to be influenced by those who have an interest in its activities, and *publicness* indicates how the means and ends of the organisation impact valuable beings and things. Organisational forms that are high in publicness include, for example, platform cooperatives, social enterprises, and multi-constituency mutuals. The relevant institutional mechanisms for openness and moral availability include, for example, deliberative collaborative governance. Such mechanisms enable members of the society of meaning-makers to hold individual organisations and whole ecosystems up against their public promises to create life value. Warren (1996) identifies how any social order is made up of a diversity of coordinative authorities, which are legitimate authorities when they are democratically authorised: 'democracy is necessary to chasten authority, to limit its claims and dangers' (p. 47). Life value organisations are democratic authorities when they are open to contestation and difference through the institution of deliberative procedures that produce 'an authoritative background of commitments and beliefs that both sustain and contain democratic challenges' (p. 47). This type of authority requires participants who are capable of autonomous judgements and informed by beliefs and commitments (pp. 54–55), and who see themselves as self-determining beings.

However, the development of this desirable form of subjectivity is hindered by oppressive structures of obedience: 'democratic authority requires a context of critical challenge that is all too easily damaged by hierarchies of status and inequalities of resource distribution' (p. 56). The equal standing of each member of the society of meaning-makers implies an equal entitlement to contributive connection in order to ensure that dominating relationships do not foster dysfunctional capability formation. This is enabled by creating a wide variety of invited and self-chosen membership options, aimed at multiplying the range of perspectives that add meanings, knowledge, and understanding into the joint task of holding the organisation to account as a legitimate authority. These options could range from full responsible member, with decision-making rights and obligations, to observer/advisor status. The value of such roles lies in providing diverse pathways for contributing to life value organisations, and at the same time addressing the interest we all have in doing something that matters, something that is significant, and gives our lives meaning and purpose.

All Affected

I adopt the all-affected principle to determine who is a member of the society of meaning-makers. Warren (2017) reminds us that, under the Justinian Code, collective decisions are justified to the extent they involve all those affected by the decision: 'what touches all must be approved by all' (p. 1). Warren translates this into 'a claim about who should, normatively speaking, be entitled to inclusion in collectivities—existing or latent—based on how their lives are affected by others' (p. 2). Under the sustainability imperative, I understand all affected, in the broadest terms, to include the people, living beings, natural ecosystems, artefacts, communities, organisations, and more, whose lives and presence in the world are shaped by the activities of an organisation. All those affected are the persons who are entitled to participate in collective decisions regarding troubling situations and who can represent non-sentient beings and things.

A basic feature of being a meaning-maker is being able to claim one's entitlement to the problem, which endows each meaning-maker with equal status when calling upon others to join with them in problem-solving.

These problems, along with the ensembles of beings and things that constitute them, must be surfaced and described by meaning-makers, who then marshal the necessary collective response. Being able to make and address the problem is a form of social power. Those affected are entitled to be involved in surfacing, framing, deliberating, and resolving the problems constituting a troubling situation. In the context of multi-stakeholder partnerships, Dentoni et al. (2018) argue that 'harnessing' the problem involves understanding how problems are characterised by knowledge uncertainty, values conflict and dynamic complexity, and non-responsive governance. 'Harnessing' is facilitated when action contexts are orchestrated by collaborative governance, consisting of processes of 'deliberation, decision-making and enforcement' (p. 334), thereby enabling all those affected to contribute to describing and addressing the problem. Dentoni et al. (2018) draw upon the case of the Roundtable for Sustainable Palm Oil (RSPO) to illustrate the challenges of using multi-stakeholder partnerships to transform social, economic, and environmental systems. The RSPO sought to develop new regulations and enforcements mechanisms for protecting forests and land. Participants, such as Unilever and World Wildlife Fund (WWF), were involved in structuring deliberative events centred upon 'pragmatism and technical rationality' (p. 347), making it difficult for local stakeholders to insert their knowledge into discourse. This allowed influential participants of the RSPO to choose solutions rather than create integrative solutions derived from the plurality of understanding and knowledge latent in the partnership. The consequent enforcement mechanisms were based on limited data collection and ignored local stakeholders' valuation of the land use for palm oil production, consequently reducing trust and weakening the capacity of the overall system to monitor sustainability practices.

Seen through the lens of the mutuality principle, such cases illustrate the interaction between the dimensions of bargaining, cooperating, and becoming. In the bargaining phase, all affected stakeholders are involved in examining the rules and norms of the deliberative forum or 'sites of negotiation' (p. 339) and in forming themselves into a public, which could be all or a subset of the relevant society of meaning-makers. In the cooperating phase, the public creates collective knowledge and joint expertise from the framing of the problem. If there is a wider society of meaning-makers, meaning-makers are constituted into a 'goldfish bowl' of critical observers, supporters, and contributors, leading to practice innovations and reflection and evaluation of governance mechanisms. In the becoming phase, problems are emergent and volatile, their unpredictable mutations requiring moral learning through whole-system multi-scalar dynamic capability formation, to which all affected members have access. The problem is made visible within a pluralist moral community, in which practices of dignifying and empathetic concern help overcome initial reluctance to interact with different others; support trust-building cycles that generate shared understanding, meanings, and knowledge; and give people confidence that it is safe to offer diverse interpretations of meanings and values that facilitate norm change and novel ways of organising.

Given the large number of people who are potentially implicated in troubling situations, the all affected principle is critiqued for being impractical. To address this worry, Warren (2017) proposes that the principle is interpreted against a contextual evaluation of the problem at hand, which assesses whose interests in self-development and self-determination are impacted by the problem. When we are enmeshed in 'extensive interdependency' (p. 3), self-development and self-determination represent core interests that democracy satisfies. Our collective ability to live successfully with complex interdependence depends upon the organisations we create. In ethical world-building, we who are affected by the activities of an organisation are entitled to co-create the organisation as a collective moral agent and legitimate authority by establishing a pattern of entitlements and obligations that enact the relevant system of power-sharing.

By focussing upon objects of shared concern, people become connected to one another through interests and needs that they have in common and especially where these provide routes for interacting with the relevant responsible collective agent. The collective agent under consideration can mobilise these potentially productive interactions, stimulating definitions of the problem, surfacing objects of shared concern, and activating collective responses. Warren (2017) argues that people may have multiple constituencies to which they belong, and they may 'self-select' their membership of organisations: 'They can bring latent constituencies to the fore; they can precisely calibrate their advocacy; they can even organize to provide collective goods that governments neglect' (p. 11). Meaning-makers therefore need to be invested with the capabilities and status for them to reflect upon what worries them and how these worries connect them to others in a potentially global sphere of influence. By self-selecting their interactions with organisations, they take on responsibilities to contribute their interpretive differences into meaning-making, thereby directing their skill, craft, and knowledge towards the purpose of life value creation.

Mutuality in the Society of Meaning-Makers

To take up such responsibilities, the society of meaning-makers must see itself as a moral community, where members are connected to one another through their equal status as co-authorities in meaning-making and their pooling of individual capabilities for organisational capability formation. The task of the society of meaning-makers is to articulate problems related to ethical organising, such as unjust distributions of burdens and benefits in social cooperation, and to demand that these problems are addressed through normatively desirable collective action, in which each member exercises equal social power. Drawing from Kantian ethics, Sherman (1993) identifies the protective benefits of organising under a mutuality principle that produces an 'ethical commonwealth', or 'a community of equals bound by the moral law—a realm of ends that is the best defence against our social vulnerabilities' (p. 295). A core element of the ethical commonwealth is the relational capabilities that underpin our rational agency, including emotional capacities to see one another in a certain moral light. Incorporated under an ethic of care, these relational capabilities include empathetic understanding, which is rooted in appreciating one another as dignified persons, each with a particular life of her own to lead (cf. Yeoman, 2014a) and through which we 'relate to one another based on an interest in each other as whole, complex people' (Jordan, 1986: 1).

I make use of Gewirth's (1996) *Community of Rights* to specify mutuality as the relational basis for constituting the society of meaning-makers as a moral community. Gewirth (1996) describes mutuality as a lively 'dynamic, interactive relation' (p. 75) that goes beyond formal equality or respect and is captured in the general formula: 'A gives some valued X to B and B gives some other kind of valued X to A' (p. 75). For mutuality to operate as a moral principle, the 'nature of the 'X' is vitally important' (p. 75), where X must possess evaluable moral content, which in Gewirth's (1996) theory is provided by the human rights we need to act as purposive agents. In the social architecture of meaningfulness and mutuality, the value of meaningfulness supplies mutuality with evaluable moral content, represented by X. This moral content specifies fair and cooperative agreements between B and A that promote the flourishing of each party as a dignified person and affords them opportunities to find meaning and purpose in non-dominating, non-alienating action contexts.

The community of rights derives from the 'mutuality of rights and obligations' that embody a 'single moral principle' (p. xiii) and requires all members of the moral community, as individuals and in collectives, to adopt mutuality as the basic moral structure of the community. Mutuality mediates the relationship between human rights and community by providing 'mutualist structural patterns of society' (p. 71), consistent with overcoming Young's structural injustice. For Gewirth (1996), the value of mutuality lies in how it facilitates moral expansiveness by moving us from our preoccupation with self-interest to an understanding of the common good. During collective processes of world-building, we gather information on diverse perspectives, enlarge our understanding of others who are different from us, and come to appreciate shared needs, common concerns, and mutual dependencies. Gewirth (1996) describes the community of rights as embodying a form of 'secular spirituality' (p. xv), where a caring society becomes 'reflective of the moral concern that all humans, as actual or prospective agents, be enabled to live lives of dignity, self-fulfillment and mutuality of respect' (p. xv). Gewirth (1996) opposes the false dichotomy between: firstly, rights accruing to people as independent individuals with no social ties, and secondly, people as part of affective communities that devalue their individual distinctiveness. The mutuality of our needs as individual purposive agents includes our need for social connection and the emotional bonds these imply, where part of our own good consists in the interest we take in the good for others. This is supported by positive emotional orientations towards others, or forms of 'fellow feeling' (p. 86) that overcome the view of society as consisting 'of 'bare' individuals who are unaware of and indifferent to one another's fates' (p. 86).

Our inherent dignity is rooted in our status as purposive agents. Gewirth (1996) argues that we should judge our actions against certain invariant features of the human condition, which he identifies as our common need to see ourselves as a purposeful being, where the conditions for action are freedom and well-being. This means that to see ourselves and others as dignified persons, we must attribute value to the abilities and goals that are the target of our agency. Our agency in the world requires a bundle of enabling rights that are guaranteed within a moral community: 'each human must respect the rights of all others while having his rights respected by all the others, so that there must be a mutual sharing of the benefits of rights and the burdens of duties' (p. 6). Thus, mutual respecting of human rights, or the moral component X of mutuality, depends upon being able to dwell in solidaristic community, bound by mutual obligations, where members are ready to help one another become purposive agents, so that they can meet their own needs whilst also contributing to the needs of others.

Gewirth (1996) outlines a 'social contribution thesis' (p. 81), wherein, because the community has contributed to realising our human rights, we have obligations to maintain that community, including promoting solidaristic values such as 'social harmony, mutual support, and fellow-feeling that overcome the divisiveness and alienation of individualism' (p. 82). We have such obligations only when the community is a moral community of rights by virtue of provisioning its members with the goods they need for purposive agency—other kinds of communities cannot oblige us to provide support and loyalty. However, we will not have such goods if we do not contribute to creating them because it 'is work that contributes to the protection and development of these necessary goods' (p. 147). But, we do not make our contribution in any way whatsoever. Gewirth (1996) says that human capital is 'primarily the possession of the individual agent and is oriented to her benefit' (p. 137). This means that others cannot require us to contribute our efforts without considering the benefits to us of doing so. In a philosophy of ethical organising, our contributions must themselves be structured by the goods of meaningful work, since it is through such correctly structured work that we are able to fulfil our responsibilities to contribute to solving problems of common concern. Such work includes participating in collective self-determination of what is meant by the common good, what rules constitute the common good of the community, and what values and institutions of mutual support and solidarity will foster fellow feeling and joint action.

At a societal level, Gewirth (1996) describes a functionalist perspective on public emotions that is reflected in more recent theories of organisational emotions. Institutional formations enact love as a public emotion through 'a system of policies motivated by a concern for the fulfillment of all persons' needs for dignity, self-respect, and more generally for the necessary conditions of action and generally successful action' (p. xv). For example, the Rana Plaza factory collapse, killing over 1,100 workers, had reputational consequences for numerous Western retailers, including Primark, J.C. Penney, Benneton, and Matalan. The disaster stimulated the formation of agreements binding corporations to collective improvements and mitigating weak state enforcement of building and labour regulations. This resulted in two types of sector-based governance innovations—an accord, consisting of a pluralist structure, grounded in a legally binding agreement and involving workers in high-level decisions, and an alliance, making use of a voluntary approach, with no formal worker voice in decision making and involving unions in an advisory capacity only (Donaghey and Reinecke, 2018).

In a further response to the disaster, the French government instituted in 2017 a corporate duty of vigilance, binding companies established in France to identifying potential human rights and environmental harms in their supply chain activities, thereby providing a legal basis for affected individuals and communities to hold corporations to account. Such legal and governance mechanisms show what is needed to elicit functional emotions in organisations and societies that stimulate the moral sensitivity of members. To render organisations morally available, practices of empathetic concern are required that augment the emotional sensitivity of organisational members, generating intersubjective feelings that help members to see each other across separations of power, culture, and distance.

Creating the Moral Community

The mutual basis for the society of meaning-makers is directed towards cultivating an expansive moral awareness of each member as a dignified person, who has contributions to make to the commonwealth or common good. I apply the idea of the capacity to dignify to the relational orientations between members of the society of meaning-makers and argue that this capacity depends upon developing empathetic awareness of widening circles of meaning-makers, who are entitled to use their capability for ethical world-building to create life value.

The Capacity to Dignify

The sustainability imperative requires a form of public meaningfulness with global reach that is capable of underpinning the social cooperation needed for planetary-scale social and economic transition. Boltanski and Thévenot (2006) argue that 'people share in a common humanity that is expressed in a common capacity to rise to occasions in the service of the common good' (p. 141). To motivate pro-social and pro-environmental behaviours, people need a sense of being recognised and cared for as dignified persons; that is, as persons with claims and obligations that signal their lives matter. Forst (2014) frames societies as orders of justification, where our dignity is connected to our recognition as a 'justifying being' who both needs and uses reasons (p. 96) and who is afforded a '*right to justification* of all actions or norms that affect them in morally relevant ways'. This imposes 'a duty to provide such justification' (p. 96) on the collectivities to which we belong. In other words, social entities, such as organisations and states, recognise human dignity by providing people with reasons they can understand for the rules, norms, and procedures that frame the circumstances of their lives. In turn, people express their dignity as justifying beings by fulfilling the reason-giving obligations they have to others. Under conditions of extensive interdependency in the society of meaning-makers, this requires an expansion of those who must be included within the sphere of reason-giving, requiring us to develop our knowledge of distant others using practices of empathetic awareness. The aim is to ensure that moral free spaces are inhabited by dignified and justifying beings, who have a right to be provided with reasons they can understand and accept for the adoption, rejection, or creation of moral principles by an organisation that is affecting their lives and work.

In an extension of dignity beyond the individual, Kateb (2011) argues that human dignity encompasses humanity as a whole, such that 'every member deserves to be treated in a manner consonant with the high worth of the species' (loc. 109). Kateb (2011) says of species dignity that 'the interdependence of individuals and groups is so extensive and deep, and so entangled, so hard, even impossible, to describe or trace, that for certain purposes we might just as well make the human species a unified entity or agent, even though we know it isn't' (loc. 147). Because of our impact on the planet and other species, human beings have a certain kind of status, or position, whereby they have 'a tremendous duty towards nature—namely, to become ever more devotedly the steward of nature' (loc. 23). The entangled nature of our lives with other beings and things is no more obviously manifest than in the webs of production and consumption, wrapped across the globe, and upon which we depend for our sustenance and our flourishing. Lane and Watson (2012) develop the idea of 'product stewardship' to capture new meanings of care and obligation in the use and reuse of products and materials at a household level, which challenges conventional understandings of ownership. Motivating pro-environmental behaviours may therefore depend upon a new narrative of human dignity, derived from our obligations to steward valuable beings and things, where the prospects for a meaningful life depend upon forming identities that are consistent with fulfilling such responsibilities.

In the society of meaning-makers, I consider dignity to be a moral act of dignifying ourselves and others. The sustainability imperative demands that we find ways to evaluate the impact of human activities upon other beings and things and in so doing establish a new basis for assigning dignity to one another. Dignifying generates the moral expansiveness by which we extend our moral boundaries to incorporate the 'breadth of entities deemed worthy of moral concern and treatment' (Crimston et al., 2018). Crimston et al. (2018) observe that 'people's moral circles have expanded over the course of history, with modern people extending moral concern to entities—both human and nonhuman—that our ancestors would never have considered including within their moral boundaries' (p. 14) Moral expansiveness, as the ability to include more morally valuable beings and things into our moral circles, is related to 'empathetic concern, perspective taking, moral identity, identification with all humanity, connection with nature, endorsement of universal values, and increased use of harm and fairness principles' (p. 16).

Moral expansiveness constructs an objectivity worth having by combining our capacity to dignify with empathetic imagination. Combined with Wallace's (2019) relational theory of morality, this suggests a cosmopolitan form of complex objectivity that sees others, from whom we are separated by distance, culture, and power, as equally real, thereby generating claims that we recognise them as persons with lives that matter as much as ours. Bagnoli (2013) observes that complex objectivity is constructed by agents who see themselves and others as 'co-legislators in a community of equals' and therefore co-creators of the norms and rules that govern their meaning-making. Ideal conditions for meaning-making permit responsible difference-making through non-alienating and non-dominative social processes that enable meaning-makers to experience themselves as dignified persons. Bird (2013) develops a social constructivist account of dignity, where dignity is not dependent upon inherent worth but consists in a status quality, which we have in our power to endow upon one another:

> [D]ignity is here construed as a common responsibility consequent upon a circumstance plausibly basic to the conditions of human life: our power to confer importance, priority, and worth on each other by respecting (or showing respect), and concomitantly upon our power to withhold such importance, priority or worth from them by treating one another with contempt.
>
> (p. 174)

Bird (2013) describes dignity as a moral practice, where the capacity to dignify enables us to bestow life value on objects: 'each of us shares in the power to dignify values, persons, achievements' (p. 175). The power to dignify entails responsibilities to recognise and maintain the dignity of others, which reflects back upon and constructs our personal dignity. Equally, we can destroy our own and others' dignity by abusing our power to dignify: 'by belittling, condemning, trivializing, and degrading people, we do not diminish a dignity that can be isolated as a possession of its immediate victims, for we at the same time debase our humanity itself' (p. 175).

The capacity to dignify is a general feature of persons that helps us to create socio-cultural and institutional common goods. Bird (2013) says that the moral rules we create 'ought to matter for *our* sake' p. 176), because they lend significance to our particular lives and ground our common human dignity. Killmister (2017) argues for a dual pathway to dignity through personal and social dignity such that 'we have dignity because we give ourselves dignity' (p. 2066). Rather than dignity being an inherent, static, unchanging quality, we confer dignity upon one another to the extent that we uphold certain normative standards that we take to be consistent with lives we have reason to value. This means that 'to violate someone's dignity is to prevent them from upholding those standards' (p. 2063). Personal dignity involves acknowledging the role in our lives of normative standards that would harm our dignity if they were violated, and social dignity means belonging to communities that recognise such standards for its members.

The capacity to dignify as personal and social dignity shapes our own and others' identities. Our lives are made up of interwoven strands of belonging and social roles that structure our practical identities. Korsegaard (2009) defines a 'conception of practical identity' as 'a description under which you value yourself and find your life worth living and your actions to be worth undertaking' (p. 20). Furthermore, Korsegaard (2009) says that 'we owe it to ourselves, to our own humanity, to find some roles that we can fill with integrity and dedication' (p. 24). In the Anthropocene, these roles will be constituted by meanings that enrich our understanding and knowledge of what is required to be a dignified person who stewards and takes care of valuable beings and things. In taking up the normative standards associated with these roles and identities, we are inviting others to confer dignity upon us to the extent that we meet those standards, where the obligations these standards entail act as a filter for the reasons we should advance into practical reasoning as justifying beings.

Moral Expansiveness and Empathy

Using the capacity to dignify as a pathway for moral expansiveness depends upon empathy. Jamison (2014) says that 'empathy isn't just something that happens to us—a meteor shower of synapses firing across the brain—it's also a choice we make; to pay attention, to extend ourselves. It's made of exertion, that dowdier cousin of impulse' (p. 23). The interactions needed for empathy building are illustrated in the following vignette. Over many years, a UK retailer had purchased flowers from the same small number of Kenyan farms. These types of long lasting corporate–supplier relationships are generally discussed in terms of how supplier integration provides mutual benefits to the participants in the form of supply chain resilience, trust, and joint practices. However, during a research interview with the author, the procurement manager noted her deep feelings of friendship, warmth, and loyalty towards the farm owners, managers, and workers. Through the long history of the retailer's connection with the farms, she had derived satisfaction from seeing children in the local communities grow and learn, and eventually took on roles in the farms. She had been personally changed by her exposure to a different culture and farming system. In other words, the person-to-person connections between the UK retailer and the flower farms created an emotional bond, mutual recognition, and mutual obligations consistent with the corporate–supplier constituting a society of meaning-makers.

Mutual relations of trust, respect, esteem, and harmony cement durable attachments that enrich our lives with meaning and significance, as well as providing ethical materials for moral agents to create their organisations as collective moral agents. Roughley and Schramme (2018) argue that relational moral agency, through which we form the right kinds of connections to one another, requires emotional orientations, or 'fellow feelings', such as empathy, sympathy, and concern. Betzler (2018) shows that the relational value of empathy lies in how it focusses our moral sensibilities upon what emotional responses particular relationships require from us. Thus, the value of empathy lies not only in enabling us to access certain kinds of knowledge about others but also in how it maintains satisfying other-regarding relationships that are valuable in themselves. Such attachments abound in organisational life. The UK retailer secured commercial advantage from its supplier connections, but the intrinsic value of the relationship created a mutual bond so that, during hard times, the procurement manager spoke up internally for the supplier's needs and concerns. The social and political benefits of empathy lie in how such feelings motivate us to act in the interests of all those with whom we are connected through webs of direct and indirect interdependence. When aroused and integrated into collective action, these feelings form the social basis for multi-scalar capability formation, including those inter-organisational capabilities needed to create the common goods that sustain associational ecosystems.

Thus, empathy has a functional role in enabling members of a moral community to 'see' one another across separations of culture, power, and distance and to augment expressive variety in deliberative processes.

Empathy helps us to identify what entities we judge to be worthy of our moral concern and should therefore be included within our moral boundaries. Slote (2007) examines how empathy, in a sensitising process of moral development, provides resources for making ethical judgements. Slote (2018) argues that empathy promotes 'situationally prudential rationality' (p. 424) by amplifying our reasons for action in collective action contexts and transmitting reasons from one person to another through emotional contagion. Empathy facilitates norm change in social cooperation by acting as the conduit for flows of meanings through collectivities. By coming to know people in the particularity of their lives and recognising their contributions to the work of social cooperation, distance, culture, and power are diminished as relevant criteria for behaving differently towards others. In societies of meaning-makers, moral learning involves sensitising organisational members to interpretive differences by seeing one another as equally entitled to advance meanings and have these considered in collective deliberation.

The value of empathy lies in its ability to help us see others in context, enabling us to acknowledge that they are as entitled as we are to the problem that lies between us. Pavlovich and Krahnke (2012) suggest that empathy enhances organisational connectedness and encourages the seeking of common ground for problem-solving. Accepting responsibility for conditions that impoverish, alienate, or otherwise harm those who are involved with us in social cooperation is activated by empathetic understanding and knowledge. Furthermore, being able to fulfil responsibilities requires 'a context for agency based in relationships, developed and borne out intersubjectively or in conjunction with others' (Borgerson, 2007: 479), where taking responsibility requires 'an active willingness' (p. 498) to adopt the relevant activities for fulfilling responsibilities. Slote's (2007) sentimentalist ethic of care stimulates such willingness by sharpening our moral vision of distant, or in other ways different and diverse, others through conscious processes of empathetic engagement. For Slote (2007), empathy 'involves having the feelings of another (involuntarily) aroused in ourselves, as when we see another in pain' (p. 13) and is a learnt capacity that can be fostered by the use of practices, such as Hoffman's 'inductive discipline'. In childhood, this involves someone noticing when a child has hurt another and using this as an opportunity to develop the child's empathetic ability by helping him to imagine how he would feel if they were harmed in the same way. An empathetic ethic of care relies upon such trained abilities to fulfil our moral obligations of care to others that cut across the varieties of separations.

The society of meaning-makers has a collective responsibility to exercise capabilities for ethical world-building in order to create life value organisations as collective moral agents. This responsibility extends to associational ecosystems of collective moral agents, which are orchestrated by systems of deliberative collaborative governance. As discussed in Chapter 4, creating collective moral agents means ensuring that organisations develop the capability for cultivating empathetic orientations and feelings in their members, where organisational responses include 'morally worthy organisational emotions' (Collins, 2018: 827).

Organisations have duties to ensure that their members' interactions cultivate empathy as a functional expression of the organisation's values, goals, procedures, culture, practices, and decisions. Morris (2019) identifies three components to empathy: 'affective sharing', or becoming responsive to the feelings of others; 'empathetic concern', or developing motivations to care for the welfare of others; and 'perspective taking', or deciding to put oneself in the position of others and imagining how this feels to them. Morris (2019) argues that empathy should be increased to the extent that doing so promotes the common good. Organisations can adopt collective practices of empathy, in the form of sharing, concern, and perspective taking, into moral learning which is aimed at life value creation. Developing functional emotions of this kind is aided by adopting socio-technical means for amplifying moral reasons through empathetic encounter. For example, Neubauer et al. (2017) describe how organisations can use 'technology enabled empathy mapping' to create virtual social spaces in which people participate in an immersive experience of a particular design problem.

Empathy and Organisational Emotions

Global companies protest that they cannot be expected to know everything concerning to the actions of factory managers, gang masters, or community gatekeepers in poorly governed and distant places. They also claim that their entitlement to corporate survival justifies low wages, poor working conditions, and lack of voice for employees. However, global information flows, including, for example, product tracing in supply chains and big data on environmental damage, means that our knowledge of distant places is extensive. Given this, we can no longer argue that it is legitimate to limit our empathetic responses to those who are knowable within the boundaries of the corporation, or that employees' right to exit limits the organisation's responsibility to respond empathetically to their needs and concerns. The moral price for doing so is to signal to others that, despite the contributions they make to our welfare, they are not in themselves sufficiently worthy of our moral concern to be included within our moral boundaries. Jenni (2016) describes such responses as moral laziness or an 'aversion to imagining the mental states of others, feeling congruent emotions, and experiencing the impulse to help' (p. 21). Organisations are capable of demonstrating functional emotions that counter moral laziness by creating practices, policies, and strategies to augment empathetic concern at an organisational level and sensitise individual members to values. In turn, members have responsibilities to maintain the organisation as a morally worthy entity, invested with the functional emotions needed to care for those gatherings of morally valuable beings and things that are implicated in the organisation's activities.

Nussbaum (2001) argues that exercising imaginative empathy makes it harder for us to deny the humanity of others. However, citing the example of Nazi Germany, she shows that ideology, values, and social conditions can block empathy, leading to moral denial: 'Brought up to have empathy for those they recognized as human, they led lives of cultivated imagination with those people; towards those whom they killed and tortured, they denied the very recognition of humanity' (p. 335). Less severe psychological devices of denial and blocking are common. They present barriers to establishing justice and care in globalised systems, where we use distance, culture, and power to obscure our moral vision of the other, rendering them invisible to us as whole human beings, thus inhibiting the expansion of our moral awareness.

Activating emotional connections to the experiences of others may be achieved through developmental processes of imaginative enlargement beyond the self to others. Nussbaum (2001) describes imaginative empathy as the 'reconstruction of another person's experience, without any particular evaluation of that experience' (p. 302). Empathy as an emotional response makes no judgement upon the goodness or badness of the experience of the distressed person, but it can act as a guide to action and as a tool for 'getting a sense of what is going on with the other person and also of establishing concern and connection' (p. 330). Imaginative empathy is a basis for seeing the other person by imagining how it would feel for oneself to be in a similar position. Organisations that are collective moral agents can overcome moral laziness when their members create multi-scalar capabilities for organisational empathy that connect the moral sensibilities of individuals to the functional emotions of organisations.

Functional emotions are more likely to be developed in organisations that create empathetic mechanisms for meaning-makers to channel meanings into collective decision-making and to contribute their interpretive differences into collective understanding and knowledge of the situation. A democratically organised collective moral agent enables people to participate in collective self-determination of the methods by which their cognitions, emotions, meanings, identities, and values will be harnessed by the organisation into collective action that they have authorised. Foss and Lindenberg (2013) argue that motivating employees to translate organisational goals into created value depends upon 'the management of cognitions of organizational members' (p. 85). Carton et al. (2015) advise organisational leaders to craft vision and values messages based upon visual imagery and a limited number of values to communicate the ultimate purpose of the organisation. The shared cognition that this creates acts as the pathway by which employees take up organisationally determined meanings into their understanding of their work.

However, encouraging organisations to use micro processes of meaning-making power to inscribe employees, and other potential meaning-makers, with their values and purposes via management manipulation of thinking and feeling is not consistent with the right of meaning-makers to justificatory reasons or their entitlement to collective self-determination. In a study of the Australian Broadcasting Corporation, Spicer and Sewell (2010) show how employees resisted values of profit maximisation. After a 40-year effort, a cultural shift towards market principles was finally achieved by focussing organisational power onto the ethos and identities of employees. In this case, the micro processes of power that underpin the creation of organisational identities were reinforced by connecting to identity-related meaning shifts in broad societal meaning-systems, thereby favouring cognitive frames shaped by market values.

Rather than inventing schemes of alienating power, organisations need to establish an emotional infrastructure that enables people to experience power as mutual influencing, including a willingness to be shaped by the meanings and perspectives of others. But Courpasson et al. (2012) argue that, even in organisations where there is dialogue and distributed authority, people need to engage in 'productive resistance' (p. 801). When resisting the organisation from a common good standpoint, people craft situations where normal power relations are suspended, allowing them to clear a space for advancing proposals, ideas, and concerns, grounded in their expertise and knowledge. By so doing, they claim their normative agency to advance interpretive differences of meanings and values, challenging managerial attempts to control their cognitions and emotional responses. Meyerson and Scully (1995) describe how 'tempered radicals' mobilise their dissent from organisationally defined ultimate purpose by bringing their differences to bear upon local visions and action contexts. They do so by steadily building bottom-up arguments for social justice in the organisation that influences change in leaders' understandings. In ethical organising, the circulation of top-down and bottom-up influencing in micro processes of power suggests the normative requirement for a system of power in which the society of meaning-makers joins its social power for meaning-making to organisational power in order to secure organisational moral availability and readiness to be open to the influence of all affected members.

Distributed Power System

The society of meaning-makers is dispersed within and between organisations. Its membership is determined by the all-affected principle, including those who self-identify as impacted by the organisation's activities, as well as those who are invited because of their direct involvement in the matter under consideration. The aim of adopting the all-affected principle in this way is to mobilise, to the highest degree possible, meanings, values, knowledge, ideas, and learning. The society of meaning-makers brings people together, as workers, citizens, family, and community members and consumers, to take care of those beings and things that contribute to the meaningfulness of their lives. As a moral community, the society of meaning-makers is constituted by relational power, connecting people through their multiple roles, obligations, perspectives, and identities, as well as their disagreements and contestations regarding what value is worth creating. Power within the society of meaning-makers is therefore concerned with how people can bring into deliberation their interpretive differences and have dignity conferred upon them to the extent they commit to and strive to fulfil responsibilities of stewarding and care.

Organisational Power

Clegg et al. (2006) point out that 'power is to organization as oxygen is to breathing' and that organisations cannot exist without a system of structural, normative, relational, and ideological power. They go on to say: 'we do not think that organizational life and politics are necessarily nasty and backstabbing. They often are, but power need not always be regarded as something to be avoided. Power can be a very positive force; it can achieve great things' (p. 3). To consider what constitutes positive power, we can ask, along with Lukes, '[W]hat interests us when we are interested in power?' (Lukes, 1986: 17). Our interest in different types of power signals how we want to relate to particular beings and things, either through extractive, self-regarding interactions or through generative, other-regarding relationships.[1] In ethical organising, we are interested in objects for their life value, which implies that we are motivated to acquire the kind of power needed to promote the good for those objects: 'power is the legitimate, the inevitable, outcome of the life-process' (Follett, 1924: 193). The relevant power for taking care of valuable beings and things often takes the form of social power, described by Fligstein and McAdam (2012) as 'the ability to induce cooperation by appealing to and helping to create shared meanings and collective identities' (p. 46). This power is a type of shared capacity to create the meanings, understanding, and knowledge needed to act into situations of common concern, where power includes the relational capacity to be open to the influence of difference and diversity.

There is no pure form of power, and different types and distributions of power infuse networks of relations in organisational life. Mansbridge (1994) argues that 'collective action requires some degree of coercion to attain even unanimously approved collective ends' (p. 57). She defines coercion as 'getting other people to do what they would not do by threat of sanction or use of force', and she distinguishes between 'procedurally fair coercion' and 'raw coercion' (p. 59). This constitutes a paradox in the midst of acting together. Even as we admit some forms of coercion to be fair because they help us to produce goods that can be derived only from social cooperation, we must, at the same time, contest and resist such manifestations of power. Mansbridge (1994) proposes that we manage this paradox by fostering 'enclaves of resistance' (p. 64). However, even when tolerated, these can end up being marginalised and pushed to the edges of the organisations and beyond. Rather, necessary coercive power must be resisted from within core strategic and operational organisational practices by submitting the power system, represented by the types and distributions of power, to the critical evaluation and authorisation of all affected members of the life value organisation.

In life value organisations, structured by the social architecture of meaningfulness and mutuality, meaning-makers use micro processes of power to resist appropriation of their interpretive meaning-making capabilities or efforts to undermine their status as meaning-making authorities. They harness discursive power to contest accepted meanings, reject impositions of meanings, and stimulate critical consciousness regarding ideological formations or subjectification projects. Often, however, meaning-makers are implicated in structures of interdependence as: 'widely dispersed persons [who] are agents of power without 'having it' or even being privileged' (Young, 1990: 33). In other words, they have responsibilities to act but no power to do so. Pfeffer and Salancik (2003) describes how firms embedded in webs of influence are dependent upon distributions of financial, material, and informational resources in order to act, to such a degree that 'extra-organisational networks can overwhelm decisions made within organizations' (Fleming and Spicer, 2014: 264–265). For example, Kahn et al. (2007) show how NGOs in the global south seek to bring business corporations under their own value-systems. Larsson (2017) identifies the potential for domination in network governance, where participants in governance shape institutional policies that affect the life opportunities of non-participants. This is enabled by forms of 'network closure' that inhibit the emergence of pluralism in networked governance (Davies, 2018).

The problem of organisational power is one of concentrated, singular power, invested in a privileged group, consequently diminishing collective power by destroying variety in the types and distributions of power. Life value organisations are 'power-full' (Clegg et al. 2006) and are pluralised by multiple sources and sites of power, which people activate and authorise depending upon the specific life value outcomes they seek to create. A pluralised system of organisational power may operate as a polyarchic bureaucracy where multi-dimensional power is dispersed across multiple sites. At the level of associational ecosystems, pluralist structures of public and private power, which take the form of collaborative hybrid governance, involve different types and scales of organisations. Macdonald and Macdonald (2010) argue that such structures enable organisations to track how their activities affect stakeholders and to establish institutional pathways for democratic control of private power in supply chains, as well as other entities of production and distribution. They describe public power as 'those forms of power that are the legitimate subject of democratic control' (p. 21). We must find ways to translate social power into public power when people's entitlements are negatively affected, making democratic control a protective requirement. For example, in supply chains, translating the social power of corporations into public power of democratic control involves combining 'foundational *normative* criteria of publicness' with '*structural institutional properties* of publicness' (p. 22), such that power is divided between various parts of the system rather than held by a sovereign body.

The design of such a power system may involve a mix of transnational corporations and non-governmental organisations exercising public power with or sometimes against government authorities and agencies. Macdonald and Macdonald (2010) identify three features of democratic representation for such ecosystem arrangements: transparency in the exercise of public power, collective preference formation and signalling among affected publics, and public enforcement. Public power inserts public norms and values into private governance, but in order for this to increase the moral sensitivity of organisations to members of the society of meaning-makers, I argue that an additional requirement must be added to the power system, and this is supplied by what Loomer (1976) describes as the relational power to be mutually influenced by one another's differences.

Relational Power

Life value organisations with mechanisms for empathetic attunement will exercise relational power, as mutual influencing, thereby making themselves morally available to be enriched by a diversity of meanings and values. Allen (1998) argues that we need to think about relational power as dynamic and continually unfolding through decision-making structures and procedures, the division of labour, and culture. Translating social power into public power requires relational orientations where all parts of the system become morally available and willing to understand how well the system as a whole is doing in fulfilling its responsibilities of care. This involves members of the moral community as seeing other beings and things as connected to them in a relational moral nexus where each member is willing to be influenced by knowledge of how the lives of others are affected by their activities.

Loomer (1976) offers a relational concept of power that he defines as 'the ability to make or establish a claim on life', where describing something as possessing power indicates the extent to which we invest that thing with worth or significance. He distinguishes relational power from linear power, which he characterises as the capacity to actualise, to effect or to bring into being, or 'power as the strength to exert a shaping and determining influence on the other, whatever or whoever the other might be' (ibid.). With linear power, our sense of entitlement to the means of life is justified by the extent to which we have the capacity to influence others. This capacity leads us to stake our claims against the competing claims of others, so that we can 'actualize the values of life, including our status and sense of worth' (ibid.). We see ourselves as independent entities who interact with others but who are not formed from those interactions. Other people exist as helpers, opportunities, threats, barriers, and means to the fulfilment of the self. We engage with one another on the basis of our relative strength, providing charity for the weak, and participating in social cooperation to the degree that doing so helps us fulfil the conditions of our independent existence. However, linear power does not direct us towards realising those aspects of life that are most likely to satisfy our need for meaning, such as our generative relationship to things of significance beyond ourselves:

> The problem of power is the problem of quality of our lives. Those qualities that make for the most complex and intense enrichment of life may not possess the greatest survival value. But they are not engendered by our dominant conception and practice of power.
>
> (Loomer, 1976)

Mutuality constituted by the relational concept of power consists in becoming persons who are equipped to influence and to be influenced by the realities, interests, and claims of others, where 'the capacity to absorb an influence is as truly a mark of power as the strength involved in exerting an influence' (ibid.). When we are capable of being influenced by others without losing our freedom and identity, we enrich and enlarge our world, and make ourselves ready to receive the dignity that is conferred upon us and to endow others with similar dignity.

> Power is the capacity to sustain a mutually internal relationship. This is a relationship of mutually influencing and being influenced, of mutually giving and receiving, of mutually making claims and permitting and enabling others to make their claims.
>
> (Loomer, 1976)

Loomer (1976) says that the value and worth of the self lies in its experiences, relationships, and learnings, through which the individual 'joins with others as a member of a complex set of causes to create the future' (ibid.). Shared concern is a mark of relational quality, or relationships that are capable of nourishing each participant, where the worth of the giver depends partly on how the relationship supports the worth of the receiver: 'The knowing and the being known are mutually creative' (ibid.). This is not a fusion of persons into a communal harmony, with the seductions of manipulative power that this implies. Rather, relational power is manifested between people in the concrete realities of their lives and work, and is connected to our capacity to dignify others as particular persons with lives of their own to lead. Loomer (1976) puts this living diversity in terms of 'the inexhaustible and variegated richness, the confusing complexity, and the omnipresent and intertwined ambiguities present in the concreteness of individual and group life' (ibid.). This involves recognising not only the people with whom we are in mutually dependent relationships but also inquiring into the helps and harms of the world we have built together and coming to terms with the disordered nature of much of this world so that we are ready to 'live within conditions which are more complex, confused, and unsettling' (ibid.).

Discursive Authority

In life value organisations, meaning-makers authorise the combinations of power that operate in particular situations. To undertake this task, meaning-makers needed to be a part of power system that combines relational power with justificatory power, as the capacity to be uninhibited in advancing one's reflexively endorsed interpretations of meanings into collective practical reasoning. The moral concern is to ensure that justificatory exchanges are underpinned by non-dominating relationships, where domination means 'having to live at the mercy of another, having to live in a manner that leaves you vulnerable to some ill that the other is in a position arbitrarily to impose' (Pettit, 1997: 4). Usurping the capacity of others for organising or preventing its conversion into the human capability for ethical world-building are made easier when relational power takes the form of domination. Thompson (2018) identifies two forms of domination: firstly, the ability to extract surplus benefits and, secondly, the ability to shape the rationality and identifications of others as subjects. The second is a form of constitutive power of elites to 'shape the goals of the community, the logics of institutions, decisions that affect the common interest' (p. 42) through hidden 'forms of legitimacy and rationalisation'. Being equipped with justificatory power enables meaning-makers to resist attempts by organisations to raid sources of meanings in order to justify subjectification projects that target their employees, suppliers, customers, and others.

To protect against unfreedom as domination, Pettit argues that members of a need discursive control, which he describes as 'the ability to discourse and [. . .] have access to discourse' (Pettit, 2001: 70), where our freedom is manifested in 'mutually discourse-friendly relationships'

(p. 70). Resisting organisational moves to impose cognitive frames and meaning-systems requires meaning-makers to be confident in their status as authorities in meaning-making. For this, they need what Forst (2014) describes as discursive justice in the social processes of justification. Forst (2014) argues that society is 'an ensemble of practices of justification' (p. 5). Each of us participates in multiple normative orders, and any efforts to identify the ethical and moral content of the good life are consistent with justice only when values, meanings, and norms associated with any particular normative order are subjected to 'the justifying authority of those affected' (p. 5). To this end, a person needs to see herself as 'a justificatory authority' (p. 4), invested with 'noumenal power' (p. 9), which operates between people in the space of reasons and consists of the ability to 'use, influence, determine, occupy, or even close off the space of reasons and justifications of other subjects' (p. 9). Noumenal power involves 'a struggle over the possibility of structuring, or even dominating, the store of justifications of others' and is 'the art of binding others through reasons'.

Justificatory justice demands that we are seen as persons whose humanity entitles us to be given reasons. In a discussion regarding peace/war, Forst characterises war as 'a flight from justification' (p. 85) and peace as a form of non-domination that 'avoids seeing the other as an enemy to be dominated or eradicated' or 'regarding him or her as a justificatory nullity' (p. 85). Being viewed as a justificatory irrelevance is the experience of many in the political, social, and economic organisations to which they belong as workers, consumers, citizens, and volunteers. In much organisational life, only managers (perhaps stretching to include shareholders) are thought of as having sufficient agency to warrant an entitlement to reason giving and receiving. Exclusion from the space of justification degrades the dignity of marginalised groups, leading to the capacity to dignify across associational ecosystems being undermined, and consequently constraining the prospects for expansive social cooperation. To remind us of Joseph Cohen's examination of slavery, a coercive system of social cooperation can be stable and sometimes very long lasting, but eventually such a system collapses under the weight of its moral illegitimacy.

In sum, the society of meaning-makers establishes the relational conditions for people to participate in ethical world-building. Ethical organising requires justice as the equal right of all those affected by an organisation's activities to participate in the processes of social construction out of which ethical worlds are created. World-building involves struggles for influence and power over meaning interpretation, where rights to exercise justificatory power is part of the interactive processes of judging what is worth creating. Being able to justify in public arenas one's positions regarding one's commitments and assessments of objective worth is a key aspect of feeling confident about the meaning content of one's life and work. Normative orders shape what justifications and reasons we bring to bear in moments of valuation, but such normative orders are legitimate only when those subject to their influence have a say in determining their content. This requires justice in the interactive processes of meaning-making and access to certain kinds of social and institutional conditions, including a resource of public meaningfulness, membership of the society of meaning-makers, and institutionalisation of agonistic republicanism. These link organisations and ecosystems into the wider social, cultural, political, and economic meaning systems. However, ethical world-building is subject to fragilities in the different elements of the social architecture of meaningfulness and mutuality. In the conclusion, I draw upon three troubling situations to explore potential breakdowns, where the trouble is a complex problem that demands a multi-perspective, multi-level response.

Note

1. Fleming and Spicer (2014) identify how power is enacted in organisations through *four faces*—coercion, manipulation, domination, and subjectification and *four sites*—in, through, over, against.

Bibliography

Allen, A. (1998). Rethinking Power. *Hypatia*, 13 (1): 21–40.

Agle, R. A., Donaldson, T., Freeman, R. E., Jensen, M. C., Mitchell, R. K., & Wood, D. J. (2008). Towards a Superior Stakeholder Theory. *Business Ethics Quarterly*, 18 (2): 153–190.

Arendt, H. (1999). 'Introduction. Walter Benjamin, 1892-1940'. In: Benjamin, Illuminations, Arendt (ed.), Zorn (trans.). London: Pimlico, 7–58.

Bagnoli, C. (2013). Constructivism About Practical Knowledge. In: Bagnoli (ed.), *Constructivism in Ethics*. Cambridge: Cambridge University Press.

Betzler, M. (2018). The Relational Value of Empathy. *International Journal of Philosophical Studies*, 27 (2): 136–161.

Bird, C. (2013). Dignity as a Moral Concept. *Social Philosophy and Policy*, 30 (1–2): 150–176.

Boltanski, L., & Thévenot, L. (2006). *On Justification: Economies of Worth*. Princeton, NJ: Princeton University Press.

Borgerson, J. L. (2007). On the Harmony of Feminist Ethics and Business Ethics. *Business and Society Review*, 112 (4): 477–509.

Carton, A. M., Murphy, C., & Clark, J. R. (2015). A (Blurry) Vision of the Future: How Leader Rhetoric About Ultimate Goals Influences Performance. *Academy of Management Journal*, 1015 (1): 10–36.

Clegg, S., Courpasson, D., & Phillips, N. (2006). *Power and Organizations*. London: Sage Publications.

Collins, S. (2018). "The Government Should Be Ashamed": On the Possibility of Organisations'. *Emotional Duties. Political Studies*, 66 (4): 813–829.

Courpasson, D., Dany, F., & Clegg, S. (2012). Resisters at Work : Generating Productive Resistance in the Workplace. *Organization Science*, 23 (3): 801–819.

Crimston, D., Hornsey, M. J., Bain, P. G., & Bastian, B. (2018). Toward a Psychology of Moral Expansiveness. *Current Directions in Psychological Science*, 27 (1): 14–19.

Dentoni, D., Bitzer, V., & Schouten, G. (2018). Harnessing Wicked Problems in Multi-Stakeholder Partnerships. *Journal of Business Ethics*, 150 (2): 1–24.

Donaghey, J., & Reinecke, J. (2018). When Industrial Democracy Meets Corporate Social Responsibility: A Comparison of the Bangladesh Accord and Alliance as Responses to the Rana Plaza Disaster. *British Journal of Industrial Relations*, 56 (1): 14–42.

Fleming, P., & Spicer, A. (2014). Power in Management and Organization Science. *The Academy of Management Annals*, 8 (1): 237–298.

Fligstein, N., & McAdam, D. (2012). *A Theory of Fields*. New York: Oxford University Press.

Forst, R. (2014). *Justification and Critique: Towards a Critical Theory of Politics*. C. Cronin (trans.). Cambridge & Malden, MA: Polity Press.

Foss, N. J., & Lindenberg, S. (2013). *Micro-Foundations for Strategy: A Goal-Framing Perspective on the Drivers of Value Creation*. Frederiksberg: Copenhagen Business School [wp]. SMG Working Paper, No. 5/2013.

Gewirth, A. (1996). *The Community of Rights*. Chicago: University of Chicago Press.

Greenwood, M. & Van Buren III, H. J. J (2010). Trust and Stakeholder Theory: Trustworthiness in the Organisation–Stakeholder Relationship. *Journal of Business Ethics*. 9 (3): 425–438.

Jamison, L. (2014). *The Empathy Exams: Essays*. London: Granta.

Jenni, K. (2016). Empathy and Moral Laziness. *Animal Studies Journal*, 5 (2): 21–51.

Jordan, J. V. (1986). *The Meaning of Mutuality*. Jean Baker Miller Training Institute at the Wellesley Centers for Women, Paper No. 23. https://www.wcwonline.org/vmfiles/23sc.pdf

Kahn, F., Muni, K., & Willmott, H. (2007). A Dark Side of Institutional Entrepreneurship: Soccer Balls, Child Labor and Postcolonial Impoverishment. *Organization Studies*, 28 (7): 1055–1077.

Kateb, G. (2011). *Human Dignity*. Cambridge, MA, and London: Harvard University Press.

Killmister, S. (2017). Dignity: Personal, Social, Human. *Philosophical Studies*, 174 (8): 2063–2082.

Korsegaard, C. M. (1996). *The Sources of Normativity*. Cambridge: Cambridge University Press.

Korsegaard, C. M. (2009). *Self-Constitution: Agency, Identity and Integrity*. Oxford: Oxford University Press.

Lane, R., & Watson, M. (2012). Stewardship of Things: The Radical Potential of Product Stewardship for Re-Framing Responsibilities and Relationships to Products and Materials. *Geoforum*, 43 (6): 1254–1265.

Larsson, O. (2017). A Theoretical Framework for Analyzing Institutionalized Domination in Network Governance Arrangements. *Critical Policy Studies*, 13 (1): 81–100.

Loomer, B. (1976). Two Conceptions of Power. *Process Studies*, 6 (1): 5–32.

Lukes, S. (1986). Introduction. In: Lukes (ed.), *Power*. New York: New York University Press.

Macdonald, K., & Macdonald, T. (2010). Democracy in a Pluralist Global Order: Corporate Power and Stakeholder Representation. *Ethics & International Affairs*, 24 (1): 19–43.

Mansbridge, J. (1994). Using Power/Fighting Power. *Constellations*, 1 (1): 53–73.

Meyerson, D. E., & Scully, M. A. (1995). Tempered Radicalism and the Politics of Ambivalence and Change. *Organization Science*, 6 (5): 585–600.

Morris, S. (2019). Empathy on Trial: A Response to Its Critics. *Philosophical Psychology*, 32 (4): 508–531.

Neubauer, D., Paepcke-Hjeltness, V., Evans, P., Barnhart, B., & Finseth, T. (2017). Experiencing Technology Enabled Empathy Mapping. *The Design Journal*, 20 (Sup 1): S4683–S4689.

Nussbaum, M. C. (2001). *Upheavals of Thought: The Intelligence of Emotions*. Cambridge: Cambridge University Press.

Pavlovich, K., & Krahnke, K. (2012). Empathy, Connectedness and Organisation. *Journal of Business Ethics*, 105 (1): 131–137.

Pettit, P. (1997). *Republicanism: A Theory of Freedom and Government*. Oxford: Oxford University Press.

Pettit, P. (2001). *A Theory of Freedom: From the Psychology to the Politics of Agency*. Cambridge: Polity Press.

Pfeffer. J., & Salancik, G. R. (2003). *The External Control of Organizations: A Resource Dependence Perspective*. Stanford, CA: Stanford University Press.

Robeyns, I. (2005). The Capability Approach: A Theoretical Survey. *Journal of Human Development*, 6 (1): 93–117.

Roughley, N., & Schramme, T. (eds.) (2018). *Forms of Fellow Feeling: Empathy, Sympathy, Concern and Moral Agency*. Cambridge & New York: Cambridge University Press.

Schuppert, F. (2013). Discursive Control, Non-Domination and Hegelian Recognition Theory: Marrying Pettit's Account(s) of Freedom with a Pippinian/Brandomian Reading of Hegelian Agency. *Philosophy & Social Criticism*, 39 (9): 893–905.

Sherman, N. (1993). The Virtues of Common Pursuit. *Philosophical and Phenomenological Research*, 53 (2): 227–299.

Slote, M. (2007). *Ethics of Care and Empathy*. Abingdon, UK: Routledge.

Slote, M. (2018). Sentimentalist Practical Reason and Self-Sacrifice. *International Journal of Philosophical Studies*, 26 (3): 419–436.

Spicer, A., & Sewell, G. (2010). From National Service to Global Player: Transforming Organizational Logics in a Public Broadcaster. *Journal of Management Studies*, 47 (6): 913–943.

Thompson, M. J. (2018). The Two Faces of Domination in Republican Political Theory. *European Journal of Political Theory*, 17 (1): 44–64.

Veland, S., Scoville-Simonds, M., Gram-Hanssen, I., Schorre, A. K., Khoury, A. E., Nordbø, M. J., Lynch, A. H., Hochachka, G., & Bjørkan, M. (2018). Narrative Matters for Sustainability: The Transformative Role of Storytelling in Realizing 1.5 C Futures. *Current Opinion in Environmental Sustainability*, 31: 41–47.

Wallace, R. J. (2019). *The Moral Nexus*. Princeton, NJ, and Oxford: Princeton University Press.

Warren, M. E. (1996). Deliberative Democracy and Authority. *American Political Science Review*, 90 (1): 46–60.

Warren, M. E. (2017). *The All Affected Interests Principle in Democratic Theory and Practice*. HIS Political Science Series, Institute for Advanced Studies, Vienna, Working Paper 145.

Watkins, E. A., & Stark, D. (2018). The Möbius Organizational Form: Make, Buy, Cooperate, or Co-Opt? *Sociologica*, 12 (1): 65–80.

Wiener, A. (2017). Agency of the Governed in Global International Relations: Access to Norm Validation. *Third World Thematics: A TWQ Journal*, July, 1–17.

Yeoman, R. (2014a). *Meaningful Work and Workplace Democracy: A Philosophy of Work and a Politics of Meaningfulness*. London: Palgrave Macmillan.

Yeoman, R. (2014b). Conceptualising Meaningful Work as a Fundamental Human Need. *Journal of Business Ethics*, 125 (2): 235–251.

Young, I. M. (1990). *Justice and the Politics of Difference*. Princeton, NJ: Princeton University Press.

Conclusion
Towards an Empirical Research Agenda

We will achieve planetary-scale social cooperation through the many organisations and associational ecosystems that make up our common life. But for transition to a more sustainable human and natural world to be successful, the processes and outcomes of social and economic change must be just.[1] This requires new forms of organising. Justice is realised when all those affected by a problematic situation exercise their human capability for ethical world-building in the development of life value models, including creating pluriversal imaginaries of economic possibilities. For example, in the agri-food system, Lamine et al. (2019) argue that the design of sustainability transitions must consider 'power relations, food justice, change mechanisms, and diversity of sustainability visions' (p. 145). Despite the considerable sustainability scholarship, Bendell (2018) says that the lack of attention given by management studies to the prospect of 'ecologically-induced climate collapse' has left people and organisations unprepared for the tasks that lie ahead. He argues that the world's overspent carbon budget and insufficient political mobilisation mean that we will soon need a multi-level change agenda focussed on deep adaptation, or type of resilience described by Bendell (2018) as 'the capacity to adapt to changing circumstances so as to survive with valued norms and behaviours'. Life value creation is therefore a tensional undertaking, captured by the idea of integrative worth as inherent worth and developmental potential, where sustainability is concerned with sustaining the beings and things that constitute lives we value, and resilience directs change to creating the economic and social arrangements by which we fulfil our responsibilities to take care of such valuable objects. Hence, in valuing what we know, we must also value what they and we could become.

To carry forward positive meanings and values into transition, the concept of sustainability must extend to the self-identities and narratives regarding how we conduct ourselves in our work, organisations, and lives. Wright et al. (2018) describe the Anthropocene as a 'powerful boundary object' for focussing organisational change. The planet is not merely one stakeholder with interests to be traded off against those of others. Nor is the planet a bundle of ecosystem services that exist to provide human beings with facilities to live, without limits, in any way they choose. Rather, the viability and meaningfulness of human lives are inseparable from the interdependent subsystems of water, food, energy, and air. Wright et al. (2018) identify five extant narratives underpinning prospects for organising in the Anthropocene: pursuing business as usual, using technology to create eco-modernity, mobilising for climate justice, initiating new forms of organisation, and exercising cultural imagination. None of these fill the 'narrative gap' between our present and our imaginaries of the future (Veland et al., 2018) with sufficient meaning for mobilising planetary-scale social cooperation, but they do indicate where we might start.

I extend sustainability justice to take account of the motivational importance of meaning in life and work in order to highlight how all those affected by a troubling situation must be involved in the narrative formation that shapes self-identities and in the collective self-determination of framing rules that constitute ways of living together in the Anthropocene. In so doing, people need to claim their entitlement to the problem, as well as their responsibilities to take care of morally valuable beings and things, where justice requires their contributive activities to be structured by the goods of meaningfulness. Ethical organising taps into narrative justice by recommending a programme of system change that orchestrates life value organisations as collective moral agents into associational ecosystems invested with multi-scalar capabilities, where the object is to create us as new kinds of people who are equipped to exercise our moral agency as meaning-makers. This will require an audit of our organisational estate against the demands of life value creation: shutting down or repurposing legacy organisations, supporting ethically viable and novel organisational forms, and encouraging economic and organisational democracy.

We must acknowledge that the undertow of anxiety produced by technological change, combined with shifts of economic power between nations, is putting at risk the fragmented mechanisms we have for scaling up the social cooperation needed to mitigate climate change. Our general capacity for organising is in danger of being hijacked by frustrations with an unfair distribution between labour and capital of the benefits and burdens of globalisation. This has spilled over into disruptive forms of organising, often in the form of political mobilisations that legitimate a retreat into economic nationalism, nostalgic populism, and hatred of difference. Reicher et al. (2005) point out that the general psychological processes involved in promoting collective action can be knowingly used for good or for ill. In the social psychology of groups, speakers who are mutually embedded in the same social categories as their audiences act as interpreters of events. Some of these speakers consciously build 'collective hate' through a process of creating in-/out-group definitions where out-groups are treated as a problem or a threat and the in-group as virtuous (see Reicher et al., 2008). People often do not speak of their experiences of collective hate and violence or cannot find an audience willing to listen. Benjamin (1936) describes how young men returned from the battlefield of World War II 'silent, not richer, but poorer in communicable experience' (p. 84), because their structures of meaning had been fractured. Organisational change worth having in the Anthropocene counters such muteness by inviting all those affected into participatory processes of narrative formation, where they are encouraged to communicate fears and anxieties in discursive spaces of empathetic imagination and caring concern .

I have sought to show that incorporating the value of meaningfulness into practical reasoning provides critical ethical resources for evaluating the ends and means of organising. Ethical organising frequently involves holding together tensions, such as cooperation versus competition, rigidity versus flexibility, and short-term versus long-term goals, identified by Das and Teng (2000) in strategic alliances. Or the paradoxes of organisational change, identified by Smith and Graetz (2011: 184), and that include rational planning with adaptive strategic thinking, cultural renewal with structural change, empowerment with strong leadership, continual incremental adaptation with radical transformation, and social goals with economic goals. Badham et al. (2012) argue that organisational change, as the 'discipline of influencing oneself and others to achieve a purpose' (p. 187), involves the exercise of *phronesis* or practical wisdom when grappling with tensions and contradictions.

In order to counter power, paradoxes, and silences, I propose that worldbuilders need to combine practical wisdom with the tactical capacity for *mêtis*. In a synthesis of meaningfulness and mutuality, these discursive resources are mobilised by mutual organisation, constituted as a democratic system that enables all affected members to authorise distributions of power over meaning-making. Instituting collective self-determination requires democratic founding, which is a change process originating in a fundamental tension between 'the paradox of democratic legitimation and the paradox of constitutional democracy' (Honig, 2007: 1). In the absence of an already existing democratic culture, democratising projects require an initiator who will have sufficient knowledge and foresight to provide the laws necessary for democracy to get going. But by so doing, the initiator undermines the autonomy of citizens, as collective self-determination. As democracy develops over time, this originating paradox re-emerges, proliferating tensions because people must think and act against a conflicted institutional context that must be responsive to the plurality of other people and things but which is also dependent upon values consolidation in moments of decision.

We find ourselves in an analogous position when we use the mutuality principle to make and remake organisations as democratic systems, in which we must learn to be worker-citizens, often starting out with little knowledge, skills, or awareness of how organisations can operate along democratic lines. Managers and owners can find themselves in the role of founding lawgivers, with enormous influence over initialising conditions, but where they cannot fully control how the paradoxes inherent in these conditions translate into emergent properties of voice, values, culture, and purpose. In order to inculcate members with the capacity for self-determination, they must simultaneously orchestrate and cede power. In other words, they must encourage the development of a capability for ethical world-building, whilst not being able to determine how such a capability will manifest or to what use it will be put.

I use the social architecture of meaningfulness and mutuality as a normative lens to examine three troubling situations (cf. Haraway, 2016) that illuminate dimensions of ethical organising. Each situation shows not only how the general capacity for organising may be thwarted or only partially translated into a human capability for ethical organising, but also how emancipatory potentials within already existing forms of organising can be activated to create life value. All three troubling situations illustrate the difficulty of ethical organising when power imbalances present advantageously positioned participants with temptations to extract the benefits and transfer the burdens of social cooperation, but where the long-term health of the associational ecosystem depends upon mutual capability formation that strengthens the capacity of the weaker party for complex contribution.

Pluralising and redistributing power, requires change in which organisational members often struggle to establish a shared position for joint critique, reflection, and inventiveness. I propose that moral free spaces can—by bringing normative concepts derived from the synthesis of meaningfulness and mutuality into critical enquiry focussed on things of common concern—provide a holding environment for multi-participant moral learning. Arendt (1999) describes conceptual exploration as 'diving for pearls' in which people investigate the historical and cultural flows of meanings, extracting from their depths 'the rich and the strange' and bringing them back into use to solve present problems (pp. 54–55). Alzola (2011) proposes an integrative relationship between business and ethics that maintains the distinct identity of their normative and descriptive perspectives. In political theory, Herzog and Zacka (2019) describe how an ethnographic sensibility can be used to investigate 'situated normative demands' arising from individuals' own self-understandings as moral and political agents. In international relations theory, Wiener (2017) proposes a bifocal approach that unite normative and empirical research to global governance by identifying the relevant organising principles and specifying practices of regular contestation that bridge legitimacy gaps. Participatory research methods using action learning, change labs, appreciative inquiry, and large-scale interventions offer structured approaches for people who are enmeshed in complex problems to express their normative agency by co-creating concepts, knowledge, and expertise.

The aim is change as ethical constructivism that produces the goods of meaningfulness, or non-domination, non-alienation, and dignity, and that refuses to construct 'a vehicle of domination for those who conspire to enact the world for others. [. . .] An alternative use of social constructionism is to create a democracy of enactment in which the process is made open and available to all' (Hatch, 1997: 367–368). In action research language, normative concepts, ethnographies, case studies, surveys, big data, network analysis, and others form mirror data that participants use to create new understanding, meanings, and knowledge, through 'an evolving process that is undertaken in a spirit of collaboration and co-inquiry' (Shani and Pasmore, 1985: 439). This data informs judging as thinking and feeling when participants, firstly, apply the value of meaningfulness in practical reasoning by asking what is worthy valuing and what they need to do to take care of the things they value and, secondly, use mutuality as an organising principle to inquire into what kind of organisation will help them take care of morally valuable objects and how they ensure fairness, care, and flourishing in the change processes that establish such organisations as collective moral agents.

Ethical organising presents us with a core moral question: 'What kind of person will I be if this system is designed in this particular way or if this decision is made in this particular way?' (cf. Freeman, in Agle et al., 2008). Or, more fundamentally, 'Will our organising help us to understand *how to become good men?*' (Shotter and Tsoukas, 2014: 377). Such questions are rarely asked during organisational change, except insofar as human characteristics are plundered for corporate-defined subjectivities. I outline three situations in which organisations already exploring the potential of meaningfulness and mutuality could deepen their ethical organising by asking, 'What kinds of people are we creating through our modes of organising? What kind of organisation are we becoming? How does this help us to determine what value is worth creating?' The first is Mars Inc.'s initiative to recreate itself as a mutual organisation, in which corporate efforts to simultaneously extend and control a stakeholder approach has produced horizontally fragmented mutuality, thereby inhibiting the emergence of a society of meaning-makers.[2] The second is the UK government's experiments in public service mutualisation that have neglected opportunities to harness constructive conflict and responsible difference-making into system-level governance, resulting in vertically fragmented mutuality. The third is the King's Cross development in London, where the normative concept of 'the meaningful city' is applied to the challenge of place-making. This draws upon heritage and culture to inform the identity and character of a large-scale associational entity and uses normative concepts to inform narratives of city living capable of binding residents, corporations, and civic associations into long-term commitments for mutual benefit.

Creating Mutual Organisation

Mars Inc. is a global manufacturer of food products, including confectionary and pet food. It operates under five principles: quality, responsibility, mutuality, efficiency, and freedom. In a 1947 letter, Forest Mars Sr describes mutuality as: 'The company's objective is the manufacture and distribution of food products in such manner as to promote a mutuality of services and benefits among all stakeholders', where stakeholders include employees, consumers, suppliers, competitors, the natural environment, and communities (Monahan, 2018: 106).[3] Mars Inc. articulates the value of mutuality as follows:

> We believe that the standard by which our business relationships should be measured is the degree to which mutual benefits are created. These benefits can take many forms, and need not be strictly financial in nature. Likewise, while we must try to achieve the most competitive terms, the actions of Mars should never be at the expense, economic or otherwise, of others with whom we work.
>
> (Michie and Roll, 2017: 1)

Or more succinctly, 'a mutual benefit is a shared benefit; a shared benefit will endure' (Roll and Cordaro, 2016).

In response to sustainability pressures, arising particularly from public monitoring of the cocoa supply chain and low producer productivity in countries such as Cote D'Ivoire (Ingram et al., 2018), Mars Inc. has explored how to use mutuality as a meta-value for orchestrating its other principles. Senior management has sought to motivate mutual value creation through an evaluative framework that captures dimensions of talent well-being, natural capital, social capital, and shared financial capital. I focus on the documented case of Maua, a base-of-the-pyramid initiative sponsored by Mars Inc. in partnership with Wrigleys, Kenya, and involving local workers, Mars Catalyst, Wrigley, and NGO partners (see Roll and Cordaro, 2016). When examined through the lens of the social architecture of meaningfulness and mutuality, collective action is fragmented across the stakeholder groups that Mars Inc. identifies as included in their understanding of mutuality. This fragmentation presents barriers to the emergence of a society of meaning-makers, through which meaning-makers come to see one another as equal moral agents and dignify one another as particular persons with lives of their own to lead.

Dolan and Rajak (2018) describe the BoP proposition as involving a process of conversion in which 'informal actors are sculpted into a cadre of self-willed entrepreneurs and acculturated into the values and virtues of maximization to render them fit for global markets' (p. 234). The Maua initiative recruits informal workers, categorised as Uplifters and Hawkers, to sell low-value products such as Wrigley's chewing gum to low-income consumers in Nairobi, as well as surrounding towns and villages (Roll and Cordaro, 2016). The profitability of the business model relies upon low labour costs and capture of the seller's social capital. Mars Inc. justifies the project as mutual, or win–win, on the basis of its profit sharing feature and training modules. Roll and Cordaro (2016) document how the Maua programme is perceived by Mars Inc. management as bringing difference to the lives of participants. This difference is understood in terms of improved livelihoods and also a particular kind of self-conception as an independent entrepreneur. This identity is delivered through socialisation mechanisms that support the corporate-defined understanding of mutuality.

In the critical perspective I have developed, mutuality is conceptualised in three dimensions of bargaining, cooperating, and flourishing. In the Maua programme, whilst phase one, *bargaining*, is expressed in mutuality as win–win, together with practices of financial sharing and training, phase, two *cooperating*, is limited by the lack of worker voice in shaping self-identities and terms of engagement. Consequently, phase three, *becoming*, has weak foundations for the complex capability formation that reduces worker dependence upon the programme. The corporation fills the space of justifications, and the contributions of informal workers to meaning-making are confined to what is necessary for demonstrating their successful adoption of behaviours expected from striving entrepreneurs. The functional reliance of the programme on local sources of social solidarity and practices of mutual aid, such as coordinating selling areas and covering for each other during illness, are acknowledged but do not ground an entitlement to influence the rules and practices of worker engagement with the corporation. To experience autonomy as collective self-determination over framing rules and identity formation, informal workers need the status and capabilities for voice. In the absence of a capability for voice, BoP initiatives maintain informal workers in a condition of dependency, facilitating the transfer of corporate risk onto already vulnerable people, such as women with caring responsibilities. This ultimately inhibits the organisational capability development that corporations need in order to become life value organisations or collective moral agents with integrated multi-scalar capabilities for ethical organising.

Greenwood and van Buren (2010) say that the moral test for an organisation is how its activities impact weaker participants who do not have the capacity to protect their interests. Mars Inc.'s approach to mutuality offers a tantalising imaginary of how organisations could rise to this moral challenge. Michie and Roll (2017) outline a pathway for Mars Inc. to become more mutual through co-ownership and stakeholder governance. They suggest creating five trusts focussed on integrating five stakeholder constituencies—employees, suppliers, customers, community, and the environment—into a multi-constituency governance architecture that converts business units and projects, such as Maua, into mutually owned organisations. If implemented, this ownership structure would institute a voice-system—a core practice of mutual organisation—in the Maua programme. The 'deaf ear' (Wilkinson et al., 2018) of the corporation to informal workers means that such workers are excluded from co-designing the framing rules that determine the nature and context of their work and organisational belonging. To the extent that there has been collective capability building, such as the encouragement of savings groups, this has been in support of corporate objectives. Indeed, even minimal efforts to build an enabling infrastructure were diverted by a decision to distribute profit share using M-Pesa mobile banking. Doing so reduced worker incentives to attend the group meetings that could have been established as moral free spaces, constituted by liberal value pluralism. A more advanced system of power sharing would encourage independent groups and institutions, including trade unions or worker cooperatives, to mobilise collective voice and influence.

Given a desire to expand their concept of mutuality, Mars Inc. has a rich repository of other principles to draw upon that would aid this task. A particularly fertile value is freedom, which is currently interpreted as 'Financial Freedom to make our own decisions, unrestricted by motivations of others' or as 'We need freedom to shape our future; we need profit to remain free'.[4] Derived from the goods of meaningfulness, freedom is a relational power that requires the non-domination of all those affected by the organisation's activities. As discussed in Chapter 7, mutuality manifests non-dominating relationships through relational power which is characterised by a willingness to be open to mutual influencing and sensitivity to the differences of others. Expanding the organisation's concept of freedom in this way offers a pathway for repairing the incomplete mutuality that inhibits flows of meanings between members of Mars's ecosystem.

Relational power, or power as the capacity to be open to and influenced by others, opens out moral free spaces as spaces of encounter, through which informal workers, employees, and other stakeholders might come to see one another across separations of power, culture, and distance as whole human beings. The Maua programme acknowledged people's need for organisational belonging by supplying workers with branded t-shirts, but the status of informal workers as independent entrepreneurs allowed the corporation to sidestep any claims by workers to be organisational members. By keeping them at a distance from the corporation, the precarious work of Uplifters stifled the construction of solidarity between workers and employees, depriving Mars Inc.'s employees of the opportunity to see the Maua workers as members together with them in the society of meaning-makers. The loss of this benefit to employees and informal workers weakens the empathetic understanding needed to aug-ment meanings and values. Mars Inc. is therefore missing moral resources for developing the sensitising ethical capabilities that would establish the organisation as a collective moral agent. Consequently, horizontal frag-mentation of mutuality between workers and employees acts as a barrier to collaborative working towards the vertical or system-level mutuality needed to transform the associational ecosystem.

Mutual Public Service Economy

The second troubling situation explores efforts to mutualise public ser-vices in the United Kingdom. Focussed on spinning out mutuals as sin-gular competing entities, these initiatives are an example of the vertical fragmentation of mutuality. Despite this, there is potential for the emer-gence of a system-level approach to the public service economy. Since the late 1980s, public service 'spin outs' have included housing associations and leisure trusts. More recently, under the 2008 Right to Request, health-care organisations are entitled to advance proposals separating them from local government control. In 2014, Francis Maude, minister for the Cabinet Office declared, 'A hundred new British businesses have spun out from the public sector and are delivering nearly £1.5 billion of public ser-vices'. The UK government has interpreted mutual ownership as a form of employee ownership, thereby neglecting the interest that other con-stituencies, such as service users and communities, have in mutual owner-ship, and inhibiting the contributions these stakeholders could make to 'the rich learning and motives for collective action' of mutual organisa-tion (Yeoman, 2016). In 2018, research for the Department for Digital, Culture, Media and Sport (DCMS) showed that a promising number of public service mutuals involved not only employees but also their benefi-ciaries and even local communities in decision-making. However, service users and local communities usually had no decision-making rights, and the voice-systems for enacting employee rights, including features such as employee representative groups, staff on boards, and voting rights, were underspecified and limited.[5]

In the absence of a re-patterning of entitlements and obligations in shared decision-making, employees have to make do with what enlightened managers are prepared to gift to them in the form of staff engagement and opinion surveys. The 2009 Ellins and Ham report, *NHS Mutual*, recommends employee ownership as a means to elevate staff engagement by making them feel valued, involving them in decision-making, and providing means for them to fulfil their desire to deliver effective pub-lic services. In 2015, the UK Cabinet Office sponsored feasibility stud-ies to explore the application of the staff mutual approach to the NHS. During this period, the author conducted research interviews with senior policymakers and NHS leaders in NHS hospital trusts and professional societies. These interviews revealed a willingness to engage with the concept of mutuality, including a strong interest in how mutual organisations could enable staff to retain public service values in their work, whilst also giving them influence when initiating the organisational change needed for productivity improvements. Interviewees perceived that the decision-making rights of member ownership could aid them in innovating novel practices, especially in system-level multi-stakeholder contexts where co-creation was demanded.

> Respondent One: Well mutuality, to me it means that if I'm a member of staff or I'm a patient at [hospital], it's mine and I've got a real stake in it and the people who run it are accountable to me and I have a responsibility.
>
> Respondent Two: So the mutuality comes from engaging the staff in the decision making, in the planning, in the development of services, making sure they're aware of what they're delivering and outcomes, and instead of saying there's a them and us, we're all part of it.

The most common discursive entry point into the concept of mutuality was staff engagement, but this rapidly expanded to encompass a variety of expressive meanings, such as mutual gains, innovation, dignity, responsibility, accountability, patient care, and meaningfulness. Respondents understood mutual organisation as potentially not only equipping staff to do their work more effectively but also improving the quality and dignity of their work, indicating an intuition that mutual organisation interlocks with meaningful work to create public value. Although public service mutualisation has been politically justified by its ability to increase efficiency through elevated staff engagement, the employee engagement construct does not entail a normative requirement for power-sharing practices, such as collective self-determination of purposes and authorisation of management authority. As an outcome measure, employee engagement obscures the active agency of employees, making the actual work they do unavailable for critical evaluation against the value of meaningfulness (Shuck, 2019).

Public service work needs to retrieve the sense of having a binding duty to public values. In their global assessment of government services, the OECD Observatory of Public Sector Innovation highlights the technological shifts affecting responses to big challenges, including those in which public services play a part. The report says, 'The combination of technological change and globalisation is reshaping the notion of work, human purpose and livelihoods' (OECD, 2018: 11). Under technological advance, our lives are becoming more varied but also more precarious and uncertain. Consequently, we need enriched expressive services to meet advanced human needs that help 'citizens demonstrate the unique combination of knowledge, skills and experiences that make up their own personal identities' (OECD, 2018: 4). These advanced needs connect identity and capabilities to meaningfulness in lives and in work. Making common goods, or those expressive services that allow us to lead meaningful lives, requires work—work carried out by public servants, in cooperation with a range of other stakeholders. Public service approaches need to go beyond short-term efficiency improvements. Rather, transformational responses are required in which public workers involve service users, civil society, private and public bodies in the ethical, operational, voice, and collaborative work needed to co-create public services. To do this, public workers must become facilitators of information flows and knowledge buiding, as well as orchestrators of multi-stakeholder relationships manifested at different scales. In other words, future public servants will be doing more complex work, involving more people and organisations, and generating more collective purpose focussed on things that really matter and are of moral significance.

This implies an expanded conception not only of public service work but also of civic work and care work more generally. Hofmeister (2019) uses care to identify new sources of work meanings that can be experienced as part of a meaningful life, where work includes 'thoughts and activities that affirm life and growth, imagine or create the future, and abate death, discomfort, and decay of minds, bodies, relationships, objects, memories, societal institutions, social life, and the natural world' (p. 319). Crafting work rooted in care requires us to exercise relational power, willing to be influenced by others, and to influence them, in order to establish the conditions for mutual flourishing. In Pavlish et al. (2019), care is a form of expansive learning in which we need 'the capability to face the responsibility of making meaning in the midst of existential free fall' (p. 251). Rochdale Boroughwide Housing (RBH) is an example of a UK public service mutual that has adopted care as a core value. In the midst of the organisation's transition to co-ownership, care was taken up by the manager of six caretaking sections—a traditionally neglected and marginalised group of employees—to build their self-respect as employee owners and to dignify their work of maintenance and repair work: the caretakers 'talked about mutuality expressed in the value of care as 'easy for us' because '*we are caretakers we take care of things*' (Yeoman, 2016: 491). As a consequence of supporting their collective meaning-making, the manager acquired deep insight into the difficulties of change. He said:

> [T]imes when we are talking, it's like it really is they've got it [. . .] he's got it. He's not got it yet, we need to [. . .] see what we can do to bring him into the culture and philosophy we want to work at. [. . .] It's strange, you can be talking and you can be thinking and feeling, do you know I've cracked this [. . .] and then you can think about things [. . .] even half an hour later, its fuzzy. [. . .] [I say] don't worry,

don't get upset about it, don't panic, we're on our ten year road here, make sure we are moving on our road to get to it, [. . .] one of the things helps us all.

(Manager, RBH, in Yeoman, 2016: 496)

Bailey et al. (2017) argue that the experience of meaningfulness is mediated by 'existential labour' (p. 416), or how employees actively respond to organisational attempts to manage the meaning of their work, which sometimes leads to reduced trust, commitment, and engagement. In RBH, the voice practices of mutual organisation, underpinned by the status of being a co-owner, became a systemically embedded practice and entitlement that enabled people to develop a positive relationship to their work: 'in the past [voice] had been at the whim of management [. . .] that can't exist anymore' (supervisor, in Yeoman, 2016: 494). In a case studied by the author of a newly converted employee-owned business, a voice-system had yet to be fully implemented, and the culture had not yet adapted to employee ownership. Staff had been transferred several times from one public service outsourcer to another. Consequently, they felt disorientated, invisible, and not valued by their employer. As a coping response, staff disconnected from organisational identification, concentrating instead upon how their work contributed to making their customer's organisation function more effectively, or how their service improved people's lives. Consequently, management requests for staff to become involved in CSR initiatives, such as painting local schools and community centres, were met with bemusement. Employees considered themselves to be already embedded in their local community through a variety of roles and belongings and argued that employee ownership should mean the organisation caring about them, so that they could care for others through their public service work.

Public service mutualisation has the potential to create a mutualised ecosystem of public service, combining governance structures with the co-design and co-delivery of integrated services. Whole-council or whole-service approaches to mutualisation could surface already existing tendencies towards meaningfulness and mutuality using polycentric deliberative governance. Ostrom (2010) describes a whole-society approach to polycentricity that extends to international governance and consists of:

> multiple governing authorities at different scales rather than a monocentric unit. Each unit within a polycentric system exercises considerable independence to make norms and rules within a specific domain (such as a family, a firm, a local government, a network of local governments, a state or province, a region, a national government, or an international regime).

(Ostrom, 2010: 552)

In the UK, the privileging of market competition presents a considerable barrier to the emergence of such a system. The Westminster Government's staff mutual approach can be compared to the Scottish Government's declared desire to put mutuality and empowerment into the healthcare system in order to create a 'more mutual NHS' in which the Cabinet Secretary for Health and Well-Being writes, 'I want us to move to a more mutual NHS where partners have real involvement, representation and a voice that is heard' (Howieson et al., 2013).[6] Here, a mutual organisation is understood to draw diverse constituencies of healthcare professionals, patients, policymakers and communities into processes of co-production through a 'common sense of purpose'. Howieson et al. (2013) connect this to the general experience of being healthy, which is grounded in the capabilities people need to lead a meaningful life. People describe this experience in terms of having a 'sense of purpose in their lives, some control over their fate, doing enjoyable activities, feeling energetic and vital, being loved, enjoying good relationships with friends, and being connected to the community' (Laverack, 2014).

In a BBC radio interview, Professor Sir Harry Burns, reflecting upon his research on the Glasgow Effect, argues that the remedy for deindustrialised communities is 'to tackle the social, environmental and economic dislocation felt by people', adding that this requires '*all* the public sector to work together to help people regain a sense of purpose and meaning in life', including innovations in social cohesion that move away from 'doing things *to* people, rather than doing things *with* people' (Inside Health, 2018). The Scottish Government's articulation of NHS mutuals captures more precisely this need of people to make a contribution that matters to their lives and to the lives of others. Public service mutuals are understood not as unitary, monovocal, and independent entities but rather as pluralist, multi-voiced, and contested organisations, bound by webs of mutual dependence into their associational ecosystems and in part motivated by the shared interest that diverse publics have in leading meaningful lives. Howieson et al. (2013) propose that this interdependence can surface through 'public interest fora', in which all affected contribute to governance of associational ecosystems of public service mutuals aimed at securing public ends through power-sharing means. These fora are similar to the moral free spaces that proliferate when the social architecture of meaningfulness and mutuality is applied to life value organisations.

The Meaningful City

Community wealth-building has emerged as an associational ecosystem approach to developing inclusive local economies, with a particular focus on cities as engines for social justice.[7] Such initiatives promise extensive multi-stakeholder engagement with public and private value creation that has the potential to develop the multi-scalar capabilities needed to produce life value. For example, Preston City Council has conceived a community wealth-building model incorporating 'anchor institutions', worker cooperatives, and credit unions to create an ecosystem in which people generate and spend wealth in the local community (Manley and Froggett, 2016). At a city level, such initiatives can be examined using the social architecture of meaningfulness and mutuality. This points towards my third example, in which the King's Cross development in London is examined through the speculative normative concept of the meaningful city (Yeoman, 2019). In the ideal form of the meaningful city, vertical and horizontal dimensions of mutuality are integrated to generate public meaningfulness at a system level. This is achieved by placing at the heart of city-making the tasks involved in provisioning people with the civic commons they need to experience meaningfulness in work and life. Public meaningfulness accumulates from the meanings that city dwellers and visitors lend to the identity and character of the city, especially its cultural and historical heritage. Here, Lefebvre's (1996 [1968]) right to the city, or the right to participate in place-making, has an important connection to what I have described as our entitlement to the problem. This entitlement is a right we have, in situations where we are affected by the activities of a collective agent, to fulfil our duties to contribute to making this agent a collective *moral* agent, invested with multi-scalar capabilities for achieving morally worthy purposes.

The concept of 'the meaningful city' is relevant to how increasing urbanisation of the world's population shapes our prospects for a sustainable future and therefore the kinds of lives people will be able to lead. City power acts as a counterweight to governments driven by regressive populist politics. Barber (2017) argues for a new politics of the city, or 'urban sovereignty' in which public power is devolved to city level but orchestrated collectively through transnational connections in a Global Parliament of Mayors. He says that urban sovereignty is justified by 'the right of self-governance' (p. 23) because cities are increasingly having to compensate for the failure of national governments to respond with sufficient urgency to a raft of social and environmental challenges, and city leaders now regard 'the acquisition of the jurisdiction and resources as a necessary condition for discharging their responsibilities' (p. 42). For example, as part of the Global Covenant of Mayors for Climate Change and Energy, cities and regions participated in the Katowice 2018 climate negotiations. These were conducted using a Talanoa Dialogue, which is a facilitative mode of engagement between private, public, civic, and other stakeholders (Hwang, 2018). The role of cities and their networks in the emerging global climate regime was reinforced through the Cities and Regions Talanoa Dialogues, which connected sustainable development goals, the Paris Agreement, and the New Urban Agenda.

Multi-stakeholder inputs into the Katowice Dialogue showed that local contributions, focussing on the need for jobs, green growth, and social justice in transitions, are disconnected from the emerging Global Climate Regime, and that cities play a vital part in integrating local, national, and international initiatives.

Cities are plentiful in potential pathways for connecting the local to the global, especially when there are mechanisms for people to participate as equal meaning-makers in the narrative framing of identities and meanings that activate pro-sustainability behaviours. Amin (2006) outlines an urban ethic for the Good City rooted in the core value of solidarity, which incorporates four elements of repair, relatedness, rights, and re-enchantment. Civic work consists of caring for the material fabric, relationships with strangers and friends, claiming one's right to contribute, and expressive difference-making. Such work of city dwelling involves 'a sense of mutability; of the moments of inspired improvisation' (Thrift, 2008: 21). In other words, myriad moments of incremental repair upon the material and immaterial fabric of the city are needed to maintain its live-ability. In caring for the city, people become responsible for looking after ensembles of valuable beings and things, and includes organising public fora around objects of common concern.

However, the general entitlements of city people (residents, workers, and visitors) to contribute to city-making have yet to be fully embedded into city governance, and there is little consideration of how involvement in city-making is incorporated into meaningful lives. Sustainability initiatives in an urban context are frequently cast in technocratic terms that miss out the human dimensions of what it means for people's lives, and their sense of who they are, if they adopt smart technologies or change their behaviour to support environmental interventions (Yeoman, 2019). With this in mind, I look at how the normative concept of the meaningful city, when activated by horizontal and vertical elements of mutuality, can be applied to the King's Cross development in London. King's Cross is a highly successful commercial venture that also produces public value. The two core partners are the investor, Hermes Investment Management, and the property management company, Argent LLP. Through their place-making work, Hermes and Argent have tapped into meanings that inhabit the heritage and culture of the area. In so doing, they have created public goods, making the repair, maintenance, and development of these goods essential to a long-term, multigenerational vision based on multiple sustainability objectives. For their part, Argent has sought to adhere to ten Principles for a Human City, which aim 'to create a lasting new place for people, one that can continue to support successfully their changing patterns of social and economic behaviour'.[8] Hermes has connected the concept of the meaningful city to proposals to develop Wellington Place, Leeds.[9] In the Hermes Real Estate 2019 Responsible Property Investment (RPI) report, Hermes make strategic connections between the meaningful city, citizen participation in place-making, and ESG value dimensions, interpreting meaningful cities as 'places that people want to work and live in and which, in turn, foster a sense of civic pride and a sense of belonging among inhabitants' (p. 9).[10]

The meaningful city specifies what is needed to institute the capability for ethical world-building, and to engage the diverse members of the city, or those city dwellers, workers, and visitors who have an interest in the city by virtue of how it affects their lives, and who are therefore entitled to contribute to making the city. Elements of the social architecture of meaningfulness and mutuality that are particularly relevant to the concept of the meaningful city include the society of meaning-makers, governance and participation rooted in agonistic republicanism, and public meaningfulness as a repository of the identity, character, ethos, culture, and history of the city. In research interviews conducted in 2018–2019, stakeholders of the King's Cross development identified the following sources of meanings to be significant: *inclusion* in an integrative value-system that incorporated values such as respect, inclusion, and recognising talent; *culture/history*, where a cultural emphasis added public and commercial value; *innovation*, or the development of an innovation hub and emerging cluster that adds value to London as a global city; *growth*, which is expressed in knowledge-based employment and diversity of the jobs onsite; and *diversity*, manifested in a mixed-used concept, including a variety of occupiers, such as diverse tenants, schools, university, students, local authorities, office space, and cultural venues.

The site development process was conducted through managed stakeholder engagement and currently uses a programme of community involvement to cultivate a sense of ownership, such as, a community garden project, a homework club, and local employment. Some communities around King's Cross are isolated, enclave populations, in which gang violence was perceived by interviewees to be rising faster than in other areas of London. There was anxiety that institutions and new developments would overshadow established communities, sandwiched between busy roads. Given this, the aspirational shops, bars, apartments of King's Cross seem out of reach for some community members, with the development described by one interviewee as a 'castle on the hill'. However, young people interviewed for the Urban Partners 2018 Destination Next Conference emphasised the vital importance of the collaborative and bridging potential of the King's Cross development for overcoming separations between corporations, communities, and residents, and called upon corporate tenants such as Google to engage with all members of the community.[11]

Doing so would establish the solidaristic basis for a society of meaning-makers, establishing moral spaces of meaning-making for generating the meanings, values, and narratives that give the city its character and identity. Such arrangements also protect against breakdowns in meaningfulness, such as impoverishing public meaningfulness by sup-pressing, silencing, or distorting meanings; disabling the society of meaning-makers through oppressive discursive practices that fail to surface diversity of meanings; inhibiting the capabilities and status of meaning-makers through exclusions and inequalities; undermining the objective and subjective dimensions of meaningfulness by using public power to endorse meanings that serve elite interests, or promote unworthy pur-poses. Breakdowns in city meaningfulness can be repaired by stakeholder-led governance that institutes vertical and horizontal mutuality though inclusive public institutions; collaborative engagements with public, pri-vate and civic organisations; deliberative practices and procedures; and public values.[12]

These three cases point towards a potential research agenda for a philosophy of ethical organising that uses the social architecture of meaningfulness and mutuality to realise the human capability for ethi-cal organising. However, mine is only one proposal among many for creating the organisations we need to negotiate the challenges of the Anthropocene. I therefore offer my framework as a resource for norma-tive reflection and empirical experimentation, with a plea that research, practice, and policy puts people, their lives, and the valuable beings and things that matter to them at the heart of sustainability initiatives. One of our most hopeful narratives lies in recognising that human civilisa-tion is an outflow of nature's production. By inviting each another into *synoikismos*, we open up possibilities for enriching our collective action with values, capabilities, and meanings, and especially when these are directed by the sustainability imperative. Complexity itself is a source of meaning and purpose, when we are called to engage in problem-solving that secures life value and flourishing. Ruskin (1985) said, 'There is no Wealth but Life'. And it is the lives of our children and grandchil-dren that will be devoted to managing sustainable transitions, if these are still possible, or will be submitted to radical, perhaps devastating change, if they are not.

Notes

1. The vast scholarly and practical literature on organisational change has barely begun its own transition towards specifying the kind of organisational change needed for multidimensional sustainability.
2. See the Mutuality in Business research programme conducted by the Saïd Business School, University of Oxford. www.sbs.ox.ac.uk/research/responsible-business-initiatives/mutuality-business
3. See Mars, 'Principles in Action'. www.mars.hu/hungary/en/about-mars/principles-in-action.aspx
4. See Mars, 'Sustainability Plan'. www.mars.com/about/five-principles
5. See 'Public Service Mutuals: the State of the Sector', Report for the Depart-ment of Digital, Culture, Media and Sport (2018).
6. See *Better Health, Better Care*, Scottish Government, 2007.

7. See Development Trusts NI (DTNI) (2019) Charter. https://cles.org.uk/wp-content/uploads/2019/05/Time-To-Build-An-Inclusive-Economy.pdf [accessed 20 October 2019)].
8. 'Principles for a Human City'. www.kingscross.co.uk/media/Principles_for_a_Human_City.pdf
9. 'Building a Meaningful City at Wellington Place, Leeds', Hermes Investment Management. https://hub.ipe.com/find-research/white-papers/building-a-meaningful-city-at-wellington-place-leeds/10030633.article
10. Hermes Real Estate (September 2019). Impactful Framework: A New Structuring Principle. 2019 Responsible Property Investment report. https://www.hermes-investment.com/ukw/wp-content/uploads/2019/09/bd004122-hermes-rpi-report-2019.pdf [accessed 20 October 2019].
11. See Urban Partners, 'Destination Next'. https://urbanpartners.london/destination-next-conference-2018/
12. Collaborative stakeholder governance, informed by meaning sources and values of the meaningful city, addresses paradoxes of city making. In King's Cross, civic pride, inclusion, and belonging is potentially in tension with efficient management, safety, and use of technology. In a different example, Toronto has experienced resistance to a smart city experiment conducted by Google's Sidewalk Labs. See 'King's Cross Investor Seeks Facial Recognition Answers'. BBC News. www.bbc.co.uk/news/technology-49394788 https://www.citylab.com/design/2018/11/sidewalk-labs-quayside-toronto-smart-city-google-alphabet/577078/

Bibliography

Alzola, M. (2011). The Reconciliation Project: Separation and Integration in Business Ethics Research. *Journal of Business Ethics*, 99 (1): 19–36.

Amin, A. (2006). The Good City. *Urban Studies*, 43 (5/6): 1009–1023.

Arendt, H. (1958). *The Human Condition*. Chicago & London: University of Chicago Press.

Badham, R., Mead, A., & Antonacopoulou, E. (2012). Performing Change: A Dramaturgical Approach to the Practice of Managing Change. In: Boje, Burnes, & Hassard (eds.), *The Routledge Companion to Organizational Change*. London & New York: Routledge.

Bailey, C., Madden, A., Alfes, K., Shantz, A., & Soane, E. (2017). The Mismanaged Soul: Existential Labor and the Erosion of Meaningful Work. *Human Resource Management Review*, 27: 416–430.

Barber, B. (2017). *Cool Cities: Urban Sovereignty and the Fix for Global Warming*. New Haven, CT, and London: Yale University Press.

Bendell, J. (2018). *Deep Adaptation: A Map for Navigating Climate Tragedy*. IFLAS Occasional Paper 2.

Benjamin, B. (1936). The Storyteller: Reflections on the Works of Nikolai Leskov. In: Zohn (trans.), *Illuminations*. New York: Harcourt Brace Jovanovich 1968, 83–109.

Das, T. K., & Teng, B. S. (2000). Instabilities of Strategic Alliances: An Internal Tensions Perspective. *Organization Science*, 11: 77–101.

Dolan, C., & Rajak, D. (2018). Speculative Futures at the Bottom of the Pyramid. *Journal of the Royal Anthropological Institute*, 24 (2): 233–255.

Haraway, D. J. (2016). *Staying with the Trouble: Making Kin in the Chthulucene*. Durham, NC, and London: Duke University Press.

Hatch, M. J. (1997). *Organization Theory: Modern, Symbolic and Postmodern Perspectives*. Oxford: Oxford University Press.

Herzog, L., & Zacka, B. (2019). Fieldwork in Political Theory: Five Arguments for an Ethnographic Sensibility. *British Journal of Political Science*, 49 (2): 763–784.

Hofmeister, H. (2019). Work Through a Gender Lens: More Work and More Sources of Meaningfulness. In: Yeoman, Bailey, Madden, & Thompson (eds.), *Oxford Handbook of Meaningful Work*. Oxford: Oxford University Press.

Honig, B. (2007). Between Decision and Deliberation: Political Paradox in Democratic Theory. *American Political Science Review*, 101 (1): 1–17.

Howieson, B., Sugden, R., & Walsh, M. (2013). Mutuality in Scottish Healthcare: Leading for Public Good. *Leadership*, 9 (2): 162–179.

Hwang, J. (2018). Cities and Regions Talanoa Dialogues and multilevel governance. *Proceedings of the Resilient Cities 2018 Congress*. https://resilientci ties2018.iclei.org/wp-content/uploads/RC2018_Proceedings_Jisun-Hwang.pdf

Ingram, V., van Rijn, F., Waarts, Y., & Gilhuis, H. (2018). The Impacts of Cocoa Sustainability Initiatives in West Africa. *Sustainability*, 10: 4249. https://doi.org/10.3390/su10114249

Inside Health (2018). BBC Radio 4, 24 January. www.bbc.co.uk/programmes/b09nvrst

Lamine, C., Darnhofer, I., & Marsden, T. K. (2019). What Enables Just Sustainability Transitions in Agrifood Systems? An Exploration of Conceptual Approaches Using International Comparative Case Studies. *Journal of Rural Studies*, 68: 144–146.

Laverack, G. (2004). *Health Promotion Practice: Power and Empowerment*. Thousand Oaks: Sage Publications.

Lefebvre, H. (1996 [1968]). *Writings on Cities*. Oxford: Blackwell.

Manley, J., & Froggett, L. (2016). *Co-Operative Activity in Preston*. University of Central Lancashire. http://clok.uclan.ac.uk/14526/1/Co-operative%20activ ity%20PrestonREPORT%20copy.pdf

Michie, J., & Roll, K. (2017). *Future Governance Options for the Mars Corporation*. Said Business School Research Papers, June.

Monahan, K. (2018). *How Behavioral Economics Influences Management Decision-Making: A New Paradigm*. Cambridge, MA, & London: Academic Press & Elsevier.

OECD (2018). *Embracing Innovation in Government: Global Trends 2018*. www.oecd.org/gov/innovative-government/embracing-innovation-in-government-2018.pdf

Ostrom, E. (2010). Beyond Markets and States: Polycentric Governance of Complex Economic Systems. *The American Economic Review*, 100 (3): 641–672.

Pavlish, C. L., Hunt, R. H., Sato, H.-W., & Brown-Saltzman, K. (2019). Finding Meaning in the Work of Caring. In: Yeoman, Bailey, Madden, & Thompson (eds.), *Oxford Handbook of Meaningful Work*. Oxford: Oxford University Press.

Reicher, S., Haslem, S. A., & Rath, R. (2008). Making a Virtue of Evil: A Five-Step Social Identity Model of the Development of Collective Hate. *Social and Personality Psychology Compass*, 2/3: 1313–1344.

Reicher, S., Hopkins, N., Levine, M., & Rath, R. (2005). Entrepreneurs of Hate and Entrepreneurs of Solidarity: Social Identity as a Basis for Mass Communication. *International Review of the Red Cross*, 87 (860): 621–637.

Roll, K., & Cordaro, F. (2016). *Maua Programme: Bettering Lives Through the Micro-Distribution of Wrigley Products*. Said Business School Research Papers, September.

Ruskin, J. (1985). *Unto This Last and Other Writings*. C. Wilmer (ed.). London: Penguin Books.

Shani, A. B. (Rami), & Pasmore, W. A. (1985). Organization Inquiry: Towards a New Model of the Action Research Process. In: Warrick (ed.), *Contemporary Organization Development: Current Thinking and Applications*. Glenview, IL: Scott Foresman, 438–448.

Shotter, J., & Tsoukas, H. (2014). Performing Phronesis: On the Way to Engaged Judgment. *Management Learning*, 45 (4): 377–396.

Shuck, B. (2019). Does My Engagement Matter? Exploring the Relationship Between Employee Engagement and Meaningful Work in Theory and Practice. In: Yeoman, Bailey, Madden, & Thompson (eds.), *Oxford Handbook of Meaningful Work*. Oxford: Oxford University Press.

Smith, C. T., & Graetz, F. M. (2011). *Philosophies of Organizational Change*. Cheltenham, UK, and Northampton, MA: Edward Elgar.

Thrift, N. (2008). *Non-Representational Theory: Space, Politics, Affect*. London & New York: Routledge.

Wiener, A. (2014). *A Theory of Contestation*. Berlin: Springer.

Wilkinson, A., Gollan, P. J., Kalfa, S., & Xu, Y. (2018). Voices Unheard: Employee Voice in the New Century. *The International Journal of Human Resource Management*, DOI: 10.1080/09585192.2018.1427347

Wright, C., Nyberg, D., Rickards, L., & Freund, J. (2018). Organizing in the Anthropocene. *Organization*, 25 (4): 455–471.

Yeoman, R. (2016). From Traditional to Innovative Multi-Stakeholder Mutuals: The Case of Rochdale Boroughwide Housing. In: Blasi, Borzaga, & Michie (eds.), *The Oxford Handbook of Cooperative and Mutual Business*. Oxford: Oxford University Press.

Yeoman, R. (2019). The Meaningful City. In: Yeoman, Bailey, Madden, & Thompson (eds.), *Oxford Handbook of Meaningful Work*. Oxford: Oxford University Press.

Index

accountability mechanisms, as economic bicameralism 105
agonism, constructive conflict 137–138
agonistic republicanism 81, 135–139; consensus and conflict 136–137
alienation 90–92
Anthropocene, life worth living in 65–66
Aristotelian teleology 125–127
Aristotle, 'the thing as what it is' 59
associational ecosystems 71, 117
associational revolution 155

base of the pyramid 197–200; and agency freedom 198; ethical organising at 197–200; impact of 198; and social interactions 199; use of 197
BlackRock 3
boundary-crossing objects 44
Burns, Sir Harry, on Glasgow Effect 245
Business and Sustainable Development Commission 3

capability for ethical world-building 185–197; collective 188–190; individual 186–187; life 195–197; organisational 190–195
capability justice 173–175; and ethical worlds 174–175
capacity to dignify 215–217
caring concern 1
changing values 44–46; sensitising process 44–45
civic work 247
climate change: and collective action 119; social cooperation needed to mitigate 234

collective achievement 11
collective action 117–145; and climate change 119; critical evaluation 120–121; effect 82; integrity 117–145; normatively desirable 118–120; psychological processes 234; purpose 117–145; work 117–145
collective capabilities 188–190
collective moral agents 120–124; emotions 123–124; integrity 121–123; reasons 123–124
collective value 57–58
common knowledge 43–44; constructing 43
constrained mutuality 96–98
constructing basic structures 180–182
constructivism, as ethical tool 176
contesting ethical worlds 182–185
corporate social responsibility 53
cosmopolitan morality, and eudaimonic reflection 27–30
creating life value 64–68
creating moral community 214–222
creating mutual organisation 238–241; bargaining 239; becoming 239; cooperating 239; moral test 239–240; relational power 240–241
creative corporation 52
cultural pluralism, and value-work 33

data, narrating 64–65
deliberative democracy, as distributed system 106
democratic world-building 103–109; harnessing mutancy 107–109; institutions 103–107; metis 107–109; overcoming muteness 107–109; structures 103–107

democratising projects, need for
    initiator 235
derogatory terms 42
dignity: capacity to 217; and society
    of meaning-makers 216
dimensions of mutuality 98–103
discursive authority 227–229
distributed power system 222–229
domination 90–92
duties of adaptation 154
duties to organise 154–156

emotions, cognitive theory 151
empathy: and moral expansiveness
    217–220; and organisational
    emotions 220–222
empirical research agenda 233–252
ethical labour, division 127–128
ethical orientations 100–103
ethical organising 2–3, 7, 90; care
    100–103; core moral question 237;
    dimensions of 236; fairness 100–103;
    flourishing 100–103; matters
    involved in 235; purpose of 8–9; and
    values 25
ethical world-building 10–14; ethics
    and economics 10; and moral
    harms 29
ethical worlds 63–64; and capability
    justice 174–175; normative
    characteristics 63
ethic of care 89–90, 158–167; becoming
    a self-determining being 161–162;
    concerns of 158–159; materialist
    160–161; separations of distance,
    power and culture 163–164; and
    structural injustice 159; and systems
    of social cooperation 162–164
ethics of attention, effect 39
eudaimonic reflection, and
    cosmopolitan morality 27–30
existential labour 244
expansive mutuality 96–98
exploitation, and fairness 97–98

fairness: and exploitation 97–98;
    interpretation 101; positive
    perceptions 101–102
France, corporate duty of vigilance
    214
framing life value organisation 69–71;
    evaluative responses 70; hybridity
    70–71; moral agency 70

free attention, meaning 38–39
freedom, nature of 36

generation of moral space 46
generativity, meaning 86
Gewirth: functionalist perspective
    on public emotions 214; social
    contribution thesis 213
Glasgow Effect 245
global value chains 164
good life, definition 37
grand challenges 51–52
gross national product, moral
    poverty 51

Hobbes, Thomas, on mutual fear 56
human capability for ethical world-
    building 8–10
human dignity 215–217
human need, and meaningfulness 84
hypernorms, importance of 35

ideology, as simplifying representation
    104
individual capabilities 186–187
integrative worth and publicness 61–66
integrity 121–123; meaning 122
interest, meaning 8

judging 146–172; ethic of care
    146–172; responsibility 146–172;
    thinking and feeling 146–149
justice 173–205; by whom 176; for
    what 176; realisation of 233; and
    social constructivism 175–185; in
    sustainability transitions 68
justice-inhibiting processes 156–157

Katowice Dialogue 246, 247
King's Cross development 237,
    247–248
Koch Industries 177–178

lex talionis 94
liberal value pluralism 36–39
life capabilities 195–197
life meaning, materialist foundation 66
life value, materialist conception 56–59
life value creation, and public-private
    distinctions 62
life value model 68–80; process 71–74;
    significance 71–74; source 71–74;
    target 71–74; world-builders 68

life value organisations 5–6, 24
life worth living in Anthropocene
 65–66

Mars Inc 237–239; and mutuality
 238–239
materialist ethics 3–4, 69; of
 care 160–161; circulation of
 meanings 64
Maua programme 238–239, 240
meaning abundance 11
meaningful city 245–249; civic work
 247; contribution to city-making
 247; culture/history 248; diversity
 248; growth 248; inclusion 248;
 innovation 248
meaningfulness: appropriate
 orientations 9–10; and collective
 action 9; desire-based account
 83–84; and human need 84;
 hybrid 83–86; hybrid account of
 9; and life-grounded projects 9;
 narrative theories 84–85; narrative
 understanding 83; objective 83–86;
 personal conceptions 87–88; as
 prudential value 8; public 86–88;
 subjective 83–86; subjective
 accounts 83; value of 5
meaningfulness and mutuality 9–10,
 81–116; social architecture 82
meaningful work 7
meaning-making, in moral free
 space 41
meanings: nature of 39; understanding
 and knowledge 41–43
meaning-talk 45
meta-governance 52
meta-organising 71
metaphysical reconstruction of
 economics 4
meta-values, meaning 81
moral agency, meaning 120
moral agents, responsibility to create
 collective 152–158
moral community, creating 214–222
moral expansiveness, and empathy
 217–220
moral free space 35–36; and
 normative concepts 236
moral imagination 40–41
moral progress 39–46
moral spaces, matters of common
 concern 42

moral worthiness 88
morally worthy organisations
 124–132
motivating humanity 6–8;
 meaningfulness 6–7
mutual fear 56
mutuality: concept 55; constraints
 96–98; dimensions 98–103;
 exclusionary potential 55; expansive
 96–98; Mars Inc 238–239, 240;
 objective of mutual organisation 10;
 as organising principle 92–98; and
 reciprocity 94–96; roots 93–94
mutual organisation 25
mutual practices, effect 81
mutual public service economy
 241–245; existential labour 244;
 potential 244; staff engagement
 242; United Kingdom 241; work
 meanings 243
mutual value 54–57; and adoption of
 service logic 54–55; creation 54–55;
 nature of 54
mutual vulnerability 56

narrative understanding, and
 meaningfulness 83
nexus of contracts 12
NHS Mutual 241–242
normative nexus 28; cosmopolitan
 perspective 29
norm-talk 45

obedience, oppressive structures 209
objects 149–152; bringing into view
 150–152; concern for 149–150;
 gathering 150; relating to 149
OECD Observatory of Public Sector
 Innovation 242–243
open-source publicness 208
organisational capabilities 190–195
organisational emotions, and empathy
 220–222
organisational integrity 122
organisational power 223–225
organisational purpose 128–129
organisational values 30–32;
 balance 31–32; definition 30–31;
 interpretative schemas 31; multi-
 domain activities 30; and relational
 power imbalances 31
organisations 12–13; ethical
 evaluation 13; and human agents

13–14; and human interaction 13;
  nature of 12
Oxfam, abuse scandals 28–29

personhood, two dimensions 72
philosophy of ethical organising
  173–205
philosophy of purpose 125–128
pluriverse, concept of 62–63
Polman, Paul 1
polyphonic moral spaces 34
power: imbalances, and social
  cooperation 165; organisational
  223–225; relational 225–227
power of naming 42
practical reasoning 24, 88–89
pragmatic idealism 6
Preston City Council 246
primary values 37–38
public meaningfulness 81, 86–88
publicness 57–58
public things, nature of 62
public value 57–58; nature of 57
public valuing 28
purpose: agents of 131; beneficiaries
  of 131; holistic approach 129;
  impacts of 132
purpose of purpose 130
purposing: as social practice 131–132;
  as social process 125–126

reciprocity 94–96; dimensions 96;
  forms of 95
relational expertise 44
relational power 225–227
republicanism, responsible difference-
  making 138–139
responsibility to see others 156–158
Rochdale Boroughwide Housing 243
roots of mutuality 93–94

S dimension 4
secondary values 37–38
securities analysts, and value
  judgements 38
seeing ourselves as world-builders
  179–180
shared value 53–54
sign meaning, sensitivity to 43
social architecture of meaningfulness
  and mutuality 82
social construction, meaning 177
social constructivism, and justice
  175–185
social contribution thesis (Gewirth) 213

social value creation, definition 58
society of meaning-makers 206–232; all
  affected 209–211; dignity 206–232;
  empathy 206–232; mutuality in
  211–214; nature of 207; operation of
  206; power 206–232
sources of meaning 86–88
space of relation 148
stakeholder theory 12
structural injustice, responsibilities for
  157–158
structure of purpose 130–131
supply chains, as systems of social
  cooperation 164–167
sustainability: as core objective 4;
  extension of concept 233, 234; and
  values 22
sustainability imperative 2, 177; and
  value 51–52
sustainability transitions 65–66
synoikismos 3
systematic malignancy 11
systems of social cooperation, and
  ethic of care 162–164

Talanoa Dialogue 246
telos, meaning 127

UK government, public service
  mutualisation 237
UN Global Compact 3
urbanisation, and sustainable future 246

value of meaningfulness 81–92
value pluralism 4, 32–33
values 22–50; committing to 22–23;
  connection to action 27; and
  ethical organising 25; forms of
  53–58; independent authority 26;
  influence of 27; intersubjective
  process 67–68; justification work
  67; Marx's theory 61; meaning of
  23–24, 51–80; and moral agents
  26; objective dimension 60; as
  public promises 26; realm of 22–50;
  relational conception 24, 25–34;
  source of 53, 72; and sustainability
  22; as sustainability imperative
  51–52
values in ethical organising 34–39;
  multi-stakeholder partnerships 34
values-work 32–34; and cultural
  pluralism 33; layered pluralism 34;
  moral free spaces 33; polyphonic
  moral spaces 34

value-systems 25–26
value worth creating 58–64
valuing in life value organisations
    66–68
voice 103–109

will to form 1–2
work: complex contribution 132–134;
    meanings 243
worth 59–61; etymology 59; intrinsic
    dimension in use value 60